He Rode with Butch and Sundance:

THE STORY OF
Harvey "Kid Curry" Logan

The West of the Wild Bunch — Late 1890s

MONTANA
Fort Benton · Wagner · Malta
Great Falls · Landusky ·
Helena · Lavina · Miles City
Red Lodge · Billings

IDAHO
Three Creek
Montpelier ·

WYOMING
Thermopolis
Sundance · Belle Fourche
Kaycee · Deadwood
Hole In The Wall
Casper · Chadron

NORTH DAKOTA

SOUTH DAKOTA

Winnemucca
Elko

NEVADA

UTAH
Castle Gate ·
Green River ·
Hanksville ·
Robbers Roost °

Tipton · Rawlins
Powder Springs ° Wilcox
Baggs Cheyenne
Brown's Hole
Glenwood Springs
Parachute
COLORADO
Cripple Creek
Cortez

Denver

NEBRASKA

KANSAS
Dodge City

ARIZONA TERRITORY
St. Johns ·
San Simon ·
Douglas ·

Folsom ·
Turkey Creek °
NEW MEXICO TERRITORY
Alma
Silver City

OKLAHOMA TERRITORY

TEXAS
Fort Worth
San Angelo
Sheffield · Knickerbocker
Sanderson · Sonora
San Antonio

• Towns & Cities
○ Outlaw Hideouts

He Rode with Butch and Sundance:

THE STORY OF
Harvey "Kid Curry" Logan

by
Mark T. Smokov

Number 13 in the A. C. Greene Series

University of North Texas Press
Denton, Texas

Printed in the United States of America.

10 9 8 7 6 5 4 3 2 1

Permissions:
University of North Texas Press
1155 Union Circle #311336
Denton, TX 76203-5017

The paper used in this book meets the minimum requirements
of the American National Standard for Permanence
of Paper for Printed Library Materials, z39.48.1984.
Binding materials have been chosen for durability.

Library of Congress Cataloging-in-Publication Data

Smokov, Mark T., 1953–
He rode with Butch and Sundance : the story of Harvey (Kid Curry)
Logan / by Mark T. Smokov.—1st ed.
   p. cm.
   Includes bibliographical references and index.
   ISBN 978-1-57441-470-7 (cloth : alk. paper)
   ISBN 978-1-57441-476-9 (e-book)
1. Logan, Harvey, ca. 1867-ca. 1910.   2. Outlaws—West (U.S.)—
Biography.   3. Train robberies—West (U.S.)—History—19th
century.   4. Frontier and pioneer life—West (U.S.)   5. Crime—
West (U.S.)—History—19th century.   6. West (U.S.)—
Biography.   I. Title.   II. Series: A.C. Greene series ; 13.
   F595.L57S66 2012
   364.3092—dc23
                        2012014392

*He Rode with Butch and Sundance: The Story of Harvey "Kid Curry"
Logan* is Number 13 in the A. C. Greene Series

To my mother and father

Contents

Preface

Harvey Logan, better known by his alias, "Kid Curry," has generally been portrayed as a cold-blooded killer, without any compassion or conscience, possessed of limited intelligence. The 1969 film *Butch Cassidy and the Sundance Kid* depicts Cassidy outsmarting a huge dull-witted Harvey Logan in a knife fight after he has contested Butch's leadership. The real Harvey Logan/Kid Curry was a stocky five feet, seven and one-half inches, and credited with a sharp mind. He has fared little better in books and western magazines, while Butch Cassidy is portrayed as the super bandit who robbed the rich to give to his friends, if not the poor. At best, Kid Curry is relegated to the position of Butch's second-in-command, but not capable of being a successful outlaw without Cassidy's cunning and planning.

In latter years, this view has begun to change. "Despite a large fraternity of Wild Bunch scholars and students," writes Richard F. Selcer, "all western historians are not equally impressed with the legend of Butch Cassidy and the Sundance Kid. In particular, longtime historian Ed Bartholomew is convinced that Butch and Sundance are largely the product of romantic mythmaking by writers Charles Kelly and James D. Horan, aided and abetted by Hollywood scriptwriters ... Bartholomew is the lonely voice of the debunker who believes that whatever fame and success the Wild Bunch enjoyed should properly be credited to Harvey Logan and Bill [or Will] Carver. This minority opinion is somewhat supported by the recollections of Joe LeFors, the famed Wyoming lawman who chased the Wild Bunch all over the country in the late 1890s, yet his memoirs mentioned Cassidy only once and Harry Longabaugh [The Sundance Kid] not at all."[1]

Another noted figure who chased Kid Curry and his gang all over the western and southern United States was Pinkerton detective Charles A. Siringo. In Siringo's *A Cowboy Detective: A True Story of Twenty-two Years with a World-Famous Detective Agency*, Harry Longabaugh, the "Sundance Kid," is paid scant attention. Butch Cassidy fares much better, being mentioned several times in the two chapters concerning Kid Curry's assaults on the Union Pacific Railroad at Wilcox, Wyoming (1899), and later at Tipton, Wyoming (1900). However, Siringo does not include Cassidy in either of these train robberies. In fact there is no concrete evidence that he ever led or participated in any train robbery; this was Kid Curry's specialty.

When Siringo refers to major crimes committed by Cassidy, it is in connection with his 1896 bank robbery in Montpelier, Idaho, and the holdup of a bank in Winnemucca, Nevada, with the Sundance Kid in 1900. The only other big robbery that Butch pulled off between these years (which Siringo does not mention) was the mine payroll at Castle Gate, Utah, in 1897, while Curry's bank and train holdup record (mostly trains) averaged one a year from 1897 to 1901. And although Siringo stated that Cassidy was "the shrewdest and most daring outlaw of the present age," he also once referred to him as "the notorious 'Butch' Casiday of the 'Kid' Curry gang."[2]

Interestingly, the friendship between Butch Cassidy and the Sundance Kid depicted in the film of the same name, could be applied more aptly to the Sundance Kid and Kid Curry. The two "Kids" were virtually inseparable from 1897 through 1900, with Sundance and Butch pairing for the first time to hold up the bank in Winnemucca in September 1900. A few months after this, Butch, Sundance, and his girlfriend, Ethel (sometimes referred to as Etta) Place, took off for New York City and South America. They tried to persuade Kid Curry and Will Carver to join them in South America, but both were adamant about remaining in the United States.

Kid Curry's reputation as a blood-thirsty killer, owing in no small portion to the early writings of James D. Horan, is mainly unwarranted. Encyclopedias of western outlaws and gunfighters (which are notoriously inaccurate, using many unreliable sources) perpetuate this myth by totaling his number of killings as high as eight or nine, with some sources stating the figure as high as forty. In addition, the Pinkerton National Detective Agency was always willing to blame Curry for any number of unsolved murders. Over the years, their detectives were never able to capture or kill the elusive outlaw, which frustrated the agency to no end. Curry even taunted his pursuers by writing that "Mr W a Pinkerton is two Slow to catch a cold in a Montana Blizzard."[3] It had been a similar situation between the Pinkertons and the notorious Frank and Jesse James in an earlier time.

The only killing that can definitely be attributed to Curry, arguably in self defense, was the result of his saloon brawl with miner "Pike" Landusky in Montana. The other killings that are attributed to him can be broken down basically into three categories: 1. killings where there is no adequate proof that he was even in that area of the country, 2. killings done with a group of outlaws who were also shooting at the same subject (posse members for example), making it nearly impossible to determine whose bullet was fatal, and 3. killings done from ambush where there were no witnesses.

It can be argued that Curry had motive for at least some of these killings. For example, a strong motive for murder would have been revenge on Montana rancher James Winters for killing Curry's younger brother John Logan/Curry. A few years after this incident, Winters was shot from ambush while brushing his teeth on the porch of his ranch house. It's a good possibility that Kid Curry was in the area at this time, since he had recently pulled off the robbery of a Great Northern train about fifty miles from the ranch. Curry was suspected, but without any witnesses the verdict at the inquest was that Winters was killed "by some person or persons unknown to this jury."[4] Another factor, which is considered in this biography, is that Winters also had made bitter enemies among the local populace.

A good example of how Horan obfuscates the facts and downright invents history in his early writings can be shown in his relating of the Winters murder. In a story published in 1957 he gives the following version of Curry calling out the rancher: "'Winters,' he shouted one wintry day [actually a day in July] as the cattleman was about to saddle up. Winters turned. He saw Kid Curry and went for his gun. The Kid outdrew him and cut him down. Then he rode over to the dying man and emptied his revolver into his twitching body."[5] This is just one of the author's many outrageous versions of incidents concerning Curry's life. To be fair to Mr. Horan, his later histories of gunfighters, outlaws, and lawmen, particularly his *Authentic Wild West* trilogy (published in the latter 1970s), contain much important well-researched information.

The latest research has made it evident that Kid Curry could not have committed the majority of murders attributed to the Wild Bunch and other loosely associated gangs. Still, there are modern writers who persist in placing him at the scene of nearly every suspected Wild Bunch killing, even when it can be shown that time, distance, and other circumstances make this highly unlikely if not impossible.

This is not to say that Curry was not a dangerous man with a violent temperament. He was capable of cruel and vicious acts, especially under the influence of alcoholic drink. When he felt taken advantage of or was threatened with losing his freedom, he didn't hesitate to use force to defend himself. He ambushed posses and shot at policemen. However, whenever a particularly brutal incident occurred during a robbery, there has been a tendency for writers to lay the blame exclusively on him. The pistol whipping of the train engineer for disobeying a bandit's command at the Wilcox robbery is one example. The facts are that all of the bandits were wearing masks, and witnesses could not identify the assailant except that he was the younger of the two robbers that had climbed aboard the engine. Of the three robbers involved, Kid Curry and the Sundance Kid were the same age, and four years older than the third bandit, "Flatnose" George Currie (no relation).

The robber who held a knife to the throat of the bank president in Winnemucca, Nevada, threatening to kill him if he did not open the vault, has sometimes been singled out to have been Kid Curry owing to the violent nature of the act. The available evidence indicates that Curry did not participate in this robbery, and that it was reportedly Butch Cassidy who wielded the knife. This goes to show that in given circumstances, even the "non-violent" Cassidy could resort to violence if the situation demanded it.

Curry's contemporaries viewed him as a very cunning criminal, possessing at least above-average intelligence. After he was captured, he came into contact with doctors, law officers, and detectives, who all believed that the outlaw had received a good education. One of his lawyers voiced his opinion that Curry had a sharp mind, and had even helped to prepare his appeal. His skilled planning of train robberies resulted in no one being killed, and the passengers were never molested for their valuables. However, the practice of shooting down the sides of the train to discourage the curious sometimes resulted in the wounding of trainmen as well as passengers. Horan states, "The likable Cassidy became the publicized personality but Kid Curry was the brains, the planner, and a ferocious menace that made lawmen cautious about going after him."[6]

An important contrast between Butch Cassidy and Kid Curry concerning their individual robberies was the fact that Butch would overlook traceable banknotes in favor of gold or silver coin. As a result, Butch was able to spend the stolen loot with little fear of detection, while Curry always had to move on after spending or exchanging banknotes, especially unsigned bills with forged signatures. This was a clear distinction of Cassidy's prudent nature versus Curry's braggadocio and lack of fear or respect for law enforcement. It ultimately resulted in Curry being convicted of forging and passing stolen banknotes, not for train robbery or murder, which would have been much more difficult to prove.

Curry's incredible escape from the Knoxville jail is included in compilations of classic escapes. The Pinkertons had repeatedly warned the chief of police and county sheriff that Curry would surely secure his freedom if not watched carefully at all times. Quoting Robert A. Pinkerton, "Logan is one of the worst [meaning one of the most successful] criminals in the West. He is a leader of train and bank robbers, and as such has no equal. He has committed three murders, and is an expert jail breaker. Suggest that you put guard on him day and night."[7] Pinkerton had made a similar statement to the press concerning Jesse James twenty-two years earlier. "No one should know more about Jesse James than I do, for our men have chased him from one end of the country to the other ... I consider Jesse James the worst man, without exception, in America."[8]

During the debate over whether Harvey Logan/Kid Curry had been killed by a posse after his last train robbery, the *Denver Post* of July 11,

1904, said of the outlaw, "Harvey Logan was known as a man of pleasant appearance and manners but of murderous passion and with a great deal of cunning and executive ability. Many railroad officials can testify to the latter phases of his character. The total amounts secured by him and others of the same crowd in express robberies would likely approximate $500,000, but it was spent as it was secured, easily. If the dead man was really Logan, the most desperate and daring of all the Western train and bank robbers has been removed from earth."

And finally, the files of the National Criminal Identification Bureau, later changed to the Federal Bureau of Investigation (FBI), state that Harvey Logan, alias Kid Curry, had the longest criminal record ever known in the United States as of 1910. Rewards for his capture, dead or alive, aggregated from $25,000 to $40,000.

This biography of the famous outlaw not only chronicles his life, but also attempts to correct the many false statements and accounts that have been written about him, in order to reveal Kid Curry's true character. By examining the available sources, much of which is contradictive, there are statements that can be found concerning Kid Curry's personality and intelligence that do not fit his image as a badman. However, he was definitely not the benevolent gunman portrayed on the 1971 television series *Alias Smith and Jones*.

In order to greatly reduce the annoying use of the Latin word *sic*, it should be explained here that words in quotations, mainly stated by unlettered cowboys, outlaws, and lawmen, are not corrected for misspellings in the text.

Acknowledgments

I t would be impossible for me to recall and thank every person and institution that contributed information in the writing of this book. However, this does not mean that I appreciate all of their help and efforts any less. A short list of a few that have impressed themselves on my mind should suffice for my intents and purposes. In no particular order they are: The Montana Historical Society, Helena, Montana; the North Central Nevada Historical Society Humboldt Museum, Winnemucca, Nevada. Pansilee Larson, the daughter of bank robbery witness Lee Case, greeted me at the door and was full of information concerning Butch and Sundance's last robbery in the United States; the Northeastern Nevada Museum, Elko, Nevada, for allowing me access to their historic photo archives on a day they were officially closed to the public; Phillips County Museum, Malta, Montana, with much information on Kid Curry's activities in the Little Rockies region; Mr. Winston Mitchell of Dodson, Montana, who guided me to the historic sites in and around Landusky, Montana, such as the graves of John Curry, Jim Winters, and Pike Landusky, Jim Thornhill's barn, and the location of the *real* Kid Curry Hideaway in the Missouri Breaks; the Harlem Public Library, Harlem, Montana; the Glenwood Springs (Colorado) Historical Society, that provided extremely valuable information from their "Kid Curry file," particularly the Parachute train robbery and Curry's death; the Nita Stewart Haley Memorial Library, Midland, Texas; Stella Brock of Hoofprints of the Past Museum, Kaycee, Wyoming, who provided much useful information concerning the history of the local ranching families; the Johnson County Library, Buffalo, Wyoming; the Milton Moffet family of Kaycee, Wyoming, for sharing their knowledge of the site and history of the Grigg homestead and post office; Sammye Vieh and her daughter Kristen of the Willow Creek Ranch (formerly the Kenneth McDonald ranch), Hole-in-the-Wall valley, Wyoming, who were gracious enough to guide me to the famous "V-notch" and other historical outlaw sites in the valley; the Jim Gatchell Memorial

Museum, Buffalo, Wyoming; the John Jarvie Historic Site, Brown's Park, Utah; the Tri-State Museum, Belle Fourche, South Dakota; the Carbon County Historical Society and Museum, Red Lodge, Montana; the Crook County Museum, Sundance, Wyoming; and the Seattle Public Library and the wonderful Inter-Library Loan service, that provided many valuable and hard-to-get sources.

It would be remiss not to thank all of the historians, writers, and researchers who have come before me, and those who are continuing to generously impart the fruits of their research for the benefit of others. As an example, I relied heavily on the research of Sylvia Lynch, Wayne Kindred, and Brown Waller for the chapters on Kid Curry's Nashville and Knoxville period.

I should note that two chapters, those entitled "The Man from Pike County, MO" and "Pay Back," were previously published in part in the NOLA (National Association for Outlaw and Lawman History, Inc.) *Quarterly* 31, no. 1 (Jan.– Mar. 2007) for an article entitled "The Death of Pike Landusky."

Finally, I would like to sincerely thank my family and friends who believed in me and gave me encouragement in the writing of this book.

CHAPTER 1

Family Matters

Harvey Alexander Logan was born to William Henry Neville and Eliza Jane (Johnson) Logan in Richland Township, Tama County, Iowa (not Rowan County, Kentucky, as written by some) in 1867, according to 1870 U.S. census records.[1] The Logan ancestors have been traced back to Harvey's great-grandparents James and Caroline Elizabeth Logan. James Logan was born in 1767 in Lewis County, Kentucky, and died in the same county in 1838.[2] Logan descendents had been living in Fleming County, Kentucky, as early as 1795, and that is where Harvey's grandparents, William Logan and Elizabeth Ray Powers, were married on August 24, 1815. Elizabeth was born to Jacob Powers and Ann (Shelton) Crosthwait on May 7, 1798.[3] The Fleming County census record of 1850 shows William to have been born in 1792 in Pennsylvania. Harvey's father and mother were both born and raised in Fleming County, Kentucky, in the vicinity of Morehead. William Henry Neville Logan was born in 1834 and Eliza Jane Johnson in 1838. They were married on October 5, 1856, being twenty-two and eighteen years of age respectively. Eliza Jane was the daughter of Zachariah R. Johnson and Delilah Evans.[4] According to one writer/researcher, Harvey's dark skin coloring can be attributed to his Grandmother Delilah's Welsh descent. This trait was not owing to an infusion of Cherokee Indian blood as has been so often stated by contemporaries of Harvey and later historians.[5]

Harvey had four brothers and a sister. The oldest brother, James William, was born in 1860, the only Logan child born in Rowan County, Kentucky. (The area in Fleming County in which the family lived, was changed to Rowan County that same year.) The family relocated to Richland Township, Tama County, Iowa, in late 1860. The next son, Denver Henry "Hank," was born here in 1862, as well as Harvey Alexander in 1867, John A. in 1870, Loranzo Dow "Lonie" in 1872, and a sister

1

Arda Alma "Allie" in 1868.[6] There has been some confusion concerning Loranzo's family nickname. Variations including "Lonnie," "Lonny," or "Louis," are not correct. In the Chouteau County, Montana, elections registrar of 1894, he gives his name and spelling as "Lonie," and stated his birthplace as Tama, Iowa.[7]

Sometime after Lonie's birth in 1872, the family moved to a farm in Gentry County, Missouri, possibly near Gentryville. The father, William, disappears from the scant records during this period, which could account for some histories stating that he had died. However, according to Logan family history, the father and the oldest son James were known to leave for long periods of time, and do carpentry or other construction work.[8] He was not divorced by Eliza, and neither one married again, contrary to what has been written.[9] Family members believe Eliza died in childbirth in 1876, necessitating the children's move to Dodson, Missouri, to live on the small farm of their aunt and uncle, Elizabeth and Hiram Lee.[10] It is not certain how the Logan children managed to travel to Dodson, since there is no record of their father accompanying them.[11] It has been said that he may have abandoned his family, except for James, sometime before Eliza died. A check of the 1880 Missouri state census records by one author indicates father and son were in the Gentry County jail in Albany, for committing an unspecified crime.[12]

Elizabeth (Logan) Lee was born in Fleming County, Kentucky, on September 26, 1828. Hiram Lee, also of Fleming County, was born in the year 1825, marrying Elizabeth there on October 7, 1849. The couple moved to Kansas in the fall of 1859, moving again in 1864 to Dodson, Missouri, now part of Kansas City.[13] At that time Dodson was a small village situated just outside the southern limit of Kansas City. They lived in a two-story frame house that sat on a small hill between Dodson Road (present 86th Street) and Troost Avenue. Hiram was an invalid who had been injured either through some kind of accident, or possibly from Civil War wounds as a result of fighting for the Confederacy. Every day during the summer months he could be seen in his rocking chair on the front porch.[14]

The Lees had eight children, six (four girls and two boys) who survived into adulthood.[15] The Jackson County, Missouri, Lee's Summit

Township census of 1870 shows the oldest Lee daughter, Mary M., as not living at home at this time. She would have been twenty years old in 1870.[16] When the five Logan children arrived on the farm in 1876, there were plenty of mouths to feed. Hank helped his cousin Edgar, the oldest Lee boy, run the farm, doing the heavier chores. He may also have hired out for wages at the neighboring farms. Later, Harvey, Johnny, Lonie, and their youngest cousin Robert E. "Bob" Lee helped out.[17]

The Logan boys were considered handsome, with swarthy complexions, dark hair and eyes, and high cheekbones. Harvey was said to have "had strong, even teeth and they lighted up his dark face when he laughed."[18] "Neighbors recalled Harvey as quiet and reserved," remarked James D. Horan, "Lonny as handsome, outgoing, and mischievous, Johnny as impulsive, a bully, and possessing an explosive temper." Older brother Hank was more even-tempered and kept some kind of control over the younger boys.[19] These personality traits would persist into their adulthood; however, Harvey's outer quiet reserve would be deceptive of an inner violence.

Justice of the Peace Alvin Douglas knew Lonie well as a boy in Dodson. "When Lonie was a boy of 10 or 12," stated Douglas after Lonie's violent death outside his Aunt Lee's house in February 1900, "he came to his aunt's house to live … Even Mrs. Lee didn't know much about his parents. He seemed to be a good sort of a boy during the eight years or so he lived with Mrs. Lee, and if he has become a desperado or anything like it, it has been since he went West eight or ten years ago."[20]

According to James D. Horan and Paul Sann, on being interviewed by a detective in later years, "Mrs. Lee said they were always 'well-mannered boys who regularly attended a Bible school every Sunday.' But in their teens, she added, they displayed signs of restlessness and were always reading Ned Buntline's wild tales and talking about the West with an old trapper who lived on the edge of town."[21] They may have idolized the exploits of the infamous outlaw Jesse James, who was killed at his home in St. Joseph, Missouri, in April of 1882. Coincidentally, in October 1881, Jesse briefly lived (as J. T. Jackson) with his family in Kansas City at 1017 Troost, on the opposite end of the avenue north of the Lee home.[22] Virtually nothing is known of the boys' formative years on their aunt and uncle's small farm, apart from some anecdotes Horan has related in one of his early biographic efforts on Kid Curry. Possibly these are recollections from descendents or old-timers who knew the family; however, without references cited, it's impossible to determine any degree of truth to them.

The "signs of restlessness" in the boys that Mrs. Lee spoke of, appeared as wild streaks that got them into trouble more than once with the law. One story relates how a twelve-year-old Harvey stole a revolver from a town drunk. He and his brothers then went to the nearby woods to practice their marksmanship on targets and small game such as rabbits. It soon became clear that Harvey was the best shot. Another time, Harvey backed the town constable against a shed and threatened to kill him if he went to his aunt with another complaint concerning the boys' behavior.[23]

These childhood anecdotes as described seem to conveniently anticipate, explain, or prove traits attributed to Harvey Logan as the outlaw Kid Curry. They show he had no compunction towards stealing, was a good shot, defied and challenged authority, and had a proclivity to violence.

In late 1883 or early 1884, influenced by the pulp western magazines and stories heard from old trappers and traders who had returned home to Missouri, Harvey and his older brother Hank decided to go west and become cowboys.[24] Another possibly more fitting reason to leave was to ease the burden the Logan children had placed on Aunt Lee by coming to live with her family. A Logan family story relates that Hank actually left a wife behind who had given him a venereal disease.[25] Hank would have been about twenty-one or twenty-two years old, and Harvey would have been sixteen or seventeen. Johnny and Lonie were too young to leave home, but would join their older brothers in a few years. It is not known where their father and oldest brother James were at this time; however, the family places them in Oklahoma Territory a few years later, still carrying on construction work.[26]

CHAPTER 2

Cowboys in Montana

hether they came up the trails from Kansas City, Missouri, a starting point for the Westward Movement, or by trailing a herd from Texas, to New Mexico, Colorado, and Wyoming, the brothers were in north-central Montana Territory by early fall of 1884.[1] It is really just conjecture as to the route they took, since there are only a few cryptic references in the available literature. The latter route can be inferred in part from a statement by Pinkerton Detective Charles A. Siringo. Kid Curry, "at an early age drifted to Texas and Colorado to become a cowboy. In 1884 he got into a 'jackpot' in Pueblo, Colorado, and had to hit the high places to escape the officers of the law, several bullets striking the buggy in which he made his getaway."[2] This is in reference to Harvey supposedly being involved in a brawl or shooting at a roadhouse outside of Pueblo.

Another brief mention is from A. V. "Kid Amby" Cheney who said he worked with Kid Curry as a "rep" with the Circle C outfit late in the season in 1890. "The ... Curry brothers ... were southern cowboys who had come north and settled on a ranch near Landusky in the Little Rockies."[3]

According to John B. Ritch, a Montana friend, the Curry boys told the Circle Bar outfit "that they came up the trail but never were they communicative as to their past or as to by what trail they had reached the ranch."[4] Another possible scenario is that they could have signed on with a trail herd coming up the Texas Trail at Dodge City, Kansas, more specifically the Western Trail, which had been in use since 1874. It "ran from the Rio Grande to San Angelo on the California Trail and due north across the Red and Canadian rivers to Dodge City. It continued north by Ogallala, Nebraska, and the Cheyenne-Black Hills stage route to Roundup, Montana."[5] The trail's main destination was the growing cattle town of Miles City, in eastern Montana. Also, since the trail went

5

through the vicinity of Hulett, Wyoming, Harvey could have somehow met later outlaw pal George Sutherland Currie there.

Contrary to what has been written in the past, and incredibly is still written today, the brothers did not change their name to Curry because of respect for "Flatnose" George Currie who they *may* have met on his

The Logan/Curry brothers in Montana, ca. 1890. Left to right: John, Harvey, Lonie. (Larry Pointer Collection, Box 21, Folder 15, American Heritage Center, University of Wyoming.)

parents' homestead near Hulett, in northeast Wyoming. If George's birth date of March 20, 1871, is accepted, he would have been just thirteen years old when Harvey and Hank arrived in Wyoming in 1884. At this age and time he was not, as he was later to become, an expert cattle rustler and horse thief. In fact, in 1886, when George was fifteen, the family moved to Chadron, Nebraska, where he found work as a grocery clerk or worked in a general merchandise store. It had to be in the late 1880s, certainly by 1890, when he left home and arrived in Wyoming to become a member of the Hole-in-the-Wall gang of rustlers.[6] Even if it could be substantiated that Hank and Harvey visited the Hole-in-the-Wall area while coming up the trail, which it cannot, George Currie would not have been there.

The brothers supposedly arrived in Miles City, Montana Territory, possibly with a trail herd. Looking for work, they were told that cowboys could get employment in north-central Montana, and were given directions to Rocky Point on the Missouri River. Their route took them northwest to the mining town of Maiden and the Fort Maginnis country, then about forty miles north to the little settlement of Rocky Point.[7]

Hank and Harvey hit town at Rocky Point, Montana Territory, in late summer or early fall, 1884.[8] It was situated on the south cliffs of the Missouri River, about twenty miles south of the Little Rockies. The town "was a trading post consisting of two saloons, a few business places, a steamboat landing and a telegraph line to Fort Maginnis, an army post on the east flank of the Judith Mountains. It was also an unloading place and shipping point for Fort Assiniboine, and at times, Fort Benton. Rocky Point was reported to be a headquarters for outlaws and thieves in 1883."[9] It was also a supply point for nearby ranches, so local cowboys would have rubbed elbows with horse thieves and cattle rustlers. A store, hotel, and one of the saloons were operated by Melton F. "Dad" Marsh, a family man of good reputation. Actually he was a snitch for the stockmen, being paid fifty dollars a month to pass on information he obtained from the brazen outlaws.[10]

The trail-worn brothers stepped down from their horses in front of Dad Marsh's saloon. Upon entering, they introduced themselves as Hank and Harvey Curry, which was their nom de guerre in Montana. There is no documentation as for the reason for the name change. Some writers claim it was necessary because of the law's interest in Harvey, over the affray in Pueblo, Colorado. The Logan family suggests that Hank instigated the name change to prevent the wife he had left in Missouri from tracking him down.[11] Hank asked Dad if there was any work in the area for a couple of waddies, and was told the Circle Bar was hiring reps at the roundup headquarters on Crooked Creek, just south of the Missouri River in present Petroleum County.[12] The Circle Bar was owned by Howes, Strevell, and Miles, an English corporation, and foreman Johnny Lea put the Curry boys on the payroll for the Judith Basin Pool fall roundup.[13] Harvey's youth soon earned him the sobriquet of "Kid."

After the fall roundup, Hank and the Kid were not about to lie around all winter, so they decided to cut fuel wood for the steamboats to operate next spring. They acquired a sled and used it to haul the wood from the breaks of the Missouri. In the spring they had forty cords to sell for about eight dollars per cord. Any idle time they had was passed at Dad Marsh's place at Rocky Point, time Marsh later claimed he spent teaching the boys to read and write. In the spring roundup of '85 they were hired again by the Circle Bar.[14] They were considered top cowhands; both were good ropers and it was noticed that Kid Curry was especially adept at peeling broncs.[15] They knew their work, and it was assumed they both had worked on another range before coming to the Circle Bar. Although the Kid was considered quiet and reserved, he gained a reputation among the hands as being the strongest man of his build and size they had ever seen. Hank was described as a much bigger man than the Kid, and also physically powerful.[16]

A. J. Davis of the famous DHS ranch (Davis, S. T. Hauser, and Granville Stuart) was impressed with the Currys. "The Curry boys were probably the best ropers and bronc peelers in Montana at that time ... They were hard working, honest for the times, of good nature and character."[17]

The reps from the DHS ranch (D-S brand) and other outfits who worked alongside the brothers had many good things to say about them. "Kid was a fine fellow ... and a good cowboy," said Con Price of the DHS. "Both the brothers were fine boys ... and would give anyone the shirt off their back if they were in need."[18] Edward C. "Teddy Blue" Abbott, who had just started working for the DHS that spring, admired Henry Curry especially. "Sure, I knew them all the time they worked for the Circle Bar. Rode about three years with them. Hank was a fine fellow; always quiet and well behaved and much liked by all the other punchers. Sort of an easy goin' fellow. He seemed to always have good control over the Kid"[19] It also may have been at this time that the Currys met later ranching partner Jim Thornhill, who had worked for the DHS and Circle Bar.[20] Some writers claim the boys knew him before this, at Dodson, Missouri; others allege he came from Texas.[21] Famous cowboy artist Charles M. Russell worked with the Currys, and portrayed them in some of his works. Hank and the Kid continued to work for the Circle Bar, and presumably wintered at Dad Marsh's place at Rocky Point.

With the summer drought of 1886, combined with the previous dry winter and spring, streams and water holes dried up and the short grass became parched. The range was overstocked and more cattle were being brought in from the south as well as from Washington and Oregon.[22] It was essential to find better range, and many of the larger outfits, such as the Pioneer Cattle Company, the Judith Basin Cattle Company, and Mc-Namara and Marlow, decided to drive their herds north of the Missouri to the untapped ranges of the Little Rockies and the Fort Belknap Indian Reservation.[23] McNamara and Marlow owned a large horse herd, and it was at this time that they contracted with the Curry brothers to establish their own ranch north of the Missouri River and break horses on a share basis. The brothers looked over the country and decided the best place for their ranch site was near the headwaters of Rock Creek just south of the Little Rockies.[24]

About this time, a trail herd belonging to the N-N (N Bar N) of the Home Land and Cattle Company arrived in Montana from Texas. A ranch was established in 1884 on Little Dry Creek near Wolf Point, with a second ranch on Rock Creek northeast of Malta added later. They also ran cattle on the open range as far south as Miles City. A young man by the name of Harry Alonzo Longabaugh accompanied the herd, and was kept on after the end of the drive. Harry was an expert with horses, and he may have met and possibly worked with Kid Curry at this time. Curry's friend Sid Willis had also been hired on to work for the owners, the Niedringhaus brothers of St. Louis. Unfortunately, at the start of winter 1886/1887, Harry was no longer needed and was laid off.[25]

Harry headed to the Black Hills of South Dakota near the Wyoming border to find suitable employment. Not finding work as a ranch hand, he was forced to work for his board for a month and a half, and sell his belongings just to survive. Later that winter he started back to Miles City to find range work, traveling through the extreme northeast corner of Wyoming.[26] On February 27, 1887, he stole a horse, a revolver, and a saddle outfit from the Three V Ranch (VVV brand) near Sundance, Wyoming, the Crook County seat.[27] He was eventually arrested and convicted of Grand Larceny, and served eighteen months in the county jail. After his pardon and release in 1889, "Kid" Longabaugh came to be known as the Sundance Kid.[28]

The disastrous winter of 1886/1887 decimated large numbers of cattle, and the disappointing spring roundup made it clear there wasn't much work for cowhands. With the help of their closest friend, Jim Thornhill, the brothers were able to complete the building of the cabin, barn, corrals, and some outbuildings for their homestead.[29] Also, over time, Thornhill filed for as many as five homesteads, all close by the Currys' Rock Creek ranch.[30] By midsummer the Currys were well into their horse-breaking deal with McNamara and Marlow, whose home ranch was now near Big Sandy and the Bear Paw Mountains to the west.[31]

A recent neighbor, the Circle C, was over on Beaver Creek east of the Little Rockies. Robert Coburn had purchased the DHS holdings on Beaver Creek from Granville Stuart, who did not like the country and was soured on the cattle business after the tragic die-off of cattle the last winter. Coburn had traded his Circle Diamond ranch on Flatwillow Creek south of the Missouri as part of the deal. When the Currys weren't busy with their horse ranch, they and Jim Thornhill worked for the Circle C. They became close friends with Coburn's sons Will, Bob, and Wallace. In fact, one winter Kid Curry saved young Bob Coburn's life during a blizzard. Curry found Coburn unconscious from a head injury, pinned under his crippled horse, far from the home ranch. Curry shot the horse, which had broken its foreleg from stepping in a badger hole, and with Bob tied to his saddle, rode to the Coburn ranch. He then rode to Malta in the blizzard to bring back the doctor, who was drunk and very reluctant to go. After threatening the physician with worse than a forty-mile ride in a blizzard, they drove to the ranch in a buckboard, reaching their destination with a much sobered doctor.[32]

Jim Thornhill also owed his life to Kid Curry when they were repping for the Circle C during the 1887 fall roundup. The two of them were swimming cattle to the north side of the Missouri River at the Rocky Point Crossing. When they reached the swift current in the middle of the river, Thornhill was suddenly in trouble when his horse panicked. Thornhill couldn't swim, and had taken in a lot of water, when Kid Curry appeared alongside. He pulled his half-drowned friend across his saddle, then grabbed hold of a steer's tail that pulled them to shore. Jim Thornhill remarked later that "the hell of it was the Kid couldn't swim a lick either." [33]

One cowboy or rancher, name undisclosed, told of knowing the Curry brothers during the time they worked for the Circle C. He said the Kid tended to be a little on the wild side, and was obsessed with the sensational literature of the day. He spent much of his spare time reading dime novels and other western pulps concerning the exploits of the James brothers.[34]

The Currys gradually built up their ranch over the next few years. They captured a few wild horses down in the Missouri Breaks to add to their own horse herd, and also acquired some cattle.[35] "When I went to Valley County in 1888 the Logan boys were well thought of," Sid Willis said of them at this time, "and had as good a start as any young men in the country. They had the best band of cattle in that section and some of the best hay land in that area." He added that "the kid is the best roper that ever rode a Montana cattle range."[36]

If a story told by Montana rancher Floyd Hardin is true, the Currys were not satisfied with what they had accumulated thus far. Seven-year-old Floyd traveled with his parents from Texas to Montana in January 1898, settling in the "Big Bend" of the Missouri River to start a small cattle ranch. Floyd later told the following story that was in "general circulation" concerning their neighbor Joe Legg and the Curry boys.

At one time Legg owned a horse ranch south of Miles City on Tongue River, and would spend winters operating a blacksmith shop in the mining town of Maiden. One day he was hunting along the Missouri River when he discovered some bottom land he preferred over his Tongue River Ranch. About the time Legg decided to move his horse operation, some big cattlemen from south of the Missouri were searching the Little Rockies region for a suitable site for their new ranch headquarters. When they chose some property located on a creek in the area, the Currys were soon on the spot to lay claim, intending to sell the cattlemen the land they desired. Deciding not to oblige the brothers, they returned to the Missouri and coincidentally selected the same bottom land that Legg had discovered. Not giving up, the Currys had followed the cattle outfit and also laid claim to their second choice of property. Realizing what the Currys were trying to pull, the cattlemen forcibly took possession of their first choice of land in the Little Rockies. In the meantime, Joe Legg moved onto the Missouri River bottom, building a log cabin complete with rifle ports on all sides. The Currys ended up with nothing to show for their schemes, losing out on both sites.

Kid Curry apparently did not hold a grudge against Joe Legg, because it is said he frequently stopped by the ranch to visit. However, Curry started to make a habit of jumping his horse over a board gate a few hundred yards from the cabin. The horse did not always clear the top board, and in these instances the gate would be damaged. In order to discourage this behavior, the next time Curry jumped the gate the rancher fired off several rounds from his old Sharps rifle. The Kid got the message and did not resume his visits to the ranch.[37]

Hank and the Kid must have written their Aunt Lee in Missouri to tell younger brothers Johnny and Lonie to come out to Montana. Johnny arrived in spring 1888 and worked for the Fergus Land and Cattle Company in the Fort Maginnis country south of the Missouri. Lonie showed up the following year and rode for the Circle Bar on Crooked Creek and later for McNamara and Marlow on the Fort Maginnis range.[38] During the winters, the two divided their time between Rocky Point and the Curry ranch. The Curry home was described by John B. Ritch "as a place of hospitality. Upon entering their ranch house, the boys deposited their guns on a table kept especially for that purpose." Guests were always welcome and Ritch characterized the brothers "as being of a kind nature and not disposed to quarrel except when under the influence of whiskey."[39]

One testimony to the kindness of the Currys is from Charles A. Smith, who later became the first merchant of the town of Harlem. In the winter of 1888/1889, he was hunting wolves with a man named "Dutch Louie," or Louis, Meyers in the vicinity of Rocky Point. Meyers, a notorious horse thief, had given up the profession after he narrowly avoided being hanged by a group of vigilantes in 1884. Within three days, a sore knuckle on Smith's hand turned into inflammatory rheumatism. Meyers put him in a nearby cabin and started for the Point for help. Meanwhile Smith was lying on the ground and wasn't able to move hand or foot. At night, rats ate the hair from his head and he couldn't move a muscle to defend himself. Meyers showed up the second night with a wagon. He put Smith in the wagon and drove forty miles to Rocky Point, where Dad Marsh and his wife took care of him for the rest of the winter. "In the spring the Curry boys got me," said Smith, "I was stranded, hadn't a cent on earth, and took me to the Curry ranch. I stayed with them for a couple of weeks" until he was well enough to pull out and look for work.[40]

Another guest who was welcomed to the Curry home was Little Rockies miner Marion I. Burke, who had known the Curry boys in Missouri. He and some other miners had fed Lonie dried venison and unsalted oatmeal when he visited their camp in winter 1893. Realizing that their food supply was low owing to a shortage of cash, Lonie told them he would charge supplies to his account at the Fort Belknap Indian Reservation store and take them to the Curry ranch seven miles from the miners' camp. The next afternoon Burke and one of his partners rode to the ranch to pick up the supplies. Burke said that for four bachelors, the Curry home was surprisingly neat and clean. Like Ritch, he noticed the gun table placed next to the washstand. Burke witnessed a shooting exhibition from the brothers and Jim Thornhill, and said it was the best he had seen in forty-two years.[41]

In Eugene Cunningham's *Triggernometry: A Gallery of Gunfighters*, one old-time gunman told of Kid Curry's speed with the poker chip draw. The gun-hand is held out at shoulder level, with the poker chip placed on the back of the hand. When the wrist is turned to allow the chip to drop, the gunman attempts to draw, cock, point, and shoot before the chip hits the ground. "Harvey Logan (Kid Curry) …could click out three shots, to beat the chip."[42]

Kid Curry's friendship with the "widow Coalchak" (actually Kolczak) has been mentioned in more than one local history. She was also a close friend of Pike Landusky's wife Julia. Elinor (or Eleanor or Elinora) Kolczak came to Montana from North Dakota with her first husband Julius Wysoski in 1888. Julius died of tuberculosis about six months after the couple's daughter Frances was born on February 22, 1894.[43] Elinor was left to manage her ranch south of the Little Rockies, and Curry would stop by from time to time to help the young widow. She later told her daughter of Curry being "a courteous, rather quiet young man who was always glad to give a hand at ranch chores or chop a supply of wood."[44] He and his brothers helped Elinor gather the cattle and brand her calves, and would often give her family butchered beef from roundups.[45] Her second husband, John Kolczak, was shot and killed in a bar in Landusky, Montana, in December 1908.[46] So, during the time of her friendship with Curry, Elinor was actually the "widow Wysoski."

Another story about the Kid also notes that he was gracious to women. Winifred Studer was born Winifred Laing Partridge on April 9, 1890. Two years later, her father moved the family from Lavina, Montana, to a ranch on Alkali Creek south of Malta to start a sheep business. Many years later, in writing a brief history of her family, she said, "Once in a while a dance would be held at someone's barn or shed and the word got around. Teams were hitched up and the whole family drove for miles to get in on the fun. Kids were bedded down on coats in a corner while the grownups danced. At several of these dances, Mother danced with a quiet, pleasant young man. His name was Logan, known as Kid Curry."[47]

Working the spring roundup for the Circle C in 1890 would have been an excellent opportunity for Kid Curry to meet up with the Sundance Kid again. Sundance was back in Montana at this time, and had been hired to break horses for Henry Ester on his ranch thirty-five miles south of Malta, not far from Circle C headquarters. Before this he had worked for the John T. Murphy Cattle Company near Lavina, Montana.[48]

While John Curry worked for the Fergus Land and Cattle Company, the Fergus County area must have met with his approval, because he filed on his own 154-acre homestead on September 1, 1891, under the name John Logan.[49] Even at this time, many writers claim the Logan brothers were being careful to cover their "back trail." If they were such notorious characters, why would John use his real surname when filing for his homestead?

There were contemporaries of the young John Curry, including Dad Marsh, who described him as a small man seeking a reputation as a badman by wearing a gun and always hankering for a fight.[50] According-ing to one story, about mid-July 1892, Curry left his brothers' Rock Creek ranch riding south toward his home. Approaching Rocky Point, he became involved in a shooting altercation with, depending on the account, a German/Dutch sheepherder, miner, or ex-cowboy turned sheepherder, named Olson. There had been previously bad blood between them attributed to various scenarios: Curry had physically beaten Olson; Olson had "pummeled" Curry; Curry had made Olson dance in a Rocky Point saloon by shooting at his feet; Curry had shot up Olson's sheep herd.

Upon meeting on the trail, they began a duel with Winchesters. Curry came out second best with his horse killed and two bullets in his right arm. The worst that Olson received was a bullet hole in his hat. Curry was left to fend for himself, and in great pain, he somehow walked to the nearest house for assistance. He was taken in a wagon to the Fort Belknap agency where his wounds were dressed. From there his brother Lonie, or possibly Hank, drove him to Harlem, where they went by rail to the St. Clare Hospital at Fort Benton. John's elbow joint was shat-tered, and after waiting a week or more, the doctors had no choice but to amputate his right arm between shoulder and elbow. The sheepherder Olson was allegedly never seen or heard from again.[51]

In the fall of 1893, older brother Hank Curry received some tragic news. He had gone to see a doctor in Fort Benton complaining of bad chest pains and a chronic cough that had him spitting up blood. He was told that he was suffering from an advanced stage of tuberculosis, and the recommendation was for him to head south to a hotter and drier climate such as Arizona. The doctor also suggested that Hank take in the curative properties of the hot springs at Steamboat Springs or Glenwood Springs, Colorado.[52]

Not long after, riding about twenty miles from the Rock Creek ranch, Hank's horse got stuck in an alkali spring. (Another story is that he came upon a couple of bogged-down steers.) Hank got soaked through in the process of freeing the animal, and faced a cold head wind while riding back home. As a result, he caught pneumonia which just about did him in. It was now imperative to get Hank south if he was to have any chance at all. Kid Curry bundled his brother up and into a wagon and they headed toward Steamboat Springs. Hank reportedly died en route in either late 1893 or early 1894.[53] The family has stated that Hank's health had steadily deteriorated after contracting a venereal disease from his wife whom he had left ten years ago in Kansas City, Missouri. The belief is that he was seeking a warmer climate to convalesce, possibly Phoenix, Arizona, when he died of syphilis.[54]

Also, according to family sources, their father, William Logan, may have died sometime in the early 1890s, possibly while in prison for murder. About this time, the oldest son James moved to Needles, California, and operated a store.[55] Some sources say Hank may have made it to his brother's home in California before he died shortly after.[56] James eventually relocated to San Jose County, where he died of natural causes at his home in 1925 at sixty-five years of age. He had been divorced and was survived by two children.[57]

CHAPTER 3

The Man from Pike County, MO

Powell "Pike" Landusky and family owned a ranch on Rock Creek a few miles from the Curry brothers' ranch. His nickname was derived from the county he hailed from in Missouri. Landusky, of Polish-French descent, was a lanky six feet tall with exceptionally long arms. His nearly 200-pound frame possessed phenomenal strength and endurance. He had the reputation of a battler and brawler, and was famous for his volatile temper, especially when he was drinking.[1]

Landusky was nineteen when he left his home in Missouri to travel to the goldfields at Last Chance Gulch (Helena) and Alder Gulch (Virginia City) in Montana Territory. The *River Press* later reported that he took passage with several friends on the steamboat *Henry Adkins* to Fort Benton. "Landusky displayed pugilistic propensities, and just before Fort Benton was reached he and some of his associates started a melee, terrorizing the passengers." They left the boat peacefully at Fort Benton after the captain received support from a group of vigilantes who were in town. Another account says he rode a horse all the way from St. Louis, sometimes with a wagon train, but mostly alone.[2]

It is commonly stated that Landusky arrived in Fort Benton in 1864 on his way to the goldfields at Last Chance Gulch. However, since his birth date is reported as March 4, 1849, he would have only been fifteen years old at the time.[3] A more accurate date for his arrival is 1868, with some accounts placing it in July of that year.[4] Apparently he was much more successful at fighting than in finding gold. He never lost and soon became known as the most ruthless and toughest fighter in the district. Later, at Rocky Point, he met horse thief Brocky Gallagher, regarded as the toughest fighter in that part of the country. These two brawlers agreed to do battle, but when Gallagher was getting the better of the fight, Landusky grabbed a six-shooter and proceeded to beat his opponent. The fight ended after Landusky threw Gallagher into the Missouri River. As a result of this victory, Landusky's fighting fame spread all over Montana.[5]

From Last Chance he went to Alder Gulch and tried his luck at panning for gold, without much success. To support himself he worked for Colonel Charles A. Broadwater's Diamond R freighting company.[6] Sometime in the fall or winter 1868/1869, Landusky and partner John Wirt began trapping at the mouth of the Musselshell River and trading with the Indians. Things went well until one day a band of Brule Sioux came into their camp and confiscated the partners' furs, traps, and provisions. When one of the Sioux grabbed a buffalo steak that was cooking over a fire, this was too much for Landusky. He went berserk, knocking the Indian into the campfire with the frying pan. He then tore off the latter's breech clout and slapped him in the face. In the next instant he grabbed his gun, using it to beat and punch any Indian within his reach. The Indians understandably thought Landusky was crazy, possessed by an evil spirit. In order to appease the evil spirit, the Sioux band gave the two white men several horses they had stolen from the Crow Indians. Landusky and his partner were lucky to have been left alive. This was the beginning of his intense hatred for the Sioux, which soon extended to all tribes.[7]

For the next decade Landusky continued to trap, hunt, and chop cordwood for the Missouri River steamers.[8] In the fall of 1879, Landusky, Joe Hamilton, John J. Healy, William Jackson, and others, established a trading post on Flatwillow Creek.[9] On December 8, 1880, a group of Blackfeet braves and their wives camped outside the post for the purpose of bartering for furs. It is certain that Landusky was filling up on the whiskey that was dispensed at the post, and the Indians may also have been partaking. Trouble started, according to J. H. "Jim" Boucher, who was at the post, when Landusky noticed a squaw sitting on the floor with a Winchester rifle. She was taking the cover off the rifle, and Landusky was worried that she would accidentally shoot herself or someone else. When he roughly took the gun away from her, a number of Indians took exception and started to protest. Landusky lost his temper and, using his fists, knocked down White Calf and Running

Rabbit. "Teddy Blue" Abbott said the trouble began when Landusky knocked down an Indian who had attempted to stab him in the back. He then threw firewood at the man as he was running away. Regardless of how it started, matters escalated until Landusky began firing his rifle into the Indian camp, purportedly at White Calf, the chief. White Calf was unscathed, but unfortunately at least one of the bullets hit the chief's wife in the abdomen, killing her. In retaliation, the Blackfeet brave Landusky had earlier struck shot him in the face, taking off his left lower jawbone. Doctors were able to save his life, but his face was terribly scarred.[10] He would slobber on that side of his face whenever the weather turned cold.[11]

In the spring of 1881 Landusky was well enough to open a store and saloon and establish a freighting business in Maiden, a mining camp in the Judith Mountains. Joining him in these enterprises was previous trading post partner, Joe Hamilton.[12] Here, in April, Landusky married Mrs. Julia Dessery, who had left Colorado and come to Montana with her five children, four daughters and a son. She had left her husband Victor Dessery in about 1879, because he had not been supporting the family. Landusky was good to his step-children; he would take the two youngest, Dora and Elfie, on his lap and sing to them. By 1888, he had two sons and two daughters of his own by Julia.[13]

During the summer of 1881, Landusky and Hamilton went to the gold camp of Alpine Gulch in the Judith Mountains, and from there located several claims. In May 1882, the partners were doing well enough financially that they sold their trading post buildings and 480 acres of land on the Flatwillow.[14] Two years later, Landusky got into the livery business in Maiden with the National Livery and Feed Stable.[15]

In June 1884, Landusky began prospecting in the Little Rockies with two partners, Frank Aldrich, and "Dutch Louie" Meyers, the latter having been a horse thief. In fact this was the reason why Meyers had left his ranch on Crooked Creek and joined the prospecting party, so as to steer clear of the vigilantes searching for him below Rocky Point. They soon discovered gold in a gulch they called Little Alder, in hopes it would be at least a smaller version of the famous Alder Gulch in Virginia City.

Landusky moved his family from Maiden to a cabin near the mouth of the gulch. The claim was on Indian land, but this obstacle was eliminated by the government ultimately withdrawing the mining district from the reservation. There was a short-lived rush, as the prospectors did not find enough placer to make it worthwhile.[16]

The dull days that followed in winter 1885 were probably the catalyst for a violent altercation that occurred between Landusky and Dutch Louie. About February 26 Landusky shot at Meyers while in the latter's tent, presumably with the intention of killing his partner. Since the incident occurred at Alder Gulch, on reservation property at the time, Landusky was arrested by a U.S. Marshal and taken to Helena to be arraigned at U.S. District Court. Charges, filed on April 1, 1885, stated that Pike Landusky "did maliciously attempt to commit the crime of murder or manslaughter with a dangerous weapon upon the person of one Louis Meyers." While Landusky was out on bond, he went to Maiden to put his business affairs in order. Among other things, he and Joe Hamilton dissolved their partnership. In November Landusky returned to Helena for his trial, but was acquitted of the charges when Meyers' witnesses did not appear at court.[17]

The winter of 1886/1887 Landusky and "Teddy Blue" Abbott rode range between the Missouri River and the Milk River to the north for Granville Stuart's Pioneer Cattle Company.[18] Landusky had moved his family to a homestead cabin near the head of Rock Creek in the Little Rockies, not far from the Curry horse ranch that Hank and the Kid were just starting up at that time.[19]

In the spring Landusky returned to prospecting the Little Rockies. In 1890 he discovered, with partner George Manning, the Gold Bug, Julia, and Gold Boy mines.[20] He also started prospecting with his son-in-law, Bob Orman, who had married Landusky's oldest step-daughter, Mary Alice Dessery.[21] In the summer of 1893, Orman discovered a rich vein of gold ore near Gold Bug Butte. He named the mine the August, the month in which it had been discovered.[22] "Bob being drunk most of the time," wrote a Little Rockies resident, "leased the mine to Landusky his father-in-law."[23] Also at this time, Landusky owned several mining claims in the

Ruby Gulch area. Another rush had started to the Little Rockies, but this time the prospectors were hard-rock miners.[24]

In a valley on the southwestern slope of the Little Rockies, about a mile above Landusky's ranch on Rock Creek, a permanent settlement was built on the site in which a few cabins remained from the earlier placer miners' camp. Since cattle had been running on the range between the Missouri and Milk Rivers for the last several years, this miners' enclave also quickly became a cow town. It was officially organized and named Landusky in a town meeting held by miners and stockmen on June 9, 1894.[25] The settlement consisted of a post office, eating house, boardinghouse, general store, assay office, stage station, livery stable, blacksmith shop, dance hall, a half dozen saloons, and about twenty cabins.[26] Some writers state that the vote to choose a town name was held in October 1894. Harvey, John, and Lonie, using the Curry name, signed a precinct election register at this time listing their residence as the Rock Creek ranch. They and other Little Rockies ranchers preferred the name of "Rock Creek" over "Landusky."[27]

The town of Landusky, Montana, today. (Author's Collection)

Charles and Augusta Chamberlain, who ran the boardinghouse, were good friends of the Curry brothers. Augusta cooked for the boys when they boarded with her one summer, and they were always very courteous to her. She considered the Kid one of her best boarders, as he would make sure that the men coming from the Landusky saloons to eat were respectful of Augusta and her family. She and Charles W. Duvall both mentioned the Curry brothers owning a saloon in town, leaving the management to John. "By September the work on Gold bug [mine] had stopped," wrote Mrs. Chamberlain. "Lone [Lonie] and kid have gone to the ranch. John kept the Saloon open and he was my only border."[28] Other saloons were operated by Jacob "Jew Jake" Harris, W. W. "Wash" Lampkin, Puck Powell, R. Curry, Clark and Cochran, with Landusky later building a saloon for his brother Antoine "Tony" to run. The reference to "R. Curry" may indicate that Curry cousin Bob Lee had joined them by this time.[29]

The Currys and Thornhill had been living peaceably with Landusky for the last few years, in great measure owing to the guiding presence of older brother Hank. Hank and Lonie would often stop by the Landusky home for a visit and enjoy Julia's cooking. Harvey's visits were less frequent, and his unassuming nature prevented him from stepping down from his horse. Hank's interest in the Landuskys' live-in schoolteacher, Mary Everett, gave him another excuse to stop by the house. However, Landusky did not want Hank going out with Mary for some reason, and he managed to convince her to stop seeing him. Julia believed her husband was also attracted to the new teacher. Even the Kid told Landusky that he should stay away from her since he was a married man. After this incident the relationship between the Currys and Landusky began to take a turn for the worse.[30]

Hank's advice to his younger brothers was to treat Landusky fairly, stay away from him whenever possible, and don't have any business dealings with him. After the death of Hank, this peaceful coexistence was fated to end.[31] Jim Thornhill threw in with the remaining Curry brothers as a partner in their ranching business, but he was not the model of exemplary behavior that Hank had been. It has been said the brothers started drinking to excess, and would go on sprees and shoot up the saloons of Landusky, although they were probably no more inclined to hurrah or whoop-up the town than the other cowpunchers coming off the range.[32]

According to Chouteau County District Judge Dudley DuBose, the Currys came before his court more than once for charges of assault. He expressed his opinion in later years that, of the three Curry brothers, Harvey was the "best of the lot," and may have turned out all right if he hadn't come under the influence of the bad men who infested the area of the Little Rockies. As for Johnny and Lonie, the judge had nothing good to say about them, and considered them "bad eggs."[33]

Little Rockies pioneer, William "Milk River Bill" Harmon, was an ex-soldier from Fort Assinniboine, who became a prospector, and then a bullwhacker for the Diamond R freighting outfit. In a 1935 Great Falls newspaper interview, he gave his opinion that John and Lonie Curry were "mean, bull-dozing cusses," and as for the Kid, "the very devil showed in his eyes." He added that it was not uncommon for the Currys to pistol-whip "some poor devil" they disliked.[34]

A dilapidated mine building in Landusky, Montana. (Author's Collection)

The Kid got into a confrontation with one William Spencer during a Fourth of July celebration in 1894. Emigrating from Sweden, Spencer had come to Valley County earlier that year and settled in the Larb Hills somewhat south of Saco and Beaverton. He earned his livelihood running sheep, logging, and building cabins. Phillips County historian, Gene Barnard, a neighbor to Spencer's son, related the incident: "He [Spencer] had acquired a mare that was exceptionally fleet of foot. Bets were placed on this mare against Kid Curry's horse and Mr. Spencer won. Curry was a sore loser, especially to a foreigner, so he roped Mr. Spencer around the arms intending to drag him. For some reason he did not take off and Mr. Spencer stepped out of the loop. Upon turning around, he saw the reason for no action. His partner had a bead on Kid Curry with a rifle. When asked later if he would have shot, his answer was the same as The Kid instinctively knew."[35]

On Saturday evening July 21, 1894, Methodist clergyman William Wesley Van Orsdel held the first religious service in the Little Rockies at the Reigel family sawmill near Landusky. It was announced that an eleven o'clock service would be held in Landusky on Sunday morning.

Jim Thornhill's barn near Landusky, Montana. (Author's Collection)

The next morning "Brother Van" stepped down from a lumber wagon that had carried him the three miles to town. Since Landusky lacked a church, Brother Van immediately set out to locate a building to hold services. He soon decided that Jake Harris' saloon would be suitable for his preaching service. His biography relates, "Van and the Reigels pushed inside the old saloon and gathered up the empty liquor bottles that were strewn around the single room. Two wooden boxes were set on end several feet apart, and a board laid across them, forming a makeshift pew that would seat several persons. A number of these benches were hastily improvised, and in a short while the room which had formerly served as a hangout for drunks, rowdies, and rustlers was well-filled with those who waited for Brother Van's sermon. At least 75 persons in all were present, and a preacher never had a more peculiar congregation than this one."[36]

Pike Landusky and saloon operator Jacob Harris were present, and the Curry brothers with friend Jim Thornhill sat together on a front bench. Taking his sermon from Matthew, "Van proclaimed a Law that

Jim Thornhill, standing at center, with Pike Landusky's family in Landusky, Montana, ca. 1890. Julia Landusky is seated front row, third from right. (Larry Pointer Collection, Box 21, Folder 18, American Heritage Center, University of Wyoming.)

over-arches all man-made laws, and told of a just and happy society which exists even now in heaven, and could be realized on earth if people cared for it enough. It was a hopeful thought, even to such as Kid Curry."[37]

The origination of the trouble that developed between Landusky and the Currys cannot be readily determined at this late date. There are two main catalysts that are mentioned in just about every biography on Kid Curry. The first is the incident of one party borrowing a new plow from the other, and it being returned with a broken handle, or it not being returned at all. The second and most understandable reason for the development of hard feelings was generated by Lonie Curry's courtship of Landusky's youngest step-daughter, Cindinilla, known as "Elfie" or "Elfia," who was only fifteen at the time.[38] Lonie had an undesirable reputation with women and Landusky protested vehemently to Kid Curry concerning the relationship. Rumor and innuendo from Landusky's saloon friends reached his ears that Elfie was meeting with Lonie secretly, and he began calling Lonie a "whoremaster" and Kid Curry a "brand artist."[39]

It was said of Landusky that he would do anything for a friend, but his dislike for someone would invariably turn into an irrational, unforgiving hatred, especially when he was drinking.[40] He made threats against the Curry brothers and began scheming of ways to get even with them. It was Augusta Chamberlain's opinion that Landusky wanted to run "the whole show. [H]e tryed hard to get the Curry boys into trouble. [I]t was a feud of long standing."[41] The oft-repeated claim by past writers that Landusky brought false charges against the Kid and John Curry for cattle rustling and brand altering cannot be substantiated. The District Court Records for Chouteau County in Fort Benton (the county seat) do not show such charges to exist.[42] It has been said that they took part in mavericking, which was largely overlooked and practiced by most of the ranchers of that day.[43] However, the court records do contain charges against Harvey Curry, John Curry, and Lee Self for assault with a deadly weapon on one James Ross. Leander "Lee" G. Self was the Currys' brother-in-law who had married their sister Allie on September 12, 1883, in Jackson County, Missouri.[44]

On or about October 3, 1894, Harvey, John and Lee got into a row with a cowboy drifter named James Ross. On October 27 Ross swore out a complaint, and the charges stated in part (capitalization and grammar left intact):

> That Harvey Curry Held a Shot Gun pointed at his, the said James Ross's Body in a threatening manner, while Lee Self and John Curry Beat him over the Head and Body with Pistols. That Harvey Curry also Beat him with a Pistol. That the said Harvey Curry, John Curry and Lee Self Beat him the said James Ross, untill his Head and Body was bruised and cut in a terrible manner.[45]

Meanwhile, Landusky boarded a Great Northern passenger train to St. Louis, Missouri, to spend several weeks visiting family. They had not seen him since he had gone to Montana as a young man, and had feared him dead. He returned to Montana in the latter part of October, accompanied by his brother Antoine "Tony" and other relatives, eager to relocate in Landusky.[46]

Undersheriff John Buckley, of Chouteau County, came to Landusky from Fort Benton about this time to arrest the two Curry brothers and their brother-in-law. In order to take time out to investigate the charges, Buckley deputized Pike Landusky temporarily, and placed the prisoners in his custody. This unfortunate lapse in judgment now gave Landusky the opportunity to vent his whiskey-soaked hatred for the Currys that he had been nursing for so many weeks. Taking them to his ranch, he handcuffed and manacled the feet of John and did the same to the Kid, with the added precaution of securing him with a log chain. Lee Self apparently somehow escaped before this treatment or had not been an object of Landusky's ire.[47]

After Landusky had secured the boys in his milk house, he left them momentarily in charge of his brother Tony.[48] Supposedly, other family members were not told of what was going on. When Julia sent Elfie for some milk, she was startled at the sight of John and the Kid in their predicament. Seeing that she was embarrassed, Harvey teased her not to let a cat get at the milk.[49]

Landusky, now well fortified with whiskey and chewing tobacco, worked himself into a rage at first by spewing curses, followed by savagely beating and kicking the brothers. He spit tobacco juice in their faces and urinated on them while they lay helpless on the floor.[50] As a final indignity, he took out his knife and said he was going to make geldings of them, no doubt wishing he could do the same to Lonie for "laying up" with his step-daughter. The Kid predicted a first town lynching if Landusky followed through with his threat. Curry also demanded that Landusky let him loose for a fair fight, promising him a thrashing he would never forget. Landusky, who appeared to sober at this challenge, put away his knife and said it was enough that he was turning them over to the undersheriff, with the likelihood of prison in their future.[51]

Buckley took them to Fort Benton to be arraigned before Judge Dudley DuBose, apparently not noting the condition of the prisoners.[52] Bail was fixed at $500 and Andrew S. Lohman and Frank Plunkett, friends of the Curry boys, signed the bond.[53] The Kid and John asked for a continuance so witnesses could be summoned for their defense. This was granted and the case carried over to the next term of district court in December.[54]

Witness Jacob Launze testified that Harvey and John Curry did not strike or attempt to strike Ross, but on the contrary, had pulled away Lee Self from his attacks on Ross and one Lou Simmons. Launze also stated that when Ross placed his hand under his coat to draw his gun, Harvey Curry drew his and told him to stop. The witness asserted John Curry did not carry any weapon that night.[55] Most accounts state that the charges were dismissed due to insufficient evidence; however, according to Kenworth, Judge DuBose did not dismiss the charges and assessed a fine of fifty dollars.[56]

The Currys claimed it was a put-up job by Landusky to get possession of their ranch and mining claims, and that he paid Ross to file false assault charges.[57] When they returned from Fort Benton, the impulsive, hot-tempered John wanted to seek out their adversary and settle the feud with guns; however, the Kid told him he would deal with Landusky in his own way when the time was right.[58] Dad Marsh said the Kid had earlier told Landusky that he would get his revenge after his return, and now he began telling several people that he was going to whip Landusky for the treatment received by him while in his custody. For his part, upon the Currys' return, Landusky tried to be conciliatory and offered his friendship, but was flatly refused.[59] He may have been trying to appease a bad conscience, but more likely he was trying to avoid the consequences of his failed scheme to rid the territory of the Curry brothers.

In November of 1894, somebody suggested the community should put on a big Christmas dance and dinner. A town meeting was held to plan a celebration the likes of which nobody in that country had ever seen. Warren Berry, the owner of a general store, proposed that something novel should be on the dinner menu, and fresh Baltimore oysters (one account says Seattle) were decided upon.[60] The task of ordering four dozen quarts of oysters fell to "Lousy" the stage driver. Not being an expert on oysters, he ended up wiring from the railroad to Minneapolis for canned oysters. As it turned out, nobody seemed to mind, even though the express rate was more than the cost of the oysters.[61]

There was a flurry of activity as everyone in town got into the spirit of preparing for the big event. The Curry boys even temporarily set aside their feud with Landusky. John had set himself up in the livery business around the time his brother Hank had died, and offered his big new hay barn for the dance. Lonie, an accomplished fiddler, volunteered to put together a band.[62] Dan Moran agreed to bring his fiddle, and Al Wise would play piano and banjo.[63] A portable Mason and Hammond organ was hauled by wagon from a ranch ten miles from town. Word of the celebration was carried by riders all over the thinly populated territory. Settlers traveled as far as sixty miles in every type of conveyance, and brought their share of food and more. By Christmas Eve more than a hundred guests had arrived, the largest assemblage of people that country had ever recorded.[64]

The closest thing to a master of culinary art in this region of the Little Rockies, as long as he was sober, was a famous roundup cook called "Tie Up George." He was enlisted to use his talent to make a very large quantity of oyster stew. John Ritch offered the use of his new home in Landusky to prepare and serve the evening meals. The men checked their artillery before joining the festivities; however, if someone felt the need to make some noise they would borrow a gun from the bartender and shoot holes in the sky. The guests danced, ate, and drank bourbon whiskey by the barrel for two days and nights.[65] Elfie recalled that Harvey walked up to her and gave her a bite of his apple. Since Lonie was busy fiddling, the Kid asked her for a dance.[66] December 27, the day after the celebration had ended, was the day Kid Curry had planned to take his revenge on Pike Landusky.

CHAPTER 4

Pay Back

There was a light snowfall the morning of December 27, 1894, and the cold was keeping several men inside the Clothing Store and Saloon run by Jake Harris. Harris' left leg had been amputated close to the hip after a gun battle with City Marshal George Treat of Great Falls in November 1891.[1] He used a shotgun for a crutch if he expected any trouble in his saloon. Harris and Landusky were friends, and Landusky had put up the money for the building with the status of silent partner. There was a counter in the back of the saloon where cheap clothing and some food items were sold. Harris had sent to Anaconda for a friend of his named Charles Annis, who went by the name Hogan, to be his clerk. Despite being frail and tubercular, he was reputed to be a gunman. It was understood that, besides minding the store, another duty of Hogan's was to keep the wild cowboy element, such as the Currys, in line.[2]

Ed Skelton, a friend of Landusky's, was present that morning: "I met Mr. Landusky at Jake Harris saloon about ten o'clock on the 27th day of December A. D. 1894. We sat there in the saloon about two hours; he got up to go home, goes out on the stoop and meets Bill McKinzie [McKenzie]. They had a talk out there quite a while and went back in the saloon and I went with them. We steped up to the bar to take a drink or smoke. I went over to the card table and left them talking at the bar."[3] Jacob Harris, George S. Allis, Thomas Smith Carter, and one other were at the card table playing whist. The time was about two o'clock.

Lonie Curry and Jim Thornhill entered the saloon at this time and walked past the bar to the back counter. They called Hogan over to weigh a quarter's worth of apples, after which they stepped toward the back door. Kid Curry then came through the front door of the saloon and walked up to Landusky who was leaning over the bar talking to miner friend William McKenzie. Curry tapped Landusky on the shoulder with his left hand, then grabbed him, pulled him around, and struck him in the face with his right hand. He then struck Landusky repeatedly, who appeared to make no defense except to keep Curry off. Pike's famous fighting ability may possibly have been hampered by old injuries, rather than by physical limitations of advanced age as many writers assert. It is often stated that he was in his fifties at the time of the altercation, but he was actually only forty-five years old.

At the start of the fight, Lonie and Thornhill told Hogan he was to take no hand in the fight. Hogan agreed, and in his testimony at the subsequent coroner's inquest, he stated that there had been no guns drawn.[4] Lonie and Thornhill then shouted to the onlookers "fair fight, fair play." At this time the combatants were scuffling and went into a clinch, and then they both fell to the floor with Curry on top. This was also when Curry's gun fell out of his pocket onto the floor. Thornhill stepped out and picked the gun up and said "No one shall interfere," followed by "See gentlemen, I don't draw this pistol, I pick it up on [off] the floor." Not one witness stated that Thornhill *pointed* the gun at anybody.[5] Meanwhile Curry was sitting astride Landusky's chest with his knees on his arms. For the next few moments he was furiously striking Landusky in the face, until Thornhill finally told Curry to let him up. Curry got up off of Landusky and told Thornhill to "give me my gun."

Landusky got up from the floor and wiped the blood from his face with his hands.[6] About half of the witnesses had gone out the back door by this time; however, those remaining all saw Landusky pull a gun from his right-hand overcoat pocket. He stuck the gun at Curry's abdomen and held it there for a second or two, attempting to fire. This is when Landusky's revolver may have jammed or malfunctioned for some other reason.[7] At this moment most of the witnesses said they heard someone, possibly Thornhill, say to kill or shoot Landusky. With his left hand Curry grabbed Landusky's right hand that held his gun, and threw it up. At the same time Curry drew his own gun from his hip pocket and fired three shots. After the first shot Landusky said, "Oh, God" or "O My." After the second shot he reeled and fell to the floor. The third shot missed him.

The Kid, Lonie, and Thornhill went out the back door with Hogan following. Thornhill and Hogan picked Harris off the ground where he had fallen while trying to escape the shooting. His crutches had not been within reach when the shooting began, so he "was hopping on one leg and holding to everything I could reach to brace myself." Harris had reached the back door about the time the third shot was fired, and he "jumped out of the door on the box used for a step, fell over and was sitting on the ground at the time Hogan and Thornhill came out and picked me up." After assisting Harris to his saloon, Thornhill went out the front door to join the two Currys as they walked toward Puck Powell's saloon. Before the shooting, two of the witnesses, E. E. Reigel and miner George Contway, had fled to Landusky's new home that was being built in town. Reigel, whose occupation was "saw mill man," mentions that workmen were there plastering.[8] Reigel saw one of the Currys go toward Powell's saloon, stop and turn around, pull his gun and point it toward Harris' saloon, then turn back and continue to walk to Powell's.

Lonie was sitting on the end of the bar in Powell's saloon when miner Tom Carter asked him for the use of a saddle horse to go after a doctor. "Tommy I think less of you for that than anything you ever done in your life," Lonie replied, and refused to let him have the horse. "It is only human," Carter retorted. At some point in this exchange Lonie said, "I hope the son of a bitch is dead." Thornhill spoke up and said, "[I] have got horses at the ranch, so help yourself," and the Kid concurred. In a few minutes John Curry drove a team up in front of the saloon. He then got in the backseat with his brother Harvey, who had somehow procured a shotgun or rifle. Lonie and Thornhill got in the front seat and they drove off.

Meanwhile, many of the saloon patrons who had fled earlier returned to view the dying Pike Landusky. Harris was among the first to enter, and he suggested someone should inform Landusky's family of the tragedy. Ed Skelton elected himself to do so. Harris and Albert L. Mathews walked to where Landusky was lying on the floor and heard him moaning. Mathews asked him if he could talk and was answered only with a groan. Then Landusky's head and neck went into convulsions, lasting for a minute or two, when he became still. Harris and Mathews took Landusky's hands and felt for a pulse but couldn't detect one. They stayed by his side for two or three minutes and "finally came to the conclusion he was dead."

Landusky's body was laid out in the bedroom of his home a short distance south of town by his mining friends. Elfie would occasionally look in on her step-father. She had wished him a Merry Christmas the evening before, and that morning the whole family ate breakfast together before Landusky left for Harris' saloon. He was buried in the frozen soil on a hill at his ranch, perhaps the same hill the children had sledded on that day.[9] Brother Van Orsdel had left that part of the country some months ago, so local layman John Ritch conducted the service.

After the shooting of Landusky, the Currys and Thornhill drove the wagon to their ranch where they deliberated on their next course of action. Lonie, John, and Thornhill thought it best to remain in the area and take their chances with the law, but the Kid was dead set against turning himself in. There is good reason to believe Kid Curry would not have been convicted of murder at trial, but he did not stay around long enough to be served. He felt that the justice system had not treated him fairly concerning the earlier assault case, and he also may have feared local

Grave of Pike Landusky on his old ranch just outside of the town named for him. (Author's Collection)

retribution. However, "With few exceptions, it was Pike's closest friends who blamed the Kid," stated Brown Waller, "and had he remained and stood trial he might have been acquitted … the mind of the citizenry was that the killing was justifiable."[10]

It was finally decided that Kid and Thornhill would hide out in an isolated cabin located in the Missouri River breaks between Antelope and Bull creeks. It would become known as Kid Curry's Hideaway in Hideaway Coulee.[11] In his memoirs, wild horse hunter Walter Duvall described it as "jist a little one room log shack, very small. I have heard that it was built by a horse thief and not by Curry."[12]

The December 31 coroner's inquest found "that one Harvey Curry did wilfully and maliciously and with a murderous intent" cause the death of Powell Landusky by firing two shots into the front of his body, "and we further find that Lonnie Curry and James Thornhill were directly imply [implicated] in the murderous assault." Bench warrants were issued for Harvey Curry for the murder of Powell Landusky, and for Louis (Lonie) Curry and James Thornhill for accessory to murder. Lonie was served with the warrant in May 1895, and Thornhill would be served in July after eventually turning himself in for trial.[13] Lonie was arrested in Chinook, and taken to Fort Benton to face the very same Judge DuBose who had presided over his brothers' assault trial.[14] His bail, set at $5,000, had been posted by M. F. Marsh and C. J. McNamara.[15] On May 14 the jury found him not guilty, the shooting was believed to be in self-defense, and this met with approbation from the judge.[16]

CHAPTER 5

Hiding Out and Future Associates

The Kid had many friends all over northeastern Montana who were loyal to him and he could turn to for help. In fact, in order to grubstake his departure from the Little Rockies, the Coburns of the Circle C bought Kid Curry's cattle and his 4T brand, and delivered the money to the hideaway.[1] Curry may have been visiting the surrounding ranches when, in about January 1895, he ran into his friend Sid Willis at the mouth of the Musselshell River. Now sheriff of Valley County, Willis was chasing three escaped convicts from the Glasgow, Montana, jail. Curry had him covered, but let him go upon learning that he was not wanted by the sheriff. Supposedly he asked Willis to extend an invitation to Chouteau County Sheriff George McLaughlin to come get him.[2]

Curry and Thornhill stayed at and around the hideaway for the better part of six months before Curry quit the country and Thornhill finally came in and asked for a trial.[3] Robert Coburn of the Circle C put up bond for Thornhill, and he retained Donnelly and Knox for his counsel. Although some sources state that Thornhill's case was dismissed without trial, he was actually tried and found not guilty on August 27, 1895.[4] Curry headed for the famous outlaw enclave known as Hole-in-the-Wall, southwest of the present town of Kaycee, in Johnson County, Wyoming.

It should be explained that "Hole-in-the-Wall" actually has two different designations. Generally it applies to the valley of Buffalo Creek that was once a prehistoric lake or river. An approximately thirty-five-mile long, 350-feet-high red wall of sandstone, running north and south, protects the valley on the east. The southern end of the Big Horn Mountains forms a barrier to the west. More specifically, the "Hole" refers to where the Red Wall cuts back sharply to the east, forming a V-shaped notch. Here the wall is steep, but not perpendicular, and covered with talus. A slab of white rock shaped like an arrowhead lies in the center of the notch, marking the trail used by rustlers driving stolen cattle and horses into the valley.

Some writers, without first-hand knowledge, describe the notch as a somewhat level trail that is wide enough to allow two riders abreast or a wagon to go through. Others question whether there is a V-notch at all, stating that it *supposedly* exists. The author traveled to the Hole-in-the-Wall valley in September 2009, and was guided to the notch by the owners of the Willow Creek Ranch (originally the Kenneth McDonald ranch). There is no gap *through* the wall; one must follow a trail *up and over* the rim of the wall, single file, on foot or horseback.

Surprisingly, with all the mythology that exists concerning the Hole, this outlaw hideout was not impregnable. To the north, south, and west it is surrounded by open rolling hills, which would not be a hindrance to any posse wishing to invade. And in addition to the V-notch, the eastern Red Wall has other openings or entrances, including one near old Barnum and a gap made by the Middle Fork of Powder River. Even so, few lawmen cared or dared to enter this outlaw domain that pastured stolen livestock. There was no actual town in the Hole-in-the-Wall valley, just a half dozen cabins. The only thing left today of the famous Hole-in-the-Wall cabin on Buffalo Creek, is part of the foundation barely exposed in the earth. Today the area is still remote and isolated, and can only be reached by a few rugged dirt roads. A few ranches dot the wide grassy valley through which Buffalo Creek runs.

If Kid Curry did not meet the young George S. Currie and his family at their ranch in Hulett, Wyoming, while coming up the trail in 1884, he couldn't help but run into him in this area of the country at this time. By 1895, George Currie had reached the pinnacle of his chosen profession, surviving the Johnson County War, and was said to have acquired the title of "King of the Rustlers" after Nathan "Nate" Champion's death. Actually, the dubious appellation of "the king of the cattle thieves" was given to Champion in the purple prose of a Chicago *Herald* reporter in April 1892, after Champion was gunned down at the KC Ranch by the big cattlemen's hired army.[5]

The Hole-in-the-Wall today. The V-notch can be clearly seen. (Author's Collection)

In 1886 when Currie was fifteen, his family moved to Chadron, Nebraska, where he worked as a store clerk. Tiring of this after a few years, he decided to make a new start. His first thought was to head to Wyoming where his family still owned the ranch near Hulett in Crook County. He found work near there riding the range for E. W. Whitcomb's Bar FS outfit on the Belle Fourche River.[6] In no time he became an expert with horses and the use of a rope in cutting out mavericks during the round-ups. Unfortunately, he and the foreman had some kind of falling out, resulting in the latter spreading word to all the cattle ranches in the area that Currie was a rustler.[7] He moved on to the Powder River country, working for the Flying E Bar ranch near Buffalo, Wyoming. Famed law-man Joe LeFors said this was about the time that Currie was stealing horses and running them north to dispose of in Montana.[8] He eventually got in with a rustling crowd in a wild area known as the Lost Cabin country southwest of Hole-in-the-Wall, and became adept at changing brands with the use of a running iron.[9] It was said he seldom had to cut

Kid Curry, the composed tramp. (Robert G. McCubbin Collection)

Rare early photo of "Flatnose" George Currie. (Courtesy of Mike Bell)

out a brand, but when it was necessary his heeler was a man named Walt Punteney.[10]

In 1893 Punteney was working for Judge Jay L. Torrey's Embar (M-Bar) Ranch on Owl Creek near Thermopolis. That summer, Punteney and two other Embar Company cowboys were in the news for relentlessly tracking down two horse thieves. The company acknowledged Punteney's dedication by promoting him to assistant foreman. But sometime within the next two years Punteney began his first steps in becoming an outlaw. He and another man were arrested for cattle rustling in December of 1896, and taken to Thermopolis. While waiting for trial, the two were reportedly confined in a store for lack of a town jail. Early one morning, Punteney escaped out the back door in his night clothes and apparently was never seriously pursued by the law.[11] By the following June he and George Currie would join Kid Curry in a bank robbing venture.

Robert LeRoy Parker, better known as Butch Cassidy, arrived in Johnson County several months after robbing the San Miguel Valley Bank in Telluride, Colorado, on June 24, 1889, with friends Tom Mc-Carty and Matt Warner. It is said that in the spring or summer of 1890 he bought some land that included two attached cabins on Blue Creek, about ten miles northwest of Hole-in-the-Wall. It is probable that he met George Currie and his rustling pal Tom O'Day, since they were in the Hole and environs at this time. However, Cassidy was forced to sell his property on Blue Creek just before Christmas 1890. He had received word that law officers or stock detectives were closing in owing to his horse rustling activities.[12]

According to Pearl Baker, in the winter of 1890/1891 Cassidy was employed working cattle at W. H. Howland's 4H Ranch, fourteen miles east of Buffalo. She says Butch also worked for the famous Pitchfork Ranch in the Bighorn Basin during this time period.[13] Research indicates Howland was actually W. H. Holland, who ranched with his family below Buffalo on Clear Creek. He owned the 4H Ranch of the Des Moines Cattle Company, which he sold in the late 1890s, taking over as manager.[14] Jesse Cole Kenworth says that Kid Curry met Cassidy when the latter worked at the 4H.[15] This is not very likely since Curry was busy

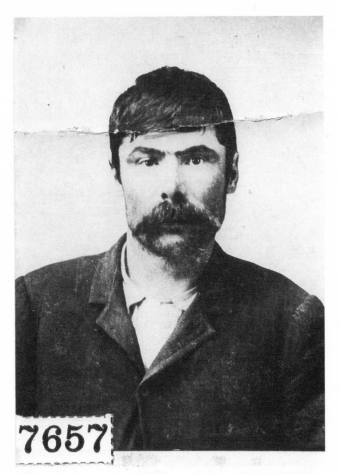

"Big, blundering" Tom O'Day. (Robert G. McCubbin Collection)

running his own ranch in northern Montana, and working part time at the Coburn Circle C.

Cassidy may have returned to the Wind River country where he and partner Al Hainer had purchased a ranch on Horse Creek, in northern Fremont County, in the fall of 1889. In April 1892 the two were arrested near Auburn, Wyoming, for horse theft. It took over two years of legal delays in the court proceedings, before the jury finally rendered their

Robert LeRoy Parker, alias Butch Cassidy upon entering the
Wyoming State Penitentiary, 1894. (Courtesy of Mike Bell)

verdict on July 4, 1894. Although Hainer was acquitted, Cassidy was
found guilty, sentenced to two years, and entered the Wyoming State
Penitentiary in Laramie on July 15, 1894. He was given a pardon by
Governor William A. Richards and released on January 19, 1896.[16] He
headed for Brown's Hole, a rugged area that outlaws favored where the
Utah, Colorado, and Wyoming borders meet.

Brown's Hole (later called Brown's Park) is a remote valley of the
Green River, thirty to thirty-five miles long and five to six miles wide.
It extends in an east-west direction, and lies mostly in northeastern Utah
and northwestern Colorado, with a small portion in southern Wyoming.
With Diamond Mountain to the south, and the O-Wi-Yu-Kuts Plateau

and Cold Spring Mountain to the north, there were very few feasible entrances into the valley. Today, in the northwestern part of the valley in Utah, access is from a very steep gravel road through a rugged canyon. There is much easier access from the relatively level terrain in Colorado on the east. The valley floor consists of mostly sagebrush and cedar plateaus, hills, and ridges, with a few cabins and dugouts that still exist from the outlaw era in various states of decay. The Green River meanders in an easterly direction along the base of Diamond Mountain, eventually turning south between the mountain's eastern slope and Douglas Mountain. It then plunges through the towering red sandstone walls called the Gates of Lodore (sometimes spelled Ladore) in what is now Dinosaur National Monument.

Matt Warner had a cabin on Diamond Mountain, and Cassidy was welcomed there by his old pal and another man going by the name of "Elzy" Lay (also referred to as "Elza").[17] In summer 1889 Cassidy had hid out in Brown's Hole after the Telluride bank robbery, and became fast friends with William Ellsworth "Elzy" Lay. They had both worked at the Herb Bassett ranch at one time or another, and also spent much of their time at the ranch of Charley Crouse.[18] Harry Longabaugh, the Sundance Kid, may also have spent time in the Hole sometime after Cassidy's release from prison in 1896. "I was well-acquainted with Butch Cassidy," Herb's daughter, Josie Bassett Morris said, "and he was a good friend. I sometimes called him my Brown's Park beau ... Now Sundance, well I don't know about, I never kept track with him. He was different from Butch. I guess I never cared that much about him anyway. It seemed he kinda tried to play the role of Elza Lay. Sundance spent a lot of his time in the Little Snake country, in Colorado. Nobody could fill Elza's shoes, not in my book."[19] Josie's sister, Ann, wrote of a Thanksgiving dinner that the outlaws put on for the people in Brown's Hole most likely in the same year, 1896. Among the hosts she names Cassidy and Lay, and also one Harry Roudenbaugh, possibly meaning Harry Longabaugh.[20]

On August 13, 1896, Cassidy and Lay headed up the robbery of a bank in Montpelier, Idaho, to obtain sufficient funds for Matt Warner's defense against a murder charge. After this successful venture they made

Early photo of Butch Cassidy's partner, William Ellsworth "Elzy"
Lay. (Robert G. McCubbin Collection)

it safely back to Brown's Hole to lie low for several months. Then, on
April 21, 1897, they robbed the mine payroll from the Pleasant Valley
Coal Company at Castle Gate, Utah. This time they hid from the law for
a few months at an isolated Utah hideout called Robbers Roost.[21]

Robbers Roost was three hundred miles south of Brown's Hole, in
southeastern Utah. The Roost "is the exact opposite of the Hole," Charles
Kelly pointed out. "Instead of being a 'hole,' protected on all sides by
mountains, it is an elevated plateau lying on the summit of the San Ra-
fael Swell."[22] The Green River and the Orange Cliffs border it on the

Brown's Hole (now Brown's Park), Utah, today. (Author's Collection)

east, the Henry Mountains to the south and west. The area is a maze of steep-walled canyons, gorges, and mesas, extremely arid, with little vegetation and few dependable water sources. Convenient supply centers for the outlaws were Green River, Utah, to the north, and Hanksville on the west. Lawbreakers, who were familiar with the few trails in and out, had the distinct advantage over any law enforcement that dared enter.

It is conceivable that Cassidy's and Curry's paths did not cross until some time after the latter's bungled attempt at bank robbery at Belle Fourche, South Dakota, on June 28, 1897. However, Harry Longabaugh had occasion to meet Cassidy as far back as 1885 when he was helping his cousin George Longenbaugh run his horse ranch near Cortez, Colorado, and Cassidy was hauling ore for a mining company in nearby Telluride. In addition, Cassidy's future bank robbing partner, Tom Mc-Carty, owned a ranch just one and a half miles southwest of the Longenbaugh homestead. Longabaugh was also in close proximity to Cassidy in early 1886, when the former was employed as a horse wrangler at the Lacy Cattle Company (LC Ranch) near Monticello, in southeastern

An old Two Bar ranch building in Brown's Park. Butch and Sundance worked here. (Author's Collection)

Utah.[23] As in the case with Kid Curry, no one really knows the first time Butch and Harry met. It is possible the meeting may not have occurred until some time after Cassidy's release from prison.

Longabaugh was arrested and convicted for Grand Larceny on August 5, 1887. He served eighteen months in the Crook County jail in Sundance, Wyoming, and was given a full pardon on February 4, 1889.[24] He was working in northeastern Montana as of spring 1890 and apparently did not run afoul of the law for the next two years. Some earlier accounts speculate that from later 1890 to 1892 Longabaugh, now known as the Sundance Kid, visited outlaw hangouts such as Hole-in-the-Wall and Brown's Hole, and may have been involved in rustling. It is now known he spent this time in Alberta, Canada, doing various jobs in the Calgary area. In April 1891 the Canadian government census showed him employed as a horse breaker on the Bar U Ranch. He also did some part-time railroad construction work. For a brief period in early 1892 he even had a part interest in a Calgary saloon at the Grand Central Hotel.[25]

The Sundance Kid resumed his outlaw career when he and two other cowboys robbed a Great Northern train near Malta, Montana, on November 29, 1892. There were few jobs available in the winter for a cowboy, and they thought robbing a train would solve the cash problem. They were obviously amateurs, and after the exploit, it was discovered their take was less than seventy dollars. To make matters worse, Sundance's accomplices were arrested, convicted, and sent to Montana State Prison at Deer Lodge. Sundance was apprehended but was accidentally released and left town before the authorities realized he was one of the train robbers. He is said to have taken temporary refuge at Lost Cabin southwest of Hole-in-the-Wall. Still running from the law, he made his way to Baggs, Wyoming, in the Little Snake River country, before moving on to Brown's Hole.[26] If Sundance did not visit the Hole-in-the-Wall area earlier in his travels and make George Currie's acquaintance, he may have met him this time as a fugitive train robber. It was a brief moment of fame however, because Sundance drifted into obscurity again for the next few years.[27]

After the N-N headquarters was moved in 1895 to Oswego in northeastern Montana, an employee roster listed Longabaugh as again working as a ranch hand. However he had moved on long before the ranch was sold in 1897 to the McNamara and Marlow holdings in northern Montana.[28] Sundance again headed for the Little Snake River country in Carbon County, Wyoming, where he was soon breaking horses for the Beeler Ranch. According to Josie and Ann Bassett, he apparently spent some time in Brown's Hole. After awhile he found employment as a wrangler on the Albert R. Reader ranch near Savery. There is every indication that the local ranchers respected his abilities, and that he was well liked.[29] In January 1897, when the Reader cattle outfit established a winter camp on the lower Snake, a local newspaper reported that "Harry Alonzo" and Bert Charter went along to look after the cattle and horses. The camp, located in an area known as Reader Cabin Draw, was close to a favorite outlaw haven called Powder Springs.[30]

Powder Springs is located about twenty-five miles northeast of Brown's Hole, just below the border of Wyoming in Moffat County,

Colorado. It was a convenient rest stop for outlaws on their way either north to Hole-in-the-Wall or south to Robbers Roost. There were an upper and lower springs, the former located in the vicinity of Powder Wash, a tributary of the Little Snake River. About two miles south in sagebrush-covered country, was the lower springs. Evidence today indicates that there were possibly outlaw cabins at each site, with enough water available to hold about 150 head of rustled cattle.[31]

As for Kid Curry, upon arrival in Wyoming in about mid-1895 after the killing of Pike Landusky, he had taken up rustling with George Currie, Walt Punteney, Tom O'Day and others.[32] Their area of operations included the Hole-in-the-Wall valley, and Nathan Champion's old headquarters at the KC Ranch, located thirty miles northeast on the Middle Fork of Powder River.[33]

CHAPTER 6

Kid Curry Loses Another Brother

About the time Kid Curry left the hideaway in the Missouri Breaks and headed for Wyoming, younger brother John Curry became involved in a water rights dispute and took up with another man's wife, not necessarily in that order.

Little Rockies pioneer Charles W. Duvall wrote that the four Curry brothers had each homesteaded their own piece of land. "The Curry ranches extended from the east boundary of the Tressler ranch down Rock Creek which swung south, just east of the Tressler homestead. As 160 acres was all one could homestead at that time these four homesteads were only about a mile and a half long. The home which the Curry's built and where they all lived was built near a large spring which came out of the north bank of Rock Creek and the homestead joining Dan Tressler. The Curry home was in plain sight from the Dan Tressler home."[1]

Tressler was building up his ranch, and he and his pretty young wife Lucy seemed to be doing well. Then a romance developed between John Curry and Lucy Tressler. When confronted by her husband Dan, she was forced to leave.[2] According to Dad Marsh, Curry wasn't the first man with whom Lucy had been intimate.[3] With marriage in mind, she moved in with Curry on a ranch on the Missouri River. Tressler remained on his ranch while he decided what to do. Becoming fed up with the situation, he sold his spread to Jim Winters in 1895, and moved to the Harlem area with his children.[4] In the winter of 1895/1896 Winters' step-brother Abraham Ditmars Gill moved from the East Coast to become a partner. Gill's father, Dr. Charles Gill of New York City, had adopted Winters after his father was killed in action in the Civil War.[5]

It wasn't long before Lucy Tressler, backed by John Curry, decided that her husband had no right to sell the ranch, and she wanted ownership or at least half the profits from the sale. It was more advantageous

49

to Curry if he could succeed in getting Lucy title to the ranch, because it had good water and graze and was adjacent to the Curry ranch.[6] They both claimed water rights to the land and Curry let it be known that Winters either had to pay up or leave the property. Lonie Curry reinforced his brother's actions at every opportunity. Understandably, Winters believed he had bought the ranch lawfully and he refused their demands.[7] During the time of this dispute Winters did not have the backing of Abe Gill, since his step-brother had gone back east for naval-reserve training.[8]

The Currys' repeated threats were punctuated not long after by an attack on a visitor to the ranch. He had borrowed a horse from Winters and was riding down a road, when a sniper's bullet passed through the crown of his hat. "They're out to get me," said Winters. "If they want me, they know where I am."[9] Winters was a stubborn as well as fearless man and he wasn't about to surrender his rights. He covered the windows of his ranch house at night and kept a loaded double-barreled shotgun just inside the door. It was well known that Winters was good with a gun.[10]

Finally, on January 31, 1896, John Curry gave Winters ten days to vacate the property or he would run him off. A witness to the threat, who had also been inside the house at the time of the later shooting, was W. W. "Wash" Lampkin, a cowboy who had often worked for the Circle C outfit over the past several years. A second witness on the property at the time of the shooting was Edward Pierson, who had come to Montana with a herd of Texas cattle in 1893, and spent the winter with Jim Winters. He had been standing inside the barn entrance when Curry rode up.[11]

For some unknown reason Curry did not wait the specified ten days, but rode up to the ranch house the very next day. At about ten o'clock in the morning on February 1, Winters saw Curry "coming riding one horse and leading another."[12] Without ceremony, Curry immediately opened fire with his .45 caliber Colt revolver, but the shot was wild and the bullet buried into the jamb above Winters' head. In no time Winters had grabbed the shotgun just within the door and fired a load of buckshot into Curry's left breast before he could shoot again. Curry's horse began pitching and bucking, causing his second shot to strike into the ground. Another blast from Winters' shotgun struck Curry in his right side. Mortally wounded, he managed to fire a last shot which again went into the ground. Curry then fell or was bucked off of his horse, and was probably already dead before he hit the ground.[13]

Winters believed that the surviving Currys and their friends would soon be gunning for him, so his first thought was to turn himself in and seek the protection of the law at Fort Benton. He quickly saddled his horse and hurried north to the railroad town of Malta. He succeeded in making it to the John Brown ranch on the Fort Belknap Reservation before his horse gave out. Certain that the Curry brothers were closing in on him, Winters wrote a note that said he had killed John Curry in self-defense and wanted to surrender, and requested an escort of a sheriff's posse to Fort Benton. The message was delivered by a rider to R. W. Garland, a merchant and rancher at Malta, who telegraphed Chouteau County Sheriff George McLaughlin. Undersheriff Charles Howell rode to the Brown ranch with a small posse, arrested Winters, then returned to Fort Benton.[14] "The officers had no trouble arriving at their destination," the Fort Benton *Daily River Press* of February 5, 1896, reported, "none of the Curry element having put in an appearance."

On the same day that Curry was killed, a coroner's inquest was held in Landusky before Justice Robert N. Cowan, at which Wash Lampkin and Edward Pierson testified. Although neither witness had seen the actual shooting, Lampkin testified that Winters was not carrying a gun when he stepped out to answer Curry's hail. It was found that Winters had acted in self-defense and he was soon acquitted.[15] John Ritch presided over the funeral, the burial plot within sight of the Winters/Gill ranch house, about a mile to the east.[16] Incidentally, the day Curry was killed, a deputy sheriff from Fort Benton was making his way along the Missouri River carrying a bench warrant for his arrest on a charge of assault. The deputy was due at Landusky the following afternoon, not aware that the long trip was a needless effort.[17]

Not long after his brother's death, a warrant was issued for Lonie's arrest for an assault on one "Shorty" Parker at the Charles Perry store on the Fort Belknap Reservation.[18] Lonie and Wash Lampkin had stopped by the store after spending time in Harlem. Lonie's story was that he had just gone behind the counter to find a match, when Parker, an employee of the store, appeared from the backroom with a gun in his hand. He and Lonie then began firing at each other, keeping the counter between them. Parker received a wound in his arm and a clubbing from Lonie's revolver.[19]

People regarded Winters as a marked man, and his friends urged him to sell the ranch and leave the territory. But he was stubborn and determined to keep what was rightfully his. He took the precaution of always having one of his hired hands accompany him wherever he went.[20] Winters was no doubt greatly relieved when he heard that Lonie had left the Little Rockies. The latter had reportedly promised to leave the country if the court saw fit to acquit him of the assault case.[21] However, one writer and researcher claims that Lonie and Elfie Landusky eloped about this time, and were married in North Dakota on March 17, 1896. They had boarded an eastbound Great Northern train at Chinook, and were gone for a week or so, spending several days at a hotel in Malta. At the end of this time they returned to the Curry ranch.[22] Nonetheless, the fact that Kid Curry could be lurking somewhere in the district, was reason enough for Winters not to relax his guard anytime soon.

CHAPTER 7

Brave Billy Deane Dies

he killing of Johnson County Deputy Sheriff William "Billy" Deane was called murder by many people, but at least one called it self-defense. "Bill Deane was a hired assassin," wrote May (or Mae) Gardner, "shooting at the Curry gang at every chance... He was as cold-blooded a murderer as Tom Horn. It was kill Deane or be killed."[1] At this point in time "the Curry gang" was in reference to George Currie, since Kid Curry and supposedly Lonie were known as the "Roberts brothers" in Wyoming.

Deane, a young Texan, was hired by Sheriff Al Sproal (or Sproul) specifically to help curb the rustling activity in the county. He was considered fearless, but his plan to capture the gang from Hole-in-the-Wall by himself was pure foolishness. He rode south from Buffalo in early April and spent the night of April 12, 1897, at the Brock home in Powder River country. Deane started out the next morning headed for the KC Ranch, but first arrived at the Alfred and Sarah Grigg homestead and post office on Middle Fork, where the outlaws often stopped for their mail.[2]

Thelma Gatchell Condit writes of the post office: "In it there had been a big fireplace with the usual sizable stack of fire length wood. One log of fair proportions near one side of the hearth was never burned but reserved as a sitting place, its top side worn smooth by the many and varied rumps it had supported through the years. It was slightly scarred here and there too, from the spurs of restless riders who had not removed their gear. Whether messages of a private nature were secreted some place in the firewood, or in this sitting log itself cannot now be proved, but it is known that men of every color and description came there and sat on that log, (always that log) and were seen reading messages that did not come by legitimate stage mail."[3]

Deane was in the post office with the Griggs and, according to one account, a mail-carrier named Rosebury, when five men rode up. Four of the men were George Currie, "Dusty Jim," and the two Roberts brothers, the latter being an alias for Kid Curry and supposedly his brother Lonie. It had been rumored that several days earlier, Deane had traded shots with possibly these same four men at Murphy Pass.[4] Historians assume that Lonie joined the Kid in Wyoming not long after the killing of their brother, John, in February 1896. But there is evidence that he may not have gone to Wyoming, and almost certainly was not present at the Deane killing. This evidence will be discussed in some detail later in the chapter.

What happened next was later described by the Griggs' daughter, Millicent "Millie" Grigg James, who was an impressionable six-year-old at the time of the incident. She stated that her mother had looked out the window and spied two men approaching the house, "one we definitely think was Kid Curry." Thinking there would be trouble between Deane and the two men, Mrs. Grigg sent her children to hide in the cellar but

The modern long-roofed house is the site of the old Grigg post office where the Hole-in-the-Wall gang confronted Deputy Sheriff Billy Deane. (Author's Collection)

they could still see what was going on. Aware of Deane's presence in the house, the men rushed in at the same time through two separate doors of the post office. When one of them pointed his gun at Deane, Mrs. Grigg grabbed it and the bullet was deflected into the roof. Then Alfred Grigg appeared with a gun to back Deane, and the "Roberts brothers" (who they were thought to be at the time) decided it was a good time to leave.[5]

In contrast to Millie's eyewitness account, is Brown Waller's assertion that it was Deane who had initiated hostilities. Waller states that when Deane saw the first of the two men enter the post office, he drew his gun "and asked whether he was looking for a fight. The man replied that he didn't know that he was." The man made it apparent he was just there to get his mail. "Tell you what I'll do," said Deane. "There are two doors to this house. We'll each go out a door and meet shooting." In response to this proposition, the man and his companion got their mail and rode off with three other men who had been waiting at the stable.[6]

Nevertheless, Deane had only a few more hours to live as he also rode out, against the advice of Millie's folks. He was next seen near the Kaltenbach sheep shearing sheds and corrals south of the KC Ranch on this day, April 13, 1897. There were twenty sheep shearers present, and one described what he saw: "Deane saw four men coming down the creek over the hill … After riding toward the four men Deane dismounted and began to shoot. They also immediately opened fire. Deane's horse broke loose and as he turned to catch it he received several shots in the back. The shots must have taken effect immediately, for Deane was dead when first reached."[7] Waller says Deane was hit three times but none of them were received in his back. A bullet entered one side of his body and exited the other; one entered above the groin; another went through a hand.[8]

The sheep shearers were afraid to go to Deane's body to see if he was dead. In the belief that the outlaws wouldn't shoot a woman, they tried to persuade Mrs. Potts, who cooked for the shearing crew, to leave the house and check on Deane. Soon her husband Jess Potts arrived and when informed of the situation, he was understandably furious. He walked up to the body and hefted it over his shoulder and carried it to the shade of the house where he placed it in a spring wagon.[9]

Sheriff Sproal and several other officials came down from Buffalo to investigate the killing.[10] There are some accounts that indicate there were more than four men involved in Deane's death, and that he had been ambushed by men hidden behind rocks or a cut bank.[11] The prime suspects were members of the Currie gang, but there was no attempt at arrest and they were never officially identified. It was as if the citizens of Johnson County wanted the killing to be hushed up and forgotten. The violence and resultant economic downturn of the county owing to the cattlemen's "Invasion of 1892" was still fresh in their minds.[12]

"Subsequent reports trace the gang to the Lost Cabin country," reported the *Wyoming Tribune*, "where they robbed Charles Bader's road ranch, pilfered sheep camps, and 'borrowed' twenty-five head of saddle horses and mules from the Swift Company sheep camp."[13] This would appear to verify Charles Kelly's statements: "In April, 1897, he [Tom O'Day] had held up Bader's ranch and moved northwest to the Lost Cabin country, seventy-nine miles from the Hole." "Besides rustling cattle, they [the Currie gang] began a series of holdups, robbing stages, sheep camps, post offices, and stores."[14]

Robert M. Divine, foreman for Judge Joseph M. Carey's CY ranch at Casper, had several run-ins with members of the Hole-in-the-Wall gang. In one of his many letters to General Manager E. T. "Ed" David, dated May 22, 1897, he indicates: "Harve Ray, Thomas O'Day, George Currey, H. Bennett, Al Smith, Bob Smith, George Smith, Dusty Jim, Ed Starr, two Robberts who helped kill Dean [,] and the Mexican he is back with them and 4 others who are strangers. They have taken 30 head of horse away from some sheep buyers near Walton [Wolton]. I think they are at least 20 men in their camp."[15] A week earlier, writing from Powder River, Wyoming, Divine informed his boss, "The Hole-in-the-Wall boys was at Johnson's Saloon on Casper creek the night before we passed there as we came out, after whiskey."[16]

Lonie Curry may not have gone to Wyoming to join his brother Harvey in his rustling activities. After John Curry's death, Lonie was living with Elfie on the Curry ranch, and still running the Curry saloon in Landusky.[17] A son, Lonie Jr., was conceived sometime in August or

September 1896, since he was born in Landusky on May 24, 1897.[18] Also there is strong evidence that he was not present at the killing of William Deane, since he was involved in an assault court case with Jake Harris at the time.

The incident that occurred in early March of 1897 served to illustrate the bitter feelings that still existed between the Curry and Landusky factions in the Little Rockies. Jake Harris was trying to get some sleep in his saloon when he was aroused by gunshots. Lonie Curry, Wash Lampkin, and a number of cowboys that made up the so-called "Curry gang," were firing into the saloon from a position on the main street. Their intent was to lay siege and drive Harris out of Landusky. Harris returned fire with a charge from his shotgun, slightly wounding both Lampkin and Lonie, which ended the affray. To gain the advantage, the latter two quickly sought out the authorities to file assault charges against Harris. In his defense Harris claimed that over one hundred shots had been fired into his saloon.

The law decided to arrest all three of them, with Harris posting a bond of $5,000 and Lonie and Lampkin ordered to post only $1,000 each. The *Lewistown Democrat* showed that it clearly favored Harris' side of the issue. "The Curry gang has long been a constant menace to the people of the Little Rockies," the newspaper reported, and referred to Lonie and Lampkin as "a couple of worthless and dangerous characters." The trial was held in Fort Benton in May 1897, with the jury taking only ten minutes to acquit Harris of the charges. To avoid similar troubles in the future, Chouteau County Sheriff Tom Clary posted a deputy in Landusky.[19] Harris figured he was no longer safe in Landusky, and with business falling off after the end of the Little Rockies mining boom, he moved his enterprise to the gold mining town of Giltedge in the Judith Mountains in June 1897.[20]

So who was the other "Roberts brother" who was seen at the Grigg post office? Possibly it was the Sundance Kid, up from his haunts around Brown's Hole and the Little Snake River country. He definitely was being referred to as one of the Roberts brothers by the time of his capture and incarceration in Deadwood in September 1897.

Alfred James Mokler's *History of Natrona County Wyoming*, a generally reliable source, contains an account of a store and post office robbery by members of the Currie gang. He states that the leaders were Kid Curry, Flatnose George Currie, and the two Roberts brothers, who "were also at the head of the notorious Hole-in-the-Wall gang." While he indicates the robbery occurred in June 1898, it was most likely the year before since he says the gang next held up the bank at Belle Fourche a few weeks later. In addition, as Divine indicated, the individuals involved were seen a short time earlier in the Wolton area. The full account is included here for an insight into one of the Hole-in-the-Wall gang's minor robberies.

Two members of this gang appeared at Wolton, an interior town sixty miles west from Casper, one evening about 9 o'clock early in June, 1898. Entering the store, they selected about sixty dollars' worth of goods. After the package had been wrapped, a third man came into the store with a handkerchief over his face and the three men drew their guns and ordered the manager of the store, R. L. Carpenter, and the clerk, Jay Harmon, to throw up their hands. While two of the men covered the manager and clerk with their guns, the third rifled the safe and robbed the post office. About $300 in money and goods were taken. Carpenter and Harmon were then marched out to the corrals and were backed against the fence while the robbers prepared to leave. The bundles were tied on the horses and a buggy team belonging to H. B. Brower, the hotel proprietor, and Carpenter's saddle horse were stolen. Carpenter and Harmon were warned if they valued their lives, not to report the robbery for twenty-four hours. The outlaws then bade the men "good night," and rode away. The next day at noon the hold-up was reported and a posse was organized and followed the trail of the robbers southwest for twenty miles, where they found Carpenter's horse, but all trace of the men was lost.[21]

On April 21, a week after the killing of Billy Deane, Butch Cassidy, and Elzy Lay robbed the mine payroll from the Pleasant Valley Coal Company at Castle Gate of $8,800.

CHAPTER 8

Belle Fourche Fiasco

The Castle Gate exploit was sensationalized in many newspapers of the time, and the Hole-in-the-Wall contingent was duly impressed with Butch Cassidy's handling of the robbery. Reasoning that they should be able to do just as well as a Mormon cowboy, they decided to rob a bank. Their first choice was the bank in Dickinson, North Dakota; however, there was something about the setup they didn't like. It was finally decided that the Butte County Bank in Belle Fourche, South Dakota, would be an easier and more profitable target.[1] Also, both Sundance and George Currie knew the area well.

Belle Fourche is situated at the confluence of the Belle Fourche and Redwater rivers and means "beautiful fork" in French. It was a central cattle-shipping railhead for a large portion of a tri-state area (South Dakota, Wyoming, and Montana). Cowboys who had accompanied the herds would celebrate in town, spending their money freely on drinking and gambling in the many saloons, and other entertainments. Additionally, the outlaws knew the town was hosting the annual reunion of Civil War veterans of the G.A.R., which was to be held from June 24 through 26. Hundreds of people would be coming from the surrounding towns such as Deadwood and Rapid City to celebrate, with the local merchants depositing all this increased revenue in the vault of the Butte County Bank by Saturday night. The time to hit the bank would be soon after it opened on Monday morning.[2]

According to Walt Punteney, the robbery was planned initially outside of Happy Jack's saloon in Thermopolis, Wyoming.[3] This may be true since the Hole-in-the-Wall gang were known to use the hot springs area for a headquarters. The boys were oftentimes seen drinking and gambling in the saloons at night.[4] When the Currie gang robbed the store at Wolton in early June and were initially seen heading southwest, they could have then turned north to Thermopolis. The purpose of robbing the store and post office may have been to stake their bank robbing venture. Nevertheless, the outlaws were in Hole-in-the-Wall no later than mid-June to organize and make final plans for the job. (A June 13 letter from Bob Divine to E. T. David said George Currie had been seen in the area riding a CY horse.[5]) They then started east toward Belle Fourche, avoiding the more populated route through Buffalo and Gillette. Crossing into South Dakota, they approached Belle Fourche from the north and were camped east of town on June 26, a Saturday.[6]

About the only real agreement among historians concerning the participants in the robbery is that Walt Punteney and Tom O'Day were definitely present. Furthermore, Jim Dullenty states that Butte County and Lawrence County, S.D., court records prove that Flatnose George Currie was easily identified by the unusual shape of his nose.[7] A Butte County wanted poster dated July 28 had the description of Currie fairly close, which included his "flat pug nose," and even spelled his last name correctly.[8]

Two more suspects listed in the poster were the "Roberts" brothers, and their descriptions resemble that of Kid Curry and his brother Lonie. Both were described as having a "very dark complexion, possibly quarter breed Indian," with the taller Roberts brother (approximating Kid Curry) listed as five feet, seven and one-half inches, age 32, weight about 140, and "formerly from Indian territory." What is rather interesting is that, in addition to Kid Curry, Pearl Baker included Willie Roberts, "a Mexican from New Mexico" who was called "Indian Billy."[9] His Pinkerton National Detective Agency file photo and description matches the taller Roberts on the wanted poster very closely. The file states he was a halfbreed with Mexican blood and had black hair, black eyes, and a "real dark" complexion. He was five feet, seven and one-half inches tall, age 36, weighed 135 pounds, and his criminal occupation was listed as train robber and hold-up. He had a brother who lived at White Oaks, Lincoln County, New Mexico.[10]

Whether Will Roberts was one of the robbers or not, most writers believe Kid Curry also participated, and given his close association with George Currie it would seem logical that he was present.[11] The fourth and last robber listed on the wanted poster was one "Harve" Ray, but nothing much is known about him. He was part of the Wyoming rustler clique, and a census listed a Harvey Ray as a rancher near Ten Sleep, Wyoming.[12] Kid Curry is said to have used the name Harvey Ray as an alias; however the latter's description on the poster is that of a heavy, round faced, bald headed, forty-two-year-old man.

The Sundance Kid has also long been considered one of the Belle Fourche robbers by most historians. It has been conjectured that one of the reasons why this particular bank had been singled out was because two of the major stockholders were John Clay and Robert Robinson. In fact the Butte County Bank was also referred to as the Clay, Robinson and Company Bank. Ten years earlier, Clay had been manager of the Three V Ranch, and Robinson had been his assistant. They were both instrumental in Sundance's arrest and conviction for horse theft at that time. The Three V was only about twelve miles from Belle Fourche, and within fifty miles was Sundance, Wyoming, where he spent eighteen months in jail. It would be understandable if he still held a grudge, and helped to plan the robbery with the idea of retaliation.[13] However, recent evidence has been brought forth that suggests he had an alibi. On the day of the robbery he was still working for rancher Al Reader in the Little Snake River Valley.[14]

On Monday morning June 28, six men were seen riding on the road to Belle Fourche. Tom O'Day and Walt Punteney rode in the lead of the group at some 300 to 400 yards. At about 9:15 O'Day and Punteney returned a "Hello!" from twenty-one-year-old Frank Miller and thirteen-year-old Noble Taylor who they passed on the road. When they approached the other four men, Miller and Taylor decided to detour off the road around them. These same four men pulled to a stop when they reached the outskirts of Belle Fourche.[15] The plan was for O'Day and Punteney to enter town first and position themselves across the street from the bank in front of two hardware stores, to prevent citizen access to the gun cases.[16]

When they hit town about 9:30, O'Day tied his horse in front of Bruce Sebastion's Saloon, and went in to buy two quart bottles of whiskey and

Belle Fourche, SD, today. The Butte County Bank is now the Wells Fargo bank on the right. The old limestone building on the left looks similar to the original bank. (Author's Collection)

an extra pint to stow in his pocket. He stuffed the quarts in his saddle bags, mounted his horse and rode to Alanson Giles' Hardware Store opposite the bank. Ten minutes later he made a second trip to the saloon for an additional two smaller bottles of whiskey, and again rode back to Giles' store.[17]

A few minutes before ten o'clock, the remaining four robbers arrived in town and tied up at the side entrance of the bank. The two-story building was constructed of limestone and was located on the corner of what are today Sixth Avenue and State Street. While leaving one man with the horses, the remaining three went into the bank. Certainly two of the latter were George Currie and Kid Curry.[18] There were two employees in the bank, cashier Arthur H. Marble and assistant (also referred to as teller or accountant) Harry Ticknor, and five customers.[19]

George Currie and the others quickly entered the side door with revolvers drawn, and ordered "Hold up your hands!" Everyone readily complied; however cashier Marble later testified it was apparent the gang were amateurs at bank robbing, and were not sure what to do next. They appeared rattled and kept running from one man to another repeating their "hands up" order. Rev. E. E. Clough spoke up to point out that he was "only a poor Methodist preacher," and took offense at such treatment. "Preacher be damned," replied one of the outlaws. "Put up your hands." At this, the Reverend ran into the bank vault.[20] Marble took advantage of this confusion and pulled a revolver from under the counter and pointed it at one of the robbers, presumably Kid Curry. He pulled the trigger, but instead of the expected explosion, there was the snap of a misfire. Marble quickly threw the gun aside and reached for the sky.[21] He was very fortunate none of the robbers were vengeful or bloodthirsty. "They didn't want to kill anybody," holdup witness R. I. Martin stated, "they just wanted money."[22]

George Currie had the presence of mind to open the sack he had brought, and ordered the customers to hand over their money. Meanwhile, from his hardware store, Mr. Giles saw several hands raised in the bank directly across State Street. He ran to the bank to investigate and soon realized what was happening, especially when Tom O'Day chased him back to his store with the help of a bullet from his gun. Giles ran through his store and out the back into the alley, and commenced to yell that the bank was being robbed. O'Day and Punteney began shooting through the hardware store windows and also those of the nearby Gay Brothers store. A bullet from this fusillade wounded Walter Gay in the cheek. The gunfire caused the already jumpy bandits inside the bank to panic, and they only took time to grab merchant Sam Arnold's previous day's cash receipts of $97 before rushing outside to their horses.[23] They left behind $1,000 in gold and silver that was stowed in a teller's tray underneath the counter, not to mention what was deposited in the vault.[24]

One bandit went out the front door while the rest exited through the side, shooting as they emerged into the street.[25] The outlaws mounted and raced south down Sixth Avenue in the direction of the railroad tracks. O'Day had not bothered to hitch his horse, and it was so spooked by the shooting, it took off running after the escaping bandits. As the gang rode west up Sundance Hill (now National Street), a shot from the aroused citizenry hit O'Day's horse in the foreleg. It was later found tied to a fence with two quarts of good whiskey still tucked in the saddlebags.[26]

About 250 yards up Sundance Hill the bandits stopped to wait for O'Day near an artesian well. They remained there for several minutes, taking a desperate chance since now several townspeople were shooting at them. An old Civil War veteran, named John McClure, was kneeling on the walk near the bank and firing several shots from an old model .44 caliber rifle. The bandits weren't in any danger from him since the bullets were falling far short of them. A more immediate threat was from Joe Miller the blacksmith, who owned a good rifle and was considered a good shot. He had run home to grab his gun and his horse, and was at that moment riding bareback up the slope toward the waiting bandits. He was about halfway up the hill, when a shot grazed his right leg and killed the horse under him. The shot didn't come from the bandits, but from an upper window of the Teall and Bennett flour mill.[27] The marksman, Frank E. Bennett, had mistaken the blacksmith for one of the robbers. Other armed townspeople were taking aim at Miller before he was fortunately recognized in time. Unable to wait for O'Day any longer, the five outlaws wheeled their horses and headed southwest for the border of Wyoming. Cashier Marble had obtained a working gun from somewhere, and City Marshal Lee Brooks observed him shooting after the bandits, even though they were not in sight.[28]

When Tom O'Day saw that his horse had left without him, he did his best to act the part of an innocent bystander. O'Day yelled at Brooks to not shoot at the fleeing bandits' horses, because they had taken one of his. He then spotted an old mule tied to a hitchrack and jumped on its back. "I'll get 'em, I'll get 'em!" he shouted as he urged the mule forward, but it started in the opposite direction his companions had taken up Sundance Hill. A crowd had gathered to laugh at O'Day's antics, but a few became suspicious. He abandoned the stubborn mule and ran up to a townsman named William F. Tracy. He told Tracy that his horse had run away from him, and asked him where he could borrow another. Tracy had observed O'Day's actions before and after the robbery, so he pleaded ignorance concerning any available horseflesh. O'Day then quickly walked west on the sidewalk until he came to a vacant lot between Sebastion's Saloon and the *Belle Fourche Times* printing office. He crossed the lot at a run and ducked into an outhouse in back of the saloon. A butcher, Rusaw Bowman, also suspicious of O'Day, followed him into the vacant lot and saw him go into the outhouse. He was in there briefly, and when he came out Bowman covered him with his gun and told him to raise his hands. O'Day's pockets were searched, which produced $392.50, a pint bottle of whiskey, and some .44 caliber cartridges. Bowman remembered O'Day had gone into the outhouse carrying a revolver, so with the help of some other men the outhouse was turned over. Someone fetched a rake and the gun and scabbard were hauled out of the hole.[29]

O'Day was soon arrested and placed in a steel cage, which was all that was left of the Butte County jail that had recently burned down by the carelessness of an incarcerated drunk. Out in the open, he was subject to the ridicule of the townspeople, who were all for hanging the culprit then and there. "Go ahead and hang me, boys," O'Day bravely responded. "You'll never see a man die any gamer than I will." Law officers soon transferred him by train to the Lawrence County jail in Deadwood for safekeeping, where he hired attorney W. O. Temple for his defense.[30]

Ex-Sheriff George Fuller had rounded up a posse, which eventually numbered about 100 men, and raced off in pursuit of the five bandits. At times the posse caught sight of the outlaws; in fact, at the head of Owl Creek, the posse got close enough for James T. Craig, the manager of the Three V, to identify them as the "Curry gang from Hole-in-the-Wall." He knew them from when he had been manager of an outfit near Buffalo, Wyoming. Word was received in Belle Fourche by early afternoon that the posse had the outlaws surrounded in a small timber tract, near the Three V Ranch twelve miles southwest of town. However, the outlaws effected an escape some time during the night, and headed north toward the Hash Knife Ranch in Montana. The last place they were heard of in South Dakota was on the Little Missouri River below Camp Crook, Harding County, near the Montana line.[31] The determined posse, according to a July 8 report, continued to follow the outlaws' trail until it was lost entirely at Box Elder Creek twenty miles northwest of the Little Missouri. This was in the vicinity of the Hash Knife horse camp just east of Ekalaka, Montana, where the gang could have obtained fresh horses.[32]

The Belle Fourche bandits eventually made their way to Wyoming and the safety of Hole-in-the-Wall. CY foreman Bob Divine commented that "8 men come from South Dakota. I hear the mail carrier saw Ray, Currey, Roberts, and 3 strangers over there by Grigg's."[33] This was the post office where the gang had had their run-in with Deputy Sheriff William Deane the previous April.

Meanwhile, O'Day's preliminary hearing was scheduled in Belle Fourche the day after the bank robbery. O'Day and his attorney showed up for the hearing but a decision was made to postpone it until the next day. There was immediate concern by the attorneys that O'Day would be lynched if the steel cage was the only thing available to contain him. In a sardonic twist of fate, it was decided to incarcerate him overnight in the Butte County Bank vault. The next day Justice of the Peace C. T. Martin, brother of bank robbery witness R. I. Martin, found sufficient evidence to have O'Day bound over to the circuit court under $15,000 bond.[34]

A $100 reward circular was posted by the Butte County Bank for each of the four bandits, George Currie, Harve Ray, and the two Roberts brothers. (Walt Punteney was not mentioned.) A later circular raised the amount to $625 each or $2,500 for the capture of all four men.[35]

CHAPTER 9

Red Lodge and Capture

I t is not certain whether the Belle Fourche bank robbers were in the Hole-in-the-Wall when the famous fight occurred there between the rustlers and some invading cattlemen on July 22, 1897. The latter party consisted of twelve men, which included two Montana livestock inspectors, and was there to round up all the stolen cattle that could be found. One of the inspectors was Joe LeFors, who would later figure prominently in tracking members of the Wild Bunch.[1] Bob Divine was there representing the CY, and according to Brown Waller, he had warrants in his possession for the Belle Fourche robbers.[2] Waller does not cite his source for this; however, it shouldn't be discounted since Divine stated in a January 1, 1897, letter that he wanted warrants turned over to him from Natrona County Sheriff H. L. Patton and Johnson County Sheriff Al Sproal, in order to bring in Currie, O'Day, and other members of the Hole-in-the-Wall gang for rustling.[3]

During the roundup three men of the rustler clique, Al Smith, Bob Smith, and Bob Taylor, rode up to the party of cattlemen. A fight ensued in which Bob Smith was mortally wounded, and Bob Divine and his son Lee were slightly wounded. Bob Taylor was captured, but Al Smith escaped after his gun was shot out of his hand. Although the cattlemen got the best of this encounter, they were afraid of rustler reinforcements and decided to pull out of the Hole, leaving behind all the cattle that had been gathered.[4]

A second roundup was scheduled to commence on July 30 with a total of fifty-four men participating. This large group consisted not only of cattlemen, but also numerous law officers from Johnson and Natrona counties (Sheriff Sproal among them), and a force of Montana livestock inspectors under W. D. "Billy" Smith. Sheriff Butts of Butte County, South Dakota, and one of his deputies, still searching for the Belle Fourche

bank robbers, were also part of the group. This time the roundup successfully recovered about 500 head of stolen cattle, and averted any serious
confrontations with the rustlers.[5] At least a few days before this second
roundup began, Kid Curry and other Belle Fourche robbers headed south
to Powder Springs to rendezvous with Butch Cassidy's gang.[6]

At the end of three months of hiding at Robbers Roost, Utah, after the
Castle Gate robbery, Butch Cassidy and his friends were getting restless
and wanted to go somewhere to spend the loot. Over the next few days
as they rode north toward Brown's Hole, they decided the best and safest
place to celebrate was in Dixon and Baggs, two small cowtowns on the
Little Snake River a few miles north of the Wyoming-Colorado border
in Carbon County.[7] Although Baggs may have been small in those days,
"Baggs was a busy town," stated Boyd Charter (son of Bert Charter), "a
crossroads of pioneer travel. The country between Baggs and Rawlins
was wide-open and uninhabited."[8] On the way the outlaws rode through
their Powder Springs hideout, located about halfway between Baggs and
Brown's Hole. Here Cassidy, Elzy Lay, and other gang members, were
joined by Kid Curry, Walt Punteney, possibly George Currie, and Sundance, who came over from Reader Cabin Draw.[9]

There is a good probability that Sundance had met and worked with
Butch and Elzy before this; however, this was possibly the first time that
Curry had met them. Butch and Sundance are said to have worked for
Ora Haley's Two Bar Ranch in Brown's Hole at various times within
the last two years.[10] The weathered and dilapidated ranch buildings now
lie deserted beside the meandering Green River. Butch was in the valley
after his release from prison in early 1896, and he also took refuge there
after the Montpelier robbery with Elzy.

They hit Dixon first on July 29, 1897, and shot up the town like a
bunch of cowboys just coming off a trail drive. After trying to drink the
town dry and chasing all the residents from the streets, the gang jumped
on their horses and rode west six miles down the river to Baggs. Here
they shot up Jack Ryan's Bull Dog Saloon, but paid for the damages
with a silver dollar for every bullet hole.[11] They also paid for drinks with
twenty-dollar gold pieces, which allowed Ryan to later open one of the

better bars in Rawlins.[12] It has been inferred that the gang became known as the Wild Bunch from such riotous celebrations as this.[13]

Some writers contend that the Wild Bunch was officially formed in 1897 when a contingent of seventy-five rustlers from Hole-in-the-Wall, led by George Currie and Kid Curry, rode south on either August 17, 18, or 19, depending on the report, to join Butch Cassidy's Powder Springs gang. This move was mainly prompted by the summer intrusions into the Hole by Bob Divine, Joe LeFors, and Sheriff Al Sproal. They were reportedly seen crossing the Lander–Rawlins stage road at Lost Soldier Pass, and again on the Union Pacific Railroad tracks near Fillmore Station, robbing several sheep camps as they passed.[14]

On August 2, 1897, two men wearing black handkerchiefs over their faces robbed the Lander–Rawlins mail stage at Lost Soldier station. The robbers held the station agent under guard in the barn while they waited for the southbound stage from Lander to pull up for a change of horses. Drawing the curtains aside they saw there were no passengers on board, and it was soon evident that the stage was also not carrying the anticipated shipment of gold dust from the Atlantic City mines. The robbers had to be satisfied with cutting open and looting the mail sacks. They then mounted up and headed west on the Lander road, making for the desolate country of the Great Divide Basin. The frightened driver described both bandits as being five-feet, eight-inches tall with light hair. Although Kid Curry could never have been mistaken as having light hair, Brown Waller maintains that he "was probably the leader."[15]

It has also been claimed that select members of the Wild Bunch soon formed a new organization called the Train Robbers Syndicate. Its mission was to rob railroad companies, particularly the Union Pacific, of their express shipments. However, owing to the gang's plans being too elaborate and involving too many people, the railroad officials were ultimately forewarned of them. The Union Pacific's guardian, the Pinkerton National Detective Agency, began to make investigations that put a halt to the syndicate's plans, at least for the immediate future.[16]

Sometime in August, Sundance quit his job at the A. R. Reader ranch and rode north in the company of Kid Curry and Walt Punteney.[17] They were in the vicinity of Red Lodge, Montana, southwest of Billings on the eighteenth or nineteenth of September. It is presumed they were there with the intention of robbing the Carbon County Bank. One of them was recognized in town while buying camp supplies, and it was reported to Sheriff John B. Dunn.[18] Dunn said in an interview that it was City Marshal Byron St. Clair who recognized the outlaws, that he had known them in Wyoming. The men told the marshal they were going to rob the bank, and advised him to leave town that evening on a fishing trip. St. Clair quickly alerted Cashier B. E. Vaill at the bank; an informer later warned the outlaws.[19]

Whether they were there to rob the bank or just to obtain supplies, all three were later observed heading north toward the Yellowstone River. Sheriff Dunn stated that George Currie and two other men had been left with thirty head of horses at Mud Springs, twenty-five miles southeast of Red Lodge. However, neither Currie nor the horses were with the rest of the gang when they were captured. Dunn was sure that the men were the Belle Fourche robbers, and he started after them with a small posse on Monday, September 20. They trailed the outlaws north to Absarokee and then to Columbus where three more men were added to the posse. At this point, according to Dunn, the posse consisted of "Stock Detective W. D. Smith of Miles City; [Jones] Dick Hicks of Billings; [Constable] H. C. Calhoun of Columbus; [and]... Attorney [Oscar C.] Stone of Red Lodge."[20] They continued to follow the trail of the outlaws west to Big Timber, then it turned northeast past the John T. Murphy Cattle Company, where Sundance had worked about seven years earlier. When the posse reached the Widow Ranch near Painted Robe, not far from Lavina, Billy Mendenhall joined them.[21]

It is quite possible the outlaws did not know a posse was trailing them when they reached Lavina on the Musselshell River, the Wednesday morning of September 22. They took time to have a drink at H. C. Jolly's Saloon, and paid their bill with a $2.50 check that the bandits had taken from the counter during the robbery of the Butte County Bank.[22] When they mounted up and rode out of Lavina, the posse was less than an hour behind them. At five o'clock in the evening, twenty miles north

of Lavina, Sheriff Dunn and his men caught up with the outlaws setting up camp near a spring. Walter Punteney and Sundance were going
for water, and Kid Curry was picketing his horse when they were surprised by the posse. Part of the posse demanded the surrender of the
two at the spring, but they jumped behind a bank determined to fight.
The posse pinned them down by firing every time the two showed their
heads. It was apparent they were outgunned, and Sundance and Punteney
surrendered.[23]

Meanwhile, Sheriff Dunn and the rest of the posse had called for
Curry to throw up his hands. Curry parleyed to give himself time to get
behind his horse, where he suddenly drew his revolver. At that instant
Dunn fired his rifle, the bullet going through the horse's neck and into
Curry's right wrist, causing him to drop his revolver. The outlaw then
jumped on his wounded horse and raced for the hills, the posse in close
pursuit. Curry's horse covered about a mile before it fell dead from another shot, or from the original wound. Curry took off running and hid
behind a sand dune, but he surrendered when the posse came up to him.[24]

The prisoners were taken to Billings by stagecoach and held for the
Belle Fourche robbery. Harry Ticknor, of the Butte County Bank, who
was summoned to help identify the bandits, arrived on Saturday, September 25. On Monday they were taken before Justice of the Peace Alex
Fraser, where Ticknor identified the men as the bank robbers. Putting up
their extra horses and gear as payment, they hired a lawyer named J. B.
Herford to defend them.[25] Ticknor's testimony prompted Herford to rec-
ommend the prisoners waive the requisition papers and return to South
Dakota. This they agreed to, and the next day, accompanied by Butte
County Sheriff Butts, Billy Smith, and Dick Hicks, they were conveyed
to Deadwood by train. They joined their partner Tom O'Day in the Lawrence County jail, who had been there since June.[26]

CHAPTER 10

Deadwood and Escape

The Deadwood *Daily Pioneer-Times* of September 30, 1897, reported the robbers' arrival. Although Kid Curry and the Sundance Kid had given their names as Tom and Frank Jones in Billings, and also at their arraignment in Deadwood, the newspaper referred to them parenthetically as "the notorious Roberts brothers." (If these two had been considered brothers all along by both the Hole-in-the-Wall residents and officers of the law, it could mean that Lonie Curry may not have been involved in any of the gang's rustling activities or the bank robbery at Belle Fourche.) Walter Punteney did not long persist in giving his name as Charley Frost, eventually admitting his real identity, although the press spelled it as "Putney." The report went on to say that all three men proclaimed innocence and insisted they didn't know anyone named George Currie. It had been determined that Currie split from the rest of the gang at Red Lodge.[1] Wyoming rancher Robert Tisdale later reported that the outlaw was seen in central Wyoming about late October.[2] Nevertheless, the posse members quickly put in a claim for the promised reward of $625 each for the three bandits who had been caught.[3]

The following day, October 1, the prisoners had their pictures taken at H. R. Locke's photograph gallery. It was reported that Punteney and Tom Roberts acted well, submitting to the process, but that Frank Roberts "acted ugly." He dropped his head and closed his eyes as the photo was snapped, with the result that only the top of his head was taken. Presumably Frank Roberts was Sundance, since clear photos exist of Punteney and Curry.[4]

On October 13 the Eighth Judicial Circuit Court for Butte County indicted Thomas O'Day, Walter Punteney, and Thomas and Frank Jones for first degree robbery. Also indicted, in absentia, were George Currie and Harve Ray. Judge Adronriam J. Plowman set bail for the four

Tom O'Day in Deadwood, SD, October 1, 1897, after being arrested for the Belle Fourche bank robbery. (Courtesy Adams Museum, Deadwood, SD)

Walt Punteney in Deadwood, SD, October 1, 1897, after being arrested for the Belle Fourche bank robbery. (Courtesy Adams Museum, Deadwood, SD)

at $10,000 each. They obviously couldn't come up with that kind of money, so the sheriff hauled them back to the Deadwood jail. Two days later the judge set the trial date for October 28.[5] The court had assigned Frank McLaughlin and W. O. Temple (O'Day's lawyer) as counsel, and they immediately filed an affidavit for more time to prove their clients' innocence. Material witnesses needed time to come from as far away as Savery, Wyoming, on behalf of Frank Jones (Sundance), and near Thermopolis, Wyoming, on behalf of Punteney. A continuance was granted and a new trial date was set for December 29, 1897.[6]

Curry's attorneys wrote his cousin Bob Lee at Cripple Creek, Colorado, saying that a man in the Deadwood jail requested financial help, but would not give his name. However, from their description, Lee stated in a later interview that he knew it was his cousin Harvey Logan.[7] Lee

Kid Curry in Deadwood, SD, October 1, 1897, after being arrested for the Belle Fourche bank robbery. (Courtesy Adams Museum, Deadwood, SD)

owned a mining claim and was known to work as a poker dealer in the saloons.[8] Before he could round up the lawyer fees, and before any defense witnesses had time to reach Deadwood, however, the prisoners escaped.

The Lawrence County jail contained a thirty-foot-square room with steel-barred windows and an iron floor. In the center of this was a twenty-foot-square cage with individual cells on one side, and a bull pen on the other. At certain times during the day, the prisoners were allowed the freedom of the bull pen for exercise. In addition, there was a ten-foot-wide corridor around the perimeter of the cage. From this corridor the jailer was able to safely lock the men back in their cells by throwing a lever that dropped a steel bar across all the cell doors simultaneously. They were supposed to be locked in their cells every night, but on Sunday evening, October 31, 1897, the four outlaws and one William Moore had somehow gained the freedom of the corridor. Moore, a local cowhand, was being held for the killing of a man named Henry Staley at Englewood two months earlier, for mistreating a dog.[9]

At 8:45 p.m., jailer John Mansfield opened the grating in the office door and saw that the prisoners were in the jail corridor. He and his wife had been on their way home from evening church services and wanted to check the prisoners. Mansfield ordered the prisoners to go back to their cells so he could pull the lever to lock them in. They countered that the bar was already in place and they were locked out of their cells. For some unexplained reason, Mansfield entered the jail room unarmed to check the cells, while his wife was to lock the door behind him. Before she could do so, Frank Roberts blocked the door with his foot, while Moore decked Mansfield with a blow to the face. One man pulled Mrs. Mansfield inside the cage, and when she resisted she was slapped and thrown to the floor. Meanwhile Tom Roberts and the others beat and kicked her husband.[10]

Locking the deputy and his wife inside the cage, the prisoners escaped through the rear kitchen door. Moore separated from the others as they fled through the courtyard gate, and he climbed a side yard fence. He was later suspected of stealing two horses from the Bassett ranch, where he had worked breaking horses. Sheriff Plunkett, who lived across the street from the jail, freed the Mansfields when he heard their screams for help. After a quick search of the jail and courthouse area, Plunkett and Deputy James Harris put out a call to the nearby towns and neighboring counties, requesting volunteers for a posse. The intrepid manager of the Three V, James T. Craig, did not hesitate, as well as Butte County Sheriff Butts and a deputy, who arrived at 2:00 a.m. on Monday. Plunkett posted a $250 reward for the capture of the outlaws, and even telephoned Lincoln, Nebraska, to request bloodhounds.[11]

It was reported that the four men had split up after leaving the jail yard, with Punteney and O'Day going to Carney Street, and from there to the railroad tracks. They continued on to the top of McGovern Hill, where they saw the lights of lanterns carried by a posse in search of them. It was later discovered that O'Day had carelessly dropped his handkerchief before they changed direction toward Blacktail Gulch and False Bottom Creek.[12]

Nevertheless, at 11:00 p.m. on Sunday, four men were seen passing Whit's Half-way Ranch on the Carbonate Road. They were presumably heading for a place in Spearfish Canyon near Maurice Station, on the B & M Railroad, where five saddled horses with supplies had reportedly been left earlier that evening. They apparently did not find any horses, and sometime during the night the four fugitives again separated. It was reported that O'Day was in poor physical shape and slowing down the rest of the party. In the early evening on Monday, a farmer met O'Day and Punteney on the Spearfish Road where it crossed False Bottom Creek near the Gunsolly ranch. They tried to take his horse, but he was able to spur away and ride to Spearfish, whereupon town Marshal Dave Craig spread the alarm. Sheriff Plunkett and Deputy Harris led upwards of sixty men toward Spearfish, and the area the outlaws were last seen was quickly surrounded.[13]

On Monday midnight, two posse members spotted a fire in a thicket, and crawled close enough to recognize O'Day and Punteney. A noise from one of the posse horses spooked the fugitives, and they jumped up and escaped into the night. Just after daybreak on Tuesday, November 2, a shot from a Spearfish boy out hunting rabbits flushed O'Day and Punteney from their hiding place near False Bottom Creek. The shot alerted the officers in the area, who rushed to tighten the cordon around the two fugitives. About one o'clock in the afternoon, the outlaws were spotted in the brush about three miles southwest of Spearfish. They were exhausted, having had little or nothing to eat for almost two days, resulting in their surrender to Marshal Craig without a fight. After being fitted with leg irons they were driven by buggy back to the Deadwood jail.[14]

About an hour before O'Day and Punteney had been routed from their campfire, Curry and Sundance stole a horse and saddle near Giesler's sawmill on Crow Creek. They then rode to Carbonate and fled toward the Bear Lodge Mountains in Wyoming. It is difficult at this point to make sense of the subsequent chase, owing to the many false sightings and conflicting reports of the outlaws' whereabouts. A posse led by Deputy Sheriff Ricks of Butte County followed a trail headed in the direction of Little Powder River, but eventually lost it. It was December when Ricks again found fresh tracks in the snow leading from Little Powder to the old TA Ranch on Crazy Woman Creek. Here the outlaws had stolen a horse and continued southwest toward Hole-in-the-Wall. The posse was out for several days but never caught sight of the robbers, and finally turned back to South Dakota.[15]

Walt Punteney's trial began in March 1898, with every reason to expect that there would be a conviction. But the people, especially the bank officials and the big cattlemen who had suffered from the gang's rustling, would be greatly disappointed. Punteney's defense witnesses from the Bighorn Basin country, Bob McCoy and Sam Brown, testified that he was eating dinner at Brown's ranch near Thermopolis in northern Wyoming, hundreds of miles from Belle Fourche, on the day before the bank robbery.[16] He was found not guilty of bank robbery, and was also acquitted of the charge of assault with a deadly weapon for shooting up the streets of Belle Fourche during the robbery.[17]

When O'Day came to trial he was also found not guilty in spite of the overwhelming evidence against him. In a final attempt to get them a prison sentence, the two were indicted for escaping the Deadwood jail. However, Lawrence County States Attorney Wilson didn't think it was even possible to prove this charge, and upon his motion the indictment was set aside.[18] The people were outraged and the papers called it a miscarriage of justice, but O'Day and Punteney were free and back in Wyoming by mid-April. They both returned to the Lost Cabin country, Punteney to go straight and ranch his homestead on Bridger Creek, O'Day to continue his rustling ways, eventually to serve a short term in the Wyoming State Penitentiary for horse theft.

CHAPTER 11

Various Endeavors

The tri-state area, which included Wyoming, Colorado, and Utah, was experiencing increasing activity from rustlers who found sanctuary in hideouts such as Robbers Roost, Brown's Hole, Powder Springs, and Hole-in-the-Wall. Owing to the rising price of cattle, the problem became so great, it was reported that "The gangs have almost depopulated the ranges within 200 miles of their retreats," with raids netting one hundred to five hundred head at a time.[1] A meeting of cattlemen was held on February 15, 1898, in Rawlins, to discuss a plan of action. It was suggested that stock detectives should be hired and a reward or bounty placed on the rustlers.[2]

It is difficult to trace the whereabouts and activities (criminal or otherwise) of the various outlaws that rode with the Wild Bunch in 1898. The Pinkertons reported that Sundance spent the winter of 1897/1898 employed at the Frank Kelsey ranch, a neighbor of A. R. Reader, in the Little Snake River Valley.[3] Within the January to March 1898 time frame, it has been stated that Kid Curry robbed a bank in Clifton, Arizona, in the company of Texas outlaw Ben Kilpatrick, and then to have taken a solo trip to Paris, France, with the proceeds.[4] Both incidents would have to be considered as hearsay, since they cannot be backed up by contemporary news reports or any other tangible evidence. It is not known if Curry was acquainted with Kilpatrick at this time, and it also seems quite out of character for him to travel to Europe, especially at this time of his life.

A story in the *Denver News* of February 27, 1898, less than two weeks after the cattlemen's meeting, may provide a clue to Kid Curry's whereabouts: "For a week news has been coming to Casper of one of the biggest 'cattle drives' ever known to Central Wyoming. It appears that Harvey Ray and other escaped Belle Fourche bank robbers have been joined by a party of Powder Springs thieves and together they are driving everything before them to the Hole-in-the-Wall region … There were upwards of twenty of the riders and they were well mounted and heavily armed."[5] Members of the two gangs, including outlaws from Robbers Roost, had assembled at Powder Springs. It is a good possibility that Kid Curry was among them; in fact, law officials believed that he was using Harvey Ray as an alias by this time.[6]

Another meeting of representatives from the large cattle concerns was held in Denver, which included the governors of Colorado and Wyoming, and a proxy from the governor of Utah. Initially, a plan was drafted to clean out the rustlers who found sanctuary in Brown's Hole. This entailed calling out the militia from the three states to establish a cordon around the Hole, then close in and preferably exterminate all rustlers encountered.[7] It was clear from past experience that simply arresting the culprits would be a waste of time, since they would shortly be out on bail, cleared of charges, or receive a short prison term at most.

Then a letter written by J. S. Hoy was published in the *Denver News* of March 11, in response to the killing of his brother Valentine S. Hoy in Brown's Hole over a week earlier.[8] In the letter he states that the proposed plan to round up all the criminals in the Hole would be impossible to carry out. He argued that the presence of a large body of militia could not enter the country without the outlaws being alerted. His idea was to have one or two men familiar with the country "acting in concert with resident citizens of good reputation," stay on the trail of a criminal until he is hunted down. Hoy approved of killing the captured outlaws instead of arresting them, and felt that "A reward of $1,000 apiece dead or alive … will put an end to them and restore peace and security to many a long-suffering and terrorized community."[9]

Hoy's letter influenced the governors' conference held in Salt Lake City three days later on March 14, 1898, in regards to the original plan of ridding the three states of outlaws. A force of fifteen special officers, five per state, invested with the powers of deputies and the authority to kill on sight was considered. Each officer, familiar with the country and the identities of many of the outlaws, would be paid $100 a month.

This plan was more in line with what J. S. Hoy and other cattlemen had been advocating. Cooperation was also sought from Governor Frank Steunenberg of Idaho and Governor Robert Smith of Montana.[10] At the end of the conference, it was not clear whether a plan of action had been approved or when it would be implemented. The governors stated only that the legality of any action would have to be determined first, and this would take some time.[11]

To show they were not intimidated by all this talk, the outlaws made a raid on the ranch of J. S. Hoy, himself. On the day of the governor's conference, they descended on one of his cattle camps not far from Powder Springs in retaliation for his letter to the *Denver News*. Livestock was stolen, wagons full of camp equipment and food supplies were driven off, and anything that had to be left behind was destroyed. Rustlers were not idle in Wyoming either, as the CY Ranch reported the theft of about 500 head of cattle and several good saddle horses.[12]

In late March, Colorado Governor Alva Adams decided to take action by singling out Butch Cassidy. He hired James W. Catron, a reputed bounty hunter, to invade the rustler sanctuaries and get Cassidy by arrest or otherwise. In a March 28 letter, Adams notified Governor William A. Richards of his scheme, but two weeks later he had to admit the venture was a failure. Catron talked incessantly about what he was going to do, and was more of a danger to himself than to any desperadoes he may have come across.[13]

This failure, in addition to the fact that Belle Fourche robbers Tom O'Day and Walt Punteney had been released and were back in Wyoming by mid-April, caused alarm in the financial institutions of that state. Foremost among them was the president of the First National Bank of Buffalo, who sent a letter to Governor Richards during the first week of May. It was an urgent plea to the state for better protection "from the lawless element which infests ... the Hole-in-the-Wall country," than the local county officers could provide. He suggested the formation of a fighting unit similar to the Texas Rangers to capture or drive the outlaws from the country. Sheriff Sproal of Johnson County was asked to visit the governor in person to talk the matter over.[14]

From the day of the secret meeting of cattlemen in Rawlins on February 15, 1898, to over two months later in April, nothing definite had been decided as to how to deal best with the rustling problem. This decision was to be further postponed after it was announced that the United States had declared war on Spain on April 25, 1898. Many of the men experienced in hunting outlaws who may have joined a tri-state strike force, volunteered instead to fight the Spaniards in Cuba.[15]

However, there were still some determined law officers left who went after rustlers, such as Carbon County, Utah, Sheriff C. W. Allred. In late April 1898, Joe Walker and three other rustlers from Robbers Roost, ran off several head of horses and cattle from the Whitmore ranch near Price, and had severely beaten two young men who were tending the cattle. On the morning of Friday, May 13, Sheriff Allred and a posse, which included Deputy U.S. Marshal Joe Bush, picked up the outlaws' trail. They caught up with their quarry in their camp near the Book Cliffs about fifty miles north of Thompson (earlier called Thompson Springs). Called upon to surrender, two of the men, Mizzoo Schultz and Sang Thompson, stood up with their hands in the air. However, Joe Walker and John Herring (or Herron) commenced shooting from their blankets with revolvers. The posse returned fire with their rifles until both outlaws were dead.[16]

Joe Bush sent a telegram from Thompson to Utah Governor Heber Wells, which stated the posse had killed Joe Walker and Butch Cassidy, and captured Elzy Lay and another man. Members of the posse identified the body of John Herring, a minor outlaw, as Cassidy, and the prisoner Schultz as Lay. When the posse reached Price, many citizens agreed that Butch Cassidy had been killed, but some had their doubts. The two prisoners, Thompson and Schultz, said the dead man was John Herring, a Wyoming cowboy. It was decided to summon two men by telegraph who knew Cassidy, Sheriff John Ward of Uinta County, Wyoming, and Cyrus Wells "Doc" Shores, a former sheriff of Gunnison County, Colorado. They both stated that the body was definitely not Butch Cassidy, much to the chagrin of the posse since the expectation of a large reward was now lost. Also, the two captured outlaws, Thompson and Schultz, were released for lack of evidence.[17]

It was spring of 1898 or later when Kid Curry was again heard from, this time in Big Piney, just below the Wind River country in western Wyoming. One report related that three men robbed Daniel B. Budd's store and post office of more than $200. The bandits, believed to be George Currie and the Roberts brothers, escaped to the north, robbing two post offices on the Wind River Divide. A Pinedale posse headed by a Sheriff Ward (John Ward of Uinta County?), and including a government postal inspector named Waterbury, followed their trail the next day. They came upon the outlaws in their camp on the Divide above the Green River Lakes region. In the resulting gun battle, the sheriff and one posse member were wounded. The outlaws then fled east across the Big Horn Mountains, with a Deputy Sheriff Huston joining the chase. They did not stop at Hole-in-the-Wall, but continued on to northeastern Wyoming, stealing thirty horses near Gillette and driving them north. They abandoned the horses before reaching the Montana border, possibly to cover their tracks. However they then stole fifteen horses from the Northern Cattle Company, and drove them to Terry, Montana, on the Yellowstone River. The Wyoming posse had given up the chase at the Montana line.[18]

By this time, Deputy Sheriff Ricks of Butte County, S.D., accompanied by Montana stock detective W. D. "Billy" Smith and Chief of Police Jackson of Miles City, Montana, was again on their trail. Pushing fifteen head of horses slowed the outlaws down, and the posse pressed them closely. They headed toward Curry's old stomping grounds in the Little Rockies, and left at least one exhausted horse along the way. After fifteen days the bandits reached the Bear Paw Mountains, and with the posse hot on their trail, they decided to make a stand. Although greatly outnumbered, they were able to hold off the posse until it was dark and then escape into the badlands. They were in such a hurry that they left all of their supplies, extra guns and ammunition, and most if not all of the horses.[19]

Brown Waller says the outlaws lost the posse somewhere in northern Montana, before escaping across the border into Canada.[20] However, Charles Kelly says they decided to head south to Wyoming and the safety of Hole-in-the-Wall. The posse continued to dog their heels, even follow-ing the outlaws to their hideout in the Hole. When the officers started fir-ing at some cabins located near Buffalo Creek, they soon found out they were outnumbered, and that their bullets were not effective against log walls. After two posse members were seriously wounded, they decided to give up the chase and withdraw to Casper.[21]

On Thursday, April 28, 1898, about the time Joe Walker and friends stole the Whitmore stock, the Ketchum Gang (a southern version of the Wild Bunch) held up the westbound Galveston, Harrisburg & San An-tonio train No. 20 near Comstock, Texas. Their take was variously re-ported to be just a small package of money to as much as $20,000. The gang struck again two months later on July 1, 1898, near Stanton, Texas, at Mustang Creek. This time the target was the westbound Texas Pacific No. 3, and again there was a wide range in the estimates of the amount taken, from $1,000 to $50,000. After this last holdup they escaped into New Mexico, possibly spending at least part of the next few months in their Turkey Creek Canyon cave hideout near Cimarron.[22]

The core of the gang at this time was brothers Tom (sometimes re-ferred to as "Black Jack") and Sam Ketchum, and Will Carver. Jeffrey Burton, an authority on these and other southwest outlaws, suggests that Ben Kilpatrick, a Texan acquaintance of the gang, may have been a fourth participant in these last two robberies, "but there is nothing to speak for it other than past and future associations, Kilpatrick's status as a fugitive, the notoriety he later achieved, and the lack of any infor-mation on his whereabouts in the spring and early summer of 1898—in other words, no semblance of real evidence."[23]

Ben and his brother George had been involved in a dispute with a neighbor in Concho County in January 1897.[24] They became fugitives and outlaws when they left Texas before an upcoming trial date of No-vember 1 of the same year. Burton asserts that the two went north to Hole-in-the-Wall, and possibly to other outlaw sanctuaries where they met principal members of the Wild Bunch.[25] Although he does not cite any evidence for this statement, the timing of the Kilpatricks' movements makes a meeting with Kid Curry, Butch Cassidy, and others, plausible.

There is a tantalizing, all too brief comment in Dick and Vivian Dunham's *Our Strip of Land: A History of Daggett County, Utah*, which contains much oral history of the northeastern corner of Utah, including Brown's Hole: "We've heard that Harvey Logan (Kid Curry) and Ben Kilpatrick spent quite a bit of one winter around Linwood, holing up, when necessary over in Hideout [presumably Hideout Canyon]." The authors state that in the early years, Linwood was "a rip-roaring, hell-raising, wide-open town, with two stores, two hotels, two blacksmith shops, a number of boarding houses, gambling hells, blind tigers, a dance hall, and plenty of tight men and loose women."[26] Since Linwood wasn't platted until 1900, it would be difficult to ascertain the actual year in which Curry and Kilpatrick may have spent time there.

Kid Curry, Flatnose George Currie, and the Sundance Kid showed up in northern Nevada by July of 1898, and were about to try their luck at train robbery. (Sundance was the only one who had any experience with this type of endeavor, but his 1892 robbery of the Great Northern near Malta, Montana, was a bungled job that he narrowly escaped, with less than seventy dollars of loot.) Pearl Baker says the three met at Robbers Roost, then traveled north to Green River, Utah, from where they hopped a freight train to Elko, Nevada. Edward Kirby says they met in Brown's Hole in June, and rode west through the Wasatch Range and the Great Salt Lake Desert in Utah, stopping just south of Winnemucca, Nevada, in Humboldt County. They spent several days scouting the Southern Pacific Railroad tracks and possible getaway routes.[27]

An 1895 travel guide described the small town of Humboldt to the tourist:

As the train stops at Humboldt, the passengers are surprised to see a beautiful little park filled with thrifty trees and carpeted with luxuriant greensward. This oasis in the desert is the result of irrigation, and the fountain of cold, clear water that throws its rainbow tinted spray into the air, tells the story as to how this magical transformation has been brought about. The charm of contrast is complete, and taking all things into consideration, I

know of no place to be met with on the trip across the continent
that the tourist will regard with more pleasure than the unex-
pected vision of this emerald of the desert.[28]

On July 14, 1898, two of the outlaws were hidden on board the tender
car of passenger train No. 1 as it left Humboldt Station about 1:25 a.m.,
traveling northeast toward Winnemucca. About one mile from Humboldt, the bandits climbed over the tender and appeared in the cab with
revolvers drawn. They ordered engineer Philip Wickland and fireman
McDermott to stop the train, and then proceed slowly to milepost #3784
where there was a large pile of railroad ties. The third outlaw was there
with the horses, and his job was to fire his revolver in order to keep the
train crew and passengers from interfering. Witnesses later described
this man as a Negro; however, this may indicate he was the dark complexioned Kid Curry. The robbers didn't know that the rear brakeman
had already jumped off the train when it first stopped, and was running
back to Humboldt. From there he telegraphed the news up the line to
Winnemucca, where a special train car was put at the disposal of Sheriff
Charles McDeid and his posse.[29]

Using Wickland and McDermott as shields, the outlaws ordered express messenger Hughes to open the door to the express car and come
out. When the messenger stubbornly refused to vacate the car, the bandits set a charge that blasted the door open, stunning Hughes. Wickland
then convinced the messenger to come out without resistance since the
engineer and McDermott were in the line of fire. The safe was blown
open, and in the process, the roof and interior of the car were destroyed.
The take was reported as low as $450 by Wells, Fargo & Company, with
local newspapers reporting it variously at $9,000, $20,000, and $26,000.
The three robbers then shook hands good-naturedly with the messenger
and the two trainmen. As the train pulled out, the outlaws were already
on their horses heading north. Two hours later, the special posse car from
Winnemucca met the damaged Southern Pacific No.1 near Mill City.[30]

The posse, consisting of Sheriff McDeid, Deputy Sheriff George
Rose, Constable Feliz of Lovelock, Phil Boyle, Clarence Sage, and

bolstered by an Indian tracker, continued on to examine the holdup site. Fourteen sticks of dynamite had been left behind by the robbers, and the tracks of their horses were found and easy to follow. However, the outlaws had more than a two-hour head start and the posse did not have enough supplies for a protracted chase, or any way to replenish their tired mounts. Although the chase was soon abandoned, Sheriff McDeid continued to investigate the case. A $1,000 reward posted for the arrest and conviction of each robber by Wells, Fargo & Company and the railroad was an incentive.[31]

When suspicion fell on two men in Oregon, McDeid and Special Agent Jonathan N. Thacker of Wells, Fargo & Company brought them to Winnemucca on January 27, 1899, to stand trial.[32] A third suspect, Daniel "Red" Pipkin of the William "Broncho Bill" Walters gang of train robbers, was arrested near Moab, Utah, in March. He was taken to Winnemucca, but was soon transferred to New Mexico for a train robbery charge. Although he evaded conviction of the latter charge, he was eventually convicted of horse theft in Arizona and sentenced to ten years in the Yuma prison.[33] The trial of the other two suspects, James Shaw and Leslie Bowie, started on April 10, 1899, and they were found not guilty on April 22. Pinkerton Detective Agency records indicate that Kid Curry, Flatnose George Currie, and the Sundance Kid were seen in the Humboldt area just previous to the train robbery.[34]

In early fall of 1898, Tom and Sam Ketchum left Texas, traveling by rail to Idaho.[35] It's possible they had visited the state before this, as well as Wyoming, Colorado, and Utah, and were acquainted with the outlaws who frequented the hideouts in those areas. In fact these southern outlaws, including Will Carver, may have introduced their northern counterparts to a remote outlaw sanctuary in the area around Three Creek, in southwestern Idaho. The Ketchums were close friends of the Duncan family, and had ranched near each other in San Saba County, Texas. Sometime in the mid-1890s, Jim and George Taplin "Tap" Duncan settled in Three Creek after seeing the area as cowboys on a cattle drive from New Mexico Territory. They filed on adjacent homesteads on May 16, 1898. Jim built a combination store and post office with creek rocks, and a later wooden addition served as a home for him and his new wife. The building was still standing and in good condition when the author visited the area in September 2007. Jim's brother Tap was forced to leave Idaho with his family not long after he had settled on his homestead.[36] The details of this circumstance as well as the connection of his name with Kid Curry's death will be better discussed later in this biography.

The Ketchums spent time in Idaho, and Carver can be placed specifically in the Three Creek and Shoshone locales. It would have been natural for them to visit their friends, the Duncans, and it would be a good bet that they informed members of the Wild Bunch of the advantages of the area. Jeffrey Burton claims that by summer of 1898 the Three Creek region of Owyhee County was known to outlaws as a convenient hideout, including the Humboldt train robbers who found safety there. Kid Curry, George Currie, Sundance, as well as Butch Cassidy and Elzy Lay, would have returned the favor by inviting their Texan associates to northern hideouts such as Brown's Hole and Hole-in-the-Wall.[37]

Burton, in his *The Deadliest Outlaws*, discusses the circumstantial evidence pointing to the Ketchums' and possibly Carver's presence in

The original store in Three Creek, Idaho, made of creek rocks. (Author's Collection)

Owyhee County by fall of 1898.[38] They also made a trip to Hole-in-the-Wall during fall of that year, probably stopping previously in Brown's Hole. It certainly had to be at this time that they recommended to Butch Cassidy and Elzy Lay, the advantages of working as cowpunchers in the southwest in order to elude the law. Butch and Elzy were tired of constantly looking over their shoulders and the possibility of being shot down by a posse as in the case of Joe Walker and John Herring. One of the ranches that hired cowboys without asking too many questions was the Erie Cattle Company, twenty miles northeast of Bisbee in Cochise County, Arizona Territory. Carver had worked there previously, and the Ketchum gang had stayed at the headquarters for a time after the first Folsom train robbery in September 1897.[39]

In late 1898, Cassidy and Lay rode to southern Arizona and were hired on at the Erie outfit by foreman Bob Johnson, using the names Jim Lowe and William McGinnis respectively. Their stay there was short, for in early 1899 they and Erie hands Perry Tucker, Joseph "Mack" Axford, Jim James, and Clay McGonagill, were hired at the WS Ranch near Alma, in southwestern New Mexico Territory. Tucker took the place of the old WS foreman who had been unable to prevent widespread rustling. Also hired at about the same time were Bruce "Red" Weaver and Tom Capehart.[40] The Ketchums did not presume to be hired by manager Captain William French, since they had stolen two of his favorite horses prior to meeting up with Carver at Hole-in-the-Wall. However, the Ketchums as well as Carver remained in the area of the WS and kept in contact with Cassidy, Lay, and Weaver.[41] Mack Axford's autobiography, *Around Western Campfires*, contains evidence of Ben Kilpatrick's presence on the range.

Axford states that French had a problem with small owners who were running their cattle on the WS range and stealing his calves. During a special roundup they found a number of large calves with the brands of the "little cowmen" following WS cows. Axford, Cassidy, and the others, under orders from Perry Tucker, would bar out these brands and rebrand with the WS iron. According to Axford, "Big Johnny Ward was one of the little men whose calves had been rebranded … when found following WS cows; he had a little chip on his shoulder on account of this."[42] The physical characteristics of Big Johnny Ward matched those of Ben Kilpatrick, most importantly the slight cast he had in his left eye that French said resembled a second pupil.[43]

The rustling on the WS range had effectively been stopped, with French remarking in his memoirs, "What seemed strange to me at the time was that there was no particular outcry or protest from the usual quarters ... The rustlers, for the time being, seemed entirely buffaloed." He later added, "[A]s long as Jim [Cassidy] and Mac [Lay] stayed on the job I wasn't greatly worried ... They were evidently doing their duty loyally to the outfit, and expressed the greatest contempt for the common cow-thieves, whom they always alluded to as the 'Petty Larceny' crowd."[44]

Ben Kilpatrick, "The Tall Texan." (Robert G. McCubbin Collection)

Some writers believe the Tom Capehart who was hired onto the WS Ranch was an alias for Kid Curry. This is not true. Capehart was a cowboy from Texas who, along with four others, had been arrested on December 12, 1897, for complicity in a Southern Pacific train robbery at Steins Pass, New Mexico. The robbery was actually the work of the Ketchum Gang, which at that time included Tom Ketchum, his brother Sam Ketchum, Will Carver, and Dave Atkins.[45] The posse, which included Deputy Marshal George Scarborough, beat the prisoners to extract confessions. "They struck Tom Capehart in the face and over the head with a gun," one of the prisoners, Walter C. Hovey, later wrote, "and jabbed him in the stomach with a cocked .45 Colt."[46] He spent a year in jail before charges were finally dismissed, joining Cassidy and Lay at the WS within the first two months of 1899. Capehart never forgot the rough treatment he had received at the hands of Scarborough and the other posse members. He was embittered from his experience with the law, and soon turned to outlawry.[47]

Kid Curry never used Tom Capehart as an alias or one that Will Carver used, G. W. Franks. According to Jeffrey Burton, this bit of fiction came about from Charles Kelly's confusion concerning the writing of William French in his *Some Recollections of a Western Ranchman*. Succeeding Kid Curry/Wild Bunch authors, such as James D. Horan and Brown Waller, basically followed Kelly and added their own surmises. As Burton states in his *Dynamite and Six-Shooter,* "French does not state or even imply that Capehart was or might have been Harvey Logan. Nor does he say that Logan was or might have been Franks. In fact, he does not make one single solitary mention of or allusion to Harvey Logan in the course of the entire book. What he does say is that he believed Capehart to be Franks."[48] This misunderstanding will become clear when the July 11, 1899, Folsom train robbery is discussed.

Although some authors claim that Kid Curry and the Sundance Kid went south with Cassidy and Lay, there really isn't any definite evidence for this. Donna Ernst, who has done much research on the whereabouts of the Sundance Kid over his lifetime, has found evidence that during the winter of 1898/1899 he was back in Carbon County, Wyoming, working on the ranch of a man named Beeler.[49] Frank Lamb, in his *The Wild Bunch*, claims that Cassidy sent word to Curry to join him in Alma, "but Curry sent back word that it was not advisable for too many of them to be in one place."[50]

Mack Axford had worked with Jim Lowe and Will McGinnis at both the Erie Cattle Company and the WS Ranch. He had been told by the WS foreman, Perry Tucker, that Lowe "was the celebrated Wyoming outlaw, Butch Cassidy."[51] Later, when Axford was working as a jailer for Sheriff Del Lewis in Tombstone, Arizona, they received a reward circular a few weeks after a bank holdup in Winnemucca, Nevada, picturing Butch Cassidy and Harry Longabaugh, the Sundance Kid. "Del brought the circular in to me and asked about the two men; he knew I had punched cows with Cassidy. The picture of Cassidy was a good likeness; *Longbaugh I did not know*." (Italics added)[52] He certainly would have recognized Sundance if he had come south with Cassidy and Lay. Axford had also worked closely with Tom Capehart at the Erie outfit, and he doesn't mention any connection between Capehart and Curry; in fact he doesn't mention Curry at all.[53]

Flatnose George Currie and Kid Curry most likely spent the winter in Wyoming, in and around Hole-in-the-Wall. They were sure to have kept in touch with Sundance for future operations.

CHAPTER 12

Train Robbers Syndicate

I n March 1899, the trio reunited at Brown's Hole and again traveled to northern Nevada, ending up in Elko.[1] They checked into Johnny Craig's rooming house under the names Frank Bozeman, John Hunter, and Joe Stewart. For about a week they frequented the saloons along Railroad Street, flourishing large amounts of money and breaking hundred dollar bills while gambling.[2] This ostentatious display may have been part of a plan to allay suspicion from the real reason they were in town. They had made plans, probably in Brown's Hole, to strike the Union Pacific at Wilcox, Wyoming, and needed a stake to finance the robbery.[3] It was rumored that the safe in the Club Saloon contained a considerable amount of cash, and would be easier to rob than the local bank.[4]

It was going on midnight on Monday, April 3, 1899, when owner E. M. James Gutridge closed up after town constable Joe Triplett had left the premises. With the safe behind the bar open, Gutridge and bartender C. B. Nichols began counting the evening's receipts, when Kid Curry, Flatnose, and Sundance entered with guns drawn. Since Triplett had left just moments earlier, Gutridge tried to yell for help, but one of the masked men hit him over the head. The robber then took Gutridge and Nichols to the front of the bar and made them sit in chairs, while a second bandit covered the front door. The third robber gathered the money in a gunny sack, the amount reported as being $550 or $3,000. The outlaws then backed out of the saloon, jumped on their horses and escaped north in the direction of Tuscarora.[5]

Three local men, J. Cook, Bart Holbrook, and John Page, were at first suspected, but after establishing alibis, Justice Morgan had to let them go. When law officials learned that Bozeman, Hunter, and Stewart had left town on the night of the robbery, they were suspected as being the saloon robbers, and possibly the same trio that held up the Southern Pacific less than a year ago at Humboldt.[6] "It seems quite possible that some of the robberies that the Wild Bunch got credit for were not of their doing," wrote Pearl Baker. "They all claimed this was so, but this particular trio stayed together and became well enough known to keep track of."[7]

The gang turned east (Baker said they went by train to Salt Lake City), and arrived in Kemmerer, in the southwest corner of Wyoming, on April 10. Here they bought a wagon and team of horses, a camping outfit, and one Winchester rifle. They also bought two saddle horses; one was a pinto from William Fenn, and the other a buckskin from John Hastie. On April 15, Kid Curry, Sundance, and Flatnose left town and were seen heading east.[8] Converse County Sheriff Josiah Hazen's posse captured the gang's horses after the Wilcox robbery, and two of them were subsequently identified by John Hastie and merchant Mike Nolen of Kemmerer, as the horses purchased by the bandits. Also, the remains of the wagon they had purchased were found in Rock Creek on June 13, broken up and parts of it burned for firewood.[9]

Railroad Street in Elko, Nevada, 1902. Kid Curry, George Currie, and the Sundance Kid robbed the Club Saloon here in April 1899. (Northeastern Nevada Museum, Elko)

It has been stated by a number of Butch Cassidy admirers that he came up from the WS Ranch to help plan or even plan entirely the Wilcox train robbery. There isn't any evidence that Cassidy was at the scene of the robbery, but it is generally accepted that he stayed in the area to later divide the loot. It has also been stated that Elzy Lay was one of the robbers, as well as a number of other Wild Bunch members. First of all, William French indicates that Jim Lowe (Cassidy) worked at the WS through the summer and fall of 1899, and doesn't mention any request for a leave of absence. He makes it clear that he hated to see good men quit or take leave from the ranch, specifically mentioning Tom Capehart and "Mac" McGinnis (Elzy Lay).[10] Lay left about the first part of May to meet Sam Ketchum and Will Carver for the Folsom train robbery that took place on July 11, 1899. Red Weaver had gone with Lay, and they were both seen in Cimarron, New Mexico, in mid-June.[11] Secondly, it is rather difficult to believe that Cassidy would have much useful input for the planning of a train robbery, when he hadn't any experience himself. Charles Kelly believed Tom McCarty, Matt Warner, and Cassidy held up the Denver & Rio Grande just east of Grand Junction, Colorado (at Unaweep Switch) on November 3, 1887, but offers absolutely no proof. The holdup itself was amateurish and the would-be robbers rode away with only about $150 in loot.[12]

Kid Curry, Sundance, and Flatnose Currie did have limited train holdup experience, and most likely received pointers from the Ketchums and Will Carver. Up to this time, Tom Ketchum and Carver had robbed five trains with varying degrees of success. For the last two robberies, the Ketchum gang had successfully used the technique of uncoupling the engine, express, and mail cars from the passenger coaches and moving them up the track. They had also discovered that showing a red light was an effective way to stop a train. They had tried this tactic earlier at the December 9, 1897, Stein's Pass robbery, but when the engineer was ordered to uncouple the express car, he set the air brakes instead. When the train could not be moved, the impatient bandits tried to gain entry to the express car on the spot. They were met with shotgun blasts from the Wells Fargo guards inside, with the result that four of the five bandits were wounded and one was killed.[13] The outlaws learned from this debacle, and pulled off the Comstock and Mustang Creek robberies of 1898 without a hitch. Kid Curry and his partners would make use of this technique at Wilcox, Wyoming, one of the boldest and most famous western train robberies. If there was any truth to the existence of a Train Robbers Syndicate, this would most likely be the beginning of its operations.

The Pinkertons suspected Rawlins saloonkeeper and Wild Bunch associate, Jack Ryan, of providing the robbers with information pertaining to express shipments on the Union Pacific Railroad.[14] After he had moved from Baggs to open a saloon in Rawlins, Ryan worked part-time as a brakeman and substitute freight conductor for the railroad. On the day of the train robbery, he sold his saloon and invested in another called the Home Ranch Saloon.[15]

At 2:18 on the Friday morning of June 2, 1899, the first section of the westbound Union Pacific Overland Flyer No. 1 was flagged down about a mile west of Wilcox Station at milepost #609, by two men waving red lanterns. It was raining heavily and engineer William R. Jones, knowing there was a small wooden bridge ahead that may have washed out, immediately slowed the train to a stop.[16] Conductor Storey, upon seeing men with guns, immediately perceived a holdup in progress, and ran back down the track to warn the second section of the train, which was running a few minutes behind.[17]

The two men, wearing shoulder-length masks, jumped aboard the locomotive and ordered Jones and the fireman named Dietrick to pull the train over the bridge, under which they had previously placed dynamite. The bandits then lit the fuse, and the end of the train just cleared the bridge when the explosion occurred. Jones was then told to uncouple the locomotive and tender, with the baggage, express, and two mail cars, from the rest of the train and pull ahead another mile or two.[18] However, as in the Stein's Pass robbery a year and a half earlier, the engineer refused the order and set the air brake instead. Unlike the Ketchum gang, these bandits knew how to remedy the situation. One of them hit Jones over the head with his pistol, inflicting a scalp wound, and threatened his life. The other robber, who appeared older, spoke up saying, "Don't kill him."[19] (Kid Curry and Sundance were both four years older than George Currie.) Jones then complied, moving the train minus its passenger cars, about two miles up the track near Como Ridge where presumably the third bandit waited.[20]

The robbers escorted Jones and Dietrick back to the mail car of chief clerk Burt Bruce, and fellow clerk, Robert Lawson. (Owing to the many conflicting reports, it is unclear whether the first mail car was attacked before moving the train over the bridge, or after.) They heard voices calling for them to open the door, and looking out saw three masked men holding guns on the engineer and fireman. Burt refused to open up and gave the order to extinguish all lights. During the next fifteen minutes the outlaws yelled repeated threats that they would blow up the car if the door wasn't opened soon. Suddenly two rifle bullets were fired into the car, one hitting the drinking water tank and passing through the stanchions, followed closely by a huge blast that destroyed one of the doors and broke the windows. Bruce thought it prudent for himself and Lawson to exit the car, particularly after the robbers threatened to blow it up with the next charge. They were then lined up alongside the mail car and searched for weapons. Curiously, at this point the bandits told the clerks they weren't after the mail, but the money in the express car.[21]

They proceeded to the express car and ordered the messenger, Charles Ernest Woodcock, to open the door. He refused, and again the bandits used dynamite to blow the door open, the blast knocking Woodcock to the floor badly stunned or unconscious. He was dragged from the car and laid on the ground, before the robbers turned their attention to the second mail car. This was occupied by clerks Robert O'Brien and James Skidmore, who wisely opened up after being threatened with more dynamite. The bandits then went back to the express car to open the two express company safes.[22] It is not certain why the mail was not searched for valuables. Brown Waller states that the bandits knew the mail personnel were army clerks and wanted nothing to do with them; however, it may have been that they simply didn't want to waste time, especially with a second section of the train so close and rumored to contain two cars of soldiers.[23]

Woodcock could not be revived enough to give the combinations of the safes, but there were plenty of explosives on hand, stolen from a railroad grading works in Cheyenne. Personnel from the second section of the train later found two sacks of giant powder behind a snow fence, each weighing about fifty pounds.[24] The roof and sides of the express car were blown out from the heavy charges used in opening the safes. "[T]here was a tremendous explosion that scattered the express car for 100 feet in every direction," according to one early newspaper report. "The end of the mail car was blown in ... Engineer Jones was slightly injured by the flying debris."[25]

It was first reported the outlaws gathered up some $34,000, but the amount was later reported to be $50,000. Part of the loot included a package of incomplete (unsigned) currency valued at $3,400 from the U.S. Treasury Department, destined for the First National Bank of Portland, Oregon. This package of bills also had the lower right hand corners blown off in the explosion, and in fact all of the stolen currency sustained some degree of powder burns from the dynamite. In addition, some of the banknotes had been stained red with the residue of a shipment of

Wreckage of express car and safe after the Union Pacific train robbery at Wilcox, Wyoming. June 2, 1899. (Robert G. McCubbin Collection)

raspberries. This obviously made the bills very easy to identify and trace.[26]

By the time the robbers had gathered up the loot, including some jewelry and watches, it was about 4:15 a.m.[27] According to mail clerk Lawson's account, after the bandits finished "their work they started out in a northerly direction on foot." "The engine of the first section [minus the damaged cars] had been sent ahead to Aurora," he continued, "the nearest telegraph station, from which place the alarm was sent out."[28] However, most accounts state that Jones ran the engine the remaining twelve miles to Medicine Bow, where he telegraphed Union Pacific officials in Omaha, Nebraska. "His message was as follows: First section No. 1 held up a mile west of Wilcox. Express car blown open, mail car damaged. Safe blown open, contents gone. We were ordered to pull over a bridge just west of Wilcox, and after we passed the bridge the explosion occurred. Can't tell how bad the bridge was damaged. No one hurt except Jones—scalp wound and cut on hand. Jones, engineer."[29]

Finley P. Gridley, a manager of one of the Union Pacific's coal mines near Rock Springs, was a passenger on the second section of the train. The bridge had not been totally destroyed, and it was able to cross safely and proceed to the holdup site. While waiting for the wreckage to be cleared, he took it upon himself to investigate the scene of the robbery. A third of a mile farther up the track, he found where the robbers had left their horses tied and hobbled.[30] After more than two hours the second section was able to proceed, "dragging along the damaged express car which knocked against sign boards and switches."[31]

Sheriffs had been telegraphed and posses formed in the surrounding counties of Albany, Carbon, Natrona, and Converse. Posses from Cheyenne and Lander were also en route to help surround the bandits. These local posses were augmented by detectives from the Union Pacific Railroad, the Burlington Railroad, and the Pinkerton National Detective Agency. Also, Governor DeForest Richards would eventually call out a company of the Wyoming state militia.[32] This would prove to be one of the biggest manhunts for members of the Wild Bunch, or for any other western outlaw gang for that matter.

A special train hauling cars containing men, horses, and supplies had been sent from Laramie by the Union Pacific, and arrived at Wilcox Station at about 8:30 a.m. A posse sent by Carbon County Sheriff McDaniel of Rawlins arrived at Medicine Bow at 9:00 a.m.[33] "The trail picked up by the first posse [to reach the scene of the holdup] ran north," Charles Kelly states, "and indicated there were but three bandits, while the train crew distinctly saw six."[34] (Engineer William Jones is the only member of the train crew that said he saw six bandits, and not all at the same time. The other crew members, express messenger Charles Woodcock, mail clerks Robert Lawson, James Skidmore, and Robert O'Brien all testified seeing no more than three robbers.[35])

A reward poster from the Office of United States Marshal, Cheyenne, Wyoming, and signed by U.S. Marshal Frank A. Hadsell, was issued on June 3, 1899. The Postmaster General of the United States offered a $1,000 reward for the arrest and conviction of each robber, with an equal amount offered by the Union Pacific Railway Company for their capture, *dead or alive*. It included a partial description of the robbers, "supposed to be six in number," making a total reward of $12,000. The descriptions were vague and not particularly helpful, one of the men described as having "black, woolly hair," and another "spoke with Texan twang."[36]

The outlaws were headed in the direction of Casper, their ultimate destination thought to-be Hole-in-the-Wall. They were within the long curve formed by the North Platte River, which was in flood, and needed to find an unguarded bridge. Natrona County Deputy Sheriff Warren E. Tubbs and six men were sent southwest from Casper to guard the bridges at Alcova and Bessemer, which they did faithfully for thirty-six hours in heavy rain.[37] However, Union Pacific Detective (Special Agent) Frank Wheeler and his posse had trailed the bandits northeast from the Medicine Bow River, forty miles across the Laramie River plains, and into La Bonte Canyon. The bandits took a shortcut over the Laramie Mountains by way of Hat Six Canyon, and followed the foothills toward Glenrock, where Wheeler lost the trail twenty miles south of there. The posse from Rawlins, following the same trail, was also thrown off the scent.[38]

Converse County Sheriff Josiah Hazen and a posse arrived in Casper by special train Saturday afternoon. Included were some special agents of the Union Pacific with Detective Vizzard of Omaha in charge. They were joined by Natrona County Sheriff Oscar Hiestand.[39] It is difficult to understand what these officials were thinking when they neglected to have the Casper Bridge guarded that Saturday evening. They may have

Converse County Sheriff Josiah Hazen. (Courtesy of Mike Bell)

thought it inconceivable that the robbers would be so brash or so fool-hardy as to ride through Casper to cross the bridge on the north side of town; or they may have thought it should take much longer to travel the 110 miles to Casper from the Medicine Bow area.

Nevertheless, about 2:00 a.m. Sunday, June 4, in a pouring rain, the three bandits were seen riding slowly down the main street past the open saloons. Although one observer was heard to joke, "There's a chance to make a reputation. There go the train robbers," they were thought to be cowboys on their way home after a night of entertainment.[40] They had actually paused in town to obtain supplies and fresh horses from friends, or possibly from a brother of George Currie who worked for the Chicago and Northwestern railroad roundhouse in Casper. Before riding out of town, they tried to raise the hostler at Bucknum's livery stable for some last minute care for their horses. The hostler would not be bothered, so the bandits continued their leisurely ride to the north side of town, and crossed the unguarded bridge over the North Platte. The newspapers were later very critical of this blunder; one headline particularly chas-tised Detective Vizzard for his lack of vigilance.[41]

Later that morning, rancher Al Hudspeth was hunting for stray horses from the CY range, and observed a man cooking breakfast near an aban-doned cabin on Casper Creek, six miles northwest of Casper.[42] He saw several horses grazing nearby, and another man watching him from the cabin door. Hudspeth rode up and asked the stranger if the horses be-longed to him. "Why in hell don't you go and see?" was the curt reply. The rancher tried to explain he was looking for some strays, when a third stranger appeared in the doorway carrying two Winchesters and handed one to his partner. Hudspeth was then told to "Hit the road and do it damned quick!" Wasting no time, he turned his horse toward Casper where he reported the incident to the authorities.[43]

Sheriffs Hazen and Hiestand gathered a posse of nine men, which included Al Hudspeth, Lee Divine, Dr. J. F. Leeper, E. T. Payton, J. F. Crawford, Sam Fish, J. B. Bradley, Charles Heagney, and Tom McDon-ald, and rode to the cabin, where they picked up the bandits' trail leading north toward Powder River. About twenty-five or thirty miles north of

Casper at Teapot Rock, they came across the remains of a camp where the robbers had eaten dinner. It was discovered that the outlaws had then followed the course of Teapot Creek for about six miles to throw off pursuit. The posse picked up the trail, and followed it easily down the muddy Salt Creek Road to a point five miles west of an old horse ranch, about thirty-five miles from Casper. This was an area called Pine Bluffs, where the bandits were waiting behind a hill or ridge to ambush the posse. It was about four o'clock in the afternoon.[44]

When the posse was within a few hundred yards, the outlaws opened up, killing one of the leading horses. Another horse was shot and two others stampeded when the men dismounted to run for cover. One of the spooked horses belonged to Sheriff Hiestand. He had the reins over his arm and was intent on adjusting his rifle, when a bullet hit the ground in front of the horse, causing it to break away and race over a hill. The sheriff walked fifteen miles before he found another horse, but it was so broken down that it could not be used for chasing outlaws. He proceeded to Casper to secure a better mount, and arrange to have supplies sent to the posse in the field. The outlaws had the advantage in the use of long-range rifles and smokeless powder cartridges. They kept the posse pinned down until they were able to escape at nightfall. Sheriff Hazen and his men decided to make camp for the night, and allow the supplies from Casper to catch up with them.[45]

On Monday morning, June 5, the posse found where the outlaws, in their haste, left behind some food and a Pacific Express Company shotgun. The train robbers had kept moving through the night, thinking the posse had been discouraged and would not follow. Feeling safe, they decided to get some rest in a protected coulee near Castle Creek, about forty-five miles north of Casper. Local ranchers say the area the outlaws stopped at is called Jumbo Water Hole. At that time it was the only available water for fifty miles in any direction, and was about forty miles from Hole-in-the-Wall. The outlaws became careless, allowing their saddled horses to stray far from camp. The saddlebags contained jewelry taken at the Wilcox robbery, and a quantity of smokeless cartridges. The posse found the horses, and set out to follow their back trail, hoping it would lead to the robbers.[46]

At ten o'clock in the morning, Sheriff Hazen and Dr. John F. Leeper of Casper were dismounted and walking up Bothwell Draw.[47] They were searching for the prints of the outlaws' horses, and were apart from the rest of the posse. Hazen called to Dr. Leeper that he had found the trail, and the latter walked over to within six feet of the sheriff. The concealed outlaws suddenly opened fire, hitting Hazen in the stomach, the bullet coming out his back near the spine. Dr. Leeper dropped to the ground as he was narrowly missed by a bullet. For the next ten minutes the outlaws fired on him continuously, and he could not immediately come to Hazen's aid. When the firing ceased, the physician gave the suffering sheriff what medical assistance he could under such conditions.[48] Hazen had to lie where he was for several hours until a spring wagon could be found to take him to Casper. Two cowboys volunteered to drive the wagon more than forty miles over rough roads to town.[49]

Meanwhile, the bandits had escaped north following Castle Creek, sometimes wading in the stream to confuse their pursuers following close behind. After a few miles the posse surrounded the bandits, who had taken refuge behind some rocks in the hills. But after nightfall, the fugitives escaped through a wash and past the fires of the possemen. Sometime during the night they came upon a freighting outfit, stole their horses, and continued north. Dr. Leeper and another posse member investigated the wash Tuesday morning, discovering their prey had escaped and were long gone.[50]

One member of the posse, Tom McDonald, had ridden ahead of the wagon, and arrived early the same morning to inform the residents of Casper that Sheriff Hazen had been seriously wounded.[51] "Genuine sorrow was depicted on the faces of our residents when it was learned that Hazen had been wounded," it was reported. "Crowds of people were on the streets awaiting the arrival of the wagon." When the wagon reached Casper, Hazen said, "he preferred to be taken to his house in Douglas if at all possible."[52] A special train took him to his home, where he died at five o'clock in the morning, before the Union Pacific's head surgeon could arrive from Cheyenne to try to save his life.[53] Sheriff Josiah Hazen was very popular and highly respected. His funeral on June 8 was attended by hundreds, and even Governor Richards showed up to pay his respects.[54] He was outraged at Hazen's death, and would use all available resources to catch his killers. Richards ultimately called out Company C of the Wyoming National Guard to join the hunt.[55]

The day after the Wilcox robbery, the newspapers were speculating that the Hole-in-the-Wall gang was responsible for the holdup, and that Butch Cassidy may have come up from the south with some of his gang to participate.[56] But by June 8 it was being reported that the three men escaping north had been identified as George Currie and the two Roberts brothers.[57] It is evident by this time that besides Kid Curry using the Roberts alias, the other was actually Harry Longabaugh, the Sundance Kid, and not Curry's brother Lonie.[58] Reward posters dated June 10, 1899, listed descriptions of the three robbers but not their identities. One had light complexion, hair, and eyes and a "peculiar nose, flattened at bridge and heavy at point." The other two men looked like brothers, one more slightly built, having very dark complexion, hair, and eyes. The poster also stated that the Union Pacific Railroad Company, the Pacific Express Company, and the United States Government offered an aggregate reward of $3,000 for each of the men, dead or alive.[59]

Union Pacific General Manager E. Dickerson told the press, "I do not believe there were over three men in the hold-up. Certainly there were no more than that left Wilcox on horses." Although he and other officers believed only three robbers were involved in the holdup, the reward poster and the newspapers reported that three other robbers, location unknown, were also involved in the robbery, which made the total reward worth $18,000.[60]

On Tuesday, June 6, the morning after Hazen had been shot, the three fugitives showed up for breakfast at David Kidd's sheep camp. For some reason, one of them, probably Sundance, separated from the other two, as it turned out temporarily. He was said to have headed for Kaycee on the old Buffalo–Casper freight road.[61] The cattlemen's town of Kaycee, named for the nearby KC Ranch, was just starting up. At five o'clock the next morning, at Jim Nelson's sheep camp on Sullivan's springs, herder John C. DeVore was joined for breakfast by two men.

They were strangers to him, and he had not heard of the train robbery.[62] The camp was about five miles southwest of E. H. French's oil wells on Dugout Creek.[63] Sometime within the last two days their horses must have given out, because on Thursday morning the two exhausted bandits walked onto Robert Tisdale's ranch on the South Fork of Powder River and demanded breakfast. Al Flood, assistant foreman, recognized them as "George Currie and one of the Roberts brothers."[64] Still on foot, the two had to swim the swollen South Powder, since all the bridges were guarded.[65]

They reportedly stopped at John Nolan's KC Ranch on the Middle Fork of Powder River, a man who was sympathetic to the outlaws.[66] Several sources have stated that the outlaws didn't obtain horses until they reached the Billy Hill ranch on the Red Fork of Powder River. However, a Pinkerton letter indicates that Mr. and Mrs. Nolan received some gold watches from the Wilcox robbery as part payment for horses and provisions supplied to the bandits.[67]

On the morning of Friday, June 9, Union Pacific Special Agent Tobin and one A. E. Minium, arrived at the Nolan ranch. They were attempting to rendezvous with the posse in the field to deliver a load of tarps for bedding. They knocked at the door, but learned only that Nolan had gone on a roundup. Also, the blacksmith and hired hands had seen nothing of a posse. They then rode to Tisdale's ranch where they finally found Union Pacific Special Agent Frank Wheeler and his posse.[68]

Wheeler and his large posse had arrived Friday morning at Tisdale's, twenty-four hours behind the robbers. U.S. Marshal Frank A. Hadsell was now riding with Wheeler after checking several false sightings of the other three, subsequently phantom, robbers reported in the newspapers. Respected Montana stock detective Joe LeFors also joined the posse at this time at the request of the Burlington Railroad. LeFors, who prided himself on his tracking ability, received permission from Wheeler to take Hadsell and seven others and try to find the foot trail of the bandits. They rode in the direction of Hole-in-the-Wall, and quickly spotted a trail indicating three men on foot. (Sundance had rejoined his partners.) LeFors sent a man to fetch Wheeler, while he and the rest of the men continued to follow the trail. After twenty-five miles of hard riding, they reached the Red Fork of Powder River at sundown, one-half hour behind their quarry. Wheeler and his men caught up with LeFors here, at the southern end of the Big Horn Mountains.[69]

The trail led into the mountains, and LeFors particularly wanted the passes watched to EK Mountain and to Billy Hill's ranch (a friend of George Currie). That evening and most of the next day LeFors's attempts to intercept the bandits were frustrated by Special Agent Wheeler's interference and unwillingness to accept advice.[70] Meanwhile, the robbers walked north to the top of EK Mountain, but paused there only a few hours in order to throw off the posse. They then doubled back to Billy Hill's ranch on the Red Fork to secure horses. LeFors's group had not eaten in a long time, so it was decided they and Wheeler's men would try to get food at A. L. Brock's ranch at the north end of EK Mountain. According to Al's sixteen-year-old son, J. Elmer Brock, upwards of sixty men showed up at the ranch and ate all the food in the house.[71]

The posse returned to where the outlaws' tracks had been discerned heading up to the top of EK Mountain. Brock wrote that "The three outlaws who came to EK Mountain were George Curry, Kid Curry ... and a former train robber, Harry Lonabaugh." It was decided to keep a guard around the mountain all night to prevent the robbers from escaping. At daylight, the possemen started up the mountain from all sides until they converged on the pass at the top. The only thing they flushed was a silver tip bear that was heard crashing through the timber, desperately trying to escape. The thoroughly frightened men at first imagined the outlaws were charging down on them, until the bear was seen running through a break in the line.[72]

By most accounts, the robbers, all but done in, reached Billy Hill's ranch in the early morning of Saturday, June 10.[73] In fact, Tom Horn, who later investigated the Wilcox robbery on his own, wrote a letter dated January 15, 1900, to Edmund C. Harris, the division superintendent of the Union Pacific in Cheyenne, stating that George Currie came to the ranch alone. It is this and the following information that Horn received from Bill Speck (after threatening to kill him) in a visit to the latter's home on January 2, 1900. Speck said he and Alex Ghent were at Hill's ranch when Currie rode up on a horse he had borrowed from the ranch of Al Smith. Currie told them he had committed the train robbery with "Harve Ray and a stranger in Powder River country, but Currie would not give his name, saying only that the stranger came from the British possessions and that he could blow Christ off the Cross with dynamite."[74] This may be in reference to the years Sundance spent in Canada, where he could have become proficient with dynamite when working on the Canadian railroad.

Currie told them that Ray was done in from all the walking, and he and the stranger were waiting at Al Smith's ranch. He had come to Hill's ranch for four horses he owned that were in the care of Ghent. Many of the ranch's horses were out on the range, and Ghent could only find two of Currie's. Currie bought two horses from Hill, with three saddles thrown in. Before Currie left, Speck said, he related how the gang had lost their horses to the posse, and that "they exchanged some shots, but did not think anyone was hurt, as Currie and his men did not want to hit anyone." It was before daylight when he started back with the horses to the Smith ranch to pick up his partners.[75]

Speck also confessed to Horn that he visited the posse camped at EK Mountain the next day, "and told them the robbers had been at Hill's ranch the night before and took some of his horses, while in reality they had been there 24 hours before the time they told the posse."[76] LeFors states that when he reached the ranch, Billy Hill also informed him of the robbers' appearance during the night. This led him to believe he was only twelve hours behind the bandits. The posse left Hill's ranch at 9:00 a.m. to resume the chase, as the trail led west into the Big Horn Mountains.[77]

The outlaws traversed the Big Horns and dropped into the Bighorn Basin, reaching the Nowood Creek drainage on Monday, June 12. They followed the valley south to John Thorn's sheep camp on Buffalo Creek, where they stopped for supper on Tuesday. From there they rode to Willow Creek (present day Bridger Creek) and French's sheep camp, where they obtained more food. By Wednesday the bandits were headed northwest into the badlands south of Thermopolis, where they attempted to confuse the posse by driving a bunch of horses over their trail.[78] Three bloodhounds, which were brought in by special train from Beatrice, Nebraska, to Casper, had scented their cold trail at Tisdale's ranch. After a thirty-six-hour chase, two of the dogs became exhausted and were lost in the badlands forty miles from Thermopolis. The last dog had more endurance, and eventually ran down two men who claimed to be sheepherders. When they said they had not known about the train robbery and pleaded innocence, their pursuers let them go.[79]

LeFors continued to track the outlaws, crossing the No Water Creek drainage east of Thermopolis. They passed a sheepherder who told them he had seen three men on tired horses late the previous evening. The trail led to Kirby Creek and the Thermopolis road, where the posse traded their jaded horses for fresh ones from J. L. Torrey's Embar Ranch. They were now more optimistic in their chances of capturing the robbers, as they continued down Kirby Creek. Former Deputy U.S. Marshal Arthur Sparhawk met them seven miles from Thermopolis and immediately went into private consultation with Wheeler and Hadsell. Specifically, Sparhawk told them he had information that the robbers were headed for Wind River Canyon. When LeFors was apprised of this, he countered that the robbers' trail clearly continued down Kirby Creek, and not to the Wind River Canyon. However, Wheeler was convinced the information was correct, and would not listen to Lefors. LeFors went along under protest, and after searching the length of the canyon, nothing was found except animal tracks.[80]

The posse then received a dispatch ordering it to abandon the chase and return to Casper. They reached town on Friday, June 23, with Lefors continuing on to Cheyenne to report to Union Pacific Superintendent W. L. Park. He explained that the chase had been thwarted by a bad tip from Sparhawk, a stranger to him. The press reported that the posse members put the blame on Wheeler's incompetence as a manhunter, and it was hinted that he may have been frightened of catching up with the killers of Sheriff Hazen.[81] It was known that outlaws from Hole-in-the-Wall used the banks of Kirby Creek near Thermopolis as a rendezvous.[82]

Some accounts state that the Wilcox loot was divided near Lost Cabin, Wyoming, and that George Currie left the others before they continued on to Thermopolis. The Kid and Sundance hid out at "Bad Land Charlie" Anderson's Hog Ranch on the Bighorn River, near old Thermopolis.[83] They celebrated with other members of the original Hole-in-the-Wall gang, which included their old friend Tom O'Day. The celebration included a shooting contest, where the men would aim at chunks of wood thrown into the Bighorn. Will Frackelton, a traveling dentist, was there and described the action: "The swift current caught the wood and whirled it about, and it required expert marksmanship to score a direct hit. Each man in turn drew bead and fired; the first to make the chips fly was the winner. It was understood that the money [that each participant had tossed on a blanket at each round] … was to be spent for drinks, and each round was followed by a visit to the bar."[84]

The dentist wanted to try his skill, so he grabbed a .45 and a battered derby hat from his buckboard and joined the outlaws. "A man whom I recognized as Louderbaugh snatched my derby and threw it high in the air while his pals blazed away. It was untouched." Frackelton grabbed Sundance's low-crowned Stetson and asked if he could have a chance. With Sundance's amused nod of approval, the dentist drilled the hat with his Colt. "It's better ventilated now," he remarked jokingly. "You shouldn't get hot-headed."[85]

Frackelton said he looked the crowd over covertly, and described "big, blundering Tom O'Day" as having an "air of genial stupidity," "who winked in a most friendly fashion." In regards to Kid Curry, he said Butch Cassidy was considered the leader of the gang, "but the real brains of the outfit was Harvey Logan, who had come from a fine Southern family." He added that the Sundance Kid told him "once that he liked to watch the expression on a face after he'd plugged its owner."[86]

After a few days' celebration, Curry and Sundance headed south toward Brown's Hole and Robbers Roost. George Currie was reported to be five days ahead of his partners, driving a bunch of stolen horses.[87] U.S. Marshal Frank Hadsell received a letter dated August 12, 1899, from Sweetwater County prosecuting attorney D. G. Thomas, informing him that one of the Wilcox robbers had recently been seen. He was not really sure of the man's name, but gave it as "Joe Curry" with attendant aliases. The attorney's informants were two Brown's Hole residents, Angus McDougal and Isam (or Isom) Dart, who had run into a man they knew south of Rock Springs, near Powder Springs in late July. He had six well-shod horses, including a packhorse, in his possession, and was exhausted from hard riding. He asked Dart for news, and was told everyone in the country was in a stir over the Union Pacific train robbery. At first the man denied any involvement, but after questioning admitted he was a participant. "[D]on't tell," he said, "for God's sake don't tell any one you saw me ... I had a hell of a time keeping away from the hounds ... Dart, you must not give me away to any one, don't tell them I was here."[88]

Sometime in the latter part of June, Curry and Sundance were spotted in southwestern Wyoming driving thirteen head of horses toward Powder Springs and Brown's Hole. The Pinkerton National Detective Agency, working for the Union Pacific Railroad, sent Charles A. Siringo and W. O. Sayles to investigate.[89] From Denver they took the train to Salt Lake City, where they were to buy horses, saddles, and supplies, and then ride to Brown's Hole. Just before they started out, their friend C. W. "Doc" Shores, a special agent of the D. & R.G. Railway, informed them that the two robbers had passed through Hanksville, Utah, still driving the thirteen horses, and headed south to the ferry at Dandy Crossing on the Colorado.

The two detectives rode east, and after five days of hard riding they reached Fort Duchesne, where they picked up the outlaws' trail. Their route took them through such towns as Price and Emery, across the desert to the Dirty Devil River and Hanksville, a ride of 500 miles. There they talked to Charley Gibbons, the owner of the hotel and store. He told them that "two suspicious characters with thirteen head of horses" crossed the Colorado River on Johnny Hite's ferry ten days earlier. Almost a week later, Gibbons' brother helped another man swim five head of horses across the river. He had inquired about the two men ahead of him, and said it was his intention to meet up with his friends. From the man's description, Siringo believed him to be Kid Curry.[90]

Siringo and Sayles crossed the river and followed the tracks that showed plainly in White Canyon. Time was wasted following the trail of the lone rider with five head of horses that went up a rocky bluff to

Pinkerton detectives Charles A. Siringo and "W. O. Sayles" (W. B. Sayers). (Robert G. McCubbin Collection)

the top of a mesa. The trail led to an arroyo where all traces were lost in the rugged canyon. Siringo was later informed by a prospector who had witnessed the scene from across White Canyon that he had been only a half mile from the lone outlaw's camp. They again followed the tracks of the two men and their bunch of horses through White Canyon, until they reached Bluff, Utah, on the San Juan River.[91]

Here they learned the two robbers were two weeks ahead of them, and that Pinkerton operatives Alvin Garman and Alvin Darkbird had arrived from Flagstaff, Arizona, a couple of days earlier. The latter two were already following the bandits' trail headed east.[92] Sayles and Siringo also learned that an unsigned twenty-dollar bill had been passed in Thompson, and another one at Charlie Gibbon's store in Hanksville. Curry had had his horse shod at the Ballard Brothers cow camp situated in the Book Cliffs north of Thompson. He paid with an unsigned twenty-dollar bill. It was now certain the men they were following were the Union Pacific train robbers.[93]

The later appearance of unsigned banknotes in Monticello, Utah, would indicate that Curry and Sundance went north to the Carlisle Ranch near that town. The foreman, an ex-outlaw named W. E. "Latigo" Gordon, kept a hidden haystack for men on the run to feed their horses.[94] He no doubt knew Sundance when the latter worked for the nearby LC Ranch, and would have given them food and supplies. From here it was a relatively short ride to sanctuary at the ranch of Sundance's cousin, George Longenbaugh, in Cortez, Colorado. It is difficult to believe that Sundance, let alone Curry, would have soon left the safety of his cousin's ranch; however, since unsigned banknotes were also later found in this area, the outlaws may have thought it prudent to move on.[95] Siringo states that he and Sayles "were born leaders of men," and did not want to follow the other detectives. Therefore, after following the trail from Cortez to Mancos, Colorado, they boarded a Denver and Rio Grande train for Durango. When they reached Durango they found they had caught up with Darkbird and Garman.[96]

Darkbird and his partner eventually lost the trail and returned to Denver, but Siringo received a tip from a friend in Lumberton, just below the border in New Mexico. His friend, J. M. Archuleta, had just happened to see the two robbers and thirteen head of horses in town. Apparently two of the horses were easy to spot by this time, one a large dappled iron-gray and the other a "pretty cream color." The detectives could not find the bandits' trail leaving from Lumberton, but an informant believed they had gone south toward Santa Fe. Not entirely convinced, they decided to separate, with Siringo going south and Sayles going north to search the Pagosa Springs, Colorado, area. Siringo's trip was a disappointment and a waste of time. A friend of his named "Cunny," who lived in the Cochiti mining district near Santa Fe, had seen the two men and their bunch of horses, but it was determined they were not the wanted men.[97]

A telegram from Sayles was waiting for Siringo back in Santa Fe, "saying that he had found the right trail, going through Pagosa Springs, and over Mosca Pass [through the Sangre de Cristo Mountains] into the Wet Mountain Valley." He caught up with Sayles south of Canyon City, but they soon lost the trail.[98]

The detectives then split up, with Sayles following a false lead to Cripple Creek, and subsequently ordered to Montana on the trail of some of the stolen money. Siringo followed what he thought was the outlaws' trail down the Arkansas River to Dodge City, Kansas. From here he continued a long wild goose chase through Indian Territory, Arkansas, Tennessee, and Mississippi. During his travels Siringo received a telegram from Darkbird to come to Nashville, Tennessee, the robbers having been seen boarding a train for there. Darkbird had been called into the field from Denver to assist Siringo, but it turned out to be a bad tip. Anyway, he contracted malaria at this point and had to return to Denver. Siringo was eventually ordered to give up the chase, the agency sending him to Montana to help Sayles with his investigation.[99]

CHAPTER 13

Finis of the Ketchum Gang

About early May 1899, during the time Kid Curry was preparing for his strike at the Union Pacific near Wilcox, Elzy Lay gave notice to manager William French of his intention to quit his horse-breaking job at the WS Ranch near Alma, New Mexico.[1] He was going to join Sam Ketchum and Will Carver in Cimarron for their strike at the Colorado and Southern Railway near Folsom. The latter two had recently broken with Tom Ketchum owing to his brutal and erratic behavior, and were setting up camp at their Turkey Creek Canyon hideout.[2]

Some authors have stated that Kid Curry participated in the robbery, or at least was onsite for the later gun battle at the hideout instead of Carver. This is easily refuted in that the Pinkertons followed Curry's trail (Wyoming, Utah, and Colorado) for weeks after the Wilcox robbery, well into the month of July. In addition, Bob Lee stated in a deposition to authorities after his arrest, that Curry went to visit his sister Allie in Kansas City, Missouri, shortly after the Fourth of July (just before the Folsom robbery).[3] The visit probably would have occurred later in the month since Siringo and Sayles were most assuredly still chasing Curry and Sundance at this time. Thus, he could not have been present at either action in New Mexico.[4]

Lay made a deal with French in which he would take charge of a trainload of cattle from Magdalena to Springer, in return for the price of the train ticket. Bruce "Red" Weaver quit at the same time to accompany Lay under the same terms. French regretted losing a top man like Lay, but didn't mind losing the services of Weaver, who was a "bit of a bluffer" when it came to breaking horses. Springer was the nearest railhead to the ranch's northern headquarters, and would put Lay and Weaver close to Cimarron. After their arrival Weaver was suspected of having contracted smallpox, and was lodged in the local pesthouse.[5] Lay loafed around Springer for a few days, and then left for Cimarron around June 7.[6]

James K. Hunt, postmaster and partner in Porter and Hunt's general store, saw Lay after his arrival in town. Hunt, suspicious of strangers, remembered seeing Ketchum and Carver in town buying supplies a week or so previous. Meanwhile, Weaver had been released from the pest-house, and joined Lay in Cimarron about mid-June. Carver, using the alias G. W. Franks, was seen in the company of Lay for almost a week in late June. He sent an order off to Denver for a .30-.40 carbine with 1,000 rounds of smokeless ammunition, which was promptly shipped to Cimarron by Wells, Fargo and Company. This gun was given to Elzy Lay, since Carver and Sam Ketchum were already thusly armed. All this activity was not going unnoticed by residents of the town. Then on July 7 Ketchum and Carver bought supplies from Hunt's store for the last time, and left for the hideout at Turkey Creek Canyon. Lay and Weaver left the next afternoon, after a few drinks in the bar at Lambert's St. James Hotel.[7]

It was 10:10 p.m. on Tuesday, July 11, 1899, when Elzy Lay and Sam Ketchum climbed aboard the blind baggage car of the southbound Colorado and Southern Flyer No. 1 while the engine was being filled from the water tank at Folsom station. They soon had a gun on the engineer, and when the train was in the Twin Mountain curve, he was ordered to stop at a fire next to the track. Will Carver was waiting with three horses tied to a snow fence, while Red Weaver may have served as a lookout nearby with another horse. The through safe in the express car was blown, and the take was reported to have been anywhere from $30,000 to $70,000.[8] The outlaws escaped toward Turkey Creek Canyon, but Weaver split from the group near Springer. The loot was probably cached somewhere in the mountains of Colfax County, until a time when they could all meet for the divvy. Weaver was arrested soon after leaving the others, but was released ostensibly owing to lack of evidence on July 20. He eventually made his way to Alma to lie low until he heard from the others.[9]

On July 15, the incautious trio, Ketchum, Carver, and Lay, rode boldly into Turkey Creek Canyon, unmindful of anyone who may have been watching. As it turned out, a freighter who had seen the three men in Cimarron previously, saw them enter the canyon. He notified authorities, which resulted in a seven-man posse locating the robbers' campsite early the next evening. The bandits had not posted a guard and were caught completely by surprise. It is uncertain whether the men had been ordered to surrender before the posse opened fire. Lay was the first to be hit as he walked toward a pool of water to fill his canteen or coffee pot. He fainted from the pain and shock from wounds in his left shoulder and back. Ketchum had time to grab his rifle and get off a few shots, but was soon hit by a bullet that shattered the bone in his left arm just below the shoulder. Carver had found excellent cover above the posse, and kept up a devastating fire. In less than an hour his bullets had killed Sheriff Edward J. Farr of Huerfano County, Colorado, and wounded at least two other possemen, one mortally.[10] (Opinion has been and still is divided among historians and writers concerning the identity of Farr's killer. Some accounts state that Elzy Lay revived from his wounds long enough to crawl to his rifle, and shoot Sheriff Farr before he again lost consciousness. For a man to recover from the shock of two serious wounds, twenty minutes into the fight, and pick out the sheriff for a kill shot would seem to be highly improbable.)

By nightfall Lay had revived enough to help Carver get Sam Ketchum on a horse, and move out of the canyon under cover of darkness. But Ketchum later stated that the pain was so great he could not remain mounted, and told the others to leave him. His partners apparently ignored his pleas, leaving him to be cared for at the Lambert Ranch house on Ute Creek. Ketchum was soon captured by a posse there and taken to Santa Fe.[11] He refused to allow a surgeon to amputate his gangrenous arm, and he died on July 24.[12] Carver and Lay eluded capture and according to one account, went into hiding near a ranch a few miles south of Elizabethtown. Lay was attended by a local man who "had a little knowledge of medicine."[13] Miguel Antonio Otero, then governor of New Mexico Territory, later wrote that Franks (Carver) paid a Hispanic couple to take care of McGinnis (Lay) at their ranch. Carver continued on by himself, traveling south toward Roswell and Carlsbad. When Lay was well enough to travel, he was to join Carver at the Lusk ranch near the latter town.[14]

Although Otero does not mention Tom Capehart, William French states that Tom attended Lay while he recuperated in Lincoln County. He made sure that Lay was well provisioned, and even tried to find employment in the area.[15] French's statement that Capehart accompanied Lay may be correct, even considering his belief that Capehart and Franks were one in the same person. Capehart had quit the WS Ranch just before Lay, and had joined him and Carver not long after the Turkey Creek Canyon fight. "It is likely, therefore," Jeffrey Burton speculates, "that Capehart was involved in the train robbing scheme from the beginning, though not as a participant. His role may have been to wait with a change of horses somewhere in the Ponil country, west of Turkey Creek."[16]

By mid-August Lay, Carver, and Capehart were camped at Chimney Wells twenty-eight miles northeast of Carlsbad, Eddy County, New Mexico. Nearby rancher Virgil Hogue Lusk saw them rounding up horses they had left some time previously on his range. He later said he thought they were horse thieves, but he certainly must have had suspicions as to their real identities. After sending word to the sheriff at Carlsbad of their presence, he invited them to join him for breakfast at his camp the next day. In the morning, Carver and Lay decided it would be better to take turns at breakfast, with one riding herd on the horses. Capehart was not on hand, as he had gone to Carlsbad to buy supplies for an excursion to Arizona. The unsuspecting Lay rode into Lusk's camp for breakfast, only to be captured by a three-man posse from Carlsbad. Carver witnessed Lay's arrest from a hill three-quarters of a mile away, but there was nothing he could do. The posse did not follow him as he rode away with a wave of his hat.[17]

Capehart returned to Lusk's camp with the provisions an hour or two after the posse had departed with Lay. Learning of Lay's capture, he rode nearly 400 miles to the WS horse camp in western Socorro County. Butch Cassidy was on hand to hear the story, and he in turn informed William French. Capehart later told French that he had been riding with Lay until just before he was captured. French mistakenly took this to mean that Capehart was the man the newspapers called G. W. Franks (Will Carver's alias).[18] Thus later writers, who believed Harvey Logan used the alias of Franks, then concluded that Logan must also have been Tom Capehart, and the man who shot up the posse at Turkey Creek Canyon.[19]

Tom Ketchum, unaware of the robbery perpetrated by his brother Sam, Lay, and Carver, single-handedly held up the C & S near the same location on August 16. Badly wounded in the attempt, he was unable to travel, and was captured the next day. Both Lay and Ketchum were taken to Trinidad, Colorado, then to Santa Fe on the same train, to enter the New Mexico Territorial Penitentiary on August 24.[20] Found guilty of second degree murder, Lay was sentenced to life imprisonment on October 10, 1899. However, with Governor Otero commuting his sentence to ten years, good behavior, and other factors, Lay was released before Christmas, December 1905. It wasn't until September 1900 when Ketchum was tried in Union County for train robbery. He was found guilty and sentenced to hang, since it was considered a capital crime in New Mexico. After his appeal was rejected, followed by a postponement and a temporary stay from the governor, he was finally hanged on April 26, 1901.[21]

Where were Kid Curry and Sundance during summer and fall of 1899, and winter of 1900? Statements in Bob Lee's deposition suggest Sundance went to Texas after the Wilcox robbery. He said the man he knew as Frank Scramble (Harry Longabaugh, the Sundance Kid) sent some of the mutilated money to Lonie Logan from somewhere near Galveston in summer 1899. It was payment for horses Lonie had furnished him and Harvey Logan in Montana after the Deadwood escape.[22] He added that Scramble had remained in the Galveston area in summer and fall of 1899.[23] Did he meet his future girlfriend whom history knows only as Ethel (or Etta as the Pinkertons called her) there at this time, or had he met her previously on some earlier trip to Texas?[24]

Sundance (going by an assumed name) went to visit Butch Cassidy in Alma, New Mexico, in the latter part of 1899, according to Wild Bunch confidant, Elton A. Cunningham, a local storekeeper. At this time Cassidy, in addition to working for the WS ranch, was a part-time bartender in the saloon run by the proprietors of the Coates and Rowe store. Ben Kilpatrick had also been hired on at the WS as Big Johnny Ward.[25] William French said that Ward "was a new-comer, and was undoubtedly one of the 'Wild Bunch'," but he apparently was not aware that his new employee had been rustling his cattle.[26] Before the end of winter 1899/1900, Sundance returned north to his friends in the Little Snake River Valley.[27]

Lee did not mention in his deposition if Kid Curry had accompanied Sundance to Texas, but he did tell the authorities that when he (Lee) and Lonie Logan were in Cripple Creek in February 1900, Lonie told him "Harvey was in Kansas City visiting his sister. Harvey probably visited my folks while he was in Missouri also ... Harvey left Kansas City about the first of February to join Frank Scramble in New Mexico."[28] Later events would suggest that one or both of them had passed some of the stolen Wilcox money while they were there. Whether Curry stayed in New Mexico or returned to Wyoming with Sundance is not certain. Meanwhile, there had been some important new developments concerning the identification and apprehension of the Wilcox train robbers.

CHAPTER 14

The Law Closes In

A reward poster issued by the Union Pacific Railroad and Pacific Express companies, dated January 12, 1900, and a Pinkerton National Detective Agency poster dated February 23, 1900, stated there was "satisfactory evidence" and it had been "definitely ascertained" that three of the robbers were Kid Curry, his brother Lonie, and their cousin Bob Lee, with the $18,000 reward still in effect. By this time the Pinkertons were publicly vacillating on the issue of whether there were more than three involved. Their poster stated there *may* have been five or six men in the robbery.[1]

"In the files of the Union Pacific Railroad," one writer states, "Harvey Logan was listed as the leader of the gang at Wilcox. What proof the UP officials had of this fact isn't known, though it may have been because they considered him the most callous and dangerous of the Wild Bunch."[2] Kid Curry's leadership role should more likely be attributed to his possessing the intelligence to plan and carry out a successful train robbery.

How did Lonie Curry and Bob Lee become suspected of participating in the robbery? Before this is answered, some background on the two men after the time of the June 1897 Belle Fourche bank robbery is in order. Kid Curry biographer Alan Lee Brekke, of Harlem, Montana, does not include Lonie at Belle Fourche. Although he acknowledges that most accounts assume Lonie went to Hole-in-the-Wall with the Kid, he states, "I have found no evidence as yet to indicate such ... To date [1898] Lonie has not showed any tendency toward being a criminal."[3]

On April 23, 1898, Lonie, with Jim Thornhill, filed an indenture on water rights to Warm Springs Creek which flowed into Rock Creek south of the Little Rockies.[4] The following September 3, Lonie sold a 160-acre tract of land in Chouteau County to a Mrs. Alice Doores of Malta,

Montana, for $2,000.[5] Lonie and Elfie had an addition to their family by the birth of daughter Della Rae on July 20, 1898, in Landusky.[6]

Lonie was apparently also spending a good deal of time in Harlem. Sometime in 1898 Chris Maloney, who owned a sheep ranch north of Augusta, Montana, traveled back to Massachusetts to marry his fiancée Agnes Murphy. On the way home they stepped off the train in Harlem to spend the night. "Agnes told about the polite bell boy at the New England Hotel," local history relates, "his name was Lonnie Currey."[7] Carrying luggage and escorting guests to their rooms certainly does not fit the image of a badman or a member of a gang of bank and train robbers.

From about May 12 to May 27, 1899, Lonie traveled to Giltedge, Lewistown, Rocky Point, Landusky, and several ranches along the way, for the purpose of visiting friends and purchasing mining equipment and properties. He was accompanied by a Miss Hattie Nichols, daughter of a Lewistown rancher, and who may have been related to Jim Thornhill by marriage. While they were in Lewistown Lonie looked into purchasing the Shufelt works, a large quartz mill for use in the Little Rockies mining district.[8] Mrs. Tressler, who was living with Jim Thornhill at this time, joined them for part of the trip. Lucy had been taken in by Thornhill after John Curry's death more than three years earlier. After stopping at the Thornhill ranch, Lonie returned Hattie to Lewistown, and spent some time with his family in Landusky before returning to Harlem. The *Harlem News* issues of May 28 and June 3 reported Lonie's presence in town during that week, the time of the Wilcox robbery.[9]

Also at this time, Lonie is said to have been a partner in a Harlem saloon with one Bill Hart. Hart operated the bar in what was to become the New England Hotel. According to Phil Buckley, sometime prior to the Wilcox robbery Lonie was approached in the saloon by a stranger in town. They had a long private conversation, after which Lonie told Hart that he would be away for about a month, and for him to take care of the business.[10] Although Buckley was an ex-lawman and brother of Sheriff John Buckley, he is the only source for the story and it cannot be verified.

As for Bob Lee's whereabouts at the time of the June 2, 1899, train robbery, defense witnesses at his later trial in May 1900 place him in

Black Hawk, Colorado. Before this he had lived and worked at Cripple Creek, Colorado, for several years since 1896. He and his mining partner, W. B. Luske, took a room in Black Hawk on April 14, 1899, and Lee was seen virtually every day by several witnesses until about June 15 or 17. A cigar merchant was able to show an entry in his account book indicating Lee had bought some cigars on the very day of the robbery. Around mid-June the partners left for Helena, Montana, to meet up with Lee's cousin Lonie Curry. However, they soon went their separate ways, Lonie going to Harlem, and Lee and his partner to try their luck placer mining at French Bar on the Missouri River. Witnesses testified seeing Lee in French Bar no later than June 21, 1899.[11]

On July 5 Lonie further strengthened his ties to Harlem by buying a half interest in George L. Bowles' Club Saloon, and changing the name to "Bowles and Curry." Within a little over three months they added a new bar. Bill Hart was asked to tend bar whenever the partners took some time off. Lonie became a close friend of editor J. D. B. Grieg, helping to put out the first issue of the *Harlem Enterprise*, by inking the printing press.[12]

By July 1899 Lee, Luske, and a placer miner named Carl Halvorson were at Washington Gulch west of Helena, working as timekeepers for mine owners John Hickler and W. H. Sudden. For some unexplained reason, Lee and Luske starting using different names, Bob Harris and John Dalton respectively. They quit on September 22 to start mining on their own. Lonie moved his growing family to Harlem, and rented the Washburn residence on September 30. On October 22 he left for Washington Gulch via Helena to visit his cousin. He arrived drunk and offered a large sum of money to anyone who would take him to the claims of Harris and Dalton. Lee's former employer, Sudden, offered to drive Lonie to the claim in the morning.[13] This is probably the first instance of Lonie attempting to spend a portion of the Wilcox money. He had received the money as payment from Sundance for the horses Lonie provided them at his Montana ranch after Sundance and Kid Curry escaped from the Deadwood jail. Unfortunately, the money was from the $3,400 Portland bundle of unsigned currency taken in the robbery.[14]

Lonie talked Lee into going back to Harlem with him, with a stop at the Mint Saloon in Great Falls, owned by former Valley County Sheriff Sid Willis, an old friend of the Currys'. While celebrating with Willis, Lonie passed one of the easily identifiable bills in town.[15] Upon arriving at Harlem on November 5, Lonie introduced Lee as his brother R. E. "Bob" Curry. On November 23 it was supposedly Lee who sent five $100 notes to the Stockman's National Bank in Fort Benton for redemption. However, after his later arrest he told authorities that Lonie still owed $300 to his saloon partner George Bowles, and sent the notes in Lee's name so that Bowles would not know Lonie had the money. Lee insisted in his deposition that he never possessed any of the stolen Wilcox money. On the other hand, Brown Waller states that Lee was at the Cascade Bank of Great Falls on November 19 to get change for a $100 Portland note.[16]

On November 25 "Bowles and Curry" became "Curry Brothers Club Saloon" when Lee bought out Bowles' interest for $1,000, half in cash and a note for the balance.[17] They remodeled the saloon in time for the grand opening and turkey shoot on December 28. Lee did most of the bartending, while Lonie played the part of a prosperous businessman by wearing suits and growing a mustache. Life was good as Lonie, Elfie, and Lee attended the Harlem New Year's dance at the Leland Hotel. Lonie helped out with the music by playing the banjo and fiddle.[18] However, unforeseen events of the last few weeks were about to drastically change their lives for the worse.

It had been a long process to trace the notes that Lonie or Lee had sent to the bank at Fort Benton in November. Although the bills had been mutilated owing to the safe explosion, the bank and United States Treasury numbers were intact. As a matter of routine they were forwarded to the bank's Chicago representative, then on to the First National Bank of Portland. Growing impatient, Lee sent two telegrams to the bank at Fort Benton, one on December 11 and another on the 20th, asking if he had been credited with the $500. Cashier Charles E. Duer's reply to both inquiries was that the money was being held at Portland. After considerable communication between Fort Benton, Chicago, Portland, and

Washington, it was finally determined the money was from the Wilcox robbery. It was this lead that prompted the Pinkertons, who represented the American Bankers' Association, to order detective W. O. Sayles to Montana.[19] It should be remembered that he had left his partner Charlie Siringo in Colorado, while the latter continued the hunt for Kid Curry and Sundance.

Sayles began by gathering information concerning the stolen money and the persons spending it, in and around Helena, Great Falls, and Harlem. He made two trips to Harlem; the first was on December 27, 1899, when he actually met Bob Lee.[20] He discovered that Lonie Curry was the brother of noted outlaw Kid Curry and that Lee was their cousin. He also learned they were raised in Dodson, Missouri, and had lived for years on a homestead in the Little Rockies.[21] In spite of the fact that both Lonie and Lee had alibis for the time of the Wilcox robbery, a report that originated in the *Lewistown Argus* stated, "A Pinkerton detective connected with the case was in Lewistown about Christmas and was accompanied to Gilt Edge by Sheriff Shaw, where the fact was ascertained that Loney and Bob Curry had been in Gilt Edge shortly before the [Wilcox] robbery occurred and had left there by private conveyance for Rocky Point in time to have reached the scene of the robbery by the date it occurred."[22]

Sayles, with another Pinkerton detective, was back in Harlem on January 5, 1900. Friends of Lee and Lonie warned them that detectives were in town asking questions, so they quickly disposed of their interests in order to leave the country. They sold the Club Saloon on the following day to local merchant George J. Ringwald. Lonie's share was $1,000, for which he received $300 cash and a promissory note for the balance, to be payable to long-time friend Jim Thornhill. Lonie then retrieved a $1,000 bill from a brown paper package of Wilcox money that had been left at Al Cecil's hotel for safekeeping. He presented the bill to the postmaster, W. E. French, and requested change. French did not have that large amount of money on hand, and told Lonie the bill would have to be sent to the bank in Fort Benton. When Lonie called for the money the next day, the postmaster said he had not received the package, and that it had presumably missed the train. In reality, the bank had notified French that the bill was from the Wilcox robbery.[23]

That evening the two Pinkertons asked the postmaster to join them in a game of pool or poker at the Curry saloon, so that he could point out Lonie and his cousin Bob. However, Lonie was already aware of the strangers' presence, and after waking his cousin in the back room, they ducked out the back door. It was reported that the two stole the receipts from a community raffle before leaving Harlem.[24] However, the *Enterprise* of January 17, 1900, remarked, "Since their stay here, or rather since we have known them, both Lonny and Bob have conducted themselves in a peaceable and law-abiding manner, in fact almost exemplary."[25]

After Lonie said goodbye to his family, he and his cousin rode west to the little community and water tank stop of Zurich. Here they boarded a westbound Great Northern Railway train, reaching Havre on January 9. With Lonie's features covered by a hat and muffler, he was not recognized by conductor Louis Bayrell until they had passed Chinook. They continued on to Shelby Junction, where they connected with a southbound train to Great Falls, Helena, Butte, and ultimately arriving in Lee's old stomping grounds, Cripple Creek, Colorado, on January 25.[26]

Lonie had arranged with Jim Thornhill to send the remainder of the saloon sale money to Cripple Creek. Using an alias of Frank Miller, he checked with the postmaster every day for the expected registered letter. Lee decided to stay in the mining camp for the immediate future, and found a job dealing stud poker at the Antlers Gambling House. When the letter finally arrived from Landusky, the postmaster was tipped off by the return address and notified the Pinkertons. However Lonie had hurriedly said goodbye to his cousin and boarded a train for Kansas City, Missouri, on February 17. He reached the home of his aunt Elizabeth Lee in Dodson, Missouri, on February 21, 1900.[27] This may have been the first time Lonie had been back to visit since he left to be a cowboy in 1889. His brother Harvey had been in the Kansas City area in January, leaving for New Mexico about the first day of February.

Soon after Sayles had missed his chance to arrest Lonie and Lee in Harlem, the Pinkertons ordered Charlie Siringo to meet him in Helena.

Sayles had accepted the position of assistant superintendent of the Pinkerton office in San Francisco, and Siringo was needed to take over the investigation in Montana. Sayles supplied him with information obtained about the Little Rockies area, so Siringo could "get in" with friends of the Currys'. According to Siringo, Sayles had been instructed to go directly to San Francisco to start his new position.[28] It has been stated, however, that he first trailed Lonie and Lee south to Cripple Creek, where he discovered that Lonie had already left for Kansas City.[29]

Lonie tried to avoid drawing attention to himself by changing his attire and even shaving off his mustache. Various explanations as to how he was soon discovered have been put forth: the Pinkertons tracking him to Kansas City, or intercepting mail from friends and relatives, or Lonie being careless enough to spend some of the forged Portland notes in Dodson. Notwithstanding, at 8:40 a.m. on February 28, 1900, a posse of Kansas City police detectives and Pinkerton agents approached the Lee farmhouse in two four-horse carriages. They separated with one group covering the west side of the house, and the other advancing on the south and east. When Lonie spotted them he had just enough time to grab his coat, hat, and Colt .45 revolver, before exiting through the back door on the north. He ran to the east side of the house, then south to the front gate. It seemed he was making for a stand of timber to the south. The detectives called on him to stop and surrender, but as he passed through the gate he drew his revolver. The posse fired a volley of twelve shots; Lonie wavered for an instant, but continued to run 150 yards across the road before he fell into the snow and stubble of a cornfield. He had been shot through the back of the head, and was breathing his last when the detectives reached him. He still clutched his revolver in his hand, but had not been able to fire a shot.[30]

His body was placed in a farm wagon, covered with a heavy robe or blanket, and driven to Stewart's undertaking parlor on Walnut Street in Kansas City. A second revolver, a .38 Smith & Wesson, was found in his pocket. Coroner Lester and Justice Alvin Douglas of Dodson accompanied the little procession. Lonie's sister Allie, of Kansas City, joined Mrs. Lee in viewing the body at the morgue.[31] Sheriff Tom Clary soon arrived from Chouteau County, Montana, to identify Lonie's remains. He sent a telegram to Undersheriff Charles Crawford informing him that he recognized the dead man as Lonie Curry, sans mustache.[32] The funeral was held at Stewart's undertaking, with only relatives from Dodson attending. He was buried at Forest Hill Cemetery in Kansas City on March 9.[33]

After the detectives had cut down Lonie, they burst into the farmhouse to find Mrs. Lee burning banknotes and incriminating correspondence in the stove. When they retrieved a recent letter from her son Bob in Cripple Creek, they quickly sent a telegram to local authorities which led to his arrest the same day. His valise contained a white-handled, single-action .45 Colt, and a newspaper clipping of the Wilcox robbery, but they did not find any of the stolen money on his person. He was taken to Cheyenne, Wyoming, to await trial on the charge of mail robbery.[34]

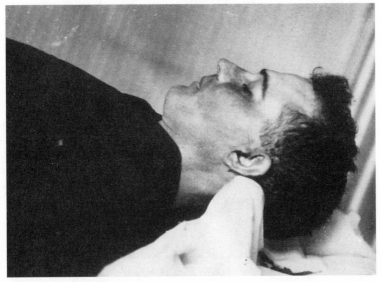

Lonie Logan in death. Shot down outside of his aunt's house near Kansas City, Missouri. (Robert G. McCubbin Collection)

Before Lonie was killed, Elfie moved back to Landusky and found work as a servant for the John Ellis family. Ellis was the proprietor of a boardinghouse, and it was here where Elfie learned of Lonie's death from a mail carrier from Harlem. Daughter Della Rae was sent to live with Paul and Mary Sunday of Harlem, who eventually adopted her. For some reason they changed her name to Mary Cecilia, which they then shortened to Maime. Elfie enrolled Lonie Jr. in St. Peter's Mission school near Cascade, just southwest of Great Falls. It is said she moved

Elfie Logan with children Lonie Jr. and Della Rae "Maime." (Larry Pointer Collection, Box 21, Folder 18, American Heritage Center, University of Wyoming.)

to Great Falls and found work, possibly through family friend Sid Willis, at the Silver Dollar and Mint saloons.[35] A. L. Smith, vice-president of the Bank of Montana at Helena, told a story concerning payment of the boy's expenses. He received a letter from a superior at the mission school stating that a $100 bill had been received from the wife of Kid Curry (actually Lonie's wife, Elfie). It was thought the bill may have come from the Wilcox train robbery, so it was mailed to Smith with a request for his advice. The banker sent for a Pinkerton agent, who readily identified the bill as one from the Wilcox loot.[36]

After splitting up with Sayles in Helena, Siringo took the train to Great Falls where he outfitted for a 250-mile ride to Landusky in midwinter. He was in Lewistown in late February, just a few days before Lonie was killed. It took him over a week to reach Landusky, owing to blizzard conditions and extremely cold weather along the route. He took shelter in Giltedge for one night before heading to the Red Barn ranch, thirty miles from Rocky Point. He remained at the ranch for a few days waiting for a Chinook wind to melt the snow. In the meantime he learned that Lonie Curry had stopped at the ranch before and after the Wilcox train robbery. When Siringo reached Landusky, he passed himself off as an outlaw on the run from Mexico named Charles L. Carter.[37]

He soon got in "solid" with Jim Thornhill, Mrs. Julia Landusky, and her daughter Elfie. According to Siringo, Elfie became his sweetheart, whereby he was able to get access to her letters from Lonie, Mrs. Lee and her daughter, and from lawyers who represented Bob Lee at his trial. He made friends with three-year-old Lonie Jr., later saying, "The little fellow was pretty and bright, and we had become greatly attached to each other." Julia Landusky gave Siringo many inside facts on Jim Thornhill's background since he had come to the Little Rockies years ago.[38] Thornhill had taken in Lucy Tressler as a "housekeeper" sometime after John Curry was killed by Jim Winters. She became his common law wife and they were later legally married on March 29, 1904.[39]

When Lucy came to live with Thornhill, she was pregnant with estranged husband Dan's daughter, Sarah. Federal census records for 1900 show she was born in November 1897. Thornhill also took in Lucy's little boy named Harvey D.[40] "They had a bright little three-year-old boy named Harvey in honor of the outlaw Harvey Logan," wrote Siringo. "This little fellow felt at home with a small [toy] pistol buckled around his waist ... This boy is pretty good material for a future train robber. He says that will be his occupation, and his father encourages him, as he says he would like to see him prove as brave a man as his namesake, Harvey Logan."[41]

Siringo stayed in the Little Rockies for many months, sometimes working for Thornhill, but the latter never revealed any information as to Kid Curry's exact whereabouts. He did tell the detective that his mail was being watched at Harlem. As a result, Siringo was convinced that the two corresponded through the Chinook post office instead.[42] Thornhill later said he was not fooled by Siringo, and knew he was a Pinkerton man.[43] He did express bitterness toward the Pinkertons for the killing of Lonie and helping to send Bob Lee to prison. He revealed that Kid Curry was presently somewhere in the south planning the robbery of another Union Pacific train, to get even with the railroad company and the Pinkertons. Siringo decided that Kid Curry was not going to return to the Little Rockies any time soon, so in late August he boarded a train in Harlem for Denver. Upon arrival in Denver he learned of a recent Union Pacific robbery near Tipton, Wyoming.[44]

Bob Lee's trial in the federal court in Cheyenne started on May 24, 1900. Although there was no direct evidence of him having participated in the Wilcox robbery, witnesses from Montana were called to testify that he had passed some of the stolen bills. Of course his relationship with the Curry brothers did not help his case either. Witnesses for the defense swore that Lee was in Black Hawk, Colorado, during the time of the robbery. Despite this, he was found guilty on May 28 and sentenced to ten years at the Wyoming State Penitentiary in Rawlins. He behaved himself in prison, earning an early release on February 13, 1907.[45]

On May 5, 1900, before Bob Lee went to trial, his lawyer arranged for him to give a deposition to United States Marshal Frank A. Hadsell and William A. Pinkerton. He hoped to clear himself by telling all he knew concerning the Wilcox robbery. He told them that most of what he knew

Bob Lee, alias Bob Curry, cousin to the Logan/Curry brothers.
(Robert G. McCubbin Collection)

about the robbery came from Lonie Logan. Lonie had said only three
men were involved, and one of them was his brother Harvey Logan. Lee
said he knew a second robber as Frank Scramble, who had escaped from
jail with Harvey Logan and a "Mulatto" prisoner in Deadwood. Harvey
and Scramble then went to the Logan ranch in Montana and obtained
horses from Lonie. With this information the Pinkertons were able to associate Scramble with "Kid" Longabaugh, the Sundance Kid.[46]

Hadsell and Pinkerton tried to get Lee to admit that Lonie, George Currie, and the Roberts brothers had also taken part in the robbery. However, Lee insisted "I never knew George Currie or either of the so called Roberts boys and if you fellows say that the Roberts brothers are in the Union Pacific robbery, then there is no use in me talking to you ... Lonnie would have told me if the Roberts boys were in the robbery. He always said there were but three in the robbery and if he [Lonie] were in the robbery he would have told me." Lonie had also told Lee "he did not know who the third man was, but he was the man who went to Utah."[47] As Wayne Kindred states, "'Flat Nose' George Currie is the only Wilcox suspect that can definitely be placed in Utah following the robbery."[48]

Lonie's and Lee's statements are supported by Kid Curry's own writings that he set down in a journal shortly before his death. He wrote (bad spelling and lack of punctuation left intact), "I am perasonally accuainted With all the facts conserning the Willcocks hold up of June the 2, 18.99," that "Mr Pinkerton and different Sheriff possies have Killed Seven Different Men and have got one in the Pris at Rawlins Wyo. all for the Willcox hold up and to my own Serton Knowlige they was only 3 to Begin With and to My own Serton Knowlige they is 2 of the 3 Still on the Seen and injoying good health [George Currie was dead at this time] and if Mr Pinkerton Noted Detective posse was all they had to contend with this world would Sail Smoth for the facts of it is Mr W a Pinkerton is two Slow to catch a cold in a Montana Blizzard."[49] In subsequent writings Curry reiterated his claim that only three men were involved in the Wilcox train robbery.

Using his brother Lonie's real name he wrote, "Lorenzo Logan, a full Brother of Harvey Logan, the Boy that the Pinkertons and possy murdered at his home at Dodson, Missour for Being implicated in the Will Cox hold up, for which he had Nothing What ever to Do With No more than his Mother Who Died When he was a Baby in the Craddle." He also wrote that his cousin "Bob Lee was mining at Black hock Colo June the 2, 18.99," which agrees with witness statements at his trial.[50]

Some authors dismiss Curry's writings as merely rants against the Pinkertons and authority in general, and an attempt at self-justification.

But there is no substantial evidence that Lonie and Bob Lee participated in the Wilcox robbery, and it is even questionable concerning Lonie's presence at the Belle Fourche bank holdup.

The temptation of easy money got in the way of their yearning to be respectable businessmen. But even the most callous person would surely agree that a bullet in the back of the head was unmerited punishment for only passing stolen money.

CHAPTER 15

Arizona Rampage

he Pinkerton's Denver office sent detective Frank Murray to Alma in about early March to investigate some Wilcox money that had been deposited in the Silver City bank by the storekeeper in Alma. Murray, who was later promoted to the assistant superintendent of the Denver office, came to the WS and questioned William French concerning Jim Lowe. When he showed French a photograph of a group of men, he recognized the only man that was sitting down as Jim Lowe. Murray then asked him if he knew that Lowe was also known as Butch Cassidy. French replied that he did not, and in return, asked the detective if he was going to try to arrest him. Murray said he was not foolish enough to attempt to arrest Cassidy in that neighborhood without the backup of "a regiment of cavalry." He was more interested in tracing the stolen money than running down Cassidy.[1]

The Alma storekeeper had told the detective earlier that a WS cowboy named Johnny Ward had spent the bills. To French's surprise it turned out to be Little Johnny Ward instead of Big Johnny Ward, the latter he knew to be a member of the Wild Bunch. Little Johnny said he got the bills from a former WS cowboy named "McGonigal" in payment for two horses. This was Clay McGonagill, who had worked with Cassidy and Elzy Lay at the Erie Cattle Company in Arizona previous to the WS. Murray was determined to track him down, not knowing that McGonagill had gone back to Arizona.[2]

Cassidy and Tom Capehart were aware of the Pinkerton's presence in the area, even buying him a drink when he returned to Alma, and alerted their friends and associates. As a result, five men, whose identities will be discussed presently, quickly prepared to leave for the north. According to Charlie Siringo, the men fully intended to kill Murray before they left. Cassidy is said to have saved the detective's life by hustling him out of town in the night. Although French had no intention of firing Butch, he quit the ranch about mid-March, or a little later, and headed north in the company of Red Weaver. On the way they stole the horse herd of one N. M. Ashby, a ranching neighbor who had been rustling WS cattle.[3]

On March 25, 1900, the citizenry of Springerville, Arizona, regarded five heavily armed men with suspicion as they rode into town. They stayed just long enough to post a letter and purchase some supplies. The townspeople became anxious when two more rough looking men arrived in the village the next day leading eight horses. The two strangers were Butch Cassidy and Red Weaver, still in possession of the herd stolen from Ashby. They went directly to the post office and picked up the letter which the earlier riders had left for them. The five men had left town that morning in the direction of St. Johns, and were seen near a freshly butchered cow by a local rancher. The cattlemen in the area had been troubled by a rash of cattle killings and horse thefts of late. At Springerville the rancher reported what he saw to Apache County Sheriff Edward Beeler. After the necessary warrants were obtained and a posse rounded up, the sheriff set out for St. Johns.[4]

Upon reaching St. Johns, about twenty-five miles from Springerville, Beeler learned that his quarry had been in town purchasing more supplies. A mail driver informed him that he had passed the five men in camp outside of town about dusk. Beeler and his men set off in pursuit, leaving word for his deputy to follow with another posse. Early the next morning, March 27, they caught up with the outlaws and there was an exchange of gunfire. The outlaws were put to flight, but the posse's tired horses could not keep after them. The second posse soon joined with Beeler's, and it was decided to form into smaller groups for a better chance of entrapping the gang.[5]

Late in the afternoon, Andrew Augustus "Gus" Gibbons and Frank LeSueur, two prominent Mormons from St. Johns, were following the outlaws' trail along a steep hillside. As they approached a group of boulders, gunfire erupted without warning, and the two men were riddled with bullets. The outlaws then took the murdered men's horses and guns before turning south toward Cochise County. The bodies were found by Sheriff

Beeler's group the next day, and were brought back to St. Johns early in the morning of March 29. Beeler began organizing another posse, but two strangers in town purchasing supplies did not escape his notice.[6]

Thus, Cassidy and Weaver were detained in the jail at St. Johns on suspicion of possessing stolen horses. They asked Beeler to telegraph French at Magdalena to confirm their identities. According to French, after he replied that he knew them, the sheriff held Weaver and let Cassidy go with the horses. It is doubtful that Cassidy was allowed to go on his way, because somehow word of the horse theft was received by the sheriff, and it was not long before the two were extradited to Socorro, New Mexico, the county seat from which they had stolen Ashby's horses.[7]

The evening of March 29 found the five outlaws southeast of St. Johns near Frisco (now Reserve), New Mexico, where they stole seven horses.[8] Traveling toward the Chiricahua Mountains, they reached Duncan, Arizona, on Sunday April 1. It was reported that Capehart was acquainted with some of the citizens, stopping long enough for a short conversation.[9] They continued in a southerly direction, camping eighteen miles northwest of San Simon, Cochise County, Arizona.[10]

Walter Birchfield, foreman for Fred Ruck's Triangle Ranch in the San Simon Valley, Arizona, discovered a freshly killed and partly eaten beef. At first he thought it was the work of Mexican rustlers or smugglers, and he later said he would not have sent for former Deputy U.S. Marshal George Scarborough of Deming, New Mexico, if he had known they were the outlaws. Scarborough was now employed as a stock detective for the New Mexico Stockraisers' Association. As it was, Birchfield wired Scarborough and met him at San Simon station, where they started on the outlaws' trail. The afternoon of April 3, 1900, they came upon the outlaws' camp at Triangle Springs in the Chiricahua Mountains. Many writers claim the two rode into an ambush; however Birchfield stated that he did not think they had been discovered. In fact, he said that he and Scarborough opened with the first shots, driving the outlaws to the cover of the rocks.[11]

When they tried for another position, the outlaws opened up and hit Scarborough in the right thigh with a .30-.40 high-powered rifle bullet. Immediately after Scarborough fell from his horse, Birchfield heard a distinctive cowboy yell he knew came from Tom Capehart. Capehart had worked for Birchfield when he was foreman for the Diamond A outfit in southwest New Mexico. Birchfield had also been slightly wounded, but he managed to drag Scarborough behind a tree and build a rock wall around him. The outlaws called on them to surrender, continuing to fire as long as there was daylight. At night, Birchfield managed to mount Scarborough's horse and ride to the nearest help at San Simon station.[12]

The next day Scarborough, weak from the cold and loss of blood, was placed in a wagon and driven to San Simon station. Dr. Samuel D. Swope and Scarborough's son Ed had come from Deming to meet him. Seeing that Scarborough was suffering greatly, Dr. Swope dressed his wound and gave him morphine for his pain. He was then taken by train to his home in Deming, where doctors tried to save his leg and his life. He died on the operating table in the early morning of April 5.[13]

Birchfield had stayed in San Simon and joined Sheriff Beeler's posse that was still trailing the killers of LeSueur and Gibbons. It was thought that they were the same five men that Birchfield and Scarborough had encountered.[14] The newspapers reported it as such after Scarborough's killing, and made tentative identifications of the culprits. At least three reward notices listing their identities were printed over time, with the last one probably being the most accurate. In addition to Birchfield's recognition of Tom Capehart's voice, his description from a reward notice in the *St. John's Herald* was almost an exact match to one contained in an 1899 Cochise County sheriff's log. He sometimes went by the name of Tom Wilson. Tod Carver, alias William "Coley" Morris, (real name Thomas C. Hilliard) was identified by a missing right forefinger near the second joint. Mack Steen was probably an alias for Ben Kilpatrick, and the description from the reward notice is a good match.[15] There was a prominent family by the name of Steen that lived in the area of Concho County, Texas, where the Kilpatricks came from. He also used the alias of Bob Johnson, the same name as the foreman of the Erie Cattle Company of Cochise County.[16] This Johnson was known to frequently hire outlaws, Butch Cassidy and Elzy Lay having worked for him for a short time.

The last two individuals thought to have been in the gang were listed as Jess Black, alias Franks, and an unidentified man.[17] There may have been some confusion between the identities of Black and the fifth man,

Franks, undoubtedly Will Carver using his alias George W. Franks. Charlie Siringo, while working undercover in Alma, New Mexico, met and made friends with Jesse Black, "one of Jim Lowe's warmest friends ... He was considered a hard case, but no one seemed to know who he was or where he came from." "One of the 'Wild Bunch' secrets given me by Bert C. [Charter]," Siringo later said, "disclosed the fact that my friend Jesse Black, of Alma, New Mexico, was a hard 'hombre' whose right name was Byron Sessions. He had been brought up in Utah and went to New Mexico with 'Butch' Cassidy after the Montpelier, Idaho, bank robbery."[18]

There is some conjecture as to George Kilpatrick's possible presence because his physical description was very close to his brother Ben's. Butch Cassidy has also been suggested as being one of the outlaws; however he was in custody in either St. Johns or Socorro while the gang was on their rampage through the southwest. Finally, and the reason this chapter has been included concerning his life, Kid Curry has been included in the list of suspects by some writers. Just as there is no evidence of Curry taking part in the Folsom train robbery, there is also a lack of evidence placing him with this gang of killers. The main reason he is considered goes back to the false assumption that he used Tom Capehart as an alias. It would be helpful to compare the physical descriptions of both men. The reward notice for Tom Capehart described him as follows:

> He is about 5 ft. 10 in. high, weighs about 175 lbs. has slightly dark complexion, dark hair and mustache, had short black beard when last seen, is stoop shouldered but quite well appearing, has blue eyes, and is of very pleasing address, but not over-talkative, has a peculiar way of ducking his head from side to side when he talks and he usually smiles a great deal when talking. He is an expert bronch trainer.[19]

A Pinkerton reward poster from 1901 described Harvey Logan, alias "Kid" Curry as:

> 5 feet, 7½ inches tall, weight 145 to 160 lbs., dark complexion, dark brown hair, can raise heavy beard and mustache, color

somewhat lighter than hair, medium build, dark eyes, nose is prominent, large, long and straight, talks slowly, is of quiet reserved manner.[20]

Clearly these are two different men. Also, whereas Capehart had motive to participate in the killing of Scarborough, Kid Curry did not, and there is no mention of him in the contemporary accounts. Capehart had not forgotten the rough treatment received from Scarborough, and his time spent in prison as a suspect for the Stein's Pass train robbery. Scarborough had also been on the trail of Capehart as a suspect for the George D. Bowman & Son bank holdup in Las Cruces, New Mexico, on February 12, 1900. It was reported that Capehart was infuriated and fed up with Scarborough dogging him.[21]

Philip J. Rasch appears to base his inclusion of Kid Curry on the similarity of his description with those of Jess Black and the unidentified man.[22] They are as follows:

Jess Black (alias Franks): Height 5′ 8″ or 9″, weight about 175 lbs., very dark complexion, black beard, black eyes.

Unidentified man: Very dark complexion, black, straight hair, short, heavy set, very quiet.[23]

The descriptions for both of these men are similar, and the one for the unidentified man is much too vague to make any meaningful identification. There is a possibility that the two descriptions could apply to the same man, Jess Black.

This problem is resolved for the most part by Grant County (New Mexico) Sheriff James K. Blair's identification of the members of the gang. While in the field with Sheriff Beeler and other officers, there was plenty of time to discuss the physical attributes and traits of each outlaw. After an interview with Blair, the *Silver City Independent* printed a list that was likely the most accurate to date. Tom Capehart continued to be one of the prime suspects, "The others were said to be Tod Carter [Carver], Jeff [Jess] Black, 'Franks' [Will Carver], and one whose name was unknown but described as a 'tall, well-proportioned man and a hard fighter'."[24] This man had been identified as Mack Steen, alias Bob Johnson (presumably Ben Kilpatrick) in the third reward poster. This list separates the identities of Jess Black and "Franks," as it should, and rids it of the possibly phantom unidentified dark man.

Therefore, if one refers to this list of outlaw identities, the only suspect who could possibly correspond to Kid Curry is Jess Black. Jeffrey Burton agrees, and states that "If he [Harvey Logan] was still in that section of country—and no evidence exists to the contrary—he is likely to have stayed close to Cassidy, Kilpatrick, and the rest."[25] Bob Lee's May 5, 1900, deposition contains a possible reference to the Scarborough killing and Las Cruces bank robbery. Lee thought Kid Curry and the man he knew as Frank Scramble (Harry Longabaugh, the Sundance Kid) might have robbed a bank in New Mexico, and when the law caught up with them, "They killed the Marshal who was close to them, also wounded an officer in the posse who subsequently died."[26] Except for this rather cryptic statement, there is equally no strong evidence that Curry did remain in the southwest, and Jess (or Jesse) Black may have been just what Siringo said he was, a hard-case friend of Butch Cassidy.

Posses led by Sheriff Beeler, Sheriff Jim Blair, and ex-Sheriff John Slaughter of Cochise County, trailed the outlaws through the Chiricahua Mountains and into Mexico. They searched the border settlements and known outlaw hideouts, but after three weeks they gave up the chase.[27] Before he left Mexico, Beeler received information that one of the Gibbons-LeSueur killers was seen working as a wood hauler near Globe, Arizona. Witnesses had identified him as one of the five men who had ridden into Springerville. Beeler found his man at a ranch on Cherry Creek, going by the name of Bill "Coley" Morris, and arrested him on May 2, 1900. He admitted that he knew the other outlaws, but claimed an alibi that would prove he was innocent of their crimes.[28] Beeler believed him and released Morris, not knowing that he had just freed Thomas Hilliard, alias Tod Carver. Another suspect, Mack Steen, alias Bob Johnson, had left Cochise County, and nothing was heard of his movements after April 1900.[29] Steen, probably Ben Kilpatrick, most likely went north to meet up with Kid Curry at Brown's Hole or Hole-in-the-Wall, in order to plan the next hit on the Union Pacific Railroad in August.

As for Cassidy and Weaver, they were taken before a grand jury in Socorro on April 27, with the result that next day they appeared in court and pled not guilty to larceny of horses. The court proceedings for May 4 show that Weaver came to trial, but there is no mention of James Lowe (Cassidy). It seems to indicate that Cassidy was released before the term of court, possibly owing to the influence of William French. He was in town during this time overseeing a train load of cattle destined for his Springer Ranch. He most likely would not have extended the same favor to Red Weaver. Notwithstanding, Weaver's case was extended to the fall term of district court, with bail set at $1,000. After clearing up some problem with his bond, he was eventually released and returned to Alma.[30]

At the fall term of court in Socorro, his case was again continued and he was still free on bail. Sometime between court proceedings he had the opportunity to dig up the Folsom loot in Colfax County. It had been over a year since the train robbery, and he must have felt it was now safe to show his face in the area. Will Carver was wanted and could not risk it, and Elzy Lay was serving a prison sentence. Weaver returned to Alma, and by early 1901 he was spending money freely in town.[31] He did not have long to enjoy his newfound wealth, because on April 9, 1901, he was shot dead by William "Pad" Holliman (or Hollimon) as a result of his inappropriate behavior towards Holliman's niece at a local dance.[32]

When Elzy Lay was released from the Santa Fe prison in December 1905, he went to Alma and looked up William French. The latter believed that "Mac" had returned to recover the Folsom loot which, "No doubt his share had been concealed somewhere in the neighbourhood." Mac "stayed in Alma for a couple of years; he evidently had something hid around out there that he was anxious to remove without attracting attention. Afterwards he went to Wyoming, where he opened a saloon."[33]

Jeffrey Burton does not believe the trail of the stolen money ended near Alma, New Mexico. By piecing together stories from various local ranchers and other sources, he infers that not long after Weaver had brought the money from Colfax County to Alma, it was removed farther south to the Mexican border by someone unknown to this day, a stranger on a dun horse. The remaining loot minus Weaver's share, exactly $58,000, was supposedly buried under the root of a juniper tree in the mountains near Bull Springs, below Bisbee or Douglas, Arizona, on the Mexican side of the border. It is assumed one of Elzy Lay's confederates somehow got word to him in prison as to where the money was buried. After his release, he waited around Alma for three or four months before he left to dig up the money.[34]

Lay eventually made his way to Baggs, Wyoming, where he courted Mary Calvert, the daughter of a local rancher. They eloped to Thermopolis, and were married on March 27, 1909. His first wife, Maude Davis Lay, had divorced him while he was in prison. For awhile he managed his father-in-law's ranch, and speculated in oil claims. Later, he and a partner operated a saloon in Shoshoni, Wyoming. His last job was head water master for an irrigation company in Los Angeles, California, when he died on November 10, 1934, after a long illness.[35]

CHAPTER 16

Death of the Rustler King

Flatnose George Currie did not accompany Sundance and Kid Curry to southern Colorado after the Wilcox train robbery, but it was too risky to remain in the area of Hole-in-the-Wall. By December 1899 he was rustling cattle in the Green River country of Utah, and had thrown in with rustler Tom Dilley. While working for the Webster Cattle Company on Hill Creek above Thompson, Dilley had got into a fight with the manager named Fullerton, and Sam Jenkins, a cowboy. All that winter Dilley and Currie built up a herd by blotching brands, particularly on Webster cattle. In April 1900 Currie was caught in the act by an employee and ordered off the ranch. The man went for the authorities after Currie warned him off with his six-gun.[1]

Grand County Sheriff Jesse M. Tyler and Uintah County Sheriff William Preece combined posses, and set out to capture the rustler or rustlers. They discovered a deserted camp not far from the McPherson Ranch on the Green River. The posse searched through the hills until, about noon the next day, they came upon Currie on foot, looking for some stray horses. He answered the command to surrender by firing at the posse with his Winchester and retreating toward the Green River. He reached the river by dark, and either swam across or built a crude raft for the purpose. The morning of April 17 found Currie settled among some boulders on a hill near the river, ready for a siege. Sheriff Preece and his men tried to pick off the outlaw from across the river, while Sheriff Tyler's posse had crossed over and was coming up behind Currie. Some time in the afternoon the answering fire from Currie had ceased. He was found dead with a bullet in the back of his head, leaning against a rock with his cocked rifle across his knees. Another bullet had gone through his cartridge belt and exited his back.[2]

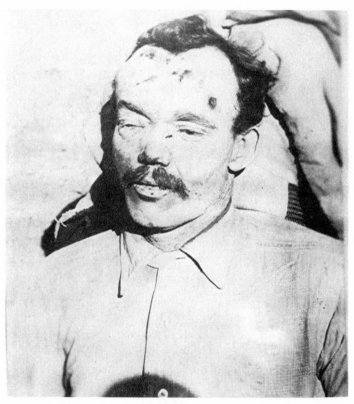

The result of "Flatnose" George Currie's shootout with a posse. (Courtesy of Mike Bell)

At the time, the law officers did not know it was Flatnose George Currie they had just run to ground. They thought he was just some small-time rustler, and his body was taken to Thompson for identification.[3] Over the next few days several people identified him as George Currie, one of the Union Pacific train robbers. These included a previous employer named Mr. Bissell of Central City, Nebraska, and one William Story.[4] Relatives in Casper were notified by wire, who presumably notified Currie's family in Chadron, Nebraska. The Union Pacific Railroad sent two men from Wyoming, Uinta County Sheriff John Ward, and John C. DeVore, who both said the body was that of outlaw George Currie.[5]

DeVore was the sheepherder who fed Currie and Kid Curry in his camp when they were on the run after the Wilcox train robbery. Pinkerton Detective Frank Murray, who knew Currie, also made positive identification. A coroner's inquest held in Thompson on April 21, returned the verdict, "[H]e George Currie came to his death by gunshot wound while resisting officers."[6]

Currie's father, John Currie, did not arrive until May 9 to claim his son's body. By this time the body was badly decomposed and made identification very difficult. Still, the father took George's body home to Chadron where, according to Murray, the rest of the family confirmed his identity before burial.[7] Controversy soon arose concerning whether the body was indeed really that of the Hole-in-the-Wall bandit of Wyoming. Contemporary news accounts reported the possibility of a scheme between detectives and Currie's relatives to recover the $6,000 reward offered by the railroad and express companies, by identifying the dead rustler as one of the Union Pacific train robbers. In 1974, Currie's niece stated that she and her cousins "have serious doubts that the grave with the headstone for George is the actual grave where George is buried."[8] However, like other major outlaws that have not been allowed to die, the plausibility of his death is in the simple fact that he was never seen again.

Just five days after Currie had been killed, three lean-faced men rode onto the Webster ranch at a rapid trot. They were riding high-quality horses, a gray and two bays, and leading a yellow pack horse. The men made it known they were looking for $3,000 that Currie had supposedly cached in the area. Apparently coming up empty, they were last seen crossing the Colorado River to the southwest. About a month later, on May 23, they passed through Moab on their way to Thompson Canyon, reaching it the next day. During their travels they frequently asked where George Currie had been killed, and the name of the sheriff who had killed him. The man who was most talkative was described as being an Indian or Mexican, owing to his very dark complexion.[9] A second man was also dark, and was about thirty-five years old, about the same age as the first. One of these dark men was of medium height and build, while the other was described as "extraordinarily" tall and stout. The third was about forty years of age, medium build, and clean shaven with a sandy complexion.[10]

Meanwhile, Tom Dilley was still wanted for his rustling activities in the Hill Creek country. In mid-May, Sheriffs Tyler and Preece, Deputy Sheriff Herbert Day, rancher Fullerton with employee Sam Jenkins, and at least three others, left Thompson with a warrant for Dilley. About forty miles north, in the rugged East Tavaputs Plateau country, they reached Post Canyon where the posse split into two groups. Tyler, Day, Jenkins, and a young boy named Mert Wade headed south, while Preece, Fullerton, and the rest of the posse started west.[11] On May 26, 1900, in the Book Cliffs, Tyler's party spotted three men they took to be Indians in camp among some willows. They were wrapped in blankets and huddled around a fire. Deputy Sheriff Day and the boy stayed back about fifty yards, while Tyler and Jenkins dismounted and approached the men for information. Tyler said "Hello boys" and, according to Day, a reply was made that he could not hear. Immediately Tyler and Jenkins turned toward their horses to flee or grab their rifles. The outlaws fired a volley into their backs, killing them instantly. As Jenkins was shot, Day thought he heard him shout "Dilley!" The outlaws fired at the deputy sheriff without effect as he raced away in the direction that Preece had taken. Mert Wade ran for cover into the nearest brush.[12]

When Day found Preece and his men three miles away, he was so agitated it was difficult for him to relate the details of the shooting. He believed a great number of outlaws must be in the area since he had seen twenty horses in the camp. From this information Preece decided to return to Thompson for reinforcements, a delay which ultimately gave the outlaws a crucial head start. He telegraphed Utah Governor Wells, authorities in Vernal, and the sheriffs at Meeker, Colorado, and Rock Springs, Wyoming. Governor Wells in turn wired his counterparts in Wyoming, Colorado, and Arizona. By the time posses from Moab, Price, and Salt Lake took the field, it was already as much as thirty-six hours since the killings.[13]

The bodies of Tyler and Jenkins were tied to mules for a two-day trip to Thompson. Two bullets had struck Tyler in his right side, and five bullets had entered Jenkins' back below the shoulders. The trail from the outlaws' camp led about twelve miles northeast to the Turner and Adams ranch in Hay Canyon. Here they picked up four fresh horses and replenished their supplies, before continuing north toward Brown's Hole. Men were sent to guard trails into every known outlaw hideout in the tri-state area. In spite of the tremendous effort expended by the various posses in tracking the outlaws over the next few days, the trail was eventually lost about thirty miles beyond the White River, just south of Brown's Hole. The greatest manhunt in Utah's history was finally called off on June 9, 1900.[14]

It was first thought that the killers were the Dilley gang, which included Jim Rose and Will Roberts. This was owing to Day's statement, and the known feud between Tom Dilley and Sam Jenkins. However, Sheriff Preece and other authorities soon ruled this out, believing the gang was not in the area at the time of the killings. Then it was believed the culprits must have been the three men who had entered Thompson Canyon two days before the murders. Some horses and five saddles the fugitives had left behind matched those in the possession of these same men seen in Moab a few days previous. The extra saddles suggested there may have been more than three men involved. The authorities also believed Butch Cassidy was one of them.[15]

In Arizona, Sheriff Beeler read the descriptions of the wanted men, and believed they matched the killers of his friends LeSueur and Gibbons. He traveled to Utah and met with Sheriff Preece, after which he was positive the killers of Tyler and Jenkins were the same men he was after. In fact it was reported the outlaws shot Tyler in the belief that he was the relentless Beeler.[16] Instead of it being a revenge killing for Currie's death as some authors have stated, it may have been just a case of mistaken identity. Beeler was quoted: "All this talk of Cassidy, Joe [Jim] Rose, and others being the slayers of the Grand county officers is moonshine. They are the same men that I have been trailing. I am positive of that."[17] Beeler continued his search for the gang, eventually picking up and following their trail to Baggs, Wyoming, where he apparently gave up the chase.[18]

The identities of the killers of Tyler and Jenkins may never be known with any certainty. We have Charles Kelly's word that, "The five outlaws who had come up from Arizona split after the killing of Tyler. Two returned; the other three kept on north over the Outlaw Trail they knew so well and were safe in Hole-in-the-Wall almost before the hunt got under way."[19] Ed Bartholomew says that after Scarborough's death (no mention of Tyler and Jenkins) contemporary newspaper reports indicated that the gang had split up. "[S]ome of them," he states, "including [Will] Carver and Logan, went north into Wyoming." However, Bartholomew is another author who transposes Tom Capehart with Kid Curry.[20]

Tod Carver may not have rejoined his friends after being released from custody at Globe, but Utah authorities believed he was one of the murderers of Tyler and Jenkins. Jeffrey Burton says a contemporary report (which he does not cite) states that Hilliard was tracked to Arizona after their killings.[21] A year later he was arrested in New Mexico for the murder of Gibbons and LeSueur. Not considering Tod Carver, the two that Kelly said had returned south would logically appear to be Tom Capehart and Jess Black. Siringo believed Black was from Utah, but a Silver City, New Mexico, newspaper report said he was from near Willcox, Arizona.[22]

Of the three outlaws who went north, certainly Will Carver would have been one of them. Ben Kilpatrick had most likely preceded him some time after the Scarborough killing, to join Kid Curry in Wyoming. The third outlaw may have been Butch Cassidy, catching up with Carver after being delayed by his Socorro court appearance. Wild Bunch informant Bert Charter told Siringo that Butch did overtake the "Kid Curry gang" at some point, but mistook them for law officers. He kept his distance from the group, but he eventually came across a blind post office the outlaws used, and found a message informing him that the riders were his friends. Did Cassidy hook up with the gang in time to participate in the Tyler and Jenkins murders? Siringo's statements clearly indicate that Butch did not come up with them until after the gang had committed their "bloody crimes."[23]

A question arises when considering whether Kid Curry played a part in this gang's depredations. If he did not accompany Sundance when he went to Wyoming, but left with the rest of the gang on their flight through New Mexico, Arizona, and Utah, why were he and Ben Kilpatrick not present at Brown's Hole or Powder Springs when Cassidy and Carver arrived sometime in June 1900? Burton says Carver joined Cassidy in Socorro after his court business was concluded about a month after the killing of Scarborough. Although not stated, he apparently infers that Carver had separated from the rest of the gang somewhere in Arizona or New Mexico as they traveled north. He also says a meeting of Cassidy and Carver, with "Kid Curry's party" was postponed owing to the Tyler and Jenkins murders and aftermath.[24] A more likely scenario is that Curry and Kilpatrick were at Hole-in-the-Wall recruiting for their upcoming assault on the Union Pacific Railroad. Evidence that one or two riders from the Hole-in-the-Wall fraternity participated in the robbery will be related in the next chapter.

Whether or not Kid Curry was a participant in these bloody crimes, Burton puts it into perspective by stating that, "Even without the apocrypha, and allowing for the tendency of some writers to debit him with murders in which his companions had an equal if not the full share, it is clear that he was one of the most ferocious and violent criminals of his day, and one of the cleverest."[25]

Sundance, who was undoubtedly in the Little Snake River Valley area at this time, hooked up with Cassidy and Carver in the gang's Powder Springs hideout. Sundance was waiting for Kid Curry to arrive from Hole-in-the-Wall. The last time he and Curry had been together, they had made tentative plans to rob another Union Pacific train. At some point, probably in New Mexico, Ben Kilpatrick was asked to join in the holdup.

Cassidy and Carver had their own plans to rob the bank in Winnemucca, Nevada, and may have hoped to persuade Curry and Sundance to join them in the venture. In fact, a story in the *Buenos Aires Standard* of April 17, 1912, is purported to be the Sundance Kid's account of the Winnemucca bank robbery told to a third party some time prior to his death in Bolivia in 1908. He states that he and "two of the boys," Cassidy and Carver, "After talking the matter over, we concluded to wait for our leader. Our Napoleon, the brainiest member of the bunch … [A]fter loafing at the Springs for a month waiting for Harry Logan (Kid Curry), we started out to take in the Winnie Bank."[26]

Mike Bell, who discovered the article, had it published with his analysis supporting its authenticity. Bell states without question that "our leader," "our Napoleon," refers to Butch Cassidy. However, it is clear from Sundance's narrative that he includes Cassidy as one of the three waiting for the arrival of their leader. He adds that they got tired of waiting for Logan, so started for Nevada without him.[27] The reference to "our Napoleon, the brainiest member of the bunch" is obviously Kid Curry. In fact, Curry was referred to as the "Napoleon of Crime" while he was later incarcerated in Knoxville, Tennessee.

CHAPTER 17

The Tipton Train Robbery

In August 1900, Butch Cassidy and the Sundance Kid were sighted in the region of Baggs and Dixon, Wyoming.[1] They and other Wild Bunch members had many friends among the residents in the Little Snake River Valley area of southern Wyoming and northern Colorado. These included Mike Dunbar, John P. "Jack" Ryan, Jim Hanson, Bert Charter, Jim Ferguson, Chippy Reid, Sam Green, Charles F. Tucker, and Robert McIntosh. Consequently, they were all under surveillance from agents of the Pinkerton Detective Agency.[2] Ferguson and Ryan both played important parts in helping the gang prepare for the strike on the Union Pacific near the small railroad town of Tipton, Wyoming. Jack Ryan owned a saloon in Rawlins, while Jim Ferguson had a ranch on the Little Snake River near Dixon.[3] Bert Charter tended bar for Ryan, and was a good friend of "Harry Alonzo," the Sundance Kid. They had both ridden for Ora Haley's Two Bar and A. R. Reader, and Charter said that "Harry was an extra good cowboy with a wonderful personality." Charter was probably introduced to Cassidy through Sundance.[4]

These friends served as contacts between Sundance and Bill Cruzan, the latter an ex-convict that Kid Curry knew, now living in Rawlins.[5] "William (Bill) Cruzan was probably the best horse thief in the Wild Bunch," James D. Horan remarked. "He knew the hidden canyons where a stolen herd could be kept, was skillful as an Apache in covering his trail, and had enormous physical stamina."[6]

According to a Pinkerton report, "In August 1900 Longbaugh agreed to take part in a train robbery on the Union Pacific road with Harvey Logan, but mean while having met Butch Cassidy he decided to go with Cassidy to Nevada and sent word to Logan by Jim Ferguson he could not keep his appointment." After the Tipton robbery, the Pinkertons found a note to Cruzan that said, "Harry Alonzo says he cannot be at that place."[7]

Charlie Siringo was investigating the robbery undercover when Ferguson told him "that 'Kid' Curry, Bill Cruzan and the 'Tall Texan', whose right name was Kilpatrick, held up the train at Tipton, Wyo."[8]

Plans were coming together for the second assault on the Union Pacific Railroad. It can be deduced that Curry, Cruzan, and Ryan spent time in Rawlins with the intent to learn about express shipments. It should be remembered that Ryan worked part time as a brakeman for the railroad.[9] Siringo said Ferguson "furnished horses and grub to 'Kid' Curry and

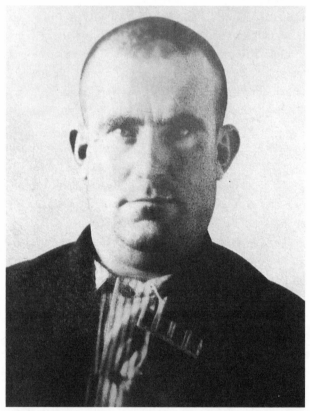

William "Bill" Cruzan joined Kid Curry and Ben Kilpatrick in the Union Pacific train robbery at Tipton, Wyoming. (Robert G. McCubbin Collection)

his gang when they started out to rob the Union Pacific train at Tipton, Wyo. ...and after the robbery Jim F. kept them hid on Black Mountain until the officers quit searching for them."[10] A brown horse that he had given to Kid Curry was later recovered by a posse. This, and statements Ferguson and Ryan made to the Pinkertons after the robbery, induced the Pinkertons to suggest they both "should be arrested as accessories before and after the fact."[11] In fact a few months after the robbery it was reported that Ryan had sufficient funds to option to buy the Club Saloon and Gambling Hall.[12] According to Siringo, another local resident who "had helped 'Kid' Curry out more than once," was Jim Hanson, owner of the Twenty-mile ranch. "He was a wealthy stock man and had furnished one of the horses to 'Kid' Curry for the Tipton train holdup."[13]

The gang next took a few days to check out the area where they intended to stop the train. After the robbery the Pinkertons interviewed several people in the towns of Tipton, Red Desert, and Bitter Creek, who said they could identify one or more of the robbers. Joe J. Maloney of Bitter Creek and A. Iverson of Red Desert, both "Saw 2 men leading 2 horses [a] couple days before the robbery." Maloney said he could identify one man who wore a blue shirt and corduroy pants. Courtney A. Joyce, a cook from Bitter Creek, said he "Sold 2 men [a] Loaf of Bread [and] would know one [for] sure, the dark complected man." Mr. and Mrs. William Running, who operated an eating house in Tipton, said the "gang may have eat there or some of them." Lizzie Warren, a waitress, remembered she had "Served one of [the] robbers a meal." On the day of the robbery the Runnings "Saw [a] short man go toward [the] Engine [and] saw a 2nd man [close-by]."[14]

The Runnings must have seen the two men around 8:10 p.m. on Wednesday, August 29, 1900, when the second section of passenger train No. 3 was stopped in Tipton to take on water. According to the witnesses, it would appear that at least one man boarded the train as it continued its run from Omaha. On an upgrade about a mile west of town, a masked bandit climbed down from the tender and placed the muzzle of a gun behind the ear of engineer Henry Wollenstein. About two and a half miles from Tipton near Table Rock, the engineer was commanded to stop the train by a small fire next to the track. The crew was quickly covered by three more masked bandits, and engineer Wollenstein and fireman Harry Weaver were ordered to step down from the engine.[15] "We had just passed Tipton and reached the 771-mile post from Omaha when I felt the train stopping," conductor Ed J. Kerrigan was later quoted. "I knew something was wrong and went up ahead to see what it was. There was a small fire by the track, and I saw some men going down toward the baggage car."[16]

One passenger stepped down from the front coach to investigate the reason for the unscheduled stop, and received the butt of a rifle to his head. Another curious passenger, a hard-of-hearing elderly man, almost got his head shot off when he stuck it out the coach window.[17] This was enough to keep the rest of the passengers in their seats inside the coaches.

When Kerrigan came up to the bandits he was told to uncouple the mail, express, and baggage cars from the passenger cars. While he was attempting to do so, the passenger cars began to roll down the steep

Inside of dynamited express car at Tipton, Wyoming, holdup, August 29, 1900. (Robert G. McCubbin Collection)

grade. He was permitted to set the brakes on the coaches, and then Wollenstein was ordered to run the front of the train ahead for about a half a mile. The bandits then ordered the express messenger, Charles E. Woodcock, the same messenger who had been dynamited at the Wilcox robbery, to unlock and open the door. He at first refused, but the conductor convinced him to come out when the bandits started preparing to blow up the car.[18] Before opening up, he was able to hide money packages totaling $600 behind some baggage. The robbers forced Woodcock to open the small local safe, before they turned their attention to the through safe. While a dynamite charge was being readied, one of the robbers conducted the crew a safe distance from the train. It took three charges to open the safe, demolishing the express car and damaging the baggage car in the process.[19]

At one point Kerrigan was asked for the time by one of the bandits. Upon pulling out his watch, the conductor said he supposed they were also going to take that. To his surprise the bandit replied, "No, we don't want anything from laboring men or the passengers. We only want what the company has got, and they have plenty."[20]

The holdup had taken about an hour. The robbers stuffed the contents of the safe in a gunny sack, walked to their waiting horses, and rode southeast in the direction of Delaney Rim. Reports of the amount of loot taken ranged from $50.40 as announced by Union Pacific officials, to $55,000 that the messenger, Woodcock, stated to the press.[21] When Joe LeFors was on the trail of the escaped bandits, he found a large amount of paper residue ripped from the money packages, tending to verify that much more than fifty dollars was taken.[22] Found on the floor of the express car were three twenty-dollar-gold pieces, suggesting that a bag or bags of coins were also taken.[23] The mailbags had netted the robbers four packages containing jewelry and watch parts.[24]

Most contemporary accounts state that there were four men that committed the holdup; sometimes a fifth participant is mentioned. There is convincing evidence that three of them were Kid Curry, Ben Kilpatrick and Bill Cruzan. Many writers have included Butch Cassidy and the Sundance Kid among the robbers. One reason Cassidy was believed to be present was owing to a report from a local rancher. He told Union Pacific officials that two weeks before the robbery, he had seen Butch and four companions riding near the site of the holdup.[25] This in itself does not prove his participation since he and Sundance had most likely not yet left for their planned bank job in Winnemucca, Nevada, on September 19, 1900.

Descriptions of three of the bandits were included in a reward poster issued by the Pacific Express Company on August 31. One man was described "as about five feet 10 inches in heighth, smooth face, sandy complexion, grey eyes, talks very fast."[26] The Pinkerton files show Butch as having flaxen hair, blue eyes, light complexion, five feet nine inches in height.[27] However, the robber's likeness could just as easily approximate Ben Kilpatrick's prison record description: Medium chestnut hair, gray eyes, sallow complexion, a shade over five feet eleven inches in height.[28]

As one writer has asserted, Cassidy may have been confused with Cruzan, because they had a similar build and complexion.[29] The second bandit's description appears to roughly fit Cruzan. He was "about five feet seven inches, sandy complexion, talks very coarse, wore canvas coat, corduroy pants, shoes badly worn."[30] His Pinkerton file states he was five feet seven inches, gray eyes, medium complexion, dark hair, rather heavy build.[31]

The Sundance Kid's reputed presence at the holdup may have been owing to his apparent likeness to Kilpatrick. When the latter was captured in St. Louis in 1901, authorities at first believed they had Harry Longabaugh in custody.[32] There is some semblance to Kid Curry in the description of the third robber, although it adds an inch and a half to his actual height: "About five feet nine inches, dark complexion, wore dark flannel shirt, no coat."[33] There was no description given for the fourth man; however a statement made by one of the robbers at the time of the holdup is important, and often overlooked by writers and researchers.

According to Wollenstein and the postal clerk Pruitt, the bandit who guarded the train crew became very talkative. One of the things he said, after the second dynamite charge to the through safe, was that the job was taking too long, "but Perry understands his business." Wollenstein said the robber quickly realized his mistake in identifying one of the gang by name.[34] It has been stated that there was no outlaw named Perry that can be associated with the Wild Bunch.[35] However, in Frackelton's *Sagebrush Dentist*, the Perry brothers are mentioned several times. While enumerating the members of the Hole-in-the-Wall gang, he includes the two Perry brothers as part of the inner circle. After the Wilcox robbery, they were both present at the shooting contest described by Frackelton at Anderson's Hog Ranch, and at a later date the dentist was obliged to work on one of the brothers' teeth at his Sheridan office.[36]

Another mention of the Perry brothers is in one of Bob Divine's letters, dated June 13, 1897, to general manager of the CY ranch, E. T. David. Apparently one of the brothers had been hired, and this is Divine's response: "How is it that Perry, the Cheyenne man, is put to work? His brother is with the Hole-in-the-Wall and he must be a friend of theirs and will give them all of the news. I understood you to say he could not work here."[37]

Despite the damage to the cars the crew was able to run the train to Bitter Creek, where the conductor Kerrigan wired news of the holdup to Union Pacific officials in Omaha at 11:00 p.m. Superintendent W. L. Park was notified at Allen Junction in Carbon County, who in turn wired Sweetwater County Sheriff Peter Swanson in Rock Springs, and both Carbon County Sheriff McDaniel and U.S. Marshal Hadsell in Rawlins.[38] Other posse members gathered at Rawlins, who had ridden with the marshal after the Wilcox robbery, were Deputy Sheriff F. M. Horton of Carbon County, Joe LeFors, now working under Hadsell as a U.S. Deputy Marshal, and Union Pacific Special Agent Frank Wheeler. According to LeFors, the Rawlins posse consisted of twelve men.[39] By 4:40 a.m. a special train had been fitted out with cars for the horses, possemen, and equipment, by Timothy T. Keliher of the Union Pacific Mounted Rangers.[40] They started for the robbery site but were delayed for two hours owing to a mechanical failure at Creston, and did not reach Tipton until 8:30 a.m.[41] Here the Rawlins posse learned Sweetwater County Sheriff Swanson had arrived by train near daylight, and with thirty men was already on the trail of the train robbers.[42] The Union

Pacific offered a reward of $1,000 each for the capture of the four men, dead or alive. The Pacific Express Company added another $1,000 each, with the same conditions.[43]

After unloading the horses the posse rode west to the robbery site, where they picked up the bandits' trail leading southeast toward the springs at Delaney Rim. South of the springs the country was flat and hard, and made trailing difficult, although LeFors was able to discern the tracks of three riders and a pack horse. After a few hours Hadsell's posse caught up with Swanson's group, which swelled the number of men to forty-two. With LeFors on a good horse and setting a fast pace, it wasn't long before the posse was strung out over two miles. Many of the more poorly mounted men began to drop out, and by the time they reached the Red Desert the posse was down to twenty men. At Soda Springs, about halfway across the desert, the water was found to be bad. The outlaws hoped this would discourage the posse from following them, as it was at least twenty-five miles until the next good water.[44]

When the outlaws reached the eastern edge of Brown's Hole, they turned ninety degrees south to a creek where they watered their horses. LeFors continued to follow their trail through the afternoon, but he realized, with the posse's slow pace, they were no longer gaining on the robbers. At 3:00 p.m. LeFors told Wheeler they were one-and-a-half hours behind the outlaws, and asked permission to take Deputy Horton and run

U.S. Marshall Frank A. Hadsell and posse going after the Tipton train robbers. (Courtesy of Mike Bell)

Wyoming lawman, Joe Le-
Fors, who chased the Wild
Bunch robbers after the Union
Pacific train holdups at Wil-
cox and Tipton, Wyoming.
(Robert G. McCubbin Collec-
tion)

Union Pacific posse and special posse car used to trail the Tipton robbers. Joe
LeFors is no. 3. (Robert G. McCubbin Collection)

Interior view of Union Pacific
Railroad special posse car.
Joe LeFors is third from left.
(Robert G. McCubbin Collec-
tion)

them down. "We must catch them now or we will have a long drawn-out
still hunt for them, as was the case of the Wilcox chase," he said, "and
you know in that case we never did pick up their trail again until now—
in another robbery." Wheeler consulted with Hadsell, with the result that
LeFors was allowed to proceed at a faster gait as long as he did not lose
the rest of the posse. Much to his frustration, the men were soon strung
out behind him for a mile and a half, and he again had to slow his pace.[45]

Nearing sundown and running out of time, LeFors spurred his horse
on for one last attempt to catch up with the robbers. With Hadsell and
Wheeler following, he reached the Little Snake River just as the outlaws were climbing the slope on the south side of the river. Although
it was obvious their quarry would continue to ride through the night,
the possemen and horses were too exhausted to follow. They decided to
make camp for the night and pick up the trail the next morning. LeFors

regretted the lost opportunity and was thoroughly disgusted with the posse's performance.[46]

In the morning they discovered where the bandits had stopped to eat and divide the loot. Pieces of money wrappers were found strewn about the site. LeFors again set out on the outlaws' trail, riding ahead of the posse that was now down to twelve men. Twenty miles south of Baggs near Horsehead Buttes, they came upon the robbers' abandoned gray pack horse. It was completely exhausted and could no longer move. After another fifteen miles the trail led to a tract of low swampy ground, thickly populated with willows. The posse proceeded slowly, with weapons drawn and alert for an ambush. In a few minutes they spotted the legs of some horses underneath the trees. The twelve men quietly surrounded the grove of willows, while LeFors began an advance on the horses. He crawled on his stomach until he was close enough to determine the legs belonged to three loose horses. He believed the outlaws had hidden fresh mounts in the willows as a relay, and were long gone. To make certain, he walked past the horses to the other side of the grove to the waiting possemen. In his autobiography, LeFors said it was evident the robbers' escape route was well planned, alluding to their use of relay horses and their attempt to set the posse afoot by leading them to bad water at Soda Springs.[47]

LeFors wanted to continue the pursuit, but Hadsell and Wheeler believed it was now impossible to catch the robbers before they reached Brown's Hole. The outlaws had fresh mounts and a good head start, while the posse had not eaten since the previous evening and were riding tired horses. Wheeler decided they should head back to the Perkins' ranch near the Little Snake River for food and rest. On Tuesday morning, September 4, they started out for Baggs, where LeFors and Hadsell returned to Rawlins by stage. According to LeFors, with a second unsuccessful chase after train robbers, the Union Pacific soon replaced their special agent.[48]

The September 5 *Rawlins Republican* reported that "the posses had followed the trail of the robbers around Haystack Mountain to the point where they had crossed the Snake River, some 20 miles below Baggs."

On Sunday, September 2, the posses "were in the vicinity of Timber Lake, in broken country between Bear and Snake Rivers. The bandits had resorted to the old trick of running into a bunch of range horses which they drove some distance and then allowed to scatter, making it almost impossible to discern which was the trail left by the horses ridden by the robbers."[49]

The outlaws then doubled back to Jim Ferguson's ranch where he hid them in a camp on Black Mountain above Dixon, Wyoming. They stayed there for three weeks, from September 2 to 23, with Ferguson supplying them with food and information on the movements of the posses.[50] The outlaws had to leave their haven after the people of Dixon ran Ferguson out of town owing to his wild ways and his association with the Wild Bunch. He and his family relocated near Palisade, Colorado, twenty miles northeast of Grand Junction.[51]

In *A Cowboy Detective*, Pinkerton operative Charles Siringo related how he was again ordered out on the trail of the train robbers: "Our agency had just received a 'tip' through an ex-convict in Grand Junction, Colo., that he talked with 'Kid' Curry and a tall companion at their camp on a Mesa twenty miles south of Grand Junction, and that they told him they were going south where the 'climate would fit their clothes,' and that they had just broken camp and started south on horseback. Therefore, I was hustled right out to get on the trail of these two men." Siringo later learned from Jim Ferguson that before the robbers reached Utah, "Bill Cruzan turned back on his mule and later was met by Bert C. [Charter] south of Grand Junction, Colo."[52]

From Denver, Siringo rode the Denver and Rio Grande Railroad 300 miles to Grand Junction. After purchasing two horses and supplies for the trail, he started south. At the Elliott ranch he learned the two outlaws had passed through only a week previous. Siringo showed Mr. Elliott a photo of Kid Curry, and he was positive it was the small dark man of the pair. The trail of Curry and Kilpatrick then led to the ranch of the "notorious Young boys" in Paradox Valley, near the border of Utah. Siringo stayed in the valley for about a week to gather information from the Young clan. He learned that the two robbers had ridden into Utah's La

Sal Mountains with outlaw Lafe Young, with the intention of obtaining fresh mounts from the range horses. Siringo followed two men into the mountains, but found out he was on the wrong trail. However, he soon determined the bandits had headed south toward the Blue Mountains in southeastern Utah.[53]

When Siringo rode into the Carlisle Cattle Ranch near Monticello, he no doubt assumed an outlaw identity to gain information. The manager of the ranch was Bill "Latigo" Gordon, an ex-outlaw who had provided refuge to Curry and Sundance when they were on the run from the Wilcox robbery. He kept a hidden haystack a couple of miles from the ranch for his outlaw friends to feed their horses. From Gordon, Siringo learned "that my men 'Kid' Curry and his tall chum, who was a stranger in that country, had left the hidden haystack the morning previous to my arrival, Lafe Young being with them." Gordon had given the robbers a supply of food, after they confessed the Tipton train robbery had been a bust and they were broke.[54] However, they probably learned their lesson from the Wilcox robbery, not to spend the marked money along their escape route.

Gordon figured the outlaws' destination was Arizona or New Mexico, since they had also told him "that they were going where the climate would fit their clothes." He informed Siringo that they were camped on Indian Creek with some other hard cases. Upon his arrival at Indian Creek, Siringo made the acquaintance of an outlaw known as "Peg Leg" Eldredge. Apparently Lafe Young had been talkative, telling Peg Leg that he was riding with two Union Pacific train robbers on the dodge. Peg Leg had met the men in their camp, and his description of the small dark man was that of Kid Curry. He also told Siringo the robbers had just struck camp, and headed south to the Colorado River. Lafe Young left them to return in the direction of Paradox Valley.[55]

Siringo did not immediately hit the trail of the robbers, but stayed in the Blue Mountains for three weeks.[56] From this and his subsequent actions, it must be inferred that he had lost their trail. "After leaving the Blue mountains I drifted south to Bluff City on the San Juan river," wrote Siringo, "thence west 120 miles over that uninhabited, rocky, desert country, over which Sayles and I passed [in pursuit of the Wilcox robbers], to Dandy Crossing on the Colorado river."[57] After he swam his horses across the river, he entered the Henry Mountains and rode north to Hanksville. He stayed with store owner Charley Gibbons, a Wild Bunch friend, but learned nothing concerning the whereabouts of Curry and Kilpatrick.[58]

Just when his trailing of the train robbers had come to a dead end, Siringo received new orders from Assistant Superintendent Frank Murray in Denver to go to Butch Cassidy's old home near Circleville, Utah. He was to gather all the information he could on Cassidy's background for later use by the Pinkerton agency. From there he was to head south to the Wild Bunch refuge of Alma, New Mexico Territory, to get information about the gang in general, and to find out who had passed the unsigned currency from the Wilcox train holdup in particular.[59]

As Siringo did not obtain much useful information from either area, Murray then instructed him to return to Denver for an assignment in western Colorado. Posing as an outlaw wanted in New Mexico, he was to locate Jim Ferguson at his ranch near Grand Junction. He got in solid with Ferguson, and was able to learn a great deal concerning the participants and planning of the Tipton train robbery. In addition, it was at this time that Siringo found out he had guessed wrong in going to Hanksville after the train robbers. Ferguson told him Curry and Kilpatrick, after leaving the Blue Mountains in Utah, had continued south into New Mexico.[60]

Their ultimate destination was Fort Worth, Texas, to rendezvous with Cassidy, Sundance, and Carver, who had successfully robbed the First National Bank of Winnemucca, Nevada, of $32,640 in mostly gold coin, on September 19, 1900.[61] In their escape from Winnemucca, the trio rode east along the Golconda Road, and a few miles before reaching that town, they turned northeast toward Tuscarora. The citizens of Tuscarora refused to mount a posse unless Humboldt County guaranteed their expenses.[62] (This is reminiscent of the scene in the 1969 film, *Butch Cassidy and the Sundance Kid*, in which the marshal of a western town is pleading with the reluctant citizens to form a posse to go after the dangerous gang of train robbers, even offering to furnish horses and guns.)

The outlaws therefore were not molested by the Tuscarorans, and continued on toward Three Creek, Idaho. Owing to the exhausted condition
of their pack horses, they could not get to a cache in Jarbidge Canyon,
so they divided the loot in a little gulch near Three Creek.[63] A posse
later trailed the outlaws there and found the empty money bags.[64] Carver
left his partners after burying at least $6,500 in an empty lard pail, and
headed for his home place in Texas.[65]

CHAPTER 18

Hiding in Plain Sight

Will Carver may have been in a hurry to get to Texas because he wanted to see his girlfriend, Laura Bullion, whom he had promised to marry. Laura was born in Washington County, Arkansas, in October 1876. When her father died in 1881, Laura's mother moved her three children to their maternal grandparents' Dove Creek ranch near Knickerbocker, Texas. Laura reportedly left home not long after her mother died in 1891, and it is believed that she worked as a prostitute in San Antonio, possibly at Fannie Porter's Sporting House. It is known that she returned to the Knickerbocker area for visits and to attend dances over the next few years. Will had been married to Laura's aunt, Viana Byler, for less than six months when she died of pregnancy complications on July 22, 1892. He was devastated by her death, and it is said he began courting her niece because she greatly resembled Viana. He had left Laura in San Antonio before going off to rob the bank in Winnemucca.[1]

However, Will forgot all about Laura when he met a girl named Callie May Hunt in October 1900 at the San Antonio Fairground's annual International Exposition.[2] Callie was born in 1876 in St. Louis, Missouri, and her mother died when Callie was a young child. Her father moved the family to Palestine, Texas, where she ran away in 1893 at the age of seventeen to become a prostitute. By July 1900, she was working at Fannie Porter's brothel, going by the name of Lillie Davis. Carver introduced himself to Lillie as Will Casey.[3]

Kid Curry and Ben Kilpatrick had also arrived in San Antonio at this time, and met up with Carver. In fact Curry had attended the fair with Carver, where he fell for Lillie's business associate, Maud Delia Moore.[4] She was described as not beautiful, not ugly, but "somewhat good looking." She had a slender build, dark complexion with high cheek bones, and thick dark auburn hair. Her "piercing black eyes ... fairly danced as she spoke," and two gold teeth showed conspicuously when she smiled.[5] She "was a pert and headstrong woman," one author said, "[with a] fiery temperament."[6] She could also turn on the charm with her cheerful, flirtatious side, which was an asset in her profession.

Maud was born in Tarrant County, Texas, in August 1875, and grew up in Kennedale, near Fort Worth. She was raised by her mother Leona, her grandmother Martha Turner, and step-father Silas D. Penny.[7] Possibly owing to problems at home, she left when she was eighteen and found work as a prostitute in Fort Worth, San Antonio, and Mena, Arkansas. Maud married a farmer named Lewis Walker in 1896, but left him three years later because she wanted excitement and did not like being poor. She returned to her earlier profession in San Antonio at Fannie's, and was using the name Annie Rogers when Kid Curry met her.[8] Annie knew Curry at this time as Bob Nevilles or Nevils.[9] When he came to visit, Curry would sometimes collapse into Fannie's bed after too much to drink, wearing his boots and spurs. Fannie did not take kindly to having her expensive satin sheets torn to shreds.[10]

Laura Bullion was abandoned with no place to go, so Fannie took her in as one of her girls, probably not for the first time. Ben Kilpatrick often visited the bordello, and soon took up with Laura.[11] There is evidence that Ben may have known Laura earlier when he worked on ranches in the Knickerbocker area and she lived with her grandparents, Elliott and Serena Byler, on their ranch at Dove Creek.[12] Ben showed off to the girls by doing tricks on a new bicycle, an incident which has been erroneously attributed to Butch Cassidy in later histories.[13]

After Carver left them at Three Creek, Sundance and Cassidy escaped through Twin Falls, Idaho, and then rode southeast to southern Wyoming.[14] By mid-October they were reported to be in Rawlins, attempting to exchange Winnemucca gold and possibly Wilcox powder-burned currency, for good paper.[15] They spent a few days at their hideout in Powder Springs before turning east to Savery, Wyoming, on the Little Snake River. Continuing on to Slater, Colorado, they stopped at Robert McIntosh's general store and post office to visit Sundance's friends on October 25. After confiding his participation in the Winnemucca bank holdup, Sundance set down a gold coin on the counter to pay back a loan from store employee David Gillespie, and said "Keep the change."[16]

The next day Butch and Sundance continued their leisurely travel south toward Texas, until they reached Wolcott, Colorado. It was time for them to meet up with their friends, so they boarded a southbound passenger train to Fort Worth. They arrived at the Union Depot in Fort Worth by early November, and met up with Carver, Curry, and Kilpatrick, who were accompanied by Lillie Davis and Annie Rogers. The city was a cattle shipping railhead, and the gang blended easily with the cowboys and cattlemen that were there for a good time. They took rooms at the Maddox Hotel at 1014½ Main Street, which leased furnished flats on the second floor. It was managed by Mrs. Elizabeth "Lizzie" Maddox, and located in the red light district of Fort Worth called Hell's Half Acre. Her husband, Kendall C. Maddox, was kept busy running a gaming room in their apartment. In a city unconcerned with bank and train robberies far to the north, the five outlaws enjoyed spending time at the various saloons, gaming rooms, and whorehouses. At 1600 Calhoun Street, only a few blocks from the Maddox, was a saloon operated by a man named Mike Cassidy. This may have been the same Mike Cassidy that had been Butch's rustling mentor in Utah.[17]

Sundance may have spent time in Texas previously, possibly to visit his girlfriend Ethel. "The beeline they [the five outlaws] took to Fort Worth," Richard F. Selcer states, "and the ease with which they melted into the local population probably indicates that they had been in town before." He speculates on "the possibility that it was the Texas connection between the Wild Bunch and their female followers that brought them to Fort Worth."[18]

At 705½ Main Street was located the Swartz View Company, a photographic studio run by John Swartz. It is not known what prompted the decision to have a group picture taken on November 21, 1900.[19] It may have been the result of a lark, or a commemoration of Will Carver's upcoming marriage to Lillie Davis, or a memento of the gang's last fling before splitting up. Whatever the reason, Cassidy showed uncharacteristic carelessness, and supposedly it was Kid Curry who strongly cautioned against the group portrait.[20] The rest of the gang should have taken his advice, because the now famous "Fort Worth Five" photograph was at least partially responsible for hastening the group's demise. The fact that they were dressed in the latest fashion of the day, with new suits, vests, and derbies, was not enough to disguise them from the authorities.

The group requested the newer, more expensive, dry-plate process for this special occasion. They then ordered copies of the photo to be picked up in a few days. Swartz was evidently quite pleased with the result of his efforts, because he placed a copy of the photo in his display window.[21] Wells, Fargo & Company detective Fred J. Dodge is usually credited with passing by and discovering the significance of the portrait.[22] The Wells Fargo office at 817 Main Street was located one block from the photographic studio.[23] When Dodge noticed the picture in Swartz's front window, he recognized one of the men in the group staring back at him as outlaw Will Carver. Dodge went inside and ordered extra copies of the photo for distribution to various law agencies. He was to also send a copy to the Pinkerton Detective Agency, having worked with them on occasion. But first he walked to the Wells Fargo office to set about trying to identify the other four men in the picture.[24]

It has been pointed out recently that Dodge could not have seen the photo in Swartz's front window, because the studio was located on the second floor. A new candidate for the photo discovery has come to light in the form of Fort Worth police detective Charles R. Scott. Scott was responsible for the department's "Rogue's Gallery" of local criminals as well as photos sent from other agencies all over the country. He would frequently take prisoners to Swartz's studio to obtain mug shots. He was there to pick up some finished mug shots, when he spied the Wild Bunch photo in the second floor waiting room. Recognizing Will Carver and Harvey Logan from wanted circulars he had received, he then wired the Pinkertons in Denver.[25]

While the Fort Worth Five were unwinding in Hell's Half Acre, they debated the idea of leaving the United States, possibly to South America. Butch and Sundance were in favor of it. They were resigned to the fact

Famous "Fort Worth Five" photograph. From left to right, Harry Longabaugh (the Sundance Kid), Will Carver, Ben Kilpatrick, Harvey Logan (Kid Curry), and Butch Cassidy. November 21, 1900. (Robert G. McCubbin Collection)

that the West was changing; robbing trains and banks was becoming more difficult. The other three did not want to leave, or were just not ready to go yet. Carver is reported to have said, "he preferred to die on dirt he knew even if he might live a hundred years in the jungles."[26] Cassidy tried to persuade his friend Kid Curry to come along, but it is evident that he felt the same way as Carver. Not long after the group picture was taken, Ben, Butch, and Sundance, left Fort Worth and headed to San Antonio. They would certainly have visited Fannie Porter's establishment, and Ben had wanted to see Laura Bullion again. Butch and Sundance may have picked up Ethel in this city or possibly in Galveston before going east, eventually leaving the country. Harvey and Will set out with Annie and Lillie for a trip to Houston.[27]

When interviewed by the Pinkertons in Cameron, Texas, on December 4, 1901, Lillie stated that the two couples "went to Houston, stopped two days and nights, then all returned to San Antonio, remained three days and nights, then went back to Forth Worth, also remained three days, and at this time, December 1st, she was married by a Justice of the Peace to Will Casey" at the Tarrant County Courthouse. She used her real name, Callie May Hunt, while Carver used the name of Casey, a variation of Causey, his step-father's name. While in Fort Worth this second time, they again all stayed at the Maddox Flats apartments. Lillie was probably referring to this time when she later stated that "Bob [Nevilles–Kid Curry] got drunk while at the Maddox Flats, and on account of the noise he made had to go to some other place."[28]

Harvey and Annie accompanied the newlyweds on their honeymoon to Denver. Lillie told what happened on that trip: "All then went to Denver and stopped at the Hotel Victor for two days, then went to Shoshone, Idaho … Maud and myself were left at the McFall House and Will and Bob were away for five days and nights, and when they returned said they had been up the road. All then returned to Denver and stopped at Brown's Palace Hotel, then went to a rooming house and stopped five days … After returning to Denver from Shoshone, Idaho, I saw Will Casey with 6 or 7 sacks filled with gold. He had the sacks in a trunk and he also had a big bundle of paper money in the trunk. The gold was in $20.00 gold pieces. Will Casey seemed to have all the money, both going out on the trip and returning, but I know he gave Bob all the money he wanted. They had a satchel stolen from them on this trip which contained a big gun, and they did considerable complaining and grieving over the loss of the satchel."[29]

It was at this time that Harvey and Annie posed for a formal, wedding-style portrait. It pictures a self-assured Annie Rogers with her hand on the shoulder of an uncomfortable looking Kid Curry. Some researchers have speculated that the photograph was the work of John Swartz of Fort Worth, or possibly a Nashville photographer; however it was definitely taken in Denver. When Rogers was later arrested in Nashville, she volunteered the information that led to Pinkerton detectives obtaining a copy of the photograph from a Denver studio.[30]

Before leaving Denver, Will spent $225 on a pair of diamond earrings for his new wife. He also bought her a fur sack for thirty dollars, and some good clothes. She later sold everything except the fur sack to pay debts.[31] The two couples boarded a Fort Worth and Denver City train, and returned to Fort Worth a few days before Christmas.[32] The girls were given some expense money and sent home ostensibly for the holidays. Will gave Lillie $167, mostly in gold, sending her to her father's home in Palestine. He mailed her another seventy dollars in currency in March 1901 from Christoval, Texas.[33] Annie later said the man she knew as Nevilles gave her five twenty-dollar gold pieces, before she went home to Kennedale to visit her mother.[34] Curry and Carver then headed for San Antonio to join Ben Kilpatrick. They registered at the Laclede Hotel on December 22 and stayed through December 30.[35]

During their stay Carver ran into his former employer of the 09 Ranch near Barnhart, Ed R. Jackson, who had recently moved to Sonora to open a bank with his partner W. L. Aldwell. They had a brief conversation, ending with Carver asking Jackson not to mention his name or that they had met. Before parting, he told Jackson that he would soon see him "out in his own country." Of course Jackson immediately telephoned his partner of this meeting, who then informed Sutton County Sheriff Elijah "Lige" S. Briant at Sonora.[36] Carver, with Curry and Kilpatrick, celebrated Christmas and possibly New Year's, before the three started for West Texas.[37]

They first stayed a day or so with Carver's mother and step-father (Walter S. Causey), just south of Bandera. From there they traveled northwest at a leisurely pace, stopping to quench their thirst at the saloons in Kerrville, Fredericksburg, Mason, and Brady. They had bought a rubber-tired buggy, and were posing as horse buyers. In actuality they were scouting potential sites for a bank holdup. Visiting his former hometown at Brady, H. E. "Boosie" Sharp, now a bartender in Sonora, spotted the men in a saloon and thought he recognized them. He informed McCulloch County Sheriff John Wall of his suspicions; however

Kid Curry and Annie Rogers
photographed   in   Denver,
December 1900. (Robert G.
McCubbin Collection)

the outlaws left town before the sheriff could telegraph for information
concerning them.[38]

They were in San Angelo on February 3, 1901, where Curry mailed
a letter to Annie's home in Kennedale.[39] When Carver found out that
one Rufus "Rufe" Thomas was in town, he supposedly vowed to kill
him. Thomas had helped to capture Elzy Lay after the Folsom train robbery in New Mexico. However, Carver gave up the attempt after finding
Thomas playing poker with a sheriff and two Texas Rangers.[40] At some
point, either Ben went alone or all three went to the Kilpatrick farm in
Concho County.[41] Regardless, the three outlaws were in Knickerbocker
by February 10, where they spent the next two weeks.[42] "About four

weeks ago," reported the April 6 *San Angelo Standard*, "four men were seen in Knickerbocker … They had a rubber tired buggy and said they were from Iowa, and while there made purchases at Tweedy's store."[43] According to the Pinkerton Archives, the fourth man was probably minor Wild Bunch member, Pat Wilson, who was traveling with them at this time.[44]

On February 1, 1901, Mr. and Mrs. Harry A. Place, and Mr. James Ryan checked into an upscale boarding house at 234 West 12th Street in New York City. Place was Harry Longabaugh's mother's maiden name. No marriage record has been found for Sundance and his girlfriend Ethel. It is not certain where Sundance met his beautiful, mysterious girlfriend, or what her real name was. Ryan was Butch Cassidy posing as Ethel's brother. The trio paid for nearly three weeks in advance for Mrs. Catherine Taylor's best second floor suite.[45]

On February 20, after seeing all the sights in New York, the trio boarded the British ship *Herminius*, and set sail for Argentina the following morning.[46] Meanwhile, the other trio, Curry, Carver, and Kilpatrick, were still in Knickerbocker. Some of the time was spent in a visit to Berry Ketchum's ranch, older brother of Tom and Sam.[47] After a few days they left in their rubber-tired buggy for Eldorado and Sonora, arriving in the latter town shortly after February 25.[48] Here, posing as dealers in polo ponies, they purchased a sorrel horse. More than once they were seen getting change for twenty-dollar gold certificates at the Jackson and Aldwell First National Bank.[49] The Pinkerton records show that by March 1, Curry and Carver were in Christoval, staying over three weeks in all, spending some of that time with Pat Wilson.[50] Presumably, some time previous, Ben had again gone ahead to the Kilpatrick family farm, located between the villages of Paint Rock and Eden, in Concho County.

During this time, Carver returned to San Angelo for another attempt at dispatching Rufe Thomas. He was unsuccessful in searching out his adversary, owing to Thomas being ill and confined to bed in his hotel room. Before Carver left town, he ran into a cattlemen friend who also happened to know Thomas. With a noticeable lack of discretion, Carver told the man of his intention to rob the bank in Sonora. When Thomas

Harry Longabaugh, the "Sundance Kid," and Ethel Place in New York City, February 1901. (Robert G. McCubbin Collection)

was on his feet again, the cattleman informed him not only of his close call with Carver, but also the latter's bank holdup plans. He thought it would be a good idea for Thomas to go to Sonora and alert the local officers. Thomas started walking down the street to think the matter over, when he suddenly ran into Sheriff Briant, who happened to be in San Angelo that day. This was Briant's second warning concerning Carver's unlawful intentions in Sonora. He immediately returned there to alert the citizens and organize his deputies against the outlaws.[51]

On March 23, 1901, Butch, Sundance and Ethel, disembarked in Buenos Aires, Argentina, and checked into the Hotel Europa. Sundance opened an account at the London and River Platte Bank, and deposited $12,000 in gold notes.[52] They had decided to go straight by homesteading a ranch to raise cattle, sheep, and horses. By June they had traveled to the foothills of the Andes in northern Patagonia, settling in the relatively isolated Cholila Valley in the Chubut Territory.[53]

Curry and Carver joined Ben at the Kilpatrick Planche Spring farm in the last week of March. There, on March 27, 1901, a grievous incident occurred that was to become one of the most controversial in Wild Bunch history. The 320-acre farm was adjacent to a pasture owned by the Molloy Land and Cattle Company.[54] The outlaws had set up camp in the pasture, and were enjoying a game of croquet with other members of the Kilpatrick family in the yard of the house. Besides Ben, the other family members present were his brothers George, Ed, and Felix, and his sisters Ola and Alice. Their parents, George W. and Mary C., and older brother Daniel Boone Kilpatrick, were away tending some sheep they kept on rented land in south Concho County.[55]

There is very little agreement in the contemporary accounts and the so-called eyewitness testimony from the Kilpatricks as to what occurred that Wednesday afternoon. About the only thing that is certain is that Oliver C. Thornton was shot and killed on the Kilpatrick farm by one of the men in the yard that day. Thornton was a neighbor to the north who worked land owned by former Concho County Sheriff Ed Dozier. Most accounts state that Thornton walked armed to the Kilpatrick farm to complain about their hogs running loose in the Dozier pasture. (There was at least one report stating he was not armed.) It is further stated that a confrontation took place, resulting in Thornton being shot a number of times by a man named Charles Walker.[56]

According to John Loomis, a neighboring rancher who knew Ben Kilpatrick and Will Carver when they were ranch hands, Dozier didn't like the idea of having outlaws living so close to him. He told the current local sheriff, in no uncertain terms, that he wanted the gang run out of Concho County. When Carver heard of this, he threatened to kill Dozier for making the complaints. Dozier reportedly became nervous over this threat, owing to Carver's reputation of being "a dangerous and desperate foe."[57] This may be why he sent his hired help to confront the Kilpatricks at their farm.

Ed Kilpatrick later said that he, his brothers Ben and George, and Walker were playing croquet, when Thornton walked into the yard armed with a Winchester and became belligerent concerning the hogs. Ed tried to explain the hogs were his brother Boone's property, and that they didn't want any trouble. He said Walker then pulled his revolver and shot Thornton, a second time as he ran, and a third time as he fell over a log at the spring.[58] However, it is possible that Thornton may have been killed elsewhere, and his body moved to the spring. According to one report, there was no blood evidence where he was found. Ed may actually have hinted at the possibility that Thornton was unarmed, when he told authorities that Thornton was shot because of his spying.[59]

Curiously absent from Ed's statements are any mention of a man referred to as Bob McDonald, the alias Kid Curry was using at the time. However, the description given for Walker, "a small man weighing from 135 to 140 pounds, dark complexion, heavy brown mustache, a bald head, and aged between 35 and 40 years," more closely resembled Curry than Carver.[60] In contrast, when George Kilpatrick was in custody, badly wounded and not sure he was going to live, he named McDonald as the murderer of Thornton.[61] "As evidence of Carver's innocence of the murder of Thornton," Jeffrey Burton postulates, "though not of Logan's guilt, this looked ironclad ... It does not exclude the possibility that George himself or one of his brothers was the actual killer."[62]

When Thornton did not show up for supper, his wife Mary went to the Kilpatrick place and found her husband's body near the spring.[63] On April 3, 1901, Mrs. Thornton went before Justice of the Peace K. W. Goher, and made out an Affidavit for Warrant of Arrest naming her husband's killers as Bob McDonald and Charles Walker.[64] The Pinkertons knew that Curry and Carver were using McDonald and Walker as aliases respectively; however, the various accounts and eyewitness testimony do not agree as to who was using which name, so it does nothing to clarify the identity of the killer.[65]

Several months later, Ben Kilpatrick was arrested in St. Louis on an unrelated charge, and his brother Boone came to visit him. The city's detectives questioned the latter concerning the Thornton murder. Boone (who was not present at the shooting) said Carver did the killing, call-ing it justifiable since Thornton was in the act of throwing a shell into his *shotgun*.[66] John Loomis wrote that "[A]fter Carver was killed it was easy to lay the blame for Thornton's killing on him and thus protect the real criminal from a sentence that could have been hanging." But Loomis never stated that the "real criminal" was Kid Curry, or a man named McDonald.[67]

Some writers, such as Ed Bartholomew and John Eaton, state that the killer had to be Kid Curry, because Will Carver was not capable of such a cruel or ruthless act. This is entirely inconsistent with what is known concerning Carver's murderous activities up to this time in his life. Bartholomew concedes that Carver was most likely responsible for the killing of Sheriff Edward J. Farr, and the wounding of several posse members (one who died later) in the Turkey Creek Canyon fight. He also writes that when Deputy Sheriff George A. Scarborough was mortally wounded by "Carver's gang" in Arizona, "Carver was seen standing, firing his rifle as fast as he could work the lever."[68] In addition, Carver was implicated in participating in the murderous ambush of posse mem-bers LeSueur and Gibbons, which so outraged the citizens of St. Johns, Arizona. There is little to no evidence in Curry's life up to this time to support the assertion that he was much more ruthless than Carver.

It is obvious that the Kilpatricks, as witnesses, were not impartial, and the truth of what really happened that day cannot be found in their highly contradictory statements. "In considering the reasons for and identity of the killer one must remember the Kilpatricks would not have brought a murder investigation to their doorsteps," Arthur Soule states. "None of the group would have wanted to forfeit the sanctuary they were enjoying by involvement in a homicide. Thornton had to have in the minds [*sic*] of one of the group, posed a threat. The one most likely to have perceived and acted quickly to neutralize the threat was Kid Curry."[69] Neverthe-less, Carver's past behavior proves he would have been just as capable as Curry in perceiving a threat from Thornton.

Still, it is difficult to believe either Curry or Carver would jeopardize their safe haven without some serious provocation. "In considering our

outlaws, Will Carver and Harvey Logan," John Eaton writes, "we …
have trouble in finding a motive. In a robbery, or in self-defense these
men would kill for the profit and preservation of their lives but never
over an argument concerning someone else's hogs … A killing would
tell the law where they are and have it close in on them just as this one
did."[70] Although Soule said the same concerning the Kilpatricks, rancher
John Loomis did not agree. In his memoirs Loomis referred to the Kilpatrick boys as "natural born criminals." He deemed it more probable
that Thornton had not been killed by Carver, but by a younger gang
member to impress the older outlaw.[71]

Loomis assuredly had either Ed or George Kilpatrick in mind, but the
person who more closely fits the criteria is the youngest male member
of the family, Felix Kilpatrick. Born in April 1884, he was just under
seventeen years old at the time of the shooting. "Felix has been characterized as a downright mean person by several sources," remarks Soule.
"A large man with a big red face, he was described by one source as the
type who would shoot at you for any reason or no reason at all. While
there was logic and rational in Ben's conflicts, it was said there was none
to Felix's."[72] The law was going to converge on the Kilpatrick ranch no
matter who did the killing, so the wanted outlaws had to flee. The remaining family members then gave confusing and conflicting testimony
concerning the killer's identity, using the Walker and McDonald aliases.
This way, none of the gang members would be directly implicated, and
it would draw suspicion from young Felix. (Four years later an arrest
warrant was issued against Felix for shooting a Mexican.[73])

Curry, Ben, and George fled with the rubber-tired buggy southwest
toward Eldorado in Schleicher County.[74] Carver left with their saddle
horses, with the intention of procuring some provisions and later meeting his friends southwest of Eldorado on the T Half-Circle range.[75] Ed
sent his two sisters to their parents' sheep camp, and waited until evening
before setting out to report the shooting at Eden.[76] The telephone line had
been found cut in the Molloy pasture to slow pursuit.[77] Concho County
Sheriff James E. Howze visited the farm to take statements from Ed and
Felix Kilpatrick before his posse followed the fugitives' trail.[78] It wasn't

long before it was discovered the wires had also been cut to Eldorado. The three driving the buggy took this precaution so that they could enter town to buy supplies, and three horses from a local rancher. The two Kilpatricks were recognized in Eldorado on Thursday the 28th.[79] For some reason they did not cut the telephone lines that connected Eldorado with Sonora, twenty-one miles south. This proved to be a big mistake.[80]

By April 1, 1901, Carver had rejoined Curry and the two Kilpatricks, camped at a waterhole on the T Half-Circle Ranch just west of Sonora, Sutton County.[81] The gang had helped themselves to a sack of oats and a quarter of a beef from the ranch headquarters. It wasn't long before the foreman discovered the men camped in a nearby pasture, and notified law officials by telephone. Sheriff Briant, of Sutton County, received word Tuesday evening, April 2, and planned to wait until morning before visiting the camp with a posse. However, his quarry was coming to him, arriving on the outskirts of Sonora just after dark.[82] They were riding horses and leading a pack horse, having previously ditched the buggy in a thicket of live oak after leaving the T Half-Circle pasture.[83]

Despite the uproar caused in that section of country by the Thornton killing, the outlaws were apparently planning to go ahead with their attack on the First National Bank in Sonora. Curry preferred trains, but he may have been swayed by how easy and lucrative the Winnemucca bank holdup had been for Carver, Cassidy, and Sundance. Yet the gang must have been aware that Sheriff Briant had received sufficient warning concerning their intentions, and that there would be organized resistance from law officers and citizens. Even if, as some believe, they entered town just to buy supplies in order to leave the country, it was extremely unwise as events proved.

They rode into the Mexican section of town ostensibly to buy a few items, mainly horse feed. Two of the men entered the Victor Castillo store at about 8:00 p.m., and bought some baking powder and flour. Not finding any oats for sale, Curry and Ben Kilpatrick rode to a small building near the end of a draw to wait for the others. Will and George rode into the main part of town in search of the horse feed. There was also no grain to be had at Beckett's livery stable across from the First National

Bank. They then rode south on Main Street and west on Concho Avenue to Jack Owens' bakery and grocery, on the opposite end of town from the bank. The *Devil's River News* later reported, "The general supposition is that this gang was arranging camp and supplies before making an attempt to hold up the First National Bank." Boosie Sharp, tending bar at a nearby saloon, recognized the smaller man as one of the horse buyers who had been in town a couple of weeks previous in the rubber-tired buggy. He also matched the description of one of the men suspected of killing Oliver Thornton. Boosie quickly related this to his brother, Deputy Sheriff Henry Sharp, who informed Sheriff Briant.[84]

Briant, along with Deputy Sharp, Deputy J. L. Davis, and Constable W. D. Thomason (also reported as W. H. Thompson), approached the bakery. Boosie joined the officers as they looked into the bakery window, but the light was poor inside. Despite this, Briant was fairly certain that the men were Carver and one of the Kilpatricks.[85] To make sure, a match was struck in order to look over the brands of the outlaws' horses. Thomason recognized one of their horses as being a sorrel the buggy men had bought in Sonora two weeks earlier. George, standing nearest the front door, noticed the flare of the match and mentioned it to Will. Carver was stooped over at the counter helping the storekeeper fill a grain sack, and appeared not to have heard Kilpatrick.[86]

Briant told his men to get ready, and they stepped into the store with guns drawn. The sheriff ordered the men to put up their hands, but Carver immediately went for his Colt .45. A surprised Kilpatrick was indecisive, and made an uncertain motion with his hands. Before Carver could cock his gun he was shot in the right lung and right arm by Sheriff Briant. He dropped his gun and fell to the floor. Thomason brought Kilpatrick down with a bullet in the left breast. The officers kept firing as long as there was any movement from the outlaws. Deputy Sharp had entered through the side door and kicked the Colt away from Carver's body. The latter was also armed with a .38 Smith & Wesson double-action pocket revolver; however he had been unable to draw it. Briant picked up a .38 Colt army revolver near the prostrate body of Kilpatrick, which had dropped from his holster when he fell. Storekeeper/baker Jack

Owens' wife and son were in a room adjacent to the bakery when the shooting started. Although the walls were thin, neither of them was hit by a stray bullet.[87] To explain why a notorious gunman like Carver did not get off a shot, Boosie Sharp later stated that the outlaw's six-shooter had become entangled in his suspenders.[88]

It is generally stated that Carver suffered seven wounds, with only the wound to the lung being mortal; Kilpatrick sustained five wounds. The outlaws were still alive when carried to the courthouse and placed on the floor. A doctor sedated them with narcotics but Carver became delirious. He began to rave and shout: "Keep shelling them, boys ... Will you stay with me? Will you swear it? Stay with the safe ... Now we have them ... Die game!" During intervals when he appeared lucid, he was asked if he was Walker or what was his real name. At first he replied that he was Franks, but later said he was one of the "Off boys." Ranchmen and cowboys who had formerly worked with Carver came to see him, and he finally confessed that he was William Richard Carver. He died on the courthouse floor late that night, about three hours after the shooting.[89]

The two outlaws wore belts filled with 30 US Army caliber steel-jacketed cartridges; however their rifles or carbines had been left at their camp. Also found on Carver's body was a photo "identified as being that of his late wife's niece," Laura Bullion. Ed Jackson was appointed administrator of Carver's estate, and Will's personal effects, along with the bandits' horses, were sold at auction.[90] The amount for his funeral expenses was withheld, and the rest was sent to his mother. Local rancher John Rae said Carver's sister had a headstone placed at the grave with just the date of his death, April 2, 1901, engraved. John Eaton was told by a local resident that the marker was placed by George Hamilton, Carver's friend from the "Sixes" ranch on Dove Creek.[91] "E. R. Byler and son Jake of Knickerbocker, father-in-law and brother-in-law to Will Carver, were in town Tuesday," reported the April 13 *Devil's River News*.[92]

George Kilpatrick's wounds did not appear to be critical, and he was confined in the Sutton County jail in Sonora. The newspapers reported that "The most dangerous wound Kilpatrick has is from a shot that entered his left breast and ranged out back of the shoulder, two shots in

the left arm and one in the knee, a glancing ball also struck him in the
left forehead."[93] He soon admitted his name, that he resided in Concho
County for sixteen years, and when asked who had murdered Thornton, he said it was McDonald. He said his dead companion was not Mc-
Donald, but a man he knew only by the name of Bill.[94] These and his
later statements concerning the killer of Thornton were contradictory.
Although the standing reward for Carver was $300, the Wells Fargo Ex-
press Company willingly paid Sheriff Briant $1,000 for the capture of
one of the last of the old Ketchum gang.[95] The company's investigative branch had been relentless in their pursuit of members of the Wild
Bunch.[96]

George's mother Mary visited him several times while he recuperated
in jail.[97] Sheriff Howze arrived in Sonora on Wednesday afternoon, the
day after the shooting, and identified George Kilpatrick and Carver. He
said they were two of the men wanted, which left Ben Kilpatrick the last
of the outlaw gang who was still free from the law. "As to a fourth man
Sheriff Howze knows nothing and thinks he is a myth," the *Devil's River
News* reported.[98] This coincides with the fact that the authorities had sent
out a description of only three outlaws. When law officials interrogated
George in jail, they were not interested in the man named McDonald
who Kilpatrick first named as Thornton's killer. They were only concerned as to the whereabouts of his brother Ben.[99]

It is apparent that no one was aware of Kid Curry's presence in that
part of the country, or even what he looked like. The newspapers revealed their confusion by attributing all the reported outlaw cognomens
to Carver. "Will Carver, alias Franks, alias McDonald, alias Walker who
was killed this week by Sheriff Briant of Sutton County, was not a Robin
Hood character."[100] However, Pinkerton detective Lowell Spence, who
had been tracking Curry through Texas, was sure of the fourth man. His
"Logan's Log" did not single out Curry as the murderer of Thornton, but
stated that he was "in it too."[101]

On April 13, Concho County issued arrest warrants for George and
Ed Kilpatrick for the murder of Oliver Thornton. Sheriff Howze appeared in Sonora, arrested George on April 25, and fetched him back to

Concho County. George was taken to Paint Rock where his bond was set at $4,000.[102] George and Ed's lawyer obtained a change of venue to Ballinger in Runnels County, the trial scheduled for November 4, 1901. After several continuances, they were tried in March 1902, with both being acquitted.[103]

Waiting near the draw on the western edge of Sonora, Curry and Ben Kilpatrick must have heard the four officers emptying their pistols into the bodies of Carver and George. It probably sounded as if the whole town was taking part, and realizing there was nothing they could do, they rode "out of town at top speed."[104] Fleeing to friends in the vicinity of Knickerbocker, they rode all night to find refuge at the home of local rancher, and minor Wild Bunch member, Bill Chaney (or Cheney).[105]

There is evidence that Curry and Kilpatrick did not leave Texas right away. After they left Bill Chaney's ranch, he (Chaney) traveled to the Lambert ranch near Douglas, Arizona, to inform Laura Bullion of Will Carver's death. According to Laura, Chaney gave her money, and accompanied her to Fort Worth to meet up with her old friend Ben Kilpatrick. She said they stayed at the Hyde Flats for several weeks, using an assumed name of Cunningham.[106]

There is also a reference to Kid Curry possibly being in San Antonio not long after Carver's death, in Lillie Davis' statement to the Pinkertons. She had left her father's home in Palestine on April 2, the same day her husband Will was killed, to return to Fannie Porter's house. There she was told by Bob Nevilles, that Will had gone to California, but she got the truth from an intoxicated Fannie Porter.[107]

In time, whether they traveled together or separately, Curry and Kilpatrick headed for their northern sanctuaries in Wyoming, and ultimately Montana.

CHAPTER 19

Robbery of the Great Northern

On April 26, 1901, while Kid Curry and Ben Kilpatrick were making their way north, Tom Ketchum literally lost his head in a botched hanging in Clayton, New Mexico, for the crime of train robbery. Four days later, April 30, Orlando Camillo "Deaf Charley" Hanks, alias Charles Jones, was released from the state penitentiary at Deer Lodge, Montana, after serving eight years for his part in a Northern Pacific train robbery near Greycliff in late August 1893.[1] He would play an important role in the Wild Bunch's next train robbery.

Over two weeks later, on May 15, a Pinkerton wanted poster was finally issued that made use of the Fort Worth Five photo.[2] It had taken what seemed an inordinate amount of time for authorities to identify the outlaws pictured. In her Pinkerton interview over six and a half months later, Lillie Davis would identify all the men in the photo by their aliases, and add some details of what she knew concerning their outlaw activities and their girlfriends.[3]

There are a number of reasons that may have influenced the gang's decision to hit the Great Northern Railroad instead of the Union Pacific. One reason was the UP's introduction of special posse cars loaded with law officers, professional manhunters, and horses built to last. These cars were coupled with the fastest locomotives available that could reach the scene of a holdup in very little time. Another reason was the UP, jointly with the Pacific Express Company, had been specifying "dead or alive" on their reward posters for the capture of train robbers. The Great Northern had not yet adopted either of these innovations. Finally, it was a great advantage that Kid Curry was very familiar with the area of operations around the selected holdup site in northern Montana.[4]

The robbery was most likely planned at Jim Thornhill's ranch or at Curry's old Rock Creek ranch. As at Tipton, Kid Curry was undoubtedly the leader of the gang. In late June, two men were seen riding through Lewistown, Montana, and camped outside of town. Among the horses in their possession were three later described by witnesses at the train robbery, a bay, a white, and a buckskin. Brown Waller states that the gang was furnished getaway horses from the Truax and Walsh ranches near Hinsdale, some forty miles east of Malta.[5] However, at the first relay after the robbery, the outlaws traded exhausted horses with the Thornhill 7UP brand for ones from a remuda on the Coburn Circle C ranch.[6]

It is not certain how, when, or where Kid Curry came to know O. C. Hanks, a native of DeWitt County, Texas, but he was quoted as saying he recruited "Deaf Charley" into the ranks of the Wild Bunch, "because he was a good man to handle the outside of the train and was an expert pistol shot." He added that "Hanks came well recommended."[7] Hanks had worked on various cattle ranches in Montana from 1889 to 1893. In 1892 he started work at the John T. Murphy Cattle Company, where Sundance had worked two or three years earlier. He quit the next year about mid-summer to go off and rob the Northern Pacific.[8] Hanks earned his nickname from the habit of leaning his head slightly to the left to favor his good ear.[9]

Hanks was seen loafing around Shade J. Denson's saloon, just opposite the railway station in Malta, Montana, on the 1st and 2nd of July 1901. At about two o'clock in the afternoon, on Wednesday, July 3, Denson noticed Hanks board the blind baggage of the westbound Great Northern Coast Flyer No. 3 and draw his gun on a trainman. The trainman, conductor Alex Smith, thought the large red-faced man was a tramp and tried to put him off the train.[10] When Smith reached up to pull the bell cord, Hanks drew his revolver and threatened to shoot if the train was stopped. The conductor hurried back to the coaches while Hanks climbed over the tender to the engine.[11]

Valley County Sheriff William S. Griffith was a passenger on the train, and conductor Smith requested that he arrest the man at the next siding. It was reported that "When the train approached Exeter, the next siding west of Malta, the conductor signaled the engineer to stop, but the train only slackened speed. The conductor signaled a second time, but

O. C. "Deaf Charley" Hanks, took part in the assault on
the Great Northern at Wagner, Montana, July 3, 1901.
(Robert G. McCubbin Collection)

the train did not stop."[12] The reason for the train not stopping was owing
to Hanks holding a gun on engineer Thomas Jones and fireman Mike
O'Neil. He told them he was going to rob the train, and ordered them to
keep the train rolling until they reached the Exeter Creek bridge east of
Wagner. This was a couple of miles west of the site where the Sundance
Kid had held up a Great Northern train over eight years earlier in 1892.
As the train came to a stop, O'Neil saw two men (Kid Curry and Ben
Kilpatrick) come out from under the bridge carrying Winchester rifles
and dynamite. Kilpatrick crossed in front of the engine to guard the north

side of the train, while Hanks fired a few shots back over the train before stepping down from the cab to take a position on the south side. Curry ordered Jones and O'Neil off the north side of the train and proceeded to the mail car, where mail clerk James Martin was ordered to jump down. Hanks and Kilpatrick kept up a steady fire down the sides of the train to keep Sheriff Griffith and any other curious passengers inside.[13] People quickly began hiding their valuables beneath seats and mattresses, although the Wild Bunch did not bother to rob passengers.[14]

O'Neil later stated that when the train had stopped, Sheriff Griffith came out of the coach and aimed his six-shooter at the bandit in the engine cab. However, when the two men with rifles appeared from under the bridge, the sheriff thought better of his chances and ducked back into the car.[15] The Malta *Enterprise* reported that he actually got off a few shots before being driven back by return fire from the bandits.[16] Still other stories claim that the sheriff didn't fire until after the robbers were out of his pistol range, making their getaway.[17]

The Great Northern was running two express cars together, the rear one containing express packages, and the forward Montana Central car carrying baggage. When the train had stopped, messenger Clarence H. Smith of the Great Northern Express Company and the baggage man were working in the baggage-express car. Hearing shots, they looked out the door and saw a man (Hanks) shooting from the engine cab.[18] Realizing it was a holdup, Smith, in a later statement said, "I tried to get back to my rear car, telling the baggagemaster I could do something if I could but reach it. I tried to unlock the other car door, when three shots were fired at me striking about my feet. The train had just then stopped and I had to return from the platform to the first car."[19]

Not long after, they heard pounding at the door on the opposite side of the car. They opened the door and saw the engineer with Curry standing behind him holding a Winchester rifle. "He told us to jump out," stated express messenger Smith. "He said 'Boys we won't hurt you.'" When the men exited the train, the bandits asked which car was the express, meaning the one containing the express packages. Smith continued, "They were told, and the baggage man was told [by Kid Curry] to go back into the first coach and tell the people to go back into the next coach behind and keep their heads in at the window, that they didn't want to shoot anybody."[20] Having an empty coach between the express car and the second coach was for the protection of the passengers when Curry dynamited the through safe. Smith also said that the coaches were not uncoupled from the rest of the train as some writers have stated.

Smith was handed a sack of dynamite, and told to accompany Curry into the express car. Ben Kilpatrick took charge of guarding the train crew, while Hanks stood between the engine and the mail car. "He [Curry] asked me to open up the local safe," said Smith. "I told him there was nothing in the safe at that time; and he said open it up anyway and it was opened up and nothing in it … [T]hen he commenced taking his dynamite from a sack and laid it on top of the safe … and he made the remark to me… 'Don't you make a crooked move, Bill' and I said 'No, I don't think I would make a crack out of myself when looking down into a Winchester … [W]hen it [the dynamite] got to sputtering I said, 'Bill I would like to get out of here' and he said 'You wait a minute and I will get out of here with you' and when it was ready we both went out."[21]

Smith may have shown too much nervousness around dynamite, because after the explosion Curry told O'Neil to carry the sack. However, the fireman was prudent enough to stay outside while Curry entered the car to check the safe. He found the safe was not open, and it took two more attempts before the door was finally ripped off. Curry was reported to have remarked that it was the toughest safe he had ever attempted to blow open.[22] It's possible that he may have tried smaller charges than had been used at the Wilcox robbery with the intention of not damaging the currency. The Davidson family's daughter Lily later remembered hearing the blasts from her home west of Malta, about three miles from the robbery site.[23] O'Neil was made to hold the emptied dynamite sack while Curry ransacked the wrecked safe. Curry began dropping money packages into the sack, and at one point the fireman heard the bandit estimate the amount at "something like $30,000 or $40,000."[24]

It may be reasonable to assume that Curry and the other members of the gang were acquainted with fireman Mike O'Neil. According to Charles

Kelly, O'Neil owned a ranch three miles from Wagner.[25] Reportedly the gang had supper with O'Neil and other friends the evening before the robbery at a roundup camp near Dodson, a few miles west of Wagner.[26]

While guarding the trainmen, Kilpatrick "talked about the hay crop and the fine condition of the country."[27] He also "made a comment about the train being late on its trip. [Messenger] Smith asked the man why they hadn't waited until the next day to rob the train. 'They wanted the money for the Fourth,' the man indicated."[28] While Curry was emptying the safe, Kilpatrick allowed the train crew to move close to the express car. Smith noticed a box in which he kept personal items had been badly damaged in the explosions. He mentioned as much to Curry who replied, "That is too bad."[29] Smith quickly thought of a way to be compensated for his loss. He said, "Bill, are you not going to give me a gun for a souvenir?" Curry pulled out a Smith & Wesson, shot it off until it was empty, and then handed it to Smith.[30]

Despite Curry's assertion that the gang did not want to shoot anybody, two trainmen and a passenger had been wounded during the course of the holdup. After the train had been stopped, brakeman Woodside stepped down from the rear of the train and started toward the engine. A bullet hit him in the right arm near the shoulder, shattering the bone. Another Great Northern employee who was wounded was Mr. A. W. Douglas of Clancy, traveling auditor for the Montana division. He received a bullet in the left arm, reportedly while resisting a robber in the express car. The third victim was eighteen-year-old Gertrude May Smith from Tomah, Wisconsin, en route to Everett, Washington, with her family. She was sitting by the window in the second coach playing euchre with her cousin when a bullet hit her right shoulder, narrowly missing her jugular vein.[31]

Six-year-old Ira Merritt was traveling with his mother, two sisters and a brother, to meet his father in Helena on the Fourth. In recounting the robbery in later years, he said a young girl (Gertrude Smith) seated in front of his family was playing cards. Curious as to what was going on, she stuck her head out of the window. A bullet struck her before she could jerk her head back into the coach. "I still remember how the blood spurted out of the wound," said Merritt. The conductor attempted to keep the passengers calm by telling them it was just a little Fourth of July celebration. Merritt said he was not believed, and when he saw the girl's clothes covered with blood, "he turned white as the driven snow and had to clutch one of the seats to keep from crumpling to the floor." Merritt also described some false bravado by Sheriff Griffith while the bandits were shooting down the sides of the train. "He had his coat thrown back showing off his star, letting it be known he had a six-gun and what he would do if the bandits tried to enter the coaches."[32]

Curry ordered the trainmen to move to the rear of the train. They were told to wait ten or fifteen minutes while the robbers prepared to make their getaway.[33] At this time a sheepherder named John Cunningham rode up on the crest of a hill to within a quarter mile of the train. The bandits spotted him and sent a bullet his way, which either struck the saddle or grazed the horse's hip. Cunningham raced to Wagner station where he reported the robbery at 3:35 p.m.[34] The holdup had lasted less than forty-five minutes.

The train crew and passengers saw only three men ride south at a "furious gait" or a "slow canter," depending on the account, to ford the Milk River. As at the Wilcox robbery, the bandits' horses were staked near the tracks and did not require a horse holder.[35] The witnesses reported seeing the men riding a buckskin, a bay, and a gray or possibly a white horse. Some accounts say the white horse was actually a saddled spare and being led by one of the bandits. As they rode away the robbers fired several revolver rounds in the direction of the train.[36]

The loot was mainly $40,000 in incomplete (unsigned) new bank notes from the U.S. Treasury Department of Washington, D.C., destined for the National Bank of Montana in Helena. There were 800 sheets, with three ten-dollar and one twenty-dollar note per sheet. The outlaws also took $500 in incomplete bank notes of the American National Bank in Helena, and 360 money order blanks of the Great Northern Express Company.[37] Eight gold watches that had not been damaged, a small quantity of silver coin, and a bolt of green silk completed the take. When Kid Curry spotted the green cloth, he reportedly said, "This will tickle the old lady."[38]

It took less than an hour to clear the wreckage and run the train to Wagner a few miles away. Auditor Douglas and the brakeman, Woodside, were taken to Columbus Hospital in Great Falls to treat their wounds. Woodside fainted when carried to the ambulance, and eventually had to have his arm amputated. Gertrude Smith's shoulder was apparently treated on the train by a druggist and his wife using cotton and Listerine. The wound later became infected and had to be treated for several weeks to prevent the spread of gangrene.[39]

On July 4, the Great Northern Express Co. issued a reward poster containing descriptions of the hold-up men, and promising a $5,000 reward for their capture. "One was, height 5 feet and 9 inches, weight about 175 pounds, blue eyes, had a projecting brow and about two weeks growth of sandy beard on chin, wore new tan shoes, black coat, corduroy trousers, and carried a silver plated, gold mounted Colt's revolver with a pearl handle."[40] This would be a close match for O. C. Hanks when compared with his Pinkerton file description: Height, 5 ft., 10 inches. Weight, 156 pounds. Eyes, blue, sunken. Mustache, sandy if any. Complexion, sandy. Color of Hair, auburn. Build, good.[41]

"Second man, height 6 feet, weight about 175 pounds, sandy complexion, blue eyes, …with slight cast in left eye; wore workingman's shoes, blue overalls over black suit of clothes, had a boot leg for cartridge pouch suspended from his neck." This is an almost exact description of Ben Kilpatrick, including the well-known peculiarity of his left eye. "Third man resembled a half breed very strongly, had large dark eyes, smoothly shaven face, and a very prominent nose; features clear cut, weight about 180 pounds, slightly stooped in shoulders, but very square across the shoulders, and wore a light slouch hat."[42] This is a very close approximation of Kid Curry, perhaps reporting him twenty pounds heavier than actual weight. Interestingly, it indicates that he had shaved off his well-known thick mustache, no doubt to confuse his future identification. A later portrait drawing done in the Knox County jail, and his death photographs, show that he continued this practice. "All three men used very marked Texas cowboy dialect," added the reward poster, "and two of them carried Winchester rifles, one of which was new. One had a carbine, same pattern as the Winchesters. They rode away on black, white, and buckskin horses respectively."

The reason for the descriptions being fairly detailed is owing to the fact that the bandits did not wear masks or blacken their faces. "Our train

Great Northern Express Co.

ST. PAUL, MINN., JULY 4, 1901.

$5000 Reward

The Great Northern Railway "Overland" West-bound Train No. 3 was held up about three miles east of Wagner, Mont., Wednesday afternoon, July 3, 1901, and the Great Northern Express Company's through safe blown open with dynamite and the contents taken.

There were three men connected with the hold-up, described as follows:

One was, height 5 feet and 9 inches, weight about 175 pounds, blue eyes, had a projecting brow and about two weeks growth of sandy beard on chin, wore new tan shoes, black coat, corduroy trousers, and carried a silver plated, gold mounted Colt's revolver with a pearl handle.

Second man, height 6 feet, weight about 175 pounds, sandy complexion, blue eyes, not very large with slight cast in left eye; wore workingman shoes, blue overalls over black suit of clothes, had a boot leg for cartridge pouch suspended from his neck.

Third man resembled a half breed very strongly, had large dark eyes, smoothly shaven face, and a very prominent nose; features clear cut, weight about 180 pounds, slightly stooped in shoulders, but very square across the shoulders, and wore a light slouch hat.

All three men used very marked Texas cowboy dialect, and two of them carried Winchester rifles, one of which was new. One had a carbine, same pattern as the Winchesters. They rode away on black, white, and buckskin horses respectively.

The Great Northern Express Company will give $5000 reward for the capture and identification of the three men, or a proportionate amount for one or two and $500 additional for each conviction.

D. S. ELLIOTT,
Auditor.

Approved:

D. MILLER,
President.

Great Northern Express Co. reward poster dated July 4, 1901, the day after the Wagner train robbery. (Robert G. McCubbin Collection) was held up at 2:10 in the afternoon by three unmasked men," said C. H. Smith in court testimony, "one of whom had a little dirt on his face, resembling the condition of a fireman after a run on the road."[43]

When the sheepherder reached Wagner to report the holdup, telegrams were sent to authorities in Glasgow and Fort Benton. Undersheriff Richard Kane of Glasgow and seven men were traveling by special train to join a posse forming in Malta.[44] When the damaged train No. 3 reached Wagner, Sheriff Griffith rounded up a posse of ten men and started for the holdup site.[45] According to Walt Coburn the Valley County sheriff had obtained horses from Malta, and made arrangements for a mess wagon and some fresh remounts to follow. A Circle C cowboy named Tim Maloney was hired to drive the four-horse team.[46] He was married to Lolly Dessery, one of Pike Landusky's step-daughters.[47] He happened to be in town to hire a hay crew when word came of the train holdup. The sheriff had been impressed with Maloney's show of bravery when he and another cowboy had raced out of town in an effort to catch up to the train robbers. This was despite the fact that they had to return to Malta upon realizing they were unarmed. Walt Coburn said this performance was all a big joke since Maloney and Curry were good friends.[48]

A local rancher named George Zimmerman saw the train robbers twenty miles south of Malta. They tried to circuit around him, but when he approached too close, the outlaws warned him off with a shot under his horse. Little Rockies rancher William Ellis passed the three outlaws on the trail leading a brown horse, two hours after the robbery. He claimed he recognized two of the men as Kid Curry and Harry Longabaugh.[49] Nevertheless, Longabaugh was in South America, and as had happened at the Tipton robbery, Ben Kilpatrick was being mistaken for the Sundance Kid. In fact, the *Great Falls Daily Tribune* of July 4 reported the leader of the gang was "Bill Longbaugh."[50]

The newspaper was much closer to the truth when it went on to state that "the large red-faced man" who had boarded the blind baggage at Malta, was identified by a Valley County officer as "Jones, who was sent to the penitentiary several years ago for train robbery on the Northern Pacific."[51] More information concerning the identity of Hanks was reported in the *Daily Tribune* of July 12. It had been determined that the robber was "Chas. Jones, alias Chas. Blackman, who was recently released from Deer Lodge, where he was confined a short term for highway robbery. Jones was the man who got on the train at Malta and stopped it near Wagner."[52] These were aliases for O. C. Hanks.

It was near sundown on July 3 when twelve-year-old Walt Coburn had finished gathering the Circle C remuda near Beaver Creek. He had shoved the horses through the west gate of the ranch early that morning, to graze on the neighboring Fort Belknap Reservation. He sighted four men on horseback, riding in pairs some distance apart. The riders joined together after spotting the remuda, and one man then rode up to where young Walt was sitting his horse. The black-whiskered man had a Winchester carbine slung over his saddle, and wore a cartridge belt with a tied-down holstered six-shooter. The dark man grinned at Walt with very white teeth and called him by name. "Jim Thornhill says you know how to keep your mouth shut." "Yes, sir," Walt replied. "Me'n my pardners need a change of horses," the man continued. "We're borrowin' the loan of some … Remember, kid, if anybody asks you if you seen four horsebackers, you ain't seen hide ner hair of me and my pardners. You don't know nothin'." Walt promised the man he would keep his mouth shut. "That's the ticket. The Circle C horses we borrow will be back in your remuda inside of a week. We're not two-bit horse thieves." He added that Walt should not give the time of day to any "henyard posse" that may show up at the ranch asking questions. "Nobody'll get anything out of me," Walt promised. "You got my word on it." The man then held out his hand and they shook on it.[53]

Black Whiskers then told the boy to ride up on a nearby high ridge and keep watch while the outlaws roped out fresh horses. When the outlaws mounted up and rode away, they left behind four sweat-covered horses with the Thornhill 7UP brand. Walt figured they would head to Kid Curry's Hideaway in the breaks of the Missouri. He had seen the wanted dead or alive posters, and he was certain the black-whiskered man was Harvey Logan, alias Kid Curry. He was equally certain "that the heavy-set gent with the yellow whiskers was Butch Cassidy"; although it was more than likely he was the heavy-set, sandy-whiskered O. C. Hanks.[54]

Sheriff Griffith halted his posse at the Circle C ranch that evening when Tim Maloney's mess wagon and the remounts had not caught up with them. He demanded a late supper and fresh horses from Robert Coburn's son Bob. An unsympathetic Bob Coburn told the sheriff that he would not get any remounts, and that if his posse wanted supper they would have to pay for it. The men slept in the bunkhouse, Maloney finally pulling in with the wagon late the next morning. He told the angry sheriff that his travel had been slowed by an overloaded wagon. The sheriff was even less pleased when Maloney told him not to look for any remounts. The livery stable owner at Malta was unable to supply any more saddle horses. Coburn advised the sheriff to take his posse to the Gill and Winters ranch where they would be welcome and most likely be given fresh mounts.[55]

The *Anaconda Standard* explained where the sympathies of the townspeople lay: "It is the general opinion of Malta people that the sheriff has not the number or quality of men or horses to pursue a successful chase. This has been the general impression here ever since the crime … Malta is a town a large portion of whose population is either in sympathy with the robbers or at least not in sympathy with the chase … [W]hen the posses to chase the train robbers were being organized, the best horses and the best men were not to be had … [T]here are more substantial men in the vicinity, who own many horses, and who could have gone themselves or who could have sent good men, who declare that it isn't their business to look after the Great Northern robbers … The justice of the peace at Malta rounded up a bunch of good horses to await the coming of the under-sheriff [Kane] and his men from Glasgow, but while waiting, someone ran the herd off. The result was the under-sheriff's outfit did not get out until midnight, and then it went poorly mounted."[56]

On July 5, newspapers reported that Sheriff Griffith's posse found signs the previous day where the robbers had forded Beaver Creek. It was also reported that the posse of sixteen men had the bandits surrounded at Buck Allen's ranch, about forty miles south of Wagner, on Fourchette Creek near the edge of the Fort Belknap Reservation. The outlaws had the advantage of cover from the many ranch buildings, so the sheriff was in no hurry to commence an attack. Upon receiving information that a posse from south of the Missouri River was on its way, Griffith decided to wait for reinforcements. It was felt that the three robbers would probably be captured before morning.[57] However, on July 6, newspapers reported that Great Northern officials did not verify the report that the bandits had been surrounded. "Officials of the express company believe that the men eluded their pursuers and are now in the Little Rocky Mountains, a wild country, well supplied with hiding places. The district will be guarded by a picket line, and the authorities hope to capture the men when they try to get out."[58] A posse discovered the bandits' horses fifty miles south of Malta, and it was believed they had secured remounts.[59]

The *Great Falls Daily Tribune* reported a story concerning a sheep-man named Morton, who owned a ranch on Little Porcupine Creek in Rosebud County. The robbers arrived at his ranch on the evening of July 5, informed Morton they were on the trail of stolen horses, and needed to reach Forsyth by the next day to recover them. They made a deal with the rancher to trade their tired horses for four of his best mounts, plus $100 in denominations of three twenties and four tens. Morton sent the bills to a bank in Miles City several days later, where they were supposedly identified as some of the incomplete notes stolen in the Great Northern train robbery. The *Yellowstone Journal* decided to investigate the story by questioning the bank cashiers in Miles City. The newspaper reported on July 20, 1901, that the cashiers insisted they had no knowledge of stolen bills being presented at any bank in that city.[60]

The General Manager of the Great Northern Express Company, D. S. Elliott, announced that Pinkerton agents from St. Paul had learned the true identity of the three robbers. However, he decided to withhold their names pending further confirmation. Elliott went so far as to say that they were dealing with men experienced in train robbery on other roads and eluding capture.[61]

The last sighting of the three bandits was probably by two cowhands from the Phillips ranch riding north to Malta. The robbers turned out to let them pass, and one of them said, "When you get to Malta just tell them that you saw us and that we were headed south."[62] It was only about four miles after the cowhands had resumed riding north, when they met Sheriff Griffith's posse. They gave Griffith the message, adding that one outlaw riding in the rear on a "nearly used up" horse had a bandage around his head and dried blood on his cheek.[63]

On the afternoon of July 6, Sheriff Griffith's posse had lost the trail of the robbers near Rocky Canyon, and the men and horses were too exhausted to continue.[64] They started to straggle back to their respective homes, Sheriff Griffith arriving in Glasgow on July 9.[65] The newspapers

Pinkerton reward poster for the arrest of the Great Northern robbers dated November 8, 1901. (Robert G. McCubbin Collection)

of July 8 supported two possibilities as to how the bandits escaped. One was that the bandits were hiding in the badlands of the Missouri, waiting for the posses to give up looking for them. The other was that they had already crossed the river and were heading south for Hole-in-the-Wall.[66] In fact, a Great Northern official stated that reliable information had been received confirming the latter theory, and that it was useless to continue the pursuit north of the Missouri. However, Sheriff Griffith dismissed these reports, informing the press that the wanted men were in the Little Rocky Mountains and couldn't possibly get away. He said he needed at least fifty more fighting men to volunteer from the outlying precincts.[67]

On July 10 Sheriff Griffith with about thirty men, including volunteers from Culbertson and Saco, left Glasgow for the Little Rockies. The following day, at the ranch of Jim Winters, he was joined by a ten-man posse organized at Chinook and headed by Chouteau County Deputy Sheriff Charles Crawford. The addition of a posse from Great Falls swelled the number of men in the manhunt to sixty-five. Over the next five days, in spite of optimistic reports from Sheriff Griffith, the combined posses appeared to be chasing phantoms. At one point early on (July 11), the sheriff reported having corralled the bandits in an area somewhere south of the Little Rockies and north of the Missouri River. This and other supposed sightings turned out to be false, and on July 17 the newspapers announced the hunt for the train robbers was over, with most of the posse members turning back for home.[68] Only Deputies Crawford and Callahan, with a few other men, continued the search along the southern boundary of the badlands for almost a month. They covered between 140 and 150 miles along the Missouri River, asking questions of anyone they met concerning strangers. It was no use, and they finally had to admit defeat.[69]

A few Pinkerton detectives had also aided in the hunt along the Missouri, and the agency continued its investigation into the Wagner robbery in the months to come. Their reward poster, dated St. Paul, August 5, 1901, listed the serial numbers, government numbers, and charter numbers of the stolen bills. This poster, unlike the earlier Great Northern Express Co. poster, gives the actual total amount of the reward. $5,000 for the capture and identification of the three robbers, plus $500 additional for each conviction, added up to a total of $6,500. Printed at the bottom of the poster, "In addition to the above there are large outstanding rewards offered for the arrest of some of these men, individually, by banks, railroads and express companies robbed by them, and by Governors of States, where individual members of this gang have committed murders and other crimes. These rewards offered aggregate upwards of $10,000."[70] Part of this total was the $1,000 offered for the arrest of the robbers by Lieutenant Governor Higgins of Montana.[71] This poster, distributed to banks throughout the United States, would bring results in a little more than two months.

CHAPTER 20

Winters' End

Kid Curry and his cohorts most likely hid out in the badlands between the Little Rockies and the Missouri River until the majority of manhunters left the area after mid-July 1901.[1] This would have been the most opportune time for Curry to leave his hideaway for a visit to his friend Jim Thornhill and Jim's common-law wife, Lucy Tressler. She was most likely the "old lady" Curry had in mind as the recipient of the bolt of green silk he lifted from the Wagner robbery. He would have been greeted at the door by three curious children, one his four-year-old namesake, Harvey D. Thornhill, nicknamed "Man." When Jim later moved to Arizona, Man became a top roper and won several rodeo competitions. The others were three-year-old Sarah, and Jim's son George, born December 27, 1899.[2]

Some histories state that Curry even took time out to visit his friend Sid Willis in Great Falls. He first took a room in the Minot block, not bothering to hide his identity. He then supposedly asked the Mint Saloon owner to act as a go-between in finding someone who would forge signatures on the unsigned Bank of Montana money. Whether Willis refused or just couldn't find anyone willing to sign the bills, Curry nevertheless left Great Falls without the desired forgeries.[3]

Jim Winters was understandably nervous and wary after he had killed John Curry in 1896. Four years later he told Siringo "that he expected to be waylaid and killed by 'Kid' Curry."[4] But it had been over five years since the gunfight, and during that time Kid Curry had not shown any inclination to seek revenge.

About six o'clock in the morning, on July 25, 1901, eight days after the posses disbanded, Winters stepped out the back door to air his blankets and feed the chickens. He was on the back porch holding a tin plate of water and brushing his teeth, when he was struck by two bullets in the abdomen. One bullet lodged in his stomach, the other passed through to shatter his spinal column.[5] According to Walt Coburn, Winters' step-brother and partner, Abe Gill, was at the ranch, along with six eastern college students from Gill's Brooklyn alma mater. They had been invited to spend their summer vacation to help with the haying and other ranch work, and had arrived at the ranch after the posses had left.[6] One press report described the six visitors only as "pilgrims," and that Gill had left the night previously for Fort Benton.[7] The inquest report lists them by name as witnesses, and the occupations of at least a couple of them are known.

Edwin F. Wetzel, an insurance clerk from Chicago, and a teacher from Pennsylvania named (A. L.?) Hoover, were able to carry Winters into the house. A friend of Wetzel's, twenty-one-year-old Boyd L. Spahr, who had been hired to cook for the haying crew, saw a man he didn't recognize running up a coulee in a crouched position over 150 yards distant. While Hoover remained to do what he could for Winters, Wetzel, Spahr, and Joseph D. Steele, tried to reach the barn for horses to ride to Landusky, but a burst of warning shots drove them back to the house.[8]

About 8:30 a.m., after the warning shots had finally stopped, Steele and Alfred Nicolovius saddled up and set out for Landusky. They pulled up at the J. B. Morrison ranch where neighbors John L. Merchant and Jim Thornhill were visiting. This provided a convenient alibi for Thornhill in the shooting of Winters. After alerting authorities in Landusky, Steele and Nicolovius continued north toward Harlem to fetch the nearest doctor, and reportedly caught up with Abe Gill near St. Paul's Mission. Gill instructed Steele to continue on to Harlem for the doctor and to notify authorities, while he and Nicolovius returned to the ranch.[9]

On the other hand, the Fort Benton *Daily River Press* of July 26, states that Gill rode the sixty-six miles from his ranch to Harlem for a doctor, and sent a telegram to Chouteau County Sheriff Tom Clary at Fort Benton.[10] He was the official who had traveled to Kansas City in winter 1900 to identify Lonie Curry's body. By the time Justice of the Peace Guy C. Manning arrived from Landusky, Winters was either dead or near death.[11]

Almost two days later, Stock Inspector Lund and jailer Coatsworth arrived from Fort Benton to investigate the shooting.[12] It was determined the killer (or killers) had fired from behind an old hog pen west of the house, where empty .30-.40 shell casings were found.[13] Also, two sets of footprints were found and followed to a campsite in a thicket of willows and brush along the creek. It showed evidence that two or three men had waited several hours for Winters to present himself. There were hand-rolled cigarette butts on the ground, shod hoof prints of possibly three horses, and many piles of manure. It was speculated that the shooter rode away from the scene, while another person or persons continued firing to give him a head start.[14] The trail of the bushwhackers was followed to the southern boundary of Morrison's ranch, thence to the head of Bull Creek, which runs southwesterly to meet Cow Creek at the Missouri River. Owing to the dry conditions their tracks were soon lost.[15]

An inquest was held at the ranch the same day of the shooting, the verdict being that Winters was killed "by some person or persons unknown to this jury ... [the bullets] being fired from a Winchester rifle or rifles of 30 U.S.G. calibre."[16] Chouteau County offered a $1,000 reward each, dead or alive, and an additional $400 for information leading to the capture of Jim Winters' killers.[17] The Fort Benton *Daily River Press* made it clear in a report the next day that members of the Curry gang were suspected. "The Curry gang and their sympathizers have had it in for Winters ever since the latter killed John Curry about five years ago, an occurrence which was justified by Curry commencing to fire at him with a six-shooter. Curry claimed the Tressler ranch, which Winters had bought and tried to enforce his claim by ordering its owner out of the country."[18] Winters was buried on the ranch across the creek and almost within sight of John Curry's grave. On September 3, 1901, after a thorough investigation that could not connect Kid Curry directly with the killing, the best that a Fort Benton grand jury could come up with was that James Winters was murdered "by a fugitive from justice: and it is, by the same source, alleged that he was one of the parties to said train robbery."[19]

"I have talked to many people who knew the Curry's intimately," stated Little Rockies pioneer Charles W. Duvall in 1940, "and have tried to characterize them from such stories and there are some who say, 'Oh no, Kid Curry never did that. That wasn't the Kid's way.' My findings are that there is not the least doubt that Kid Curry did kill Jim Winter as I have never been able to find any thing courageous or brave about the Curry's. The ambushing of Jim Winter fits them to a T ... They were an overbearing cowardy [*sic*] lot and never brought anything but a bad name to Landusky."[20]

Although the *River Press* stated that "Mr. Winters is known and respected throughout northern Montana as a good and reputable citizen, but has been feared and detested by the rough element that has succeeded in terrorizing that part of the country," he had other enemies. It continued, "During the recent hunt for train robbers the different posses made the Gill & Winters ranch their headquarters and this may have had something to do with the crime."[21] Indeed it could have had something to do with Winters' killing, but possibly not in the way the newspaper intended. In fact notices, purportedly originating in Landusky, had been

James Winters' grave, with ranch house site in the distance. (Author's Collection)

posted in the surrounding area warning anyone who had aided the various posses to leave the country or suffer the consequences.[22]

The residents of the Little Rockies were not happy with the fact that Gill and Winters had invited the augmented Valley County posse to camp on their ranch, while it supposedly scoured the country for the presence of the bandits. More than once, members of the posse rode into Landusky to fill up on whiskey, and then proceed to shoot up the town.[23] "Justice of the Peace Guy Manning issued warrants for their arrest," one writer states. "When Puck Powell and George Bowles, who had taken over Jake's saloon, refused to allow the possemen to shoot up the place, they repaired in a body to Grant McGahn's bar. There McGahn joined his visitors in filling the joint with bullet holes."[24] Outside of town they cut down barbwire fences and rode through the grain fields of Winters' neighbors. One intoxicated manhunter shot a fellow posse member's saddled horse in the brush, having mistaken it for a train robber. Still, Winters allowed the possemen to remain on his ranch, even after some of his neighbors complained of their conduct.[25] According to one account, one neighbor even threatened that "Winters would pay him for the damage done to his property by the posse or get what Johnny Curry got."[26]

As for Abe Gill, "Gill, unlike his partner Jim Winter was thoroughly disliked," Charles Duvall wrote. "He was a man of the highest morals and his character was above reproach, but he tried to impose his beliefs on his friends and neighbors ... After the cold blooded murder of Winter, Gill became more active than ever in his one man drive to down lawlessness. He kept the authorities informed of all lawless acts of his neighbors and his ranch was headquarters for officers of the law when in the Little Rockies."[27] There was also animosity toward Gill ever since he had been appointed a U.S. land commissioner a few years previous. His integrity in administering homestead applications and deeds that divided up what was left of the open range, did not make him popular with the big ranchers.[28]

Pinkerton Detective Charles Siringo received information that Kid Curry visited Jack Ryan in Rawlins, Wyoming, after the Great Northern train robbery, and had cached some of the stolen money on Jim Hanson's

Twenty-mile ranch south of that city.[29] From there he traveled southeast to Dodson, Missouri, and visited his aunt, Mrs. Elizabeth Lee, and his cousin Lizzie. The Pinkerton files list a mid-July time frame for this visit. Does this mean that Curry left Montana after the Great Northern robbery and before the killing of Winters on the 25th? This would all but furnish him an alibi for the murder since he was reported to be spending a great deal of time in Kansas City with a Miss Carrie Hunter, whom he had met seven years previous. During that time she had been married and apparently divorced, and was now employed as a cook in a private home.[30] Of course it is possible, but not really logical, that Curry could have made two trips to Kansas City, killing Winters in between.

Curry and Miss Hunter met up with a man named A. B. Hill, identity unknown, in Kansas City on August 30, 1901. Could A. B. Hill have been an alias for O. C. Hanks? Pinkerton archives indicate that all three, including Bob Lee, went to Cripple Creek, Colorado, and stayed until September 3. However, Lee could not have been with his cousin Harvey, because he was in prison at this time. Curry left Miss Hunter, who probably returned to Kansas City, and traveled to Fort Worth, meeting Ben Kilpatrick and O. C. Hanks at the Maddox Hotel flats on September 7.[31]

The "Logan's Log" Pinkerton document shows that on September 14, Curry was celebrating at Fannie Porter's house in San Antonio. Although not named, Hanks was most likely with him since later events would indicate that he was acquainted with Porter. The log also does not specify that Ben Kilpatrick accompanied them from Fort Worth.[32] Whether it was in Fort Worth or San Antonio, Ben hooked up with Laura Bullion and they began traveling through West Texas visiting his relatives, and her relatives at Lambert's ranch near Douglas, Arizona.[33] Laura's grandparents had recently moved in with their daughter Lucinda, and her husband James W. Lambert (Laura's uncle).[34] Ben's brother Boone was later arrested in Sheffield, Texas, for having some of the stolen banknotes in his possession. The charge was eventually dropped for insufficient evidence.[35]

After Kid Curry had left Annie Rogers at Fort Worth in late December 1900, she visited her mother's home in Kennedale in January of the new year.[36] Possibly for reasons of boredom, the need for money, or both, she would leave home frequently over the following months to spend time at Fannie's house in San Antonio. Finally, she left for Mena, Arkansas, where she had worked previously, and was there in September when she received a message from Fannie that Bob Nevilles was in town asking for her. Annie decided it would be better, if not wiser, for Bob to come to her, so she replied with a telegram saying she "Will wait till parties come."[37]

CHAPTER 21

Caught in the Act

Kid Curry didn't waste any time getting to Mena, Arkansas, to meet his girlfriend Annie Rogers. The short time they were there, they rented a frame house using the names Mr. and Mrs. Bob Nevilles.[1] On September 18 they left for Shreveport, Louisiana, registering for a week's stay at the Serwich Hotel.[2] Their hurried departure from Mena may have had something to do with the imminent arrival of a Pinkerton operative. He may have picked up Curry's trail in San Antonio, or had possibly been alerted to the appearance of Montana bills that the couple was spending. Nevertheless, within a few days the agent was in Mena, canvassing the neighborhood for any leads. One neighbor recognized a photo of Curry as the man he knew to be Bob Nevilles.[3]

During their stay in Shreveport, the couple played cards and drank in various saloons. Curry was generous with his worthless money, and gave Annie a number of ten-dollar bills to spend. Tiring of Shreveport, they traveled to Jackson, Mississippi, and found lodging for a few days near the state capitol. They generally had a good time making the rounds of the saloons.[4] Next, they took the train to Memphis, Tennessee, arriving in late September or early October, according to a Miss Corrine Lewis. She was the proprietress of a red light district "resort" that the couple stayed at for nearly two weeks.[5] They registered as R. T. Moore and wife of St. Joseph, Missouri.[6]

In Memphis it was more of the same. They would patronize houses of prostitution to buy beer and pay for each round with a Bank of Montana bill. Each time they received the change, Annie would hide it in her stocking.[7] Miss Lewis later related her astonishment at the amazing amount of beer the couple could drink, without showing any effects. She also remarked on how Annie was dressed very plainly when she first arrived at her establishment.[8] However, Annie soon remedied that when she subsequently went on a shopping spree. She spent $150 at Edward Hunter's Dry Goods, buying clothing that included a black tailor-made suit and a black hat decorated with black plumes.[9] Annie later estimated that she and Mr. Nevilles unloaded about $300 or $400 of the Montana bills on doing the town and having a good time in Memphis.[10] Annie also had managed to keep $400 for herself, mostly forged money, when they left Memphis on October 10 and headed to Nashville.[11]

Upon arrival in Nashville the next day, they checked into the Linck's Hotel, registering as Mr. and Mrs. R. J. Whalen of Memphis.[12] They occupied room number two for three days and according to testimony from the hotel proprietor at Annie's trial, "the couple stayed largely isolated, took many of their meals in their room and ... used several of the stolen bills during their stay."[13] However, according to Annie, "Nevils preferred barrooms to hotel rooms and continued to stay out late at night."[14] She received more money from her companion, and had accumulated quite a stash, over $500. In Lillie Davis' statement to the Pinkertons she said, "Maudie [Annie] had written to Fannie Porter that she had five hundred dollars, and that she was going to put it in the bank, and Fannie wrote Maudie not to put the money in the bank."[15] Apparently Annie took her advice, deciding to just exchange her wad of tens and twenties for larger bills at the bank to make it easier to carry. This is probably not what Fannie had meant; she may have been warning Annie to stay away from banks altogether owing to the risk of being caught with questionable money.

On Monday afternoon, October 14, with Nevilles out on the town, Annie walked up the steps and entered the Fourth National Bank of Nashville. The *Nashville American* of October 16, 1901, tells what happened next to turn Annie's happy, carefree world upside down.

> Monday afternoon about 2:45 o'clock, just before the close of banking hours a well dressed woman, wearing several rings on her fingers, appeared at the Fourth National Bank. She walked up to the teller's window, and, pulling a big bundle of crisp new bills from her pocket, placed them on the marble slab and requested

that she be given some $100 or $50 bills for the $550 worth of tens she had. ...The teller, Mr. [Spencer] McHenry, thought of the circular ... sent to every bank of prominence in the United States ... and after consulting the paper, arrived at the conclusion that the woman's identity warranted investigation. He engaged her in conversation, stating that he would get the money for her in a few minutes. In the meantime he called up police headquarters and informed the officials of his suspicions. Lieut. Marshall and City Detectives [Jack R.] Dwyer and [Austin] Dickens went immediately to the bank, and after securing possession of some of the bills, placed the woman under arrest. [16]

Before the police arrived, Annie was taken into an office by bank president Samuel J. Keith, accompanied by McHenry and Cashier J. T. Howell, who had determined the bills were forged. They told her the bills she tried to pass were forged, of which she immediately denied any knowledge. She said she had been traveling for about two weeks with a blonde man she had met in Omaha named Charley, and he had given her the bills when they separated in Shreveport. Charley then headed for New Orleans, while Annie traveled to Nashville alone. Annie was briefly questioned again upon arrival of Detectives Dwyer and Dickens, and then taken to the station house to be interviewed by Lieutenant Marshall, the chief of the city detectives. Annie repeated her story about meeting the blonde man, and said she arrived in Nashville alone on Sunday, October 13. She insisted she took no part in forging stolen bills. No matter how they persisted, Annie's interrogators got very little information from her. She did confide that her name was Annie Rogers (later changing it to Maud Williams), she was from Texas, and she had been married to a farmer at one time, but became dissatisfied and left him.[17]

The next day a warrant was sworn out before Justice of the Peace Hiram Vaughn, charging Annie Rogers, alias Maud Williams, for attempting to pass forged bank bills of the National Bank of Montana with the intent to defraud the Fourth National Bank of Nashville.[18] For her immediate future, Annie was housed in a cell on the second floor of

the local police station. Not believing her story that she was in Nashville alone, the police started a search for anyone who may have been
seen with her, and hopefully find more of the stolen bills. Pinkerton
General Superintendent E. S. Gaylor of the Chicago office arrived in
Nashville to help with the investigation at the request of the authorities.
Meanwhile, Annie spent the evening of the 15th contentedly reading a
book.[19]

On Wednesday the 16th, the *Nashville American* reported a description of Annie, and that it was thought she was directly connected with
the gang who robbed the Great Northern near Wagner, Montana, on July

Maud Delia Moore, alias Annie Rogers. (Robert G. McCubbin
Collection)

3, 1901. When a *Nashville Banner* reporter came to interview her on the same day, she was quite cheerful, flirting with him and Detective Dwyer.[20] She also used her charms on a well-known southern photographer named Giers, who took her police mugshot. He was surprised to learn she had once been a secretary as well as a photographer in Texas. She confided that the one thing about photography she did not like was the messy developing process. Giers later stated that he found her pretty, as well as good humored, witty, and well spoken.[21]

However, at her preliminary hearing at 10:00 a.m. on Thursday, October 17, her demeanor had changed to one of defiance. When she appeared before Justice Hiram Vaughn, the newspapers commented on how becoming she looked in her black tailor-made suit and plumed hat. He asked Annie if she pleaded guilty or not guilty to the warrant charging her with attempting to pass forged banknotes. "Guilty of what?" she replied. "Of taking those bills to the bank? I taken them bills to the bank. Yes I did that."[22] The Justice repeated the charge, whereupon Annie pled not guilty. Her bail was set at $10,000, and upon stating she could not give bond, she was remanded to jail. He then asked if she had a statement to make. "Nothing, but I came by those bills honestly, and I don't see why I should be taken and treated this way. I had used some of the bills before, and I thought they were all right. I got them from a gentleman, a little blond man."[23] It was at this moment that she realized the full impact of her legal troubles, and she broke down in tears before the court. The fact that she quickly regained her composure, and refused to admit any wrongdoing, would only last overnight in her cell.

The next day, Annie was ready to make a second, much more revealing statement. She confessed that her real name was Delia Moore, born in Tarrant County, Texas, and she had left home to work as a prostitute. She told of her brief marriage, and going to work for Fannie Porter after leaving her husband. She admitted the story concerning the blonde man named Charley and his going to New Orleans was not the truth. Her traveling companion was named Bob Nevilles, whom she had met in San Antonio in the fall of 1900. Annie even told of her and Nevilles having accompanied Will Casey (Carver) and Lillie Davis to Denver and other points. When asked the occupations of Nevilles and Casey, "she said she didn't know; that they were just good fellows ... said she supposed they had secured their money gambling."[24] Nevilles later joined her in Mena, Arkansas, from where they traveled to Shreveport, then to Memphis, and finally to Nashville, registering under assumed names.

With Annie's statement, detectives were soon able to determine the couple had registered at the Linck's Hotel in Nashville as Mr. and Mrs. R. J. Whalen. When Kid Curry arrived back at the hotel on the day Annie was taken into custody, he waited for her until 11:00 p.m. Thinking she had quit him, he checked out and went to the railway station. He took a midnight train to Birmingham, Alabama, and checked into the Franklin House.[25] Owing to Annie's reticence and false statements during the past few days, the authorities in Nashville were frustrated in their attempt to apprehend her companion. While at the Franklin House one morning, Curry started to rush up the stairs and was startled by someone calling after him, "Where are you going? Wait a minute!" He immediately pulled a gun and pointed it at a man who turned out to be the desk clerk. Curry realized his mistake and quickly made up a story to explain away his strange behavior. "Oh, I am so nervous. My wife has just sued me for divorce up at Nashville, and the least thing agitates me. I thought she was about to cause me some trouble, but you must not mind my actions."[26] Fortunately for Curry, this explanation was accepted by the clerk who had not yet heard of Annie's capture, and had no reason to be suspicious of the well-dressed stranger. However, when the clerk was later shown photographs of the Wagner train robbers, he was surprised to see this man among them.[27] Alerted of Curry's presence in the south by the Nashville police, Alabama authorities soon picked up his trail to Mobile, where it was just as quickly lost.[28]

On Monday, October 21, it was discovered that some of the forged bills had been successfully passed at the American National Bank in Nashville, not noticed until the teller counted his till at the end of the business day. Authorities could only speculate as to whether these bills were circulated by Annie before her capture, or if it meant the presence of more of the Great Northern bandits in the city. To further complicate matters, over the next few days more stolen bills were being spotted by alert bank tellers in New Orleans, St. Louis, Baltimore, and Chicago.[29]

Annie was still being held in the cell at police headquarters, which she much preferred to the county jail. Shunning typical jail food, she ordered her meals from local restaurants.[30] A reporter from the *Nashville American* interviewed her there on the evening of October 25. She would not answer any personal questions, but did state she was wrongfully accused and came by the money honestly, in fact justly. When asked if she had employed a lawyer, she said that she hadn't, but she had talked to a lawyer (Richard West) who had been sent by a person who sympathized with her. The story went on to say, "While the woman would not admit that she had heard from friends with regard to money or the employment of a lawyer she intimated very strongly in an unguarded moment ... that someone would be to her rescue soon."[31] For some reason, the day after Annie's interview, she was escorted to a cell at the county jail by Detectives Dwyer and Dickens. It may have been owing to the fact that she continued to be uncooperative with authorities in their investigations. Coincidentally, on this same day, she retained General W. H. Washington as her attorney.[32]

News of Annie's predicament was eclipsed by an electrifying police chase through the streets of Nashville on Sunday morning, October 27. At about 10:30, a red-faced man of large build entered the Newman & Company dry goods store at 417 North College Street, and presented a twenty-dollar bill in payment for some clothes he had selected. This may have been the same man who had been hanging about the area for the past few weeks. He never gave the same name twice, so the local crooks just called him "Red." He was considered a very desperate man, and thought to be a counterfeiter because of the bills he carried. "He was arrested as a vagrant, fined $10 in the City Court and placed in the workhouse," reported the *Nashville American*. "He was there but a couple of days, when friends came to his rescue and paid him out. It is known that he left town at once, but only a couple of days ago."[33] According to Pinkerton agent Lowell Spence, Kid Curry met with Charley Jones about ten miles outside Nashville around this time.[34] Charley Jones was in fact,

O. C. "Deaf Charley" Hanks, and he was back in Nashville attempting to pass more of the stolen bills.

Clerk Gillock could not make change for the twenty-dollar bill, so Mrs. Newman tried to secure change next door at Harwell's Drugstore. From there she made for the businesses of Charles Zickler's grocery and J. G. Greener & Company, druggists. Zickler looked at the crisp note suspiciously and recognized it as one of the stolen Montana bills. He quickly phoned the police station, which was only two blocks away. Lieutenant Tanksley dispatched Detectives Dwyer and Dickens to the Zickler store, where the groceryman filled them in on the situation at Newman and Company.[35]

When the detectives walked into the store, they saw Hanks leaning against the counter with his back to them. Dwyer walked up to him and asked if he was a stranger in the city. Hanks replied yes, whereupon Dwyer asked his name and where he came from. He quietly said his name was Ferguson, and that he was from Memphis. Dwyer then identi-fied himself and Dickens as officers, and that they were arresting him in regard to the stolen bill. Hanks instantly straightened up, and said, "The hell you will!" At the same time he pushed back his coat and started to pull two pistols. Dwyer grabbed the outlaw's wrists before he could fire his guns. As the two men struggled, Dickens began striking Hanks on the head with his billy club filled with shot. What happened next is best described by the *Nashville American*: "For three minutes the three men struggled in a small space near the front of the store, only a few feet from the stove. In some unaccountable manner the desperado, a man of hercu-lean strength, threw the officers from him and made a sensational dash into College Street."[36] Dwyer later reported that he got off two shots after the fleeing bandit, believing one of them had taken affect.

Hanks ran north on College Street, desperate to find a means of es-cape. He spotted a large, heavy wagon of the Nashville Ice Company on the street, with three men on board. He caught one of the horses by the bridle, ordered the men off the wagon at gunpoint, and then climbed up to the driver's seat. Grabbing the reins and whip, he lashed the horses into a run up the street grade. Dwyer ran after the cumbersome vehicle, quickly outdistancing fellow officer Dickens, but was unable to catch the ice wagon as it increased speed. Dwyer fired several shots at the escaping bandit, hitting the wagon four times, but missing Hanks.[37]

Just up the street, off-duty patrolman W. H. Kiger heard the gunfire, and joined in the chase. He ran up to Dwyer as the latter was asking for the use of William Bransford's horse and buggy. Bransford refused, but they were able to secure a buggy from J. F. Stacey, Superintendent of the Nashville Gas Company, and started after the fugitive. In the meantime, Hanks had just driven across the Cumberland River Bridge at what was, for an ice wagon, breakneck speed, barely avoiding other vehicles in the heavy traffic. At the corner of Bridge Avenue and First Street, the team ran across the sidewalk, knocked down a fire plug, and hit a brick wall. One of the horses fell and fractured its leg in the collision.[38]

Hanks then commandeered a fine horse and buggy owned by coal merchant J. H. Dodson. With Dwyer and Kiger close behind, he raced up Woodland Street to Fourth Street. Hanks continued to Fatherland Avenue, heading in the direction of the river at Ninth Street. Leaving the road he crossed a field to the Davidson Lumber Mill, and passed through an area known as Shelby Bottoms. Suddenly he found his route blocked by a storage yard containing several hundred cedar telephone poles. Without a second thought, he whipped the horse into pulling the buggy over the poles, until he came to a fence. He had time to tear down a section, because the officers' horse became entangled in the poles, and they had to continue the chase on foot. Hanks drove through the opening, exchanged parting shots with Detective Dwyer, and sped on across the country not stopping for any obstructions. Once during his wild ride, the buggy turned over, and he lost no time setting it upright. However, it became evident that his horse was beginning to tire, and soon could not pull the buggy any further. Before Hanks abandoned the buggy, he threw nearly $1,300 of the Montana bills in the air, hoping to delay the officers when they stopped to pick up the money.[39]

Hanks began to run toward the river, through a region called Shelby Park. He soon came up to a horse tied in a field, mounted it bareback, and rode off at a gallop over the remaining few hundred yards to the river.

This is where Dwyer and Kiger had their last glimpse of the fugitive, as he quickly outdistanced any pursuit from the officers. It was another hair-raising ride, jumping over fences, and gullies and ravines from ten to fifteen feet deep. The ride finally came to an end at a wire fence with a thirty-foot gully just beyond. He was last seen on foot entering a thicket near the river. About 200 men, including Police Captain Henry Curran with most of the police force, Sheriff Lewis Hurt with all of his deputies, several constables, and many armed citizens, all converged to search the area and several miles upriver. The search continued throughout the night and the next four days, including the use of bloodhounds, but Hanks had vanished.[40]

The truth concerning his escape was finally learned from a man named J. T. Johnson, who told police of an incident that occurred on Sunday, about 11:00 a.m. He had loaded a skiff with wood that he and his young son had gathered from an island in the Cumberland River, and was rowing upstream, when a stranger hailed them from the east bank. The stranger explained he had got the better of two men in a fight, and wanted to get across the river to escape from a pursuing mob. Johnson noticed the blood on the man's head and face (the result of Detective Dickens' billy club), and concluded he was telling the truth. The stranger was ferried to the west bank of the river, and before entering the thicket along the shore, he tossed a silver dollar to Johnson's son.[41]

At first authorities were sure that the fugitive's identity was "none other than George Parker, alias 'Butch' Cassidy," but by the end of the month, Nashville Police Captain Curran was not so certain.[42] Curran professed that the description could just as easily fit Wild Bunch member, Harry Longabaugh, who authorities believed was in the area.[43] By now the police force was clearly frustrated, and ready to forget the whole ice wagon incident. The November 1 *Nashville American* ran a headline declaring, "Parker Has Gone."[44] The Pinkertons, who had been helping with the search, would later identify the bandit as Charley Hanks.[45]

Although the police were not certain of the bandit's identity, they were sure he was one of the train robbers. To make matters worse, the day after the ice wagon chase, they received a special dispatch from Memphis, informing them that Annie Rogers' companion while in Memphis and Nashville was the notorious Harvey Logan. It had taken some time, but identification was finally ascertained when photographs were shown to Memphis merchants and anyone else who had come in contact with the couple. Memphis Police Captain Mason was able to identify Annie as the woman he had often seen walking by the police station.[46] The Nashville police force had enough troubles trying to apprehend "Parker," let alone a dangerous outlaw such as Harvey Logan, alias Kid Curry.

Ben Kilpatrick and Laura Bullion had also been traveling through the South, and by October were enjoying a carriage ride through the Happy Hollows section of Hot Springs, Arkansas. The prosperous-looking couple was seen by a local reporter who took their photograph. It was published in the November 7 edition of the *St. Louis Daily Globe-Democrat*, in which they were identified as Mr. and Mrs. J. W. Rose.[47] Their next destination was Memphis, Tennessee, where they spent a few days before continuing on by train to St. Louis, Missouri.[48] They arrived in town at the Union Pacific Railroad Station about 7:00 on the morning of November 1, 1901. They registered at the Laclede Hotel near the train depot, as J. W. Rose and wife from Vicksburg, Mississippi. The well-dressed couple was assigned a good room on the third floor. Ben and Laura ordered their meals brought up and rarely left the room for the first few days, which had also been observed of Curry and Annie when in Nashville.[49] They may have spent the time forging the unsigned Montana bills.

In Nashville the next day, November 2, Annie Rogers, alias Maude Williams, alias Mrs. R. J. Whalen, was indicted by the grand jury on eight counts.[50] Also on this day, Kid Curry, uncertain as to how to contact Annie, mailed a letter through a Rosa S. Wilson in Kennedale, Texas. It eventually reached her in the Nashville jail on November 19.[51]

After being cooped up in the hotel room for three days, Ben decided it was time to spend some of the forged banknotes. He went to the Globe Loan Company and bought an expensive watch from broker Max Barnett, using four twenty-dollar bills as payment. Barnett later presented the bills at the Mechanic's National Bank, and teller Victor Jacquemin recognized them as part of the stolen Montana money. He took them to Mr. Austin, the head cashier, who notified Mr. John E. Murphy of the U.S. Secret Service. City detectives, provided with Kilpatrick's description, began questioning businesses in the red light district.[52]

The following day, November 5, Kilpatrick set out alone to tour the town's saloons and brothels, much as Curry had done in Nashville. That evening he was tracked to the parlor of a house of prostitution on Chestnut Street, surrounded by several women. Unlike Hanks, Kilpatrick was not given a chance to resist arrest, as two detectives took him by surprise, pinning his arms to an upholstered chair. When he was searched, the

Ben Kilpatrick prison photo. (Robert G. McCubbin Collection)

police found two revolvers, $400 of the stolen banknotes, and a room key from the Laclede Hotel. He at first refused to answer any questions, but eventually admitted his name was John Arnold. Authorities were quick to identify him as Harvey Logan, alias Kid Curry, then later as Harry Longabaugh, alias the Sundance Kid.[53]

Laura became worried when Ben didn't return to the room that evening. She made the fateful mistake that Curry had not, and that was her decision to wait until morning before leaving the city. Laura was paying her bill to the hotel cashier at about 7:00 the next morning, when several detectives surrounded and arrested her. When she was searched, about $7,500 of the stolen money was found in her valise. After the police searched her hotel room, she was taken to the city jail where Ben was being held, but was not allowed to see him.[54]

The prisoners were interrogated separately by Chief of Detectives William Desmond using the "sweat treatment," and after a couple of days Laura admitted her real identity. She further confessed that she had

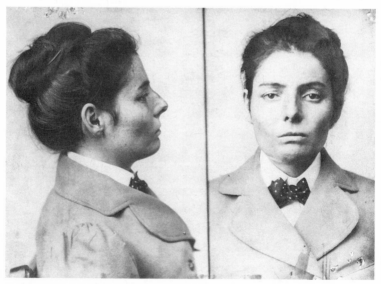

Laura Bullion mug shots. Ben Kilpatrick's devoted girlfriend. (Robert G. Mc-Cubbin Collection)

forged the signatures on some of the money she possessed from the Great Northern train robbery. Ben held out longer, but after several days he became so exhausted from the ceaseless questioning and lack of sleep, he finally gave in and admitted he was Ben Kilpatrick.[55] The November 1901 term of the Federal Grand Jury indicted Ben and Laura on seventeen separate counts of forgery. They were arraigned on November 16, and both pleaded not guilty, to be tried together on December 12, 1901.[56]

The same day Ben and Laura were arraigned, Kid Curry mailed another letter to Annie Rogers, again using Rosa Wilson as a go-between. Fannie Porter also received word from "Bob" (Kid Curry) on November 27, informing her of Annie's imprisonment. Fannie then wrote to Annie promising to help her out as much as possible.[57] Although the exact date is not known, it was most likely also in November when Fannie received a mysterious visitor one night. According to Lillie Davis' statement to the Pinkertons, "She [Fannie] turned down the lights in the hall inside the door and let the man into her own room. I heard considerable weeping and wailing in Fanny's room, and her saying 'Poor Maudie', and blaming Maudie [Annie Rogers] for what she had done. Then Fanny Porter came out of her room, drove all the girls in the house upstairs, turned out the lights in the hall and left the house with the man who was in her room ... Fanny Porter came back that night about 3:00 A.M. alone." Lillie intimates that the man gave Fannie some of the "new Montana bills."[58]

Lillie said one of the girls in the house thought it was Bob Nevilles in disguise; however it was probably O. C. Hanks. He came back in the evening two days later, and Lillie said it was "Bob or Harry on horseback outside. He was dressed in a cowboy suit and on horseback, and said before daylight he would be fifty miles away." It is obvious that Lillie was not very certain about the visitor's identity. Lillie's statement continued: "The last time Bob was at Fannie Porter's house he gave Fannie his diamond ring and Fannie said she was going to pawn it to get money to help Maudie out." Fannie was angry with Lillie for not agreeing to sell her diamond earrings (that Will Carver had bought her), and send the money to Annie's lawyer, General Washington, to help with her bond. Lillie finally loaned Fannie fifteen dollars, and added to the amount Fannie had raised, they were able to send $200.[59]

On December 12, the day of their trial, first Ben and then Laura agreed to plead guilty to just one count of the indictment on advice from their counsel. This was accepted by the court and the other counts were dropped. This was very fortunate for the defendants, since authorities had asked for a fifteen-year sentence for each forged note they had passed. If they were convicted on all counts, and the sentences set to run consecutively, this would most likely have meant life imprisonment. Ben was sentenced to fifteen years in the Ohio State Penitentiary at Columbus, and was transferred to the federal penitentiary at Atlanta, Georgia, in 1905. Laura was given five years, to be served in the Missouri State Penitentiary at Jefferson City.[60]

CHAPTER 22

Kid Curry Captured

id Curry continued to travel through the South, hiding out for a time in late November 1901 in the Unaka Mountains, a rugged region where western North Carolina's border meets southeastern Tennessee. He was accompanied by a native of the area named Sam Adkins (or Atkins), who was wanted for murder in Texas. The two fugitives had become acquainted during the time Curry had been in Texas.[1] Curry also spent some time in early December in Asheville, North Carolina, northeast of the Unakas. He was seen in the company of two men, Luther Brady and Jim Boley.[2] All three of these men would figure importantly in Curry's future during his sojourn in Knoxville, Tennessee.

On Monday, December 9, Curry arrived at the Southern Railway Station in Knoxville from Chattanooga, Tennessee. Two pieces of his baggage were to be sent later on Train No. 36, actually arriving on Thursday the 12th.[3] By Tuesday he had checked into a room at the Central Hotel where he kept two grips, but he made his headquarters for the week at Ike Jones' saloon (known as the Old Central Bar) in the red-light district called the Bowery. Going by the name William Wilson, he was soon seen in the company of two of the better-looking prostitutes in the Bowery, Mayme Edington and Lillian Sartin (or Sartain). He was especially fond of Lillian, spending the nights in her room upstairs over the bar at Ike's place on Central Avenue and Commerce Street. He ate many of his meals at a nearby restaurant run by the wife of Edwin Jackson "Uncle Jack" Harrison.[4]

Curry took the women out on the town, spending his wad of money on expensive food and drinks in the more high-classed establishments on Gay Street, in the city's main business district. He liked to window shop at the stores with glittering Christmas displays. The girls thought him rich and generous with his money, good looking, but rather vain concerning his appearance. At a shooting gallery on Gay Street, he showed off his shooting prowess to Lillian and an approving crowd. He won so many prizes, that the proprietor was compelled to ask him to stop shooting. He spent much of his time during the week at the Central Bar, but also frequented such places as Badgett's Saloon, the Climax Saloon, the Custom House Bar, and the Cumberland Pool Room. Many times he was joined by the two men he met earlier in Asheville, Luther Brady and Jim Boley, along with another local small-time crook named John Whipple.[5]

Curry liked to play pool, always standing treat for the games and drinks. He was described as "a drummer [traveling salesman] type," friendly but not very talkative. He drank apricot brandy exclusively, smoked expensive cigars, and told his fellow pool players that he made his living as "a railroad man."[6] He regularly flashed his money roll of twenty-dollar bills and showed off two revolvers. When full of liquor he would tell people he was "something of a man himself," and boasted of having made three men "bite the dust."[7]

On Wednesday evening, Patrolman William M. Dinwiddie paid a visit to Lillian's room and spoke to Curry about the noise the couple was making. Upon his polite assurance of good behavior, the officer left the room. Dinwiddie later saw Curry at Harrison's restaurant, and also at J. D. Finley's bar where they enjoyed a cigar together.[8] According to Mayme and Lillian, by the end of the week, the man Wilson became quarrelsome, especially when drinking. On Friday night Curry was drinking more than usual and was in a sullen mood. His ill temper frightened the girls so much that they became hysterical.[9] Curry's disposition was probably the result of whatever business he had with Brady and Boley going sour. Curry may have paid the two men to use their connections to exchange the stolen money for good money, and he had realized he was being taken for a ride.

The day before, Curry had gone to the Southern Railway Station to meet the train carrying the rest of his baggage. Witnesses said he was accompanied by a man described as being taller and fairer than Curry. They retrieved the two bags and were seen to remove a few articles before checking them into the station baggage room. They drove off in a buggy together, but nothing more was seen of Curry's companion.[10]

It was about 8:20 p.m. on Friday the 13th when things came to a head between Curry, Brady, and Boley, during a game of pool at the back of the Central Bar. Curry, partnered with John Whipple, played against Brady and an unidentified man. Frank Humphreys (or Humphries), the owner of the billiard table, Jim Boley, and a man named Sterling "Sterl" Stewart, were spectators. Curry looked out of place in the dingy, darkened, malodorous, Bowery "resort." He was wearing a stylish dark brown suit of first quality, the fabric speckled with green or blue thread, and a dark blue crusher hat. He had deposited an expensive black silk-lined overcoat upstairs in Lillian Sartin's room. The pockets contained a silk handkerchief, kid gloves, and silver-rimmed glasses with smoked lenses.[11]

The men were betting on the games, and were clearly intoxicated. As Brady took his turn to shoot, he slipped and knocked the tip off of his cue. He didn't bother to exchange it for another cue, but continued to use it when it was next his turn. Curry objected to this, and he began to trim the ragged end of the cue using his pocket knife. Humphreys, anxious about the abuse of his property, interjected, "Don't cut that stuff up … it's mine." In a menacing mood, Curry stepped up to Humphreys and asked, "What have you got to do with it?" Brady intervened, explaining that the man had only one leg and it was not worth hitting a cripple. Curry relented saying, "He need not be so damned insulting if he is a one-legged man."[12] Willing to forget the altercation, he shook hands with Humphreys, but Brady would not leave it at that. He was obviously spoiling for a fight with Curry, and began to berate him for his behavior. In an effort to contain his temper, Curry walked to the bar to toss down a drink. He then returned to Brady, who said something to Curry in a low voice that could not be heard by any bystanders.[13]

Curry suddenly flew into a rage, grabbed Brady around the throat and pushed him backward into an empty sugar barrel in a corner of the room. Curry continued his stranglehold until Brady's face began to turn red, then purple. Jim Boley rushed over to help his friend, prepared to strike Curry on the head with a cue stick, when some bystanders grabbed his arms. Outside, Patrolman W. M. Dinwiddie, who had become acquainted with Curry earlier in the week, was walking his beat with Patrolman Robert T. Saylor. Upon hearing the commotion from inside Ike Jones' saloon, the two officers forced their way through the crowd to witness Curry choking Brady with one hand, while trying to fend off an attack from Boley with the other. "You'll have to stop that," Saylor shouted at Curry. At the same time Dinwiddie rushed up to Brady to arrest him on outstanding warrants for unlawfully carrying a gun, and shooting someone.[14]

Curry drew a hammerless .38 Smith and Wesson, held it close to his side, and said, "By God, I am here to protect myself," before firing a shot in the direction of Boley. Saylor later stated that the bullet hit Dinwiddie; however Dinwiddie was just as certain that the shot wounded Saylor. Regardless of who was the target, apparently the newspapers were correct in reporting the first shot hit no one. Curry had pulled his gun and fired so fast that witnesses believed he had fired through his pocket. However, a later examination of the coat did not reveal any damage. Saylor, a big and powerful man, then charged into Curry and hit him over the head with his billy. Curry was able to get off a second shot which hit the officer in his right side, ranging downward. Saylor was staggered for a moment, but came at the gunman again. Curry fired a third shot into Saylor's left arm just below the shoulder. When this failed to stop the 250-pound officer, a fourth shot hit Saylor in his left side. This was too much for the big man, and he finally fell to the floor.[15]

During this time Dinwiddie had not been idle, clubbing Curry with his billy whenever there was an opening. After his partner went down, Dinwiddie stepped in and gave Curry such a tremendous blow over his head that the club split lengthwise. As Curry dropped to his knees, Dinwiddie was able to grab Saylor's billy which had fallen to the floor nearby. However, Curry quickly regained his feet to fire his fifth and last bullet into the officer's breastbone, lodging near the neck arteries. Before Dinwiddie went down, he was able to wrench the gun from Curry's hand, ripping the skin of his trigger finger to the bone. Bleeding badly from the gashes on his head, Curry's fuzzy thoughts turned to escape. He staggered to the rear door and managed to vault the porch railing, dropping ten to fifteen feet to First Creek below, without further injury. A number of witnesses to the fight had followed him to the porch, and watched as his stumbling figure was swallowed up by the darkness of night.[16]

Other members of the crowd laid Saylor on the billiard table with a chair supporting his head, while Dinwiddie was placed on the carpet near the door. Someone had telephoned police headquarters to have some doctors sent over as quickly as possible. The first to arrive were Doctors W. S. Nash, J. C. Carter, and C. E. Lones. A. B. Lutrell, Nash's assistant, would also lend a hand. The officers' uniforms were removed in order to treat their wounds, the first priority being to stem the flow of blood. Dinwiddie's shirt contained powder burns from Curry's last shot at close range. His prognosis was good, and after his wounds were dressed he was taken to his home on Grand Avenue. However Saylor wasn't expected to survive his terrible wounds. Even his arm wound was serious, the bone being split to the shoulder.[17]

Deputy Sheriff Charles McCall arrived on the scene with his bloodhounds, and was joined by a number of Knoxville police officers under Lieutenant George W. McIntyre. The fugitive's trail was picked up on the western bank of First Creek behind the saloon. Curry had crossed to the other side, followed the creek to the Tennessee River, and then turned east for a couple of miles to an abandoned barn in East Knoxville. A small pool of blood found on a rock suggested he had sat down to rest for awhile. However, the bloodhounds were not able to pick up his trail beyond this point. Witnesses began to report sightings of a bare-headed man covered with blood. A janitor on his way to work saw the man on Reservoir Hill some time after 8:00 p.m. At about 11:00 p.m. another resident, Nelse Miller, saw the man exit an alley near Mabry Street heading in an eastward direction.[18]

Curry had left his overcoat, hat, and gloves behind when he ran from the saloon, and it wasn't long before a cold, heavy rain began to fall. The temperature dropped to ten degrees above zero, and was expected to reach zero by Saturday morning. Curry later said that at one point he had passed out under a tree, and was awakened by a pouring rain. The police found evidence that he had returned to Knoxville to buy medical supplies, so he could bandage his head. He then hired a hackney in Central Avenue to drive him to the tracks of the Southern Railway. All that night every available police officer searched the buildings and neighborhood houses in the Bowery district.[19]

By daylight Saturday morning a man with a bloody head was seen by several people near Chilhowee Park and Caswell Station in East Knoxville.[20] County officers, dispatched by Sheriff James W. Fox, joined the police as they continued to follow up every lead concerning Curry's whereabouts. It had stopped raining, but the temperature had dropped close to zero during the night. While the search continued without results, Sergeant William "Will" Malone received a phone call at the police station that would soon lead to an explanation of the previous evening's events in the Central Bar. Mr. Will Haynes of Bradley and Haynes Company on Gay Street, described three men who had bought three suits apiece using Montana bills from the Great Northern robbery. The police were well aware of the trio's identities, and decided to pay a visit to the home of John Whipple and Jim Boley. There they found the two men and Luther Brady trying on the suits they had just purchased.[21]

The men denied any knowledge of stolen banknotes, claiming they won the money in pool and poker games with a Mr. Wilson. They were taken to the station, while the police began to investigate reports from other merchants that had received some of the bad money. It was soon discovered the men had used the notes at two other clothing stores, and several saloons in the Bowery. Two merchants had sent some of the money to the bank where it was immediately recognized as stolen. President W. H. Goss of the Knoxville Banking Company notified the police when an employee of the Climax Saloon asked for change from a twenty-dollar note. Brady used one of the twenty-dollar bills to pay an outstanding fine at the court of Squire William Sellers. Ironically, later in the morning the three men were taken before Squire Sellers for a preliminary hearing. They were charged with passing stolen banknotes, and bound over to await trial at circuit court. The three were taken to jail when they could not make bond set at $5,000 each.[22]

Police interviewed residents of the Bowery who related how the man Wilson had frequently flashed a large roll of twenty-dollar bills in saloons and expensive restaurants around the city. One resident disclosed a plan that Brady and friends came up with to rob Wilson. While Brady provoked him into a fight, Boley or Whipple would intervene and relieve Wilson of his bank roll. The police thought this scenario could explain Wilson's choking of Brady, to make him confess where the money was. Further investigation led to the recovery of $3,680 in unsigned twenty-dollar bills that the men had left in the safekeeping of bar owner Dennis Finley.[23]

Later, at Kid Curry's trial, the three would change their story from winning the money at gambling with Wilson, to Whipple finding the fugitive's red wallet on the floor after the saloon fight. Whipple gave the wallet to Boley and Brady, who testified that it contained about $4,000 in new twenty-dollar bills. They removed the money before throwing the wallet into a creek in back of Finley's bar. Brady took $200 or $300, and wrapped the rest of the money in a paper bundle to give to Finley to hold. Further testimony revealed their finding a photo of a man and woman in the wallet, which Brady tore in half and threw away. Boley thought it might have been the same photo as the one of Curry shown to him in court.[24]

There is another possibility that could explain Curry's violent attack on Luther Brady. Assuming that Curry still had possession of his wallet before the fight, what had Brady said or done to cause him to go berserk? Surely not because of the unsportsmanlike conduct of Brady while playing pool. The answer could be that Brady may have already been in possession of the $4,000, given to him by Curry earlier, to exchange for good money using his criminal contacts. It is possible the money came from one of the bags Curry had checked at the railway station. If Brady didn't think his percentage was enough, he may have reneged on the deal. It was learned at the preliminary hearing for Brady, Boley, and Whipple, that Wilson had planned to leave town on Saturday to travel to Kentucky.[25] His actions in the saloon on Friday evening may have been to force Brady to go through with the deal, or to return his money. Conversely, the trio's intention could have been to get Curry in trouble with the police, so that they would be free to spend the money, which is exactly what happened.

With a description of William Wilson, the police believed their city had entertained one of the Great Northern train robbers, who had recently been in Nashville. Knoxville and Nashville newspapers conjectured that the man's identity was Harry Longabaugh or possibly the "Ice Wagon Man," George Parker (actually O. C. Hanks).[26] By Sunday morning, December 15, authorities were following up reports that the man had been seen in several towns within a fifty-mile radius of Knoxville. Sergeant Will Malone and a county deputy checked out a reported sighting twenty miles away in Strawberry Plains.[27] They found nothing, and sightings in Newport and Madisonville also proved to be false.[28] It was difficult to believe the fugitive could have traveled very far with his serious head injuries. The wet and freezing weather and lack of warm clothes just added to his weakened condition.

There was some very good news that morning concerning the conditions of Patrolmen Dinwiddie and Saylor. The men had undergone surgery to remove the bullets that Curry had put into their bodies. Although in considerable pain, especially Saylor, it appeared both men would recover from their wounds. Saylor's condition was so grave that the doctors thought he wouldn't survive the chloroform. He rallied however, and the doctors believed he would survive as long as infection did not set in. He was treated for his high fever, and was given large doses of opium for the severe pain.[29]

As doctors continued to attend the two officers, a man with a bloody bandage on his head was seen around noon in Jefferson City, less than thirty miles northeast of Knoxville. The fact was mentioned to Mr. William B. Carey, a merchant of Jefferson City, who afterwards saw the man walking furtively through an alley. Carey noticed he wore a beat up hat on his bandaged head, and overalls covered with blood. He knew about the search for the wanted man, so he called police headquarters in Knoxville between three and four in the afternoon. Police Chief J. J. Atkins dispatched Lieutenant George W. McIntyre, Sergeant William Malone, and Patrolmen Sid C. Giles and Tom Dewine, on the next train to Jefferson City, which turned out to be about four o'clock.[30]

Carey didn't want to wait around for the police to arrive, so he formed a citizens' posse made up of Frank Rhoton, George Carey, Walter Padgett, James and John Clevenger, and possibly a man named J. Jennings. The posse, armed with shotguns, learned that the fugitive had been seen in the company of another man, assumed to be another one of the train robbers. W. B. Carey and his brother-in-law, Walter Padgett, split from the main body to search for the second man. They came upon him as he followed the railroad tracks into Jefferson City to get something to eat. He was easily captured and held at the depot, giving his name as John Drees. The rest of the posse had struck out to investigate some smoke they had seen rising from thick brush about 250 yards from the depot. They approached cautiously, and came upon a half-frozen man trying to keep warm by a small fire. It was the wanted man known as Wilson, and he was ordered to throw up his hands. Although he said he would not be captured that way, he compromised by extending his arms directly in front of him. He remained calm while being searched for weapons, and appeared resigned to his immediate fate.[31] Curry was quoted as saying, "You didn't give me a chance," to which his captors replied, "You didn't give those Knoxville policemen a chance either." Curry allowed that they had made their point.[32]

The posse started back to the depot with Curry in tow, meeting the train carrying the Knoxville policemen as it pulled into the station. Lieutenant McIntyre ordered Sergeant Malone and Patrolman Giles to take charge of the two prisoners. They were handcuffed and quickly searched again before they boarded the train for Knoxville. Before departing, McIntyre acknowledged that the men of the Jefferson City posse were entitled to the reward, and that William Carey deserved first credit for the capture.[33]

Word of the Bowery shooter's capture reached the city ahead of the train. When the train arrived at the Knoxville station at 6:35 Sunday evening, it was mobbed by over 2,000 curious and excited citizens. They sent up a cheer as Lieutenant McIntyre stepped down with the first prisoner, his clothes and hair covered with dried blood. He wore a tattered hat without a crown, in which he had fashioned some wooden pins to close the opening in the top. The crowd surged around the waiting patrol wagon, necessitating the use of police force to keep a pathway open. People even climbed onto the roof of the nearby Union News Company building to get a better view of the desperado. There was much yelling and cheering as the wagon, loaded with the two prisoners, was started toward the city jail. Someone in the wild throng fired a shot into the air, which surprisingly did not cause much alarm.[34]

A smaller crowd of five or six hundred citizens met the patrol wagon at city hall to see the prisoners escorted to jail. Both prisoners were taken to a room and ordered to strip, so they could be examined for any identifying marks. Their clothes were also given a more thorough search than previously, resulting in the discovery of $2,000 of the Montana bills wrapped in newspaper in one of Curry's inside coat pockets. An old wallet containing an additional $240 of stolen money was also found, along with fifty dollars in good money and two Southern Railway baggage claim checks.[35]

The police wired the Pinkerton Detective Agency in Chicago with the descriptions of both prisoners. A scar from a gunshot wound on Curry's right wrist was very important in verifying his identity. The Pinkertons knew he had received this wound during a shootout with a posse near Lavina, Montana. The gunshot wounds on the prisoner's back added to the certainty that he was Harvey Logan, alias Kid Curry. His description included the fact that he was smooth shaven, and that he had one decayed tooth missing in his lower jaw.[36] Drees' general build, sandy hair, and light complexion, were a close match for Butch Cassidy. Atkins requested that they send an agent to Knoxville who knew the prisoners well enough to identify them. While he waited for a reply to his telegram, the police chief searched through a stack of wanted circulars distributed by the Pinkertons.[37]

Curry and Drees were issued jail clothing and then asked some questions concerning their identities.[38] Curry chose to remain silent, but Drees became talkative, realizing that he was facing something worse than a vagrancy arrest. He stated his name was John C. Drees, an iron moulder from Louisville, Kentucky, who had been working at a local foundry in Knoxville. He had left town on Friday after a drunk, and having no money, walked to Jefferson City. His intention had been to hitch a ride on a train going east to Bristol, Tennessee, before his arrest by the citizens' posse.[39] He told a reporter, "Soon afterward I heard Logan was arrested but knew nothing of him and it aroused no interest in me. I had not seen the man before, never saw him and don't want to see him. I had no connection with him whatever."[40]

They were brought before the court of Squire William Sellers for the swearing of warrants. Curry was served with two felonious assault warrants, one for unlawfully carrying a pistol, and one for being a fugitive from justice, with bond set at $20,000. When the Squire asked Curry to state his name, he said he had none and had never had a name. When an officer asked him how he got the injuries to his head, he said with a smile, "Damned if I know." With no useful information coming from Curry, he and Drees were handcuffed together and transferred to the Knox County jail. A local restaurant sent over an evening meal for the ravenous prisoners. Drees was so nervous he ate very little; however Curry, who hadn't eaten anything for two days, proceeded to do justice to everything on the plate. He enjoyed a cigar after supper, supplied by one of the policemen guarding him.[41]

The severe cuts on the top of Curry's head needed medical attention, one being three inches long and open to the bone. He said he would make do with some warm water to wash his head, but did not object to Dr. C. E. Lones dressing his wounds.[42] The doctor later said, "He has plenty of grit and a bucket of coarse sand to spare."[43] The police officers couldn't help but concur. While Curry's wounds were being treated, the officers began asking questions concerning his identity and the shooting incident in the Central Bar on Friday evening. He said his name was Charles Johnson (perhaps not a coincidence that Johnson was his mother's maiden name), and had lived his first ten years in Chelsea, Iowa.[44] He admitted shooting the patrolmen, but had done so in self defense since they were beating him on the head. (Both of the billy clubs used on him had been splintered.) He spoke briefly of his escape, and of his following the railroad east toward Jefferson City. His brain was addled from the beating, and he recalled waking up under a tree in a pouring rain. His rain-soaked clothing had soon become frozen when the temperature plummeted.[45]

Before the two prisoners were escorted to the jail cell they would be sharing, Sheriff Fox introduced "Charlie" to the employees, reporters, and curious visitors. As Curry waited in the corridor to be let into his cell, one brash reporter thrust his hand through the bars and said, "Good evening, Mr. Longabaugh." Curry looked at the man and coldly said, "I don't know you." The reporter was withdrawing his hand when Curry added, "That is, by that name. My name is Johnson. When you shake hands, be careful and take only three fingers, and don't squeeze my hand. My first finger is very sore." After shaking hands, Curry said good evening to his visitors before being placed in his cell. He pretended not to know how to hang the hammock that had been given him, explaining, "I've never been in jail before." Drees immediately lay down in a corner, while Curry stood there gripping the bars and watched everything going on around him.[46]

During the time the prisoners were being processed and questioned, the police were busy examining the baggage Curry had left in the checkroom at the Southern Railway Station. The two claim checks found in his wallet were presented to the baggagemaster by Lieutenant McIntyre and Patrolman Giles. The first bag the lieutenant opened was an expensive alligator leather grip. Among various toiletries he found a fully loaded, blue-steel single action Colt .45 with a ten-inch barrel. Underneath other personal articles, which included some expensive men's underwear, was found $3,130 of the Montana currency wrapped in part of a *Cincinnati Times-Star* dated December 4. There was also pen and ink used to forge the unsigned notes. The other grip was made of canvas, containing more underwear and several suits with Denver clothing store labels. There was nothing, however, to indicate the identity of the owner of the two bags.[47]

Before this long, eventful Sunday had ended, Chief Atkins received an answer to the telegram he had sent earlier to the Pinkertons in Chicago. "Congratulate you, Harvey Logan is undoubtedly the most desperate murderer, train robber and outlaw in the United States," William Pinkerton had replied. "Partner with him may be O. C. Hanks, alias Deaf Charley or George Parker, alias Butch Cassidy. See photos on our circular. Our representative left here last night for Knoxville."[48] He received another wire from R. A. Pinkerton of the New York office, which stated, "Send you and all concerned hearty congratulations on important arrest made. Logan is one of the worst criminals in the West. He is a leader of train and bank robbers, and as such has no equal. He has committed three murders, and is an expert jail breaker. Suggest that you put guard on him day and night. One of our men en route from Chicago representing the Great Northern Express Company."[49]

CHAPTER 23

Reward and Jurisdiction Squabbles

On the train that carried Curry to Knoxville, W. B. Carey and Walter Padgett, with their attorney Frank Parks (or Park), struck up a deal with Lieutenant McIntyre concerning the reward. They agreed that the men of the Jefferson City posse would split the reward with McIntyre and the other three policemen. When the train reached the city, the agreement that had been drawn up by Parks was signed by Carey and McIntyre, with police Chief Atkins as witness. However, the next day, Monday, December 16, the other members of the Jefferson City posse hired legal representation in the firm of Pickle and Turner. Frank Rhoton and John Clevenger publicly stated that Carey had made the agreement without consulting them, and that they did not agree with the division of the reward. The terms specifically stated that the four officers would divide half of the reward, leaving the other half to divide among the seven posse members. The Jefferson City men argued that the officers had nothing to do with the actual capture of Curry, and therefore did not deserve to receive such a large portion of the reward. Rather, the money should be divided among the sole captors of Curry, and W. B. Carey who saw the fugitive in the alley and initiated the search.[1]

A legal notice, signed by George Carey, Frank Rhoton, J. A. and John Clevenger, and J. Jennings, was served on Sheriff Fox. It essentially notified the sheriff to hold onto Curry, and not surrender him to anyone until the reward was paid to the above parties; otherwise he would be personally held responsible for damages.[2] Later, other claims appeared for a share in the reward or rewards. Two men who deserved it were the wounded patrolmen, Dinwiddie and Saylor; one claimant who did not was Luther Brady.[3]

During the morning of the same day, the *Knoxville Sentinel* sent a photographer to the jail to take Curry's picture. Knowing nothing good could come from it, the veteran outlaw said, "You have got no use for my picture, and I don't care to have any taken."[4] He turned his back to the camera for emphasis, thinking that would put an end to such foolishness. However, someone then made the suggestion that a rear view picture could be taken. This was quickly forgotten after Curry turned his head and gave them such a look of hostility, that they were afraid he would kick the camera to pieces. He settled down when Dr. C. E. Lones visited the jail to stitch and dress his head wounds. He appeared unconcerned with the pain and even joked with the doctor. Meanwhile, the *Sentinel* made another attempt to capture Curry's image by sending an artist to sketch his portrait. Curry was sufficiently distracted by Dr. Lones, that Lloyd Branson, an artist of national repute, was able to complete the portrait. It was an excellent likeness, and was printed on the front page of Monday's issue of the newspaper.[5]

Dr. Lones said Curry's weakened condition was the result of a large quantity of blood loss and exposure to the extremely cold weather. He remarked that his patient's rawboned muscular frame, slightly bowed legs and turned in toes, were the result of a life on horseback. The doctor and reporters assumed that Curry had a good education because he used good, apt language, hardly any slang, and little or no profanity.[6] Curry complimented the doctors concerning their treatment of him, and made efforts to ingratiate himself with the police officers. He gave a fine gold watch to Sergeant Will Malone, and said he would probably not have any need of it for some time. He also gave one of his two expensive rings to Patrolman Sid Giles, explaining that the officers had been kind to him on the train after his capture.[7]

Curry then took the opportunity to request some new shoes, since his had been ruined during his attempted escape. He asked Sheriff Fox to buy him a pair of number 7E Douglas brand shoes, and some number 10 Lisle socks. He did receive some new shoes but not the Douglas brand, as it was commonly known their manufacture incorporated a steel shank which could be made into a file or saw. Also the particular brand of socks could be unraveled for the purpose of making a rope.[8]

Later in the day, authorities learned that Lowell Spence, the Pinkerton agent due to arrive at 5:55 p.m. from Chicago, would not reach Knoxville until Tuesday because of a wreck on the Cincinnati Southern.[9] However, Tuesday brought plenty of activity at the jail, as hundreds of people stood in line for a chance to gape at the prisoner who had been getting so much press. They would pause in groups of four to six at his cell to just look or say a few words. It wasn't only the men who were curious to see "Charles Johnson," as many inquisitive women also took a place in line. He joked with his visitors, calling out to one group, "Right this way boys, ten cents a peep." People began to leave dimes on his cell railing, which Curry accepted for a short time. But he soon put a stop to it, saying that he had enough money for his needs.[10]

Lowell Spence finally arrived in the city at about 8:00 a.m. on the delayed southbound train. He checked into the Hotel Imperial and immediately found his way to the dining room for breakfast. Afterwards, he met Chief Atkins and Sheriff Fox in the lobby and accompanied them to the jail. All visitors were cleared from the cell area except for a few reporters. The prisoners had been let into the inner corridor between the two cell rows and were milling about. Fox called for Charlie Johnson, and as Curry came forward to grip the bars, Spence whispered to the sheriff, "He's the man." The detective asked the prisoner, "Would you mind showing me your arms?" Curry assented, but those present noticed it was with some trepidation. Spence saw what he was looking for, a scar from a gunshot wound on the man's right wrist. When Curry was given permission to go, Spence assured the sheriff that "He is, beyond doubt, Logan."[11]

Spence also looked at John Drees, the man who had been captured with Curry. After a careful examination, the detective announced that he didn't know the man, and was sure he was not one of the Great Northern robbers. Spence then had Curry called over to the bars again to ask, "Is there anything I can do for you?"

Curry replied, "Not that I know of, unless you have a cigar about you."

"I have none, but will send you down some when I go uptown," said the Pinkerton man.

"I will be obliged," Curry responded.[12]

Before departing, Spence congratulated the authorities on their capture of the notorious Harvey Logan. He added that they were lucky the policemen had not been killed, since he considered Logan to be much more prone to violence than his associate Parker (actually O. C. Hanks).[13] He then went to the telegraph office to wire his superiors in Chicago and the Great Northern Express Company that the man in jail was Harvey Logan, and that over $9,000 of the Montana bills had been recovered.[14] This amount, added to what had been recovered in St. Louis and Nashville, totaled close to $19,000.[15] This approached half of all the money stolen, and the express company was understandably pleased. Chief Atkins received a complimentary telegram from D. S. Elliott, the company's general manager, congratulating him for Logan's capture.[16] Spence next went to city hall to examine the two bags Curry had checked at the train station. He found several items that had not been noted in the original list by Lieutenant McIntyre, including Annie Rogers' telegram from Mena, Arkansas, to Miss Fannie Porter in San Antonio, Texas, that stated, "Will wait till parties come." News clippings from two St. Louis papers pertaining to Ben Kilpatrick's arrest, and the Fort Worth Five photo were also found.[17]

In the afternoon, Spence and McIntyre, along with Sergeant Malone and Patrolman Dewine, went to visit Curry at the jail. He denied ownership of the bags at first, but later changed his mind for want of some of his clothes.[18] He joked with McIntyre when he glimpsed the Colt .45 from one of the grips, saying, "I don't believe I will need that in here."[19] Curry was pleased when Spence gave him the supply of cigars he had promised earlier, and someone handed him a glass of whiskey.[20] He was in high spirits when he spotted Luther Brady mingling with other prisoners in the jail corridor and asked, "Did I hurt you?" When Brady answered to the negative, Curry said, "Well, I'm glad of it."[21] The authorities did not think Curry's concern for Brady was heartfelt, so the latter was soon moved to another floor in the jail to prevent any trouble between the two.

Curry's head injuries began to worsen and it was evident he was in much pain. Dr. Lones, assisted by Dr. Nash, dressed his wounds again. He wasn't getting much sleep, and he requested a soft pillow to help ease the pressure on his head.[22] The pain and discomfort tended to make him even more bad-tempered and uncooperative than usual. Unfortunately, Fox and Spence made another attempt to get Curry to sit for a photograph. The Sheriff tried to persuade him to allow for a picture, but he would have none of it, and kept his face covered with his hand. "It's customary to take pictures of all criminals when arrested," Spence explained, "and we will get yours sooner or later." "Well, you won't get mine," Curry replied with finality.[23]

Curry's preliminary hearing was held at the jail the next afternoon, Wednesday, December 18, with Squire Sellers presiding. He had hired city attorney and chairman of the election commission, Reuben L. Cates, to represent him. Cates would soon come under fire from the newspapers questioning why a city attorney was defending someone who had violated city ordinances when it was his duty to prosecute him. While the contents of Curry's bags were on view, Sellers began asking him a number of questions. No doubt owing to legal counsel he had become reticent, and at one point said he would do his talking at his trial. In answer to questions concerning his family, he said his parents and siblings were living, but he wouldn't say where.[24] A continuance was agreed upon until Saturday, December 28, one reason being that policemen Dinwiddie and Saylor had not sufficiently recovered from their wounds to attend the hearing. The cause of much of the delay in his case was in determining whether Curry should be tried in state or federal court. Needless to say, Curry could not make his $20,000 bond and remained in jail.[25]

After Curry's identity had been confirmed, the number of visitors he received increased from hundreds to thousands during the rest of the week and into the next. He said he didn't mind the people who would converse with him, but he lost patience with those who would "just stand there with their eyes sticking out of their heads so you could knock them off with a stick."[26] The day after his preliminary hearing, Curry was honored by a fifteen-minute chat with Governor Benton McMillin of

Tennessee. He had taken care to bathe and shave before the governor's arrival at the jail. They joked about various subjects including the chase of the ice wagon bandit in Nashville.[27] Curry was impressed with the governor, and one newspaper reported, "The prisoner himself is a Democrat and he seemed pleased to learn that the governor was of the same political faith."[28]

A visitor Curry was not pleased to receive on Friday, December 20, was a Pinkerton superintendent named Andrew Irle. He had come to verify Spence's identification of the outlaw, and to discuss with authorities where Curry should stand trial. When Curry realized the reason for the stranger's visit, he lay down in his hammock and hid his face with a newspaper. However, Irle was able to confirm without a doubt that the so-called Charles Johnson was Harvey Logan, the infamous Kid Curry. A reporter described him as more noted, more daring a desperado than Jesse James. Irle also looked at John Drees, and concurred with Spence that he was not a member of the gang of train robbers.[29]

One visitor Curry particularly enjoyed was a constable from Cocke County, just east of Knoxville. James Horan recites an account from a *Knoxville Sentinel* reporter who had witnessed the visit:

> He [the constable] did not say how long he had been an official but his experience with criminals had not been extensive … Jailor Bell took the constable to the cell and Watchman Clark introduced him to Logan who said he was delighted to meet him.
>
> "I'm sure glad I didn't meet you on the outside," smiled Logan who saw at a glance what he was up against.
>
> The constable was somewhat embarrassed but his mountain nature soon overcame him.
>
> "I 'spect it better ye didn't," he replied in much the same tone and showed in a moment that he could "give and take" as they say in the mountains …
>
> "Have you made many arrests?" asked Logan.
>
> "Yes, a few but I have studied the business a heap."

"You'll find that's the safest part of your business," Logan said solemnly.

"How's that?"

"I say the studying part is the safest."

The constable laughed and Logan fairly roared.

When they shook hands Logan told him:

"You just keep on studying. Don't be in a hurry to gradu-ate and be careful when you go and put your detective edu-cation into practice, for some farmer might beat you with a cornstalk."[30]

Sheriff Fox sharply curtailed the number of visitors soon after Curry received a suspicious letter on Saturday, the day after Irle's visit. The authorities had read the letter and passed it on to the prisoner, without revealing its contents. His reply was printed as a public notice in the *Journal and Tribune* on the 23rd: "Charlie Johnson, prisoner at the jail, received an important message from a friend in Knoxville, and would ask this friend to come and see him and give further particulars about the matter referred to in the letter."[31] There was speculation that the letter may have contained a plan of escape, and it was rumored that Curry's friends would attempt to free him some time on Christmas. Conse-quently, a man did soon visit Curry at the jail, who was later described as tall with red hair and beard. After the stranger had left, one of the door locks showed signs of tampering in order to learn its combination.[32]

Nothing came of the incident at the jail, and Curry enjoyed a fine Christmas dinner of turkey and sweet potatoes. He was also given cake, candy, fruit, and nuts from his many male and female admirers of Knoxville.[33] Fellow prisoner John Drees had finally been released on Christmas Eve on a writ of habeas corpus.[34] Shortly before the new year, Curry received a love letter in a scented pink envelope mailed from out of town.[35] Annie Rogers was no doubt aware of his incarceration, and it may have been she who sent the letter. In fact, Lowell Spence firmly believed Annie had received funds from Curry to help pay her attorney, General Washington. In addition, a few days after her arrest, a Nashville cigar salesman named Morgan Roop came to her rescue. Mr. Roop felt Annie was being subjected to unfair, if not unlawful, treatment by the police, so he hired attorney Richard West to represent her.[36]

By the time of Curry's preliminary hearing continuation on Saturday, December 28, four more warrants had been sworn against him. Added to the original four, he now had a total of eight state warrants, which included an assault and battery charge on Luther Brady.[37] Meanwhile, Curry had been in contact with his good Montana friend, Jim Thornhill, who had sent money for his defense. Curry used it to hire additional legal talent, Charles T. Cates, Jr., and former Republican state senator John C. Houk. Houk was the only experienced criminal lawyer of the three on the team; however Reuben Cates and his cousin Charles wielded powerful political clout in the county and state. Charles Cates was a particularly close friend to Sheriff Fox and Circuit Court Judge Joseph Sneed.[38] Curry's attorneys would use this influence to full effect in the debate over jurisdiction in this case.

The defense wanted the case tried in state court, arguing that Curry would not get a fair trial in federal court. His lawyers maintained that those favoring federal prosecution were motivated by the reward that would be paid out. Their contention was that the Great Northern Express Company was more apt to pay the reward for a federal conviction, as had been the case with Ben Kilpatrick. Furthermore, the testimony of witnesses who would appear against Curry could be influenced by a chance of receiving a share in the reward. Also, there were those who wanted to see Curry punished for the shooting of the police officers, which would not be possible in federal court.[39]

In addition to the express company, those who sided with the federal authorities were the Pinkerton Agency and the Knoxville police department. The prosecution believed that if Curry was convicted in federal court for the passing of stolen and forged banknotes, he would receive a stiffer sentence. The federal authorities went to the jail where the hearing was again set to take place, and tried to serve warrants on Curry. Under orders from Sheriff Fox, the jailer Thomas Bell denied them access.[40] He also refused admittance to three police officers who showed up and asked to have Curry released into their custody. Sheriff Fox later backed up his jailer's actions, and Charles Cates defended the sheriff for doing his duty under the law. Meanwhile, Curry's attorneys were informed that the magistrate had no intention of attending a hearing at the jail.[41] However, they were able to delay their client's first court appearance until the next meeting of the circuit court in February 1902, with Judge Sneed presiding.[42]

Curry spent the slow month of January 1902 playing solitaire, reading novels, and perusing the daily newspapers for stories about himself. He was careful to shave and comb his hair every day, and sometimes put on a neat pink shirt. For exercise he often played football in the corridor with the other inmates using a ball made of rags. He was also considered excellent at wrestling and boxing.[43] He continued to receive visitors, including U.S. Marshal Frank Hadsell, who had chased Curry after the Wilcox and Tipton train robberies, and Union Pacific Railroad Chief Detective William T. Canada. They were traveling to Alabama on business and stopped in Knoxville for a look at the man who had eluded them.[44] Curry's popularity in Knoxville continued; someone even used Harvey Logan's name as a write-in for mayor of Knoxville during the city elections. However, he received only one vote.[45]

The state grand jury convened on January 21 and found three indictments against Curry: two for felonious assault with the intent to commit murder in the first degree on Dinwiddie and Saylor, and the third for assault and battery on Luther Brady. But Curry was not present, and would not be taken from his jail cell for a hearing until almost mid-February.[46]

As January came to a close, the *Knoxville Sentinel* interviewed Patrolmen Dinwiddie and Saylor, who continued to convalesce. Both of them preferred Curry to be tried in federal court so that he would be given a heavy sentence. Surprisingly, Dinwiddie said he had no malice toward Curry, and that they had become friends before the shooting. Saylor's wounds still caused him much suffering, but he continued to slowly improve.[47] The two policemen were still not well enough to appear at the term of circuit court on February 11. For that reason Judge Sneed granted a continuation in Curry's case until the next term of court in

May. The prosecution made a motion requesting permission for federal authorities to serve warrants against the prisoner. The judge explained he did not want to surrender state's authority, so he denied the motion.[48]

Sheriff Fox began to tighten security at the jail owing to repeated warnings from the Pinkertons and the federal authorities concerning Curry's desperate nature. The sheriff placed a restriction on visitors which included refusing admittance to citizens who had been supplying the prisoner with home cooked meals. It was reported that Curry became quite upset that his source of good dinners had been stopped.[49] Since Curry's trial was to be delayed for at least three months, Lowell Spence returned to his Pinkerton office in Chicago. Spence's offer to pay the cost of a special guard over Curry had been refused by Sheriff Fox. When the agent had left the city, however, the sheriff did hire a guard, paid for by the Great Northern Express Company.[50]

As the month of March arrived, the federal authorities determined to make their move concerning Curry's participation in the Great Northern train robbery. Patrolman W. M. Dinwiddie, Luther Brady, Jim Boley, Lillian Sartin, and Mayme Edington were subpoenaed to appear as witnesses before the federal grand jury on the twelfth of the month. The attorney general stated that it was not the intent of the federal government to interfere with the state courts. Admitting that the state courts had jurisdiction in the case, he said the move was made so that the government would be ready to take over if the prisoner was acquitted. State authorities did not object, as long as they got first crack at Curry.[51] The U.S. Court opened with Judge C. D. Clark presiding, resulting in a true bill found against Harvey Logan for passing stolen and forged notes. Thus, as the newspapers pointed out, the legal strategy to stall Curry's case in the state courts for a lighter sentence had backfired. After serving a sentence in state prison, he would have to face federal charges and the likelihood of another sentence in federal prison.[52]

No doubt owing to Curry's latest legal entanglements and his long confinement, it was reported that Curry was disposed at times to be sullen and morose. There were periods when he refused to talk or mingle with the other prisoners. He kept in good physical condition in case an opportunity presented itself for escape. He would run around his cell and climb the bars, and continued to participate in the ball games conducted in the corridor.[53]

One day in April, Curry learned that Joshua and Moultrie Jones were being housed in the Knox County jail for murder charges. From reading the local newspapers he knew they were the brothers of Ole Bull Jones, one of the best solo violinists in the country. He soon sent an invitation to Moultrie, who also played violin, to visit him in his cell. When Moultrie showed up with his instrument, he was surprised to learn that Curry was a knowledgeable music enthusiast. The other prisoners in the cellblock were amazed when he expounded on the works of the great composers. He was delighted when Moultrie played some classical music, and when the violinist struck up a reel Curry broke into effusive laughter.[54]

CHAPTER 24

A Violent Affray at Flo's

fter his miraculous escape from Nashville authorities in late October 1901, Orlando Camillo Hanks headed to his native state of Texas. On the way, he stopped long enough in Little Rock, Arkansas, to buy a pair of spectacles.[1] Hanks was probably the mysterious visitor that Fannie Porter received in her room one night in November, telling her of Annie Rogers' arrest. He was no doubt well aware of Kid Curry's urgency in getting Annie some help. However, a visit to his mother and brother near Abilene, Texas, may have taken priority over San Antonio. His mother, Mrs. Laura A. Cox, later made a sworn statement that she had last seen her son Camillo "in the early part of November, 1901, when we were together for several days."[2]

Mrs. Cox also stated that Camillo had told her of receiving nearly $11,000 for his share of the Great Northern train robbery, and that he had buried about $5,000 of the loot on her son Wyatt's ranch in Callahan County. Wyatt later told her that, before leaving the ranch for good, Camillo dug up the buried money and took it with him.[3] His mother and brother were worried that something bad would happen to him, so it was decided to write his brother Wyatt's name in ink on the label of O. C.' s coat. The label read: "O'Dowd [the maker], Little Rock, Arkansas. Mr. Wyatt Hanks, Oct. 1901."[4]

The whereabouts of Hanks is uncertain for the next few months. Some sources indicate he traveled to Calaveras County, California, spending time carousing and brawling in the saloons before returning to Texas.[5] However, he reappeared in Texas from the east by way of Longview, and then traveled south to Beaumont where he bought a second pair of spectacles.[6] It was reported that he was seen boarding a train at Flatonia on about April 10, 1902, headed west to San Antonio. He was remembered because of a pistol he was carrying.[7]

247

DeWitt County Sheriff Thomas M. Stell, an old schoolmate of Hanks, estimated the outlaw's arrival in San Antonio as late March or early April 1902. He checked into a boarding house, regularly keeping to his room during the day and reading newspapers. The landlady observed his habit of going out in the evening after supper, and returning no later than 10:00.[8] Unfortunately for him, he decided to change his routine on Tuesday night, the 15th of April. Instead of returning to his room, at around 10:00 p.m. he entered Flo Williams' "resort" at the corner of South Laredo and West Nuevo streets and began to drink. A few hours later he became loud and obnoxious, bragging to Flo and the saloon girls that he had recently served time in prison for murder. The women became frightened when he displayed two pistols, a Colt .45 six-shooter and a .38 double-action revolver, the latter having a sawed-off barrel protruding only half an inch from the cylinder. This was to make it extremely difficult for someone to grab the gun from his hand in a close encounter.[9]

By now it was early Wednesday morning, sometime between 1:00 and 2:00, and Flo decided it was time to notify the police. She sent her bartender, W. T. Souter, who soon located three officers at the Chapa & Driess drugstore just down the street. Policeman Frank Harvey entered the room first, followed by mounted officer Pink Taylor and policeman D. E. Hughes. Souter pointed out Hanks, and the officers were almost upon him before he rose from his seat and fired a shot into Harvey's midsection. The bullet was stopped by the policeman's large belt buckle, saving him from serious injury or death. Hughes and Harvey grabbed Hanks to stop him from getting off another shot.[10]

Hanks had used his .38 double-action revolver to shoot Harvey, but in his excitement he had not thought to release the trigger for another shot. He just kept pulling harder on the trigger as he struggled with the officers. This gave Taylor the opportunity to step forward and shoot Hanks twice in the left breast, the bullets passing through the aorta. A third shot went through the top of his head and exited behind his right ear. Needless to say, he died instantly, all three shots being fatal. Harvey's left eye received powder burns from the closeness of Taylor's first shot.[11]

A search of Hanks' clothes turned up a wallet containing $100, as well as a second wallet containing $240. In addition, the officers found sixty-five dollars stuffed in his socks, and cases for his two pairs of spectacles were in his pockets. It was soon determined that the money was part of the Montana loot stolen in the Great Northern train robbery.[12] His body was then taken to the undertakers, Zizik & Shelly. The only identification that could be found was his brother Wyatt's name written on the label of his coat. Addison Kilgore, a former sheriff of DeWitt County, happened to be in town at the time. He identified the dead man as Wyatt Hanks, having arrested him a few years earlier for horse theft. Others in town believed it was a man they had seen around DeWitt County they knew as Charley Hanks.[13]

The next day, Thursday, Detective John Womack and U.S. Deputy Marshal Fred Lancaster were on hand with a Pinkerton circular for O. C. Hanks. The description on the wanted poster matched closely with the body laid out at the morgue. Hanks' boyhood friend, Sheriff Thomas Stell, had been notified, arriving on Friday from Cuero. He had brought a cousin of Hanks to help with the identification. They viewed the body at the morgue and both agreed it was that of Camillo Hanks. Hanks' mother and her nephew Lewis Burns were in San Antonio on Saturday to confirm identification. Mrs. Cox said it was her boy, Camillo, and Burns made a sworn statement saying he believed the body was that of his first cousin Camillo Hanks.[14]

His burial was delayed for five days per a request from D. S. Elliott of the Great Northern Express Company. A detective was on his way from Denver, as well as the express messenger at the Wagner train robbery, C. H. Smith, to verify identification. After agreeing to the delay of her son's burial, Hanks' mother and her nephew took the Saturday afternoon train to Cuero.[15] Lowell Spence arrived the next evening and verified the body was that of the man who had escaped authorities in Nashville, confirming that the ice wagon bandit was O. C. Hanks instead of George Parker.[16] When Smith looked upon the body a few days later, he could not state positively that the dead man was one of the train robbers. However, the express company was apparently satisfied it was

Hanks, because the body was released for burial.[17] Thousands of people had viewed his body while it lay wrapped in a white sheet at the morgue. But except for Addison Kilgore and his son, who represented the family, there were no mourners or religious services at his burial in the City Cemetery at 10:00 a.m. on April 24, 1902.[18]

When Harvey "Kid Curry" Logan received news of the killing of his train robbing associate, O. C. "Deaf Charley" Hanks, he was outwardly unconcerned.[19] But he would soon receive more unwelcome news that would begin to chip away at his resolve. His traveling companion, Annie Rogers, appeared in criminal court on April 21 to request her bail be reduced from $10,000 to $1,000. With Curry and Fannie Porter contributing what they could, it was all the money she could realistically raise. Sitting with her attorneys Washington and West, holding a white handkerchief in one hand and wearing a black kid glove on the other, Annie faced Judge W. M. Hart. She showed a marked deterioration in her physical and mental condition from spending six months in the Davidson County jail. Her cheeks were sunken and she appeared sad, tired, and strained. In spite of this, she was reported to have been well dressed, with particular emphasis placed on her ostrich-plumed black picture hat.[20]

The prosecution, Attorney General Hiram Vaughn, called two witnesses to testify during the first day of the hearing. The first witness was Spencer McHenry, the astute bank teller who had recognized that the bills in Annie's possession were from the Great Northern train robbery. The second witness was express messenger C. H. Smith, who described the robbery in detail. He was positive the man he had seen in the Knoxville jail was the robber who had blown the safe. He also identified him as the same man when shown a photograph of Curry taken with Annie in Denver. After Smith's testimony, court was adjourned until the next day.[21]

Annie seemed in better spirits at the beginning of her second day in court. She smiled, chatted, and laughed with the people around her. But as the witnesses appeared against her, she became anxious and disconcerted. Pinkerton Detective Lowell Spence's testimony was especially damaging to her case. He confirmed that the man standing next to Annie in the photograph was Harvey Logan. The detective also testified that a portrait of Annie had been found in the gold watch Curry had given away at the time of his arrest. General Vaughn stated, in the context of these photographs, there was proof enough of a long-term intimate relationship between Annie and Curry.[22]

When it was the defense's turn, General Washington began by calling Lieutenant Marshall who had taken Annie's statement after her arrest. He pressured the officer into admitting that Annie had not been advised of her right to have an attorney present during questioning. Moreover, he accused the police of actively preventing her from employing counsel, and that they had interrogated her using the "sweatbox" treatment.[23] Under cross examination by Vaughn, it was learned that Annie professed to know the man in the photograph as Bob Nevilles, not Harvey Logan. She admitted to being a prostitute, and that her trip through the south with Nevilles had started in Arkansas. She also claimed her companion never told her where his money came from.[24]

Nothing was to be decided this day concerning Annie's bond reduction, as General Vaughn informed the court that several of the state's witnesses were not present. Since they were expected in a few days, court was adjourned, and scheduled to resume on Monday, April 28. When the witnesses did not show up in court that day, Judge Hart made the decision to reduce her bail to $2,500. This was still an amount that she and her supporters could not possibly raise. This ended her hope for freedom anytime soon, and a tearful Annie was escorted back to her cell.[25] It would be another month and a half before her trial would commence.

Curry's own confinement was taking its toll on his body and frame of mind. He tried to stay fit with daily exercise, but his once stocky frame had been reduced by about twenty pounds. He continued to read books and newspapers to occupy the long hours of idle time, but his spirits were flagging. When Curry read of Annie's plight in the Knoxville papers, it affected him deeply and he could no longer maintain his resolve.[26] Concerning the pair's relationship, one writer may have said it best: "Some have suggested that her relationship with Curry was one of convenience since she was a woman whose loyalties drifted toward the biggest bankroll. But it would be a mistake to assume there was no affection between these two social misfits … They apparently hit it off from the start. Yes, she loved for money and Curry could be a savage outlaw with a hair trigger, but there was substance to their unconventional relationship, as strange and unorthodox as it was …

"Annie was one of the few stable influences in Curry's reckless, troubled young life. She calmed him and he must have loved her for it. At times, Curry could be moody and sullen, if not a bit angry, but Annie knew when to leave him alone and when to talk … she was one of the few real relationships he had."[27]

D. S. Elliott, of the Great Northern Express Company, had been continually warning Knoxville authorities to watch Curry closely in order to foil any escape attempt. Sheriff Fox received Elliott's latest letter on Friday, April 25, which was printed in a Knoxville newspaper the following Sunday. In the first paragraph he stated that "The death of Hanks, from which Logan has no doubt expected aid, will rather tend to increase Logan's desperation and he will make an effort to get away before his trial." It ended with the warning, "If this man is allowed any freedom whatever or is not carefully watched at all times he will manage to get away as sure as the world."[28]

It was also on Friday that Curry decided to give vent to his feelings of desperation, frustration, and helplessness. In the afternoon he threw a bucket of cold water on Samuel Calloway, a guard he disliked. He then punched out all the windows he could reach with a broom he had been given to sweep out his cell. "He tore out the lighting apparatus and, seizing the massive door to his cell, he began to swing back and forth on its hinges, thus making an unbearable noise and yelling like a Comanche Indian." He kept up the disturbance for more than an hour, after which he decided to go to sleep for the night. In the morning he seemed to have forgotten his outburst of the previous night, and "was given a breakfast of beef, biscuits, coffee and sweet milk. He had no more than partaken of his meal than he began the din. He would strike his door and the bars with the hickory broomstick, making a dreadful noise, and then would give vent to an awful yell." He would intersperse his ranting by singing songs about life on the plains. One of them ended with a line that would come uncannily close to predicting Curry's future: "In the saddle of my favorite broncho I will die."[29]

Curry continued his outrageous behavior through the weekend, but by the following Monday morning he appeared to have finally settled down. Curry blamed his tirade on the poor quality of food and other jail conditions. This explanation did nothing to appease Sheriff Fox; he had had enough of Curry's antics. Acting on Elliott's advice, the sheriff immediately took away Curry's freedom and other privileges. He was confined to his locked cell and not allowed use of the corridor. His interaction with the other prisoners was stopped when they were removed from his floor. He was not allowed visitors, and was kept under watch twenty-four-hours a day.[30] Reporters were apparently exempt from Curry's visitor restriction, because a few days after his tantrums had ceased, they recorded an apology of sorts. He said he had wanted to break the monotony of his confinement with a little fun, and was sorry to have caused anyone worry.[31] He offered whiskey to the carpenter, Burrell Badgett, who came to repair the broken windows.[32]

Curry's old friend and partner, Jim Thornhill, wrote attorney Reuben Cates on April 22, inquiring when the trial was to be held and what were the chances of acquittal. He requested that Curry write him to let him know if he could do anything. Thornhill had been providing funds to help with Curry's legal defense. Curry replied to Thornhill on May 11 telling him he needed more money, "as Much as $1000" if his case was continued until the next term of court. He told his friend to only send what he could if he was not "Fixed for Ready Cash."[33]

On May 13, Curry was given the chance to aid Annie as a witness in her defense. Her lawyer, Richard West, accompanied by Davidson County Assistant District Attorney G. B. Kirkpatrick, had come to Knoxville to get a sworn statement from Curry. Also present were Curry's attorney John Houk, Sheriff Fox, two deputies, and a court stenographer. The resultant thirty-five-page deposition made it apparent it was his intention to absolve Annie of any knowledge of the train robbery or where the money had come from. He admitted he was pictured in the now famous Fort Worth Five photograph. He told of meeting Annie in San Antonio, and traveling with her through much of the western and southern states. He admitted having given her money frequently, but would not say how it had come to be in his possession. In order to help Annie, Curry was being cooperative and honest for the most part. However, he would not answer any questions that would jeopardize his own case, especially concerning his role in acquiring the Montana bills.[34]

Curry was not present during the May term of court, his attorneys having succeeded in moving the date forward to Tuesday, June 3.[35] This gave him plenty of idle time to tell his guards about a trip he had taken to France, which just happened to be at the time of the Great Northern train robbery. Knowing that the newspapers would pick up on the story, it was his attempt to establish an alibi.[36] When Curry was escorted into the packed courtroom in June, he was noticeably thin and pale. He told reporters that without any chance of exercise, life in jail was killing him.[37] Assistant Attorney General John R. Holloway of the prosecution made a motion to allow federal warrants to be served on Curry. The judge did not accept the motion and overruled.[38] The defense then asked for a continuance in regard to the felonious assault cases. Initially Judge Sneed overruled this request, but when it was found that the state's witnesses were not in court, he ordered the case to be continued until the September term of court.[39]

When Curry was returned to his cell, he continued to pass the days scanning the newspapers for any information pertaining to Annie's upcoming trial. He couldn't have failed to notice a *Knoxville Sentinel* story of June 11 that reported the arrest of Wyatt Hanks and two others in the Abilene, Texas, area. It stated that the men were charged with passing some of the Montana bills.[40] Wyatt may have lied to his mother about Camillo coming back for the $5,000 buried on his ranch; or Camillo may have just given his brother a cut of the loot.

The first day of Annie's trial began on June 14, 1902, in the Davidson County Courthouse, with Judge Hart presiding. She looked tired and defeated as she sat in court for two days listening to a procession of prosecution witnesses. Many of the same witnesses took the stand who had appeared at her hearing for a reduced bond in April.[41] One of them,

Detective J. R. Dwyer, on cross-examination by the defense, admitted that Annie had not been advised of her right to an attorney and that her statements could be used against her in a court of law. He also stated that when she was searched at police headquarters, she began to cry when asked to remove much of her clothing.[42]

New prosecution witnesses had been summoned to testify in order to establish a relationship between Annie and Curry. Among these were Lieutenant McIntyre and Sergeant Malone from Knoxville, and Corrine Lewis, the proprietress of the Memphis "resort" where the couple had stayed. Miss Lewis testified that the two arrived together, flush with money, in about late September 1901. She said they spent large amounts of money drinking in the various resorts of the red light district, and on new clothes for Annie.[43]

On Tuesday, June 17, Annie took the stand in her own defense and gave much the same testimony as she had in April. She reiterated that she had traveled with a man she knew as Bob Nevilles, and that she had not known the bills he gave her were stolen. She said she never wrote on them and had never seen Curry write on them. She concluded her testimony by stating that the detectives had handled her roughly while she was under arrest.[44]

Nashville cigar salesman Morgan Roop was then called to testify on behalf of Annie. He said he hired attorney Richard West to defend Annie, after he learned of the unjust treatment she had received from the police. He also testified that a Pinkerton agent had tried to persuade him to withdraw his financial assistance. Defense attorneys Washington and West were, in effect, showing the court that the Pinkertons were in collusion with the police in an attempt to deny Annie legal representation.[45]

The jury heard from several more witnesses before the defense wrapped up their case by reading Curry's deposition into the court record. Court was adjourned and closing arguments were scheduled for the next day, Wednesday, June 18.[46] Wayne Kindred sums it up nicely: "The opposing attorneys painted conflicting pictures of Annie in their closing arguments. General Vaughn described her as a greedy opportunist who gave false statements to the police and helped Harvey Logan avoid arrest. Defense Attorney West argued that she was an unsophisticated country girl who had been taken in and used by a crafty criminal."[47] After receiving instructions from Judge Hart, the jury deliberated for only about two hours. Foreman A. J. Howington read the verdict of "Not guilty" to a packed courtroom. The crowd cheered in approval and rushed to shake Annie's hand. She was both surprised and delighted that she had received what she termed a fair deal, and shook hands with her attorneys, the judge, and every member of the jury.[48]

Annie was free, but she was not yet finished with the court. With the help of her attorneys, she filed suit for the return of the $500 she had attempted to have changed at the bank in Nashville. It was her assertion that she should be compensated since she had not known the bills were stolen. Annie stayed in Nashville for the next few months while her suit for damages slowly progressed through the legal system. Ultimately the court would deny her claim, ruling that she did not acquire the money in complete innocence.[49] Mr. Roop continued to support her while she remained in the city. During Curry's September hearings, the newspapers reported the attendance in court of a mysterious woman dressed in black.[50] If it had been Annie, she would have been immediately recognized by her widely publicized photographs. She and Curry no doubt realized there would be nothing for either of them to gain by her presence in Knoxville.

James Horan, who possessed copies of Annie's love letters to the Kid in jail, states that she wrote Curry telling him there was nothing she could do for him. She said visiting the jail would only bring unwanted attention from newspaper reporters and "snoopy" detectives. After denouncing the press in one of her letters, she said, "Oh, if it was only me in that place instead of you … you must believe I have been a good girl for you ever since I was released … I know we will be together soon…"[51]

CHAPTER 25

"Manny a Vote He Would Lose"

J im Thornhill received several letters from Curry's attorneys over the next few weeks. The September term of court was approaching, and they were insisting on payment for their fees. Thornhill, angered at being continually badgered for money, wrote Reuben Cates telling "him to keep his shirt on as he was dealing with a man of principal." On August 15 he wrote to "Mr. Charley Johnson" from Landusky, Montana, promising that $1,000 would be sent down in a week to ten days.[1]

Both Reuben and Charles Cates did well as political candidates in the August election. Reuben won the office of attorney general for Knox County, while Charles was elected attorney general for the State of Tennessee. Not surprisingly, their friends Sheriff Fox and Judge Sneed were reelected.[2] In fact, the election commission, of which Reuben Cates was chairman, was accused of unethical practices.[3] Soon after the election, things started going bad for Curry. He was brought before Judge Sneed in criminal court on the afternoon of September 5 for an unscheduled hearing. Reuben Cates could not act as attorney general and defend Curry at the same time, so the court appointed Jerome Templeton as special prosecutor. As was expected, a move was made by the prosecution to turn Curry over to the federal authorities. This time however, over the objection of the defense, Sneed permitted federal warrants to be served on the prisoner. He then ordered concurrent jurisdiction with the state court, continuing Curry's state cases until the next term of court.[4]

Curry voiced his anger to the newspapers, and later wrote (but never mailed) a scathing letter to the editor denouncing Judge Sneed and Charles Cates, Jr. He stated that the reason Sneed refused to turn him over to the federal court for several months, was because "he knew if he turned me over Before the election manny a vote he would lose." Curry also wrote that Charles Cates sold out to the Great Northern Railroad Company, and "he Maid it a point to turn Me over to the federal athoreties."[5]

On September 13, Curry walked to the federal courtroom in the government building handcuffed to a guard on each side of him. He was dressed nattily in a light gray suit and was in good spirits as he appeared before Judge C. D. Clark to answer four federal indictments against him.[6] His attorney Charles Cates immediately made a motion to quash, claiming the charges in the indictments were not specific enough. A sworn affidavit from "Charles Johnson" was also entered, listing other reasons to quash or grant a continuance of the indictments. One of the main reasons stated was that Curry's attorneys were not given enough time to prepare his defense.[7] The defense also needed more time to locate one James Stewart, whose last known address was Chicago, Illinois. If found, the witness could give proof that Curry was in France from early June to August 1901, during the time of the Montana train robbery.[8] The prosecutor, U.S. Attorney General Will D. Wright, stated that the defense had been given adequate time to prepare and was against any further delays of the trial. Judge Clark said he would announce his decision on Monday, September 15, and then adjourned court.[9]

When court opened on Monday morning Judge Clark ruled that the federal indictments against Curry would be quashed. However, Attorney General Wright informed the court that a new indictment was ready to be served on the prisoner. A warrant was served on Curry by the U.S. Marshal's office, and a hearing was set for Wednesday the 17th. The court ordered bail set at $15,000, and as he walked back to jail he appeared confident and joked with his guard.[10] At the Wednesday hearing Curry was served the new indictment containing nineteen counts, mainly for counterfeiting, possessing, and passing forged and unsigned banknotes. After the indictment was read, the case was ordered continued until November 17.[11]

Sometime after the September hearings and before the November 17 trial date, Charles Cates excused himself from Curry's defense team to concentrate on his new duties as state attorney general. He was replaced by former State Attorney General E. F. Mynatt and L. C. Houk, while

John Houk and Reuben Cates remained with the case.[12] In another letter intended for the editor of a Knoxville newspaper, Curry clearly states what was on his mind. "Charles T. Cates … quit me cold he quit trying to Rob Me alltogeather. But Reuben stayed with Me, not with My Lawsuit But with my Pocket Book with the intention of Robbing Me and My Loyal Friends."[13]

On the morning of Friday, September 19, a package intended for Curry was hand-delivered to Sheriff Fox by an elderly painter and wallpaper hanger named Edwin Jackson "Uncle Jack" Harrison. Curry had eaten several meals at the Knoxville restaurant run by Mrs. Harrison, before his fight in the Central Bar. The package had been mailed to Mr. Harrison with a note inside asking him to deliver it to Charles Johnson at the county jail. It contained packages of smoking and twist chewing tobacco, and six long stemmed cob pipes. The sheriff inspected the tobacco and found nothing wrong, but he was suspicious of the six pipes wrapped in brown paper. Each bowl was sealed with a paper label which the sheriff broke open. He found that each pipe contained a coiled steel saw twenty-two inches long. He then looked at the mostly illegible postmark with a magnifying glass, and determined the package had been mailed from Nashville on September 17. The note had been signed by a Martin Roberts, but the handwriting appeared to be feminine. The sheriff had no doubts that Annie Rogers had sent the package. (It may not have been a coincidence in the similarity of the two names.) Harrison was arrested and held for trial in the court of Squire Fitzgerald on September 26. However, he was quickly acquitted since it could not be proved that Harrison knew the pipes contained saws.[14]

In late October Patrolman William Dinwiddie returned to the police force to walk a beat in the better part of town on North Gay Street. Robert Saylor never fully recovered from his wounds, and eventually took a position as bail bondsman.[15] It was eleven months since the shootings when Curry's trial finally opened in federal court.

In the afternoon of Monday, November 17, Curry was escorted under heavy guard to the Knoxville Customs House where his trial was to be held. He was handcuffed to his guards as usual, and his legs were shackled. Always fastidious in his dress, he looked dapper in a new dark gray suit and vest. Thousands of curious people accompanied him as he walked down the street to the government building.[16] In fact, a local judge would later remark to Curry that only President Theodore Roosevelt had attracted a larger crowd when he visited the city on a day in September.[17] As case no. 3472 opened to a packed courtroom, it was soon evident that the defense was to continue its delaying tactics. Most of the afternoon was taken up by Curry's attorneys objecting to the jury selection process and requesting a continuance. Because of the late start of the trial, Judge Clark adjourned court until the next morning.[18]

On Tuesday morning it was more of the same from the defense, until the prosecution informed the court that there was no excuse for any more delay in the proceedings. The defense attorneys had had adequate time to prepare for their case and gather their witnesses. Judge Clark assented and called in the jury to start the long awaited trial of the *United States vs. Charles Johnson*. After the nineteen counts of the indictment had been read, Curry pleaded not guilty to all charges.[19] The jury heard testimony from thirty-four witnesses over the next three days, twenty-seven of them for the prosecution. The first two witnesses called by Attorney General Wright were A. L. Smith, vice-president of the Bank of Montana at Helena, and R. L. Livingston from the U.S. Treasury. With testimony from these and other witnesses, Wright carefully traced the banknotes from their origin in the Treasury, to shipment in the express car of the Great Northern Railroad, to the robbery of the train in Montana, and finally to their recovery from Knoxville businesses and from Curry's possession.[20] On cross-examination, Reuben Cates attempted to prove there was no evidence his client had signed the notes.[21]

Express messenger C. H. Smith of the Great Northern Express Company and fireman (now engineer) Mike O'Neil both positively identified Curry as one of the robbers.[22] The fact that O'Neil appeared anxious during his testimony may have been from fear or a guilty conscience. There is a possibility he may have come in contact with Curry and the other bandits before the robbery. Other prosecution witnesses called to testify were Lieutenant McIntyre, Sergeant Malone, Patrolmen Dinwiddie and Saylor, Ike Jones' bartender Horace Burnett, as well as Brady, Whipple, and Boley.[23] Of Curry's prostitute companions in Knoxville, only Mayme Edington testified, because Lillian Sartin had disappeared and could not be found.[24]

On November 20 the prosecution recalled several witnesses to testify before resting their case. The defense team did not make a good showing, calling just seven witnesses, with Curry refusing to testify in his own defense. Closing arguments began in the afternoon and were continued the next morning.[25] Houk and Cates both pointed out errors in the indictment and the lack of evidence against their client for forgery. Houk further stated that testimony determined there was nothing illegal about circulating unsigned national currency.[26] The district attorney argued that the prosecution's case was airtight, and warned the jury not to focus on any technicalities brought up by the defense that would allow the defendant to walk.[27] After receiving instructions from Judge Clark, it took the jury only three hours to find Curry guilty on ten counts of the indictment. His attorneys made a motion for a new trial which Clark denied on Saturday, November 29. The judge then sentenced him to 130 years at hard labor at the federal penitentiary in Columbus, Ohio, and fined him $5,000. Time to be served was really only twenty years, since sentences for some of the counts ran concurrently.[28] This was the same prison in which Ben Kilpatrick was incarcerated.

Wright had written the Department of Justice several times beginning September 11 concerning the decision of where Curry should be confined. He had explained that the Nashville state prison would not be secure enough for an escape artist such as Curry. He also expressed the concerns of the Great Northern Express Company and the Pinkerton Detective Agency that the outlaw should not be sent to any western prison where he would be among friends. They preferred that he be sent to an eastern prison, specifically the one in Albany, New York. The court finally decided on the federal prison at Columbus, despite assertions from Wright, the Pinkertons, and the railroads that it was unwise to confine Curry and his pal Kilpatrick together.[29]

The *Lewistown Democrat News* of December 5 printed a letter allegedly written by Kid Curry to Edward Hanlon, a rancher friend in Montana's Little Rockies.

> I will get out of this scrape yet. I will show these people that they are not dealing with a soft thing. They call me "the Napoleon of Crime" and you should see how they flock to see me when the trial is on.
>
> And when I get out of this, Ed, look out for me. They talk about Harry Tracy, but if I don't give them a better run for their money, my right name is not Harvey Logan. I'll cut my way through h—l before they'll take me again.
>
> I am now waiting for my sentence. It will be a light one for the people out here are with me and I've got all sorts of friends. Well, goodby old friend, it won't be long before I'll be back in Montana and when I am there'll be h—l to pay![30]

Since Curry reveals in the letter that he was waiting to be sentenced, he must have written it sometime between the 21st and 29th of November.

When Judge Clark overruled on the motion for a new trial, Curry appeared calm. After his sentencing however, he lost control and had to be removed from the courtroom. Between curses, he alluded to the fact that certain public comments from one of the jurors during the course of the trial had seriously compromised his case. As he was being escorted back to his cell, someone asked Curry if he was going to appeal. He replied hotly, "Of course I am going to appeal. I am not going to have a juror sit on my case after he has expressed an opinion."[31] Attorney Houk intended to ask for an appeal on a writ of error for the case to be heard at the U.S. Circuit Court of Appeals in Cincinnati. Back in his cell, Curry complained of a persistent cough which the doctors diagnosed as acute bronchitis. He said confinement in a northern prison such as Columbus would be damaging to his health, and requested to be sent to a southern prison. His request was denied.[32]

Annie Rogers was still in Nashville in the latter part of November, waiting for the court's decision concerning the return of her part of the

Montana bills.[33] It is not certain when she left the city to return to Texas, but it was probably not long after Curry's sentencing. She continued to write to him, but there is no evidence that they ever saw each other again. It has been stated that Annie was tired of the life of a prostitute, and intended to move in with her mother and brother in St. Louis, where her brother owned a department or dry goods store.[34] However, the Pinkertons reported her working as a prostitute in May 1906, above Dee Picchi's Saloon in the red light district of Hot Springs, Arkansas.[35] There is no reliable record of the whereabouts of Maud Delia Moore alias Annie Rogers after this.

Knowing that the appeals process could further delay Curry's prison confinement, Wright wrote the Department of Justice on December 4 requesting that the defendant be sent to Columbus as soon as possible. He believed the Knox County jail was not secure enough to contain a man as desperate as Curry. Sheriff Fox was in agreement and made it known that he no longer wanted to be responsible for the prisoner. However the U.S. Court of Appeals ruled that it was illegal to confine Curry in a federal prison during his appeal.[36]

Later in December, Judge Clark granted the defense's request to present a writ of error to U.S. Circuit Court Judge H. H. Lurton in Nashville. Curry also filed a pauper's oath to be included with the petition for a writ of error.[37] Legal fees had already cost him between $2,000 and $3,000, and another $300 to $500 would be needed for the appeal. Until the petition was heard in January, Curry was ordered to remain in the Knox County jail.[38] On January 8, 1903, the newspapers reported that Judge Lurton had granted the petition for a writ of error, and ordered the federal authorities to hold Curry in Knoxville until the appeals case before the U.S. Circuit Court was concluded.[39] His appeal on the pauper's oath was not allowed; he would have to pay cash for each step of the process.[40] The defense was given thirty days to prepare a record of the case for the U.S. Court of Appeals in Cincinnati, and it was completed on January 29.[41]

Curry had been confined to his cell ever since his rebellious outburst in April of the previous year. Sheriff Fox finally responded to his complaints in the latter part of January. He told Curry he would be allowed more freedom if he gave up his shaving razor. Curry wrote Houk on January 30 telling him of his response to Fox's condition: "i told him he could not have it he said i could stay in My cell then i told him all right that i would Before i would give him My Razzor i gave it to him once and i went 2 Months without shaving."[42] With the help of Charles Cates and some of the sheriff's other friends, Houk eventually succeeded in inducing Fox to lift some of his restrictions.[43] By March, the jailer Thomas Bell informed an inquisitive reporter that Curry was a model prisoner. "He is locked in his cell at night and given the freedom of the corridor during the day."[44]

Curry's appeal had been scheduled for April in the federal court of appeals, but his attorneys were informed that it would be continued until the May session. His case was heard on May 5, and it would take almost a month for the court to reach a decision.[45] On June 2 it was announced that the U.S. Circuit Court of Appeals had upheld the lower court's conviction of Curry. He and his attorneys were given thirty days to file an appeal to the U.S. Supreme Court in Washington.[46] Curry left it to his legal counsel to prepare for the appeal, while he began to put a plan of escape into motion, a plan he had been working on for several months.

CHAPTER 26

"He's gone!"

ver since his capture, Curry had been planning and preparing for the eventuality of his escape.[1] The first night, as he gripped the bars of his cell, he was alert to every move that went on in the jail. The following day, he asked for a special brand of shoes and socks made of materials that could aid an escape. That same day he probably secured some rope or strips of canvas before being given a replacement for his "torn" hammock. He succeeded in obtaining pieces of window molding and lengths of broom wire during the tantrum he threw in April 1902. Subsequent violent outbursts resulted in additional materials which he would use in his escape.

Curry was running out of time. His attorneys had to file an appeal before the U.S. Supreme Court by July 10, 1903, or else Curry would be transported under heavy guard in a steel-lined mail car to the Columbus, Ohio, federal penitentiary.[2] However, on Saturday afternoon of June 27, he was ready to put his escape plan into action. Curry was housed on the second floor of the jail with only one guard, Frank Irwin, for company. At about 4:15 Curry was pacing the corridor between the two rows of cells when he struck up a conversation with the guard, Irwin. Irwin was walking around the outer corridor between the main cage and the jail wall. He stopped at the window in the south wall where there was a good view of the Tennessee River. "I think, Charley, that the river is rising slowly for so much rain," Irwin said to Curry. As Curry responded to the guard's statement, he began walking to the south end of the inner corridor. He was standing directly behind Irwin with only the bars of the cage between them, when he called the guard's attention to an object in the river.

Irwin had his back to the bars and was looking at the river, when Curry suddenly threw a loop of twisted wire over the guard's head and around his neck. He jerked on the lasso, slamming Irwin against the bars.

According to Irwin, Curry said, "I have got the advantage of you, Frank, and I am going out of here. If you move I will kill you; just do as I tell you and don't yell, and you are all right." He forced the guard to turn around and place his hands through the bars. Curry held the wire loop tightly against Irwin's throat with his left hand, while he used his right hand and teeth to tie the guard's hands together with canvas strips torn from a hammock. After making sure the knots were secure, Curry then said, "I am going out of here. Yell, and you are a dead man. I like you, Frank, and it may be that I will be stretched out here dead in a few minutes. I don't want to hurt Tom [Bell, the jailer downstairs], but he has got to turn me out." Irwin begged Curry not to hurt Bell, saying Tom had nothing against him.

Curry then retrieved a long pole he had put together from pieces of molding and kept hidden in the bathroom. At one end of the pole he had fastened a hook made from what looked to be the rusty handle of a bucket. He stuck the pole through the bars of the north corridor with the intention of hooking a pasteboard shoebox located at the northwest corner of the main cage. Inside the box were the guards' pistols, a .45 caliber Colt and a .38 caliber Smith & Wesson. With a few minutes' effort he was able to drag the box within reach and retrieve the pistols. He took care to return the box to its original position, so that the jailer would not notice anything amiss. Curry then returned to Irwin and took the watch from the guard's pocket. "I only want to see what time it is. I don't want anything that you have got," he said.

It was 4:30, about the time jailer Bell routinely left his office on the first floor to check on his second floor prisoner. Curry waited for him at the north end of the cage opposite the second floor entrance. He had planned his break down to the minute, and he was anxious that Bell was taking too long. To hurry things up he rapped on the bars with his medicine bottle. The jailer soon climbed the stairs and confronted Curry, thinking that he needed something. In a flash, Curry had one of his pistols pointed at the jailer's face, and said, "Open up, Tom, I am going out of here. I don't want to hurt you, but I will kill you if you do not open the door. I have nothing against you, but Fox had better stay out of my way. I am going out of here." Curry tied one end of a six-foot-long spliced rope to one of Bell's wrists. While he held onto the other end of the rope, he ordered Bell to close the circular door that opened onto the second floor cell block. He then told him to open the combination lock on the steel door to the inner corridor.

Bell failed at his first attempt to work the combination, and Curry warned the jailer not to fool him. After another attempt the combination finally clicked and the door swung open. He ushered the jailer back to his cell, explaining, "Just keep quiet, I want to get my coat." In addition to his coat, he picked up his razor and shaving brush, a bar of soap, and one good suit of clothing. Curry kept Bell covered with his pistol all the time, which made the jailer nervous. "That thing will go off accidentally, Charley, and you would shoot me," Bell said. "No, it will not," Curry replied. "I am watching that. I won't hurt a hair of your head. I may take you a good piece with me, Tom, before I am done with you, so let's get out of here." He marched Bell downstairs to the main office, then down the basement steps to the rear entrance which opened into the back yard. Here they met R. P. Swanee, a jail helper and former prisoner. Curry held a pistol in each hand, and had his slouch hat pulled low over his eyes. Pointing a gun at Swanee's rather "prominent abdomen," Curry coolly said, "Fall in line."

They went to the stable where he ordered Bell and Swanee to saddle a mare owned by Sheriff Fox. When Swanee couldn't find the saddle and bridle, Curry swore and told him to look everywhere. He finally found the saddle but not a bridle, so a halter would have to do. As Bell led the animal from the stable, Fox appeared on the rear porch of his residence adjoining the jail and asked what was the matter. Bell replied, "that he would soon find out what was the matter if he did not get back into the house." The sheriff had just returned about a half hour earlier from the funeral of his close friend, James C. Roberts, and was not armed, so he turned to rush upstairs for his pistol. The sheriff's housekeeper, Sallie Robinson, later said she knew something was wrong when she saw Bell in the yard looking as pale as a ghost.[3] Curry had intended to have Bell mount behind him to use as a shield, but decided against it since no one was around at the moment to fire on him. Holding a pistol in his right hand, he rode out of the jail yard into Prince Street.

He spied a little girl standing on property opposite the jail, recognizing her as the child whom he had often waved and called hello to from the second floor jail window. However, this time he motioned to her to not make a sound as he rode by. As Curry turned into Hill Avenue, a man named Bud Woods saw him ride past and by chance noted it was 5:05. He soon turned into Gay Street and rode south across the bridge over the Tennessee River, then onto Martin Mill Pike. He was seen by several people, but it was generally thought that he was a liveryman returning a customer's horse. Those that recognized him called friends along the route ahead of Curry so they would get a last glimpse of the famous prisoner through their shutters or from front porches.[4] In the meantime, jailer Bell and Jim West, the cook, had rushed to the jail's second floor to release guard Irwin from his bonds. By the time Sheriff Fox had retrieved his pistol, Curry was going up Hill Avenue and out of range. He later commented that he did not have a rifle at his residence. While Bell and Irwin telephoned police headquarters, Fox went uptown to spread the alarm.

At about 5:30, U.S. Marshal R. W. Austin left his office with U.S. Attorney W. D. Wright, and saw Sheriff Fox walking toward them in a leisurely manner. "Fox, how is Logan?" asked Austin. "He's gone!" the sheriff replied. "You must be joking," Austin said. "No, it is a fact," Fox replied. They all went to Austin's office where Fox related the story of Curry's escape. Upon learning that Curry had been allowed use of the inner corridor, both Austin and Wright reminded the sheriff that they had given him orders not to let the prisoner out of his cell. Fox also told them that he had found a map in Curry's possession two weeks previous to the jailbreak, showing the country south of the river. The marshal then asked the sheriff if anything had been done concerning the hunt for Curry, and Fox said he was going to send out a posse. It wasn't until 6:00, about an hour after Curry's escape, before a posse rode out of town after him. The three men agreed to meet again at Austin's office at 8:30 that evening.

Deputy Sheriffs Epps and Hardin, and Constable C. G. Gamble followed Curry's trail out Martin Mill Pike. Officer McIntyre and Deputy Sheriff W. G. Lea (or Lee) started on their way to search Sevier County. Meanwhile, Austin began calling all available deputy U.S. marshals and sheriffs of neighboring counties. The sheriffs of Blount and Sevier counties promised to send out posses to aid in the search. Austin also notified Federal Judge C. D. Clark, the U.S. Department of Justice, the Pinkerton National Detective Agency, the Great Northern Express Company, and the Great Northern and Union Pacific Railroads. The Pinkerton office in Chicago responded by sending two of their agents, E. S. Reed and H. Beardsley, to Knoxville. After notifying officials by telephone in nearby cities and counties, Sheriff Fox took time to conduct tours of Curry's second floor confinement.[5]

Curry left Martin Mill Pike and rode east on Magazine Road to where it connected with Ford Valley Road. About the time the sheriff's posse left Knoxville, Curry rode up to Robert H. Griffin's country store on Ford Valley Road. He struck up a friendly conversation with the men there, but decided to leave when they began to huddle and look at him with recognition.[6] About 6:30, he was seen by a farmer named Lee Wrinkle (or Winkle) near the Sevierville Pike. He asked in which direction was the Maryville Pike.[7] He then left the Ford Valley Road, turning onto a little traveled road into McCall (or McCall's) Woods.[8] Near there, close to the New Prospect Church, a man named Haz Johnson saw a horse grazing by the road at about 10:00. As he approached the animal, he noticed it was wearing a halter in place of the usual bridle. The next moment he was surprised to see a man rise up from the ground, jerk the horse's reins, and give a slight cough. This stopped Johnson in his tracks, giving the man time to mount and ride slowly away. The rider kept looking back over his shoulder to make sure he wasn't being followed. Johnson later gave a description of the horse and rider which was a match to Sheriff Fox's mare and Curry.[9] He may have been the last person to have seen Curry while he was in Tennessee. Although James Horan, without giving a time, states that "A boy last saw him at the junction of Martin Mill Pike and Pickens Gap Road."[10]

The posse eventually picked up his trail on the Pickens Gap Road, and then onto a dirt road that led over Brown's Mountain. Once he left Brown's Mountain, Curry again entered the Pickens Gap Road in the direction of Neubert Springs, roughly seven miles from Knoxville, where the posse lost all trace of him.[11] It was believed the fugitive would head for the Chilhowee Mountains to the south by way of the Dupont Springs Road. Officers of the Sevier County posse guarded this and other mountain roads.

When Sheriff Fox did not show up for the 8:30 meeting at Austin's office, the marshal and Mr. Wright went out looking for him a half hour later. They soon learned the sheriff wanted them to meet him and several others in the office of Charles T. Cates. Also present were William Epps, E. E. McMillian, and Curry's attorney, John C. Houk. Fox again told how Curry escaped jail, and mentioned evidence of the wire used on Irwin's neck. Wright disagreed with the latter statement, saying he had examined the guard and found no marks on his neck. Austin and Wright then left the office after declining any further conversation concerning Curry's escape in the presence of his attorney. Before the night was over, a total of $1,250 was offered for Curry's recapture, $500 from Sheriff Fox, another $500 from the Great Northern Express Company, and $250 from U.S. Marshal Austin. A Pinkerton reward poster issued on July 3 substituted the $250 offer from Austin with $100 from the U.S. district attorney of Knoxville.[12] It would soon be announced that the original reward for the capture and conviction of Curry would not be paid. Even though he had been convicted, the case had not reached its limits in the courts.

In the early morning hours of Sunday, people began to gather all about town, with thousands waiting in the vicinity of the jail for news of the escape. More newspapers were sold on this day than on the morning after the previous record-breaking event, the assassination of President William McKinley.[13] At about 8:00 it was discovered that the sheriff's mare had returned to the jail without saddle or halter. She was lame and missing a left hind shoe, evidence that she had been ridden hard. The horse had first been seen two miles southwest of Knoxville, grazing along the Maryville Pike. She made her way to the Martin Mill Pike, and then to the south end of the A.K. & N. (Atlanta, Knoxville and Northern) railroad trestle over the Tennessee River.[14]

A man who lived near the trestle heard a commotion in the night that sounded like a horse falling. When he got up Sunday morning he found the sheriff's horse in his corn lot. Tracks found near the river were later examined by detectives, and it was determined the horse had been ridden. Hoof prints showed clearly that its front legs had dropped into a gully, resulting in the rider being thrown forward over the horse's head. The rider's size seven footprints were found a little further into the deep gully.[15]

McIntyre and Lea returned to the city at about 10:00 a.m. after searching for Curry all night. They reported his trail had been lost near Neubert Springs, and also that they had seen the sheriff's mare near the river about midnight.[16] It was speculated that Curry may have turned back to the city, and had thrown the saddle and halter into the river in an effort to throw off pursuit.[17] Sheriff Fox said Curry was trying to fool authorities into believing he had switched to another horse, but they were not fooled.[18] It was also conjectured that he could have hopped a slow moving freight as it crossed the railroad bridge in the night.[19] Fox didn't believe that either, saying that Curry would lie low for the first few days of the search, and then escape to North Carolina.[20]

After being in the saddle all night, the sheriff's posse returned at noon on Sunday with no new developments to report.[21] Sheriff Fox was kept busy defending himself against questions and accusations pointing to possible complicity in the escape. He said he had rejected Curry's pleas to be allowed out of his cell, and granted Curry freedom of the inner corridor only after repeated requests from his attorneys. He further stated that he had made several requests in writing to have Curry transferred to another jail or prison, but they had all been ignored.[22]

Guard Irwin defended his actions or lack of action by explaining, "I simply knew that he had me and that if I created any trouble he would cut my throat or kill me. He could have done that and accomplished his purpose in getting away as easy as not." Jailer Bell stated, "I was so taken by surprise when he shoved the pistol in my face that I hardly realized what had happened. He would have killed me if I had not complied with his request, and I opened the door to save my life. I do not regret my action, and knew Logan would have shot me if I did not do what he asked me to do. He would have covered every man that came up until the door was unlocked. With those pistols, he had control of the situation … I would not have had the escape happened for anything on earth, but Logan had me at his command, and to resist would have been death. I don't care what is said about the case. I knew the man, knew what he could do, and did his bidding to save my life."

The accusations continued on Monday, with Austin and Wright stating that Fox should be held accountable because of his decision to let Curry have the run of the corridor. Austin made sure to cover himself by stating that in January, with Wright's approval and the urging of Sheriff Fox, he had submitted an affidavit to the U.S. Circuit Court of Appeals, requesting Curry be transferred to the jail in Cincinnati, Hamilton County, Ohio. He believed that the Hamilton County jail was more secure than the Knox County jail, and that Curry would have fewer possibilities of escape. The court did not bother to acknowledge the affidavit.[23] Austin also related that in June, two weeks previous, Fox revealed to him that Curry's friends had attempted to bribe the watchman and were prepared to pay up to $10,000 to assure his escape. Austin said he immediately repeated his request to the U.S. Circuit Court of Appeals to issue an order for Curry's transfer to the jail in Cincinnati, but had not received the order up to the present time.[24]

Monday's *Sentinel* reported that Sheriff Fox told the newspaper in February that Curry "was a very dangerous man to have in his jail and would by some means make trouble for him and his deputies." He said it was his wish that Curry would soon be taken away to the penitentiary in Columbus.[25]

Fox welcomed the investigation ordered by Judge Clark that very same day. Witnesses were examined, and a reenactment of the escape was performed with the same tools Curry had used.[26] Deputy Epps stated that Curry's cell had been routinely kept clear of any materials that could have been used in an escape.[27] However, upon inspection his cell floor was found covered with trash and old clothing. Among some old newspapers and magazines was a book entitled *The Life of Napoleon Bonaparte*.[28] One of the first things learned was that Irwin was mistaken in the origin and description of some of the materials. The hook was not made from an old bucket, but from a type of metal fastening used in shingle baling. Also, the canvas strips that the guard said Curry had used to tie his hands could not be found.[29] Unless someone had carried them off as a souvenir, Irwin was most likely tied with two short lengths of rope found at the scene. The results of the reenactments performed by Fox, Irwin, and Bell, proved that Curry's escape could have occurred as they had stated. A report of the findings was sent to Washington, D.C.[30]

Over a year later in August 1904, Attorney General Wright, still claiming negligence on the part of Sheriff Fox for Curry's escape, convinced the federal government to bring suit against him for $10,000 in damages.[31] The case was scheduled to be heard at the September term of U.S. Circuit Court, but eventually a settlement was reached out of court.[32] Fox reportedly was fined $3,000, or possibly as much as $5,000.[33] Although Fox and the jail guards were accused of taking bribes from Curry, there is no evidence to suggest it. This is not to say that Curry didn't actually make an attempt. He tried to bribe several of his guards during his incarceration, at one time offering Deputy James May and Charles Hood $800 in exchange for some steel saws.[34]

The question that needs to be asked is what was his source of money? Financially, Curry relied heavily on his friend Thornhill, as shown by the letters that were sent back and forth between them and Curry's lawyers. Proof that he had run out of money months before his escape, is in the fact that he had tried to appeal his case on the pauper's oath in early January 1903. In fact, Attorney John Houk believed Curry escaped by nerve and cunning alone, as he had only two dollars in his pocket when he broke jail.[35]

Still, William Pinkerton believed there was every indication that Curry used bribes to facilitate his escape.[36] In one of his letters to the editor, Curry takes issue with Mr. Pinkerton, "the Noted Detective as he calls him self. he says it Was a clear case of Briberry that got Logan out of the Knox Co jail that is one mor of the manny Lies he has Publched [published]."[37] In another letter he begrudgingly absolves Sheriff Fox of any involvement in his escape: "[A]ll Becose he Was such a Dirty Kur i have Been thinking of never Saying a Word and Let the Dirty cur Pack the name of selling out to me But that is one thing he is Not guilty of So We will give the Divil his Dews."[38]

Monday afternoon the Pinkerton agents who had been sent from Chicago arrived in the city, setting up their investigative headquarters at the Hotel Imperial.[39] Assistant Superintendent E. S. Reed and Detective H. Beardsley were joined in the investigation by Deputy Sheriff Abner Epps and U.S. Deputy Marshal Charles McCall. Their purpose was to determine what had become of Curry after his escape, not how he escaped. Early the next morning, the two operatives hired horses at the livery stable and, supplied with maps, had Deputy Epps guide them over Curry's escape route.[40] They learned that the fugitive had indeed returned to the city by a circuitous route, and met up with his old pal Sam Adkins. This was the same man who had accompanied Curry in the Unaka Mountains in the fall of 1901. He was a well-known hardcase in western North Carolina and northern Georgia, the latter area being his home. Apparently Adkins had spent the last few months in the vicinity of Knoxville, and somehow had gotten word to Curry that should he escape, he would be waiting for him south of the Tennessee River near the Cherokee Bridge.

Sheriff Fox had been correct in saying that Curry had not changed to another horse, for it was discovered that he and Adkins had walked to Black Oak Ridge in North Knoxville the night of the escape. In fact the question of the mare's missing saddle was answered by Jim Thornhill in an August 20, 1905, letter to John Houk. He stated emphatically that Curry had thrown it into the Tennessee River from the A.K. & N. railroad bridge. This information surely proves that some time following his escape, Curry had been in communication with his friend.[41] From Black Oak Ridge the two fugitives hopped a northbound freight train, and got off at a coal chute just before Coal Hill (or Coal Creek). Curry stayed out of sight in a house for four days, while Adkins scrounged for much needed supplies.

They headed north for some distance on foot, and then turned east, traveling at times by rail from Campbell to Greene Counties toward Johnson City. Agent Reed and Deputy Marshal McCall followed their trail that led into Unicoi County and then crossed the line into North Carolina. The fugitives then traveled southwest, keeping to the mountains along the Tennessee and North Carolina border, in order to reach the Unaka Mountains in Graham County, North Carolina. On July 12 the two stood on a bank of the Cheoah River about twenty miles northwest of Robbinsville, not far from the Little Tennessee River.

Adkins and Curry called out to an old man in a canoe, crossing to the river bank opposite them. As "Old Man Melton" paddled back to them, he recognized his cousin Sam Adkins. The smaller man was a stranger to him, and did not say anything. Melton took them across the river to his cabin where Adkins began visiting with the family. Curry, who was out of condition from his inactivity in jail, was limping badly and did not enter the cabin. Adkins was anxious to hide out in a natural rock shelter, called a rock house, high up on the mountain. When he asked Melton to guide them to one that was near water, the old man was reluctant. Melton became alarmed when his cousin made threats that frightened the women in the family. In the end it was some pointed remarks from Curry that convinced Melton it would be better to go with them.

Besides eight heavy revolvers, the two men had been carrying their provisions which included a lantern, a frying pan, part of a sack of flour, and a half side of meat. Curry was finding it difficult to walk and could only manage to carry the meat, with the rest of his share of the supplies carried by Melton. By the time they reached the top of the mountain and found a place to rest, he could barely walk. He immediately took off his shoes, revealing his swollen feet covered in blisters. As he and Adkins began cleaning their guns, they told the old man that as long as they were on the mountain they were not afraid of an army of officers, and that they would rather die than be captured. Adkins said they planned on staying in the mountains until his friend's feet were healed enough to enable him to walk to a railroad. He told Melton their supplies would need to be replenished every few days, but he was not to come up to the rock house. He was to use a prearranged signal from the ridge further down the mountain, and they would come down to meet him. Before Melton left them, his cousin warned him it would be unwise to bring a posse back with him. However, Curry indicated it would be fine with him as long as Melton was accompanied by only one or two officers.

One day Melton signaled from the ridge, and when he did not receive a response he continued on to the rock house. He found the camp deserted, discovering that the fugitives had left the flour sack in the crotch of a tree to show they had gone. When the officers later questioned Melton and his family, it was obvious that they did not know anything concerning Curry's escapades in Knoxville. Nobody in the family was literate, and they had not heard of the famous outlaw's escape from jail. However, their description of the bandit matched that of Kid Curry. In addition, Melton was able to give the detectives a lead concerning his possible whereabouts. Adkins had talked of going to a cattle herder's shack he knew of near a remote and rugged region of dense thickets in Monroe County, Tennessee, called Jeffrey's Hell. More men would be needed to flush the dangerous pair from that immense wilderness.

On July 21 Assistant U.S. Attorney John M. Simmerly received news in Knoxville that Pinkerton detectives had learned where Curry was hiding. With concurrence from the Pinkertons and the Great Northern Express Company, he asked the Department of Justice to send federal marshals to Jeffrey's Hell to capture Curry. Two days later, the DOJ finally gave the authorization needed for the marshal for the Western District of North Carolina, J. M. Millikan, and a force of deputies to attempt the capture and arrest of the outlaw. The next afternoon, July 24, U.S. Deputy Marshal McCall and Pinkerton agent Lowell Spence joined the posse at Murphy, in western North Carolina. Although there was some dispute as to whether Curry and Adkins were near Jeffrey's Hell or many miles from there, the officers planned to search the herder's shack and the nearby home of a man named Edwards, who was related to Adkins in some way.

The officers started into the mountains from Andrews, North Carolina, on July 25, and by late afternoon they were within a few miles of the shack and Edwards' home. A check of both locations the following morning came up with nothing. Curry and Adkins were gone, or else they had not been there in the first place, and with no new leads, Millikan abandoned the search. At this point the federal authorities gave up any further attempts to recapture Curry. However the Pinkertons continued the search through the first half of August, before finally calling it quits.

A year later there was still tremendous interest by the citizens of Knoxville concerning the exploits of Harvey Logan/Kid Curry. Plays were written about his life of crime, but concentrated mainly on the time he spent in their city. One play performed at the Park Theatre to sold-out audiences was particularly popular for its portrayal of his escape from the Knox County jail. Sheriff Fox's actions during Curry's escape were shown in a humorous light to the delight of the audience. In a scene where the jailer informs Fox that Curry was escaping, the actor who plays the sheriff stumbles and falls over furniture as he runs back into the house.[42]

CHAPTER 27

Back in the West

A westbound Great Northern train was stopped by three men near Malta, Montana, on August 28, 1903. The bandits were frustrated in their holdup attempt when guards on the train prevented them from boarding the engine. Giving it up as a bad job, they rode away toward the Bear Paw Mountains. The railroad said it was the work of the Curry gang, and the outlaw leader had been reported seen in Malta earlier in the week.[1] Another robbery attempt on the Great Northern took place on September 2 in Great Falls, in which the bandits rode the train into the city limits.[2] It is difficult to believe that Curry would have attempted a train robbery so soon after his escape. Wild Bunch members were known to take several weeks and even months to plan their robberies. The need for money would not have overridden his innate caution. Also, the *modus operandi* of the holdups did not fit Curry's style. In fact, northern Montana may not have been his first destination after eluding the Pinkertons and federal officers in the mountains of North Carolina. The detective agency would most likely have sent agents to watch Jim Thornhill and other friends of Curry's.

An incident that took place in the Hole-in-the-Wall area may establish that Curry was in Wyoming some time in the latter half of July or very early August 1903. Alfred J. Mokler relates, "A few months afterwards [after his Knoxville escape] Logan was seen near Kaycee, in Wyoming, by a man who knew him well. He was on foot and was with another man."[3] Some writers believe Curry's companion was an old friend named Charlie Howland, alias Stevens, whose father, W. H. Howland, had owned the 4H Ranch near Buffalo.[4] The latter was actually W. H. Holland who was managing the ranch at this time. The rancher did have a son named Charles Turner Holland, but he was killed in a winter horse riding accident when only eleven years old.[5]

278

From Kaycee the two men walked to the Hole-in-the-Wall country, hoping to obtain horses. It so happened that Robert Tisdale and John May were staying the night at the Kenneth McDonald ranch. During the night May's horse, saddle, and six-shooter and one of McDonald's horses and a saddle were stolen. Deputy Sheriff Leonard Beard was notified at Kaycee, and with another officer, Alva Young, took up the trail of the horse thieves. The trail led them "up the Red Valley to Buffalo creek, and from there they followed the trail to Walt Putney's [Punteney] ranch, on Bridger creek, about forty miles southwest."[6]

Walt had taken part in the Belle Fourche bank robbery failure, but was now raising cattle near Lost Cabin. Vigilance was kept in the ranch house for any officers of the law. "When the officers came in sight of the Putney ranch," Mokler states, "they saw two men riding over a hill to the west." The lawmen rode after them, which was something Curry liked to discourage. Dismounting, he walked back from the top of the hill and began firing at the officers. A gun battle ensued in which Curry was

The old Kenneth McDonald ranch cookhouse today in Hole-in-the-Wall, Wyoming. Kid Curry stole horses from here after escaping from Knoxville. (Author's Collection)

wounded, and had to be helped on his horse by his companion. Despite Curry's wound, the two men were able to escape into the hills. Natrona County Sheriff Frank K. Webb joined Beard in trailing the two thieves.[7]

According to Picard family history, the outlaws rode up Bridger Creek to Dave Picard's 2B ranch on Lysite Mountain. The men were gone from the ranch, and the women were tending to their children who had whooping cough. The family was acquainted with certain members of the Wild Bunch, but not necessarily by their real names. When Curry had visited their ranch in years past, he went by the name of Ed Howard. For the present, the women dressed his wound and hid him in the cellar with his partner standing guard. The next day Curry was taken to Picard's Lake Creek winter camp on the opposite side of Lysite Mountain, twenty-five miles from Thermopolis. He was again put in a cellar away from the cabin, while his partner maintained guard. Two men then rode to Thermopolis to fetch a doctor.[8]

Mokler's history takes up the story: "Two nights after this fight occurred two men rode into Thermopolis at about nine o'clock. They were wearing masks when they called at Dr. Julius A. Schulke's [actually Schuelke] office … They ordered him to gather such instruments and procure such medicine, bandages and other things necessary to treat a human being suffering from a serious gun-shot wound … He was then blindfolded and led out to a buggy and assisted into it. The men then drove away with him, and they were on the road several hours, but the doctor did not know how far or in what direction he was from Thermopolis when the team stopped … [He was assisted into a house where] the blindfold was taken from his eyes, and he saw a man of very dark complexion lying on the bed. The man had been shot through the groin with a soft-nosed rifle bullet … The wound was dressed and the physician left medicine and directions for the treatment of the patient. The doctor was then blindfolded again, and was taken from the house to the buggy and returned to his home in Thermopolis … He was given a liberal fee and was told to remember nothing that had transpired that night."[9]

The men appeared a few nights later and the same procedure was followed as before. However, the wound had become infected and the doctor voiced his opinion that the man would die within a few days. Mokler says it was supposed the patient was "Harve Logan," but there were some who believed he did not die or that it was another outlaw.[10] Indeed, other versions of the story state that Curry was taken care of by friends until he eventually recovered. In fact the Picard family story substitutes a Dr. Richards for Dr. Schuelke, and relates how Curry's condition improved enough so he could be moved to a ranch below Thermopolis. He was hidden on an island in the Bighorn River where the rancher kept his milk cows. Supplies were taken to him twice a day when the cows were milked. Curry was not moved again, and he stayed on the island until he recovered.[11]

The sheriff and deputy had followed the outlaws' trail to the cabin on Lake Creek, where they found bloody bandages lying in a corner of the room. The sheriff supposedly did not try very hard to pick up the trail and lost interest in continuing the chase.[12]

Some local accounts place this episode in May 1904, a date that would make it impossible for Curry to have participated in the June 7, 1904, Parachute, Colorado, train robbery, since he would not have had time to recover from his serious wound. However, Mokler states that Dr. Schuelke told his story to his closest friends before his death on August 7, 1903. Also, Ray Picard intimates that the incident took place when he was a child at the 2B ranch (1902–1903). "Stevens [Curry's partner] knocked and stuck his head in the door. Ray thought it strange for a man to be wearing a cap during the warm weather of *late summer*."[13] (Author's emphasis.)

Dave Picard and his partner Vince Hayes were later arrested by Sheriff Webb, Deputy Sheriff O'Brien, and Joe LeFors. They were suspected of giving Tom O'Day, who had worked for the 2B, a false alibi for a rustling charge. It was their contention that the arrests were made in revenge for giving aid to Kid Curry, a friend they knew as Ed Howard. The officers' attempt to get even did not materialize however, as Picard and Hayes were ultimately found not guilty.[14]

Another story places Kid Curry back in northern Montana on September 23. He still had many friends and informers who would have sent word to him when it was safe to return. James T. Moran's ranch house was located near Yantic (present day Lohman), a town situated between Havre and Chinook. It was close to midnight when he responded to a loud knock on his door. A man stood on the threshold whom he took for one of the hobo fraternity who frequently rode the passenger-freight trains. Moran was surprised when the man introduced himself as his old friend Kid Curry, because he looked like a tramp. Curry told him that he had come by to borrow a horse with saddle and bridle. Curious, but still not recognizing the man, Moran invited him into his home for a visit. Curry was aware his appearance had drastically changed since his earlier days in Montana. He told the rancher he had been to Fort Benton and Havre, and no one had recognized him, even Sheriff Buckley. When he recalled past incidents that the rancher had since forgotten, it ignited a spark of recognition.[15]

Moran went out to saddle a horse for Curry around two o'clock in the morning. He had told the rancher he was heading north, but he rode east toward Chinook. The next day Moran found that his horse had been returned, with a package of money tied to the saddle for payment. After deliberating over the tramp's visit for several days, he came to the conclusion that it was indeed Kid Curry. It was reported that the outlaw stayed at a ranch near Chinook for the next four nights.[16]

This may have been the Simon Pepin P-Cross ranch, located about twenty miles south of Chinook and Havre in the Bear Paw Mountains. It was one of the first big outfits to run cattle north of the Missouri River. Foreman "Sleepy Tom" Conant, who knew Kid Curry, told a story that supposedly occurred years later in Vernon, British Columbia. He ran a livery stable there, and hired a hobo who had asked for work. Although his appearance was disheveled, dirty, and unshaven, he was good with horses. When he drew his pay each day he would spend it on drink. Similar to Moran's story, Conant did not at first realize it was Kid Curry. Then while particularly under the influence one evening, Curry talked of his past life in Montana. When he quit his job the following day, Conant concluded that the man he had hired was Kid Curry.[17]

Curry probably headed south through the Bear Paw Mountains to see his old partner Jim Thornhill, as well as other friends in the Landusky area over the next few months. At the time, Ruel Horner was the Zortman to Malta stagecoach driver. Horner had arrived in the Little Rockies in 1903, and acquired some land near the old Curry ranch. Many years later in 1959, he claimed to have seen Kid Curry with a local rancher at Zortman sometime after his Knoxville jail escape. He commented that the Kid was well-liked, so no one publicly admitted his identity.[18] Zortman resident Bill Kellerman claimed to have played poker with Curry in Grant McGahn's saloon in Landusky in winter 1903. "The Kid came into the saloon and bought a drink. We all knew him, of course, but no one spoke his name. He strolled over to the poker table and asked ... if he could join the game. He bought a $10 stack of chips, lost the pile and walked out saying we were too tough for him."[19]

During Curry's sojourn in central Wyoming, it would be safe to say that he met up with his old rustler friend, Tom O'Day. Some accounts even include O'Day in the horse stealing episode at the McDonald ranch in the Hole-in-the-Wall valley. One thing that is certain is that he was captured by Natrona County Sheriff Frank K. Webb in the Big Horn Mountains on November 23, 1903, with twenty-three horses in his possession. Having stolen them in Natrona and Converse counties, he was attempting to drive the herd out of the country to associates in Montana. He was captured at a cabin in the mountains and brought to Casper two days later by the sheriff and two deputies. His trial was set for the February 1904 term of district court. The first jury could not come to an agreement, and neither could the second. O'Day was finally found guilty at his third trial, and sentenced to six years at the Wyoming State Penitentiary.[20]

In February 1904 Curry's whereabouts were reported by the *Great Falls Daily Tribune*. He checked into the Oxford Hotel in Denver and was recognized by the desk clerk who knew him from Missouri. (Curry's winter respite must have restored him to a semblance of his former self.) He declined the bellhop's offer to carry his luggage, but asked for a pitcher of water to be sent to his room. Apparently Curry didn't think anyone would enter his room without knocking, but that is exactly what happened. He was bending over two opened grips containing bundles of new currency (the balance of the unsigned Bank of Montana money?), when the bellhop entered the room carrying the pitcher of water. The latter also couldn't help noticing a large revolver next to the suitcase. With an oath Curry ordered the startled bellhop out of his room. He then escaped through a side entrance before the police, alerted by the desk clerk, arrived at the hotel. The Denver Pinkerton office sent agents to try to follow the trail of Curry.[21]

Curry headed south to Texas to find recruits for a train robbing venture. He needed to find men more suitable to the profession than rustlers like his previous partner or Tom O'Day. The Kilpatricks were living in the area of Ozona in Crockett County, not far from the town of Sheffield where they had lived previously. The family had moved there from Concho County in 1901 after the killing of Oliver Thornton.[22] Here he found former associate George Kilpatrick, brother of Ben, and Dan Sheffield, a known outlaw whose sister Truda had married D. Boone Kilpatrick.[23] Pinkerton Assistant Superintendent Lowell Spence of Chicago stated in an interview that since Curry's escape from Knoxville, he had resided at

Rare photo of Tom O'Day under arrest in Casper, Wyoming, 1904. (Courtesy of Mike Bell)

the Kilpatrick home in Texas using the alias of "Tap Duncan."[24] It would be reported that sometime in March 1904, George Kilpatrick, Jack (Dan) Sheffield, and "Tap" Duncan left Crockett County, "well armed and mounted and prepared for a long journey."[25] It will be seen that if Spence's statement is correct, it serves to help clear up the later controversy surrounding the identification of Curry's body.

The Denver Post of July 11, 1904, reported that Curry was in southern Wyoming about early April. "Three months ago Harvey Logan was seen at Rock Springs, Wyo., and the Union Pacific officials were immediately informed. Then it was that a special train was put on the Wyoming division ... This train consisted of a special engine and two cars, one of the tourist sleeper variety [a Pullman], with the addition of being a complete armory on wheels; the other for the accommodation of a dozen horses. This train ... runs back and forth between Laramie and Green River, ready for any attempt at train hold-ups and for instant pursuit."

CHAPTER 28

Parachute

he first week of June 1904 found three men, obviously not used to hard labor, working on sections 8 and 9 between Parachute and DeBeque, Colorado, for the Denver and Rio Grande Western Railroad.[1] Hired under the names J. H. Ross, Charles Stubbs, and John Emmerling, they worked just a few days in order to become familiar with the area and the train schedules. On Saturday, June 4, they went to New Castle to pick up their discharge checks from agent Folger of the Rio Grande Railway. Upon learning they would have to wait until Tuesday to receive their pay, they worked at the restaurant of Stephen Groves for their meals. About 11 o'clock on Tuesday morning, June 7, J. H. Ross, in reality Kid Curry, signed a voucher in good hand acknowledging payment of $1.75. It is rather ironic that Curry used an alias very similar to the man (James Ross) who filed assault charges against him almost ten years earlier in Montana. The other two men, who were George Kilpatrick and Dan Sheffield, were each paid $2.05.

Sometime that same morning, the three traveled to nearby Glenwood Springs to transact some business with the Globe Express Company. Giving his name as J. H. Ross, Curry asked agent Otto Barton to express a valise to Pueblo, Colorado. The agent became suspicious, owing to the fact that the valise was of very good quality and the sender appeared rather seedy. He also noticed two rough-looking men, one being tall and the other of medium height, waiting outside for their associate.

After receiving their pay in New Castle, it was reported that the trio then hopped a westbound freight train to return to their old campsite near Parachute, a small fruit shipping station. In the afternoon a rider was seen a few miles from there leading two horses. This later led to speculation that there may have been a fourth member of the gang, even though only three had been seen during and after the robbery.

This time Curry's plans did not include setting up horse relays as was usual with Wild Bunch robberies. Curry had expected to get the horses from their "hangout" east of Grand Junction, but could not get them for some reason.[2] Uncharacteristically, Curry decided to do without any relay of fresh horses.

It has been speculated that the head injuries Curry received from the Knoxville patrolmen, and his long confinement in jail, affected the planning of and his performance at his last train robbery. He may have just believed his time was up. Attributing the words to George Kilpatrick, Frank Lamb states, "that on the last trip he [Curry] did not have any of the old-time good spirit and carefree disposition that had characterized him in all of his former associations with the Wild Bunch. Everything he did was more or less mechanical and habitual and his plans were indefinite and indecisive. He tried to keep up the old traditions, but it was plainly apparent that there was very little of the old spirit left."[3]

It was about 9:30 p.m. when westbound train No. 5, the San Francisco express on the Denver and Rio Grande Western Railroad, left Glenwood Springs. Shortly before 11:00 p.m. it slowed up at Parachute, where it was not scheduled to stop, to let off a passenger. At the same time another passenger boarded the train to ride the "blind baggage." Fireman John Anderson spotted the man as he climbed over the tender, and ordered him to get down. The new passenger pulled a revolver and in turn ordered Anderson back to the engine cab. Engineer Ed Allison was soon looking down the "glistening gun barrel," and he stated afterwards that it "looked as big as a small cannon."[4] Some writers assume the man behind the gun was Kid Curry; however it could have been George Kilpatrick since the fireman described him as a "big masked fellow."[5] The tall bandit ordered the engineer to run the train "like hell" until he spotted a small campfire beside the track on Streit Flats, about midway between Parachute and the Una siding. As the train began to slow down, he was told to sound the whistle as if to frighten cattle off the track. This was to allay any suspicions from the train crew, and also to alert the two other masked robbers waiting at the fire.

When the train came to a halt, Mrs. Effie Egbert, traveling with her baby, thought it was her stop at DeBeque, and began to gather her luggage. Conductor Charles C. Ware told her to remain seated, that it was just an emergency stop. She later told an interviewer that she had not been aware of the holdup until a neighbor mentioned it on the telephone the next day.[6] Stepping from the train, conductor Ware and brakeman J. E. (Ed) Shellenberger started walking toward the engine to determine the reason for the stop. The bandits fired at the trainmen, and Shellenberger was hit either in the left calf, leg, thigh, or hip, depending on which report is to be believed. Ware's lantern was shot from his hand, but he was not injured, and he was able to run back to Parachute to give the alarm. When mail clerk Fred Hawley heard the gunshots, he concealed the first class mail sack, and stuffed a large amount of the registered mail inside his overalls.[7]

The engine, express and mail cars were detached from the rest of the train and pulled ahead about a half mile. The express car was probably in combination with the baggage car since the various contemporary news reports alternated between one or the other when describing the car that was blown and the two safes plundered. One bandit covered the engineer and fireman, while the other two demanded admittance to the express car. Express messenger D. J. Shea refused to open up, and had piled luggage against the door in an attempt to keep the robbers out. The standoff was resolved by one of the bandits placing a charge of dynamite against the door. The resultant explosion blew the messenger off his feet, and he was found in a corner covered with debris. Fortunately he was not injured, and was now more than willing to leave the express car. Another charge placed against the large through safe (with a smaller safe on top) blew out twenty feet of the sides of the car along with most of the roof. Needless to say, the baggage was badly damaged; however the express goods were relatively untouched.

The robbery had taken place 600 feet from the Grand River (the present day Colorado), where the bandits were seen to be heading on foot with their plunder. Shea reported that the robbers secured only one package containing thirty dollars, sent from Salida to be delivered at Grand Junction. The robbers took the messenger's revolver, and also his gold watch that he had placed in the small safe for safety. "They didn't get enough cash out of the safe to pay for their dynamite," said D. D. Mayo, manager of the Globe Express Company.[8] As was usual with Curry's operations, the passengers were not molested. It was thought that the outlaws robbed the wrong train, and had really been after the Wells Fargo through safe carrying $150,000 in gold bullion on the No. 105 Colorado Midland, which ran ten minutes ahead of the D. & R.G. train No. 5. (Some accounts state that the Midland train was far behind schedule, and the Rio Grande flyer was running ahead of it.)

Engineer Allison was able to back the damaged express car and mail car to the passenger coaches. The train was run back to Parachute where the express/baggage car was sidetracked, and agents along the line notified of the robbery. Although Shellenberger's wound would prove not to be serious, he was taken to the Sisters' Hospital in Grand Junction. He was soon moved to the D. & R.G. hospital at his home in Salida. Conductor Ware, also of Salida, returned to his home and wired his official report to the general offices in Denver. The Globe Express Company later rewarded messenger Shea for his bravery "and for his general willingness to defend the company's property with his life."[9]

The railroad responded swiftly, owing to the fact that Vice-President Charles H. Schlacks and Manager J. A. Edson happened to be riding in a private car on the train that followed No. 5. They soon ordered their offices at Glenwood Springs, DeBeque, and Grand Junction to organize posses. Garfield County Sheriff Frank Adams responded by dispatching a special engine bearing a number of deputies from Glenwood Springs to the holdup scene. Mesa County Sheriff W. G. Struthers, Deputy D. M. Hardy, former railroad detective Cyrus Wells "Doc" Shores, with a posse of cowboys and ranchers, started from Grand Junction by train. By Wednesday it was estimated that 100 men, along with bloodhounds, were in the field tracking the outlaws. A reward of $900 was offered for the three robbers by the D. & R.G. and the Globe Express Company.

Curry, Kilpatrick, and Sheffield crossed to the south side of the Grand River by means of a rowboat they had stolen from the O'Toole family earlier. They mounted their horses that had been hidden in the trees near the river bank, and rode the trail east toward Battlement Mesa. The rough going through thick timber and brush-choked canyons soon caused their horses to tire. They stole some fresh mounts from R. O. (Rollin or Rolland) Gardner's ranch before continuing in an easterly direction toward Holmes Mesa. A heavy rain that had fallen immediately after the robbery at first made it difficult for the posse to discover any trace of the bandits. The trail of their freshly shod horses was eventually picked up, and it was easy tracking all day Wednesday. As evening approached the tracks were lost on Cache Creek, but it was supposed that the outlaws would cross the mountains to the south and strike for the Gunnison River country. For some unknown reason they continued their easterly course into the more populated area south of Rifle and Silt.

At five o'clock Thursday morning they arrived on foot at Joe Banta's ranch on Mamm Creek, their horses presumably left behind from exhaustion. They ordered breakfast from Mrs. Banta, paying her a dollar for her trouble. They took three horses from the barn, and were careful to cut the telephone line before starting toward Divide Creek. Their next stop was at the Fred Toland ranch, where the outlaws helped themselves to more horses. Meanwhile, it wasn't long before Mr. Banta had repaired the phone line, and had notified the authorities of the bandits' location. Soon a fifteen-man posse from Grand Junction and DeBeque was on their trail, with about twenty-five more men en route from New Castle. Much to their detriment, the outlaws did not bother to cut the telephone line at every ranch house they passed.

The outlaws rode past Marshall Nuckolls' ranch, and stopped at the Gustafson ranch just south of there. They needed to exchange one of Banta's horses that had come up lame. At first they tried to rope a wild bronco, but after a warning from Mrs. Gustafson they settled for one that was broken. From there the robbers rode north for some distance before swinging southeast in the direction of the Larson and Schweitzer places. They stopped at the Larson ranch for a last change of horses, with the posse hard on their heels. Mrs. Larson accosted the thieves in the corral, but she was chased into her house. Her two young sons ran out of the house with their rifles and fired at the outlaws as they raced from the ranch. From the divide overlooking Gibson Flats, about fifteen miles from New Castle, the posse came up on the bandits at about 11:00 a.m. After a running fight the latter abandoned their horses and took cover in Gibson Gulch on East Divide Creek.

Rancher Gardner and Deputy Sheriff Elmer Chapman were in an exposed position about fifty yards from the outlaws. Some contemporary accounts substituted Gardner's brother-in-law, Joe Doby (or Dobie), for Chapman in this action. Curry shot Gardner's horse from under him, and he (Gardner) dropped to the ground behind it. The outlaw evidently believed the rancher had been taken out of the fight, because he turned his fire on Chapman, grazing his cheek. At the same instant Gardner fired at Curry, and the bullet "entered the fleshy part of the bandit's left arm, upraised, supporting his gun, passed clear across the breast beneath the skin, shattering the breast-bone, and breaking two ribs and plowing its way through the muscle of the right arm almost identically as it had injured the left."[10] Curry's companions shouted, "Are you hurt Sam?" or "Come on Sam." "Don't wait for me," he replied. "I'm all in and might as well end it right here."[11] Placing his revolver to his right temple, he pulled the trigger for the last time, sending a bullet through his brain.

Sheffield and Kilpatrick kept up their fire as they ran up the north side of Gibson Gulch, using the dense growth of scrub oaks as cover. Their horses had broken and run during the gun battle, in which it was estimated that about 200 shots had been exchanged. One witness stated that "it is the greatest wonder in the world that some of the posse were not killed in the melee, as they were exposed to full view and only poor marksmanship saved them."[12] It was supposed they were making for Garfield Creek, and the posse following them found the country so rough they had to leave their horses behind. A party of local ranchers and cowboys left from Garfield Creek to head them off. Another posse was in the field headed by Garfield County Deputy Sheriff Mohn. The newspapers made much of the fact that the telephone had been a great aid to the pursuers.

At 4:00 p.m. it was reported the two robbers had not yet been sighted, although their tracks indicated they had been cut off by the posse coming from Garfield Creek and forced to turn back. As night began to fall, the various posses stationed guards near water sources in the area and kept a close watch on their horses. Early Friday morning bloodhounds from Leadville were put into service, but they soon lost the trail. About 5:00 that evening, the last trace of the bandits was lost within two miles of the Grand River. Although there were many rumors as to their whereabouts, the Glenwood Springs newspapers had to concede that "the two remaining bandits have succeeded in eluding their pursuers."[13]

There were reports stating the fugitives had entered a cabin about four miles from Parachute, forcing the occupants to feed them. Local rancher Ed Walker was said to have been threatened with death if he did not go to town for food and ammunition. It was later learned that Walker had been sent to town to obtain supplies for a posse, not by the bandits.[14] Apparently Walker had become acquainted with the Parachute robbers about two weeks before the holdup. They would ride to his ranch now and then to purchase hay for their getaway horses.[15]

The outlaw's body was strapped onto a horse, and taken by Deputy Sheriff Mohn to New Castle Thursday evening, arriving at 4:30. At the time he was killed, he had in his possession two revolvers, a rifle, a sawed-off shotgun, and plenty of ammunition. A search of his pockets revealed a compass, field glasses, railroad timetables, maps of the area, and money to the amount of five dollars. The body was laid out in the railroad freight house until it was brought on the train to Glenwood Springs by Sheriff Adams later that evening. The man's face was clean shaven and sunken in, and his overall appearance indicated he had been sick. A number of people in both towns readily identified the body as that of J. H. Ross, including railroad agent Folger. When his ragged clothing was removed by the coroner at J. C. Swartz undertakers in Glenwood Springs, the badly flattened posse bullet fell out.[16]

Although it was said that the robbers had taken nothing of value, the *Daily Avalanche* of June 9, 1904, reported, "When the three robbers left the ranch of Joe Banta ... it was noticed that each had a bundle on his saddle and one of them carried a box. When the saddles and horses were found later no bundle was attached to them and the box is nowhere to be found ... It is now said by one who should know, that the safe blown, instead of being empty, or nearly so, as supposed, really contained $12,000." Ed Walker said the two surviving bandits returned to the area in the latter part of June, possibly searching for loot they had buried from the holdup.[17]

If this is true, they may have been returning from the Big Horn Mountains in Wyoming, where Grand River valley rancher Jim Cox said they went after obtaining horses near Glenwood Springs. Cox had been with the posse when it battled the outlaws on East Divide Creek. He somehow picked up the trail of the two remaining robbers after the posse had quit the chase. Keeping a safe distance, he supposedly followed them all the way into Wyoming, where they stopped for supplies in Shoshoni. When the outlaws entered the valley of Hole-in-the-Wall, Cox decided it was time to return to Parachute.[18]

More than one author has stated that George Kilpatrick was wounded during the posse's fusillade, and died before reaching his home in Texas. In fact, there is evidence that he received the wound prior to the Gibson Gulch fight. Arthur Soule says it occurred when Curry ambushed the posse near Teepee Creek. After a brief gun battle the robbers rode to the Gustafson ranch to obtain a fresh mount. One of the men did not approach, but sat his horse on a nearby hill. Mrs. Gustafson noticed him and said he appeared to be hurt.[19]

While Ben Kilpatrick was serving his sentence at the federal penitentiary in Atlanta, Georgia, he received a letter from his brother Felix dated April 7, 1905. After informing Ben that he (Felix) was wanted for shooting a Mexican, he says, "I hope G [George Kilpatrick] will come back before too long, I am getting awful tired of this country"[20] In a letter to Laura Bullion on January 20, 1906, Ben wrote, "[N]o I'm afraid something is rong or G would have wrote."[21] Ben wrote a note to an inmate friend named Andy Brigham on January 31, 1906, revealing, "I guess none of the folks have heard from G. Yet it looks as if none of us will ever hear from him any more."[22]

Writers Carolyn Bullion McBryde and Jeffrey Burton agree that George did not return home, but that he did come back to Texas. Their evidence relies primarily on a letter dated March 9, 1905, from Marlin, Texas, that Soule and Horan say was sent by George Kilpatrick, Sr., to his daughters following a bitter separation from Mrs. Kilpatrick.[23] Burton believes the letter was actually sent by George, Jr., to his sisters, since it contains the latter appellation.[24] "Sister you don't have any idea how bad I want to be with you girls. It does seems like sometimes I can't baer it. I could come home and things might be worse, so I don't see what I am to do, I don't fear any danger on your parts never blamed you but little older heads is what done the mischief."[25] The writer also mentions that the mineral baths he had been taking did not relieve his medical condition, specifically his "rematics [rheumatics]."[26]

If the report of the train loot is true, and George Kilpatrick did survive the Parachute robbery, he and Dan Sheffield would have ended up with the entire $12,000, which was quite a bit of money for that time. In fact, according to an interview with Sheffield descendents by Donna Ernst in 1994, their unemployed Uncle Dan always seemed to have enough money to buy new cars.[27]

It is fairly certain that Dan Sheffield and possibly Felix Kilpatrick were indirectly involved in Ben Kilpatrick's last robbery on March 12, 1912.[28] Ben was released from the Atlanta prison on June 11, 1911, and promptly arrested by the sheriff of Concho County, Texas, for the murder of Oliver Thornton. When his case came up on September 4 in the county courthouse at Paint Rock, he was either acquitted or released for lack of evidence.[29] Finally free and clear, Ben and his loyal girlfriend Laura Bullion, went to live at his brother Boone's ranch near Sheffield, Texas. Laura had been released from prison early for good behavior on September 19, 1905. She at first ran a rooming house in Atlanta, Georgia, to be near Ben and work for his parole. Owing to constant harassment from the Pinkertons and the press, she moved to Birmingham, Alabama, finding work as a seamstress until Ben was released.[30] After all the waiting, Laura and Ben would be together for only a few months.

Ben and a former Atlanta prison inmate called Ole Hobek, also referred to as H. O. Beck and Ole Beck, made plans to rob the westbound
Galveston, Harrisburg, & San Antonio train No. 9 between Dryden and
Sanderson, Texas. They left two staked out saddle horses and a packhorse east of Sanderson near the planned robbery site. There may have
been another accomplice whose job it was to watch over the horses.
Sheffield was to wait in his automobile about a mile south of the site,
and would take the loot to be hidden and later divided.[31]

The two bandits boarded the train at Dryden late in the evening of
March 12, 1912, twenty miles east of Sanderson. It was 12:05 a.m. the
next morning when they forced the engineer to stop the train about

Ben Kilpatrick and Ole Hobek (alias Ole Beck). They were killed in a failed
train holdup between Dryden and Sanderson, Texas, March 13, 1912. (Robert G.
McCubbin Collection)

halfway between the two towns. The robbery went terribly wrong sometime between 12:30 and 1:00 a.m. During this time Ben turned his back on messenger David Trousdale, bending over to examine a package in the express car. The messenger, seeing his chance, picked up a nearby ice mallet and hit Ben three times over the head, breaking his neck and crushing his skull. Trousdale then picked up the dead bandit's Winchester, and waited in the dark for over an hour for Hobek to appear. Not wanting to wait any longer, Trousdale fired a shot into the express car roof. When Hobek soon appeared to investigate, the messenger sent a fatal bullet into his head. The bodies were taken to Sanderson, photographed, and eventually identified, before being buried together in the local cemetery.[32]

Sheffield went to Sanderson the day after the holdup to find out why Ben and Hobek didn't meet with him. He arrived in time to see their bodies, and then decided it would be wise to leave town. The sheriff stopped and questioned Sheffield briefly, but with no evidence of complicity was obliged to let him go.[33]

Ben Kilpatrick obviously had not been reformed by the years he spent in prison. All of the outlaws pictured in the famous Fort Worth Five photograph would die violently, with Ben being the last. Alone again, Laura asked her uncle Jake Byler for train fare to return to the South. She spent the last years of her life in Memphis, Tennessee, supporting herself as a seamstress in local drapery shops and department stores. She had few friends and kept to herself for the most part, until she died on December 2, 1961.[34]

CHAPTER 29

Kid Curry in His Grave?

A great crowd came to view Curry's body when it arrived at Glenwood Springs Thursday evening, June 9, 1904. Several people recognized the dead man, including Globe Express Company agent Otto Barton. It was the same man who gave his name as J. H. Ross on Tuesday morning, and asked to have his valise sent to Pueblo.[1] After viewing the body, Barton checked his files for a circular he had recently received from Wells Fargo Express Company on one George W. Hendricks (or Kendrick), alias James Keith, George W. Kayser, George Hess, and A. S. Keith. He was wanted for robbing their office at Sparkill, N.Y., and the United States Express Company office in Bernardsville, N.J., both in April 1904. There was a reward of $500 for his capture. Barton, accompanied by a Dr. Hotopp, "examined the body very minutely and found it to tally to the smallest particular with" the description of Hendricks. Although the general physical characteristics really weren't a close match, and the comparison was never considered seriously, it is interesting that the tally included a "small scar above right wrist."[2] The significance of this scar will be seen in the subsequent controversy that occurred over the identification of the bandit's body. For some reason, researchers have failed to observe the importance of Dr. Hotopp noting this scar in an early examination of the body before serious decomposition began.

The Ross identification fell through on June 12 when two men, one named J. H. Ross and the other identified as William or Charles Stubbs, reported to the sheriff in Pueblo. They informed him that they had worked as part of the D. & R.G. railroad section gang near the continental divide, and had quit two days before the train robbery.

They were able to prove they had been in Pueblo looking for employ-ment the night before the robbery. "When I read how I had stood on the summit of a high ridge," said Ross, "and, after being struck through the shoulders with a Krag-Jorgensen bullet, let out a wild de-finance [*sic*] at the enemy, and sent a ball crashing through my brain, I thought it was about time to make myself known. I didn't want anybody to try to collect my life insurance, and thought that perhaps my friends might be interested to known that I was really alive. So I suggested to Stubbs that we had better make ourselves known to the proper authorities."[3]

Dr. R. R. Macalester, the resident physician of the Glenwood Hot Springs company and acknowledged as a prominent criminologist, ex-amined the body of the unknown suicide bandit. He used techniques that were popular at the time, which included phrenology and palm reading. The *Denver Post* of July11 printed his findings:

It is common to find in criminals the marks of their crimi-nal natures. It sometimes happens that men commit crimes who are not criminals by nature, but more often men are criminals because of hereditary tendencies or because of a perverse life.

The man killed by the posse, after the train robbery of sev-eral weeks ago, can be easily placed in the latter class, as a man, criminal because of hereditary tendencies, and because of a perverse life.

Every line in his face indicates a degenerate, and while his head indicates a man of considerable brain power and intel-ligence, that intelligence evidently took the form of cunning, if the rest of the lines of his face are to be believed.

He was a man of small stature, slimly built, but very muscu-lar. His hands and feet indicate that he never performed much manual labor, in fact, his fingers are thin and flat, seemingly the fingers of a train dispatcher or telegraph operator. But I do not think he spent much time at work of any sort.

His head is especially good, the forehead is broad and the skull roomy. His nose is good, and the angle of his jaw is strong, indicating a man of considerable will power.

His mouth and chin, however, are very weak. His ears are those of a degenerate. They are unlike in their formation, and the lobes are especially large and flabby, for a man of his small stature. Although his ears are his most prominent features, even considering his nose, because his nose is not too large for the upper part of his head. His ears are very prominent, and one could tell him by studying his ears, even though he did not see any other feature.

The mouth recedes, and the chin tapers off very suddenly from the strong angle of the jaw. The whole lower part of his head nullifies the development of the upper part and indicates the degenerate. The angle of the jaws, while indicating a strong character, show also the degenerate by their bulging.

The man's hands are very good, and show none of the marks of the thug. The fingers are tapering, and the thumb well formed. The hand of a thug is usually blunt, and the thumb unusually short. The dead man was [a] cunning criminal, possibly a forger or criminal of some similar nature.

There are scars on the man's body showing disease, and other marks indicate that he led a very perverse and viscious [sic] life.

The lines of his hands indicate that he was a man of strong passions. His heart line is the most prominent on his hand, and shows that whatever he did was done in response to his passions and not to his judgment. His life line is unusually short, and all the lines of his hands are peculiar.

His whole appearance marks him as a moral coward, although he might be considered physically brave, but a closer analysis of his actions, marks him more as a desperate man, swayed by uncontrollable impulses, than a man of real courage.

The doctor was probably the source of the dead bandit's physical description that appeared in the same paper.[4] Next to this was a description of Harvey Logan provided by a Pinkerton circular:

HARVEY LOGAN	THE UNKNOWN
Eyes—Dark.	Eyes—Brown.
Height—5 feet 7½ inches.	Height—5 feet 7½ inches.
Weight—145 to 150 pounds.	Weight—150 pounds.
Build—Medium.	Build—Stocky.
Complexion—Dark, swarthy.	Complexion—Dark.
Hair—Jet Black.	Hair—Dark, mingled with gray; partly bald.
Nose—Prominent, large, long and straight.	Nose—Very pointed, prominent cheek bones.
Scars, Etc.—Gunshot wound on right arm between wrist and elbow; two scars on back, evidently from buckshot; left shoulder lower than right, due to wound; long arms and fingers.	Scars, Etc.—Scar back of head running toward neck; scar butt end of nose; buckshot scars on abdomen; scar right hand middle finger; scar above left breast; disease scars on legs.

On June 14, a week after the train robbery, the body was placed in a cheap pine coffin and buried in a pauper's grave in the potter's field section of the Glenwood Springs cemetery. Sometime before the burial, hand impressions had been taken and a death mask (or masks) made.[5] In addition, four photos were taken of the corpse at different angles, one without his hat. These were sent to the various law enforcement agencies and railroad officials. Lowell Spence, Assistant Superintendent of the Pinkerton agency's Chicago office, believed the photographs showed an excellent likeness of Kid Curry, a man he had been chasing for years.

Four days after the dead bandit's burial, guards were still stationed at various escape routes it was believed his two fugitive partners would take, with orders to let no one pass. The evening of June 18, rancher Jess

Moore was accosted by four rancher guards as he was riding back from Battlement Mesa. He ignored their order to halt, and continued on his way. The guards then blocked his path, again ordering him to stop and to identify himself. Moore belligerently responded, "If you want to know who I am, come over and find out." The guards immediately replied with a volley of gunfire, several bullets perforating the crown of his hat, and one nicking or passing through his horse's ear. Only their poor marksmanship saved Moore's life.[6]

It is not certain why it took so long for the Pinkertons to begin their investigation into the dead bandit's identity. It wasn't until July 7, 1904,

Kid Curry in death. After being wounded by a posse, he committed suicide on June 9, 1904. (Robert G. McCubbin Collection)

Kid Curry in death without his hat. (Courtesy of Mike Bell)

that Robert Pinkerton in New York sent a telegram containing instructions to his brother William in Chicago. "Suggest Spence go at once to Knoxville with photograph. Have him show it thoroughly. If identified please advise us. Notify all western offices to publish on instructions from you ... If Spence succeeds in getting photograph identified then he is to telegraph Chicago. We will notify all eastern offices to arrange for publication of an article showing that identification has been made of the dead outlaw as Harvey Logan, alias, Kid Curry."[7]

The *Daily Avalanche* of July 11 ran a Knoxville article headlined ANOTHER NAME, describing Spence's sojourn in that city. "Rowel E. Spence, a detective employed by a Chicago agency, has returned to that city after securing identifications of two pictures which he had in his possession, supposed to be photographs of the famous Montana bandit and train robber, Harvey Logan ... Believing the photographs to be those of Logan, Spence came here to identify the bandit through jail officials where Logan had been confined over a year. Sheriff Fox, from whom Logan escaped, positively identified the photographs as those of Logan. So did Jailor Thomas Bell, whom Logan held up at the point of a pistol while escaping from jail. The outstanding reward for the bandit is variously estimated at between $18,000 and $30,000. It is probable that the remains will be exhumed and further identification established, as Logan had many bullets marks on his body."

In actuality, the majority of the large rewards were withdrawn after Curry was convicted at his Knoxville trial. The only reward that could be collected at this time was the $1,100 offered soon after his escape from jail. Sheriff Fox and the Great Northern Express Company were still offering $500 apiece, and the United States district attorney of Knoxville put up $100.[8]

Others in Knoxville who identified the photographs as Curry were his attorneys Charles T. Cates, Jr. and Reuben L. Cates, Police Chief J. J. Atkins, and Lieutenant George W. McIntyre. Of all the officials who had been in close contact with Curry in Knoxville, only U.S. Attorney General Will D. Wright expressed some doubt as to the identity of the man in the photographs.[9] Spence was sure it was Curry, but not everyone at the Pinkerton National Detective Agency was convinced that the body was the famous outlaw. A July 9 memo in the agency's archives indicates that William Pinkerton was one of them. After receiving a telegram from Spence that he had secured positive identification of Curry, William wrote his brother Robert to advise him that, "I am inclined to believe it is Duncan, yet the people in Knoxville who know Logan well assert positively it is Logan ... Naturally the people at Knoxville, who are crooked in this matter, including the Sheriff, would try to make it appear that Logan is dead, to save their own skirts. Personally, I am inclined to believe the Knoxville identification is wrong."[10] Although Spence stated at this time that Curry had used the alias of Tap Duncan

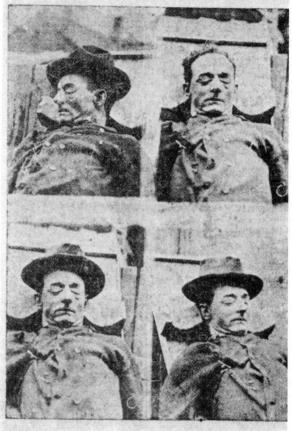

Death photos published in the *Saint Paul Pioneer Press*. (Courtesy of Mike Bell)

while sojourning in Texas, it is interesting that William Pinkerton believed the body may have been that of the real George Taplin Duncan.

William's memo also noted that the description of the dead bandit that had been made public, did not mention "a gun shot wound on his wrist, which we all know Logan had." Both the superintendent of the Pinkerton Denver office, John C. Fraser, and his assistant, Frank Murray, stated they needed to see the scar on the right wrist before they would be totally convinced it was Logan. Union Pacific officials and D. S. Elliott, General Manager of the Great Northern Express Company, also would not be satisfied until an exhumation was done.[11]

Under the headline BODY OF THE SUICIDE BANDIT TO BE EX-HUMED, the *Denver Post* of July 11 asked the question, "Was the Rio Grande train robber who committed suicide to avoid arrest, near New Castle, June 9, Harvey Logan, alias 'Kid' Curry, etc., the most notorious train bandit in existence?" The story continued, "To decide this question the body of the bandit suicide will be exhumed at Glenwood Springs to see if there is a gunshot wound on the right forearm near the wrist. The Pinkerton National Detective agency, which has ferreted out the identification of the Rio Grande robber, announces positively that the dead man was Logan, bank and train robber and murderer, but the exhumation must take place, in order to make the matter a certainty. Every big railroad company in the West insists on this, and if it is proved that the body now buried at Glenwood Springs is that of Harvey Logan, there will be relief in many a railway official's breast."

Since the physical descriptions of Curry and the dead bandit were almost exact, the exhumation would be needed to compare the body's scars with Curry's known scars. When Spence first visited Curry at the Knox County jail, he noted a "very slight scar" on one wrist.[12] As time went on, this slight scar came to be described in newspapers and circulars as a deep gunshot wound on the right forearm. Dr. Charles P. McNabb of Knoxville, who had Curry strip before examining him in jail, recorded finding "two mean looking scars in the back," but did not make any mention of a wrist scar.[13] Another physical feature of Curry's that was noted at the time of Spence's jail visit, was a missing lower front tooth, and was reiterated the day after his escape.[14] Dr. Macalester's examination of the unknown body before burial also reported the absence of one tooth in the lower jaw and his upper teeth intact.[15] The doctor did not note the existence of a wrist scar however.

The *Daily Avalanche* of July 12 reported that officials of Glenwood Springs referred to the *Denver Post* article as space filler. "The announcements ... of yesterday that the dead bandit, supposed to have been one Ross, who participated in the D. & R. G. robbery at Parachute, is Harvey Logan, alias Kid Curry, a member of a gang of desperadoes and a much wanted one, has revived not a little talk. It is the opinion of the officials here that the article as published, smacks over-much as a spacefiller. It is by no means certain that the dead man who was buried here is the one wanted."

There had been speculation that the other two robbers were Butch Cassidy and Harry Longabaugh. However, the Pinkertons announced that one of them was George Kilpatrick, and declined to state the identity of the other. Both newspapers mentioned that the address of Ola Kilpatrick, sister of Ben and George, had been found in the dead man's pockets. The *Avalanche* stated, "This address gave a clue that the dead robber perhaps had some connection with the old 'Black Jack' Ketchum-Carver-Logan-Kilpatrick gang of train robbers ... and investigation has been carried on from that end of the clue but with what result is not known. Her location was given as Pecos, Texas."

The July 13 *Avalanche* reported that the majority of D. & R.G. officials did not believe the Pinkerton announcement that the body was that of Curry. "To the casual observer it looks like a case of wanting to believe something with the Pinkertons." The Pinkertons were accused of floating the story for the reward, but as they had not taken part in the pursuit of the robbers, the agency was not eligible. "Messrs. A. W. Brown of the D. & R. G. detective agency and R. Brunazzi for the Globe Express [C]ompany, were here today and place but little credence in the story, according to an authority. They are working along entirely different lines and are going right along trying to locate the surviving robbers." The *Avalanche* reacted to the Denver newspaper stories concerning the exhumation by stating, "The officials here know nothing of any proposed movement to exhume the body, and question whether the mystery would be cleared up at this stage of the game if this were done."

The address of Ola Kilpatrick was checked out prior to digging up the grave, and she supposedly identified a photo of the body as that of Tap Duncan of Knickerbocker, Texas.[16] Lowell Spence and Union Pacific Railroad chief special agent William Canada arrived in Glenwood Springs on the morning of July 16 to begin the exhumation. Some newspapers referred to Canada as a Northern Pacific detective. Others in the examining party were Globe Express Company special agent R. Brunazzi, Garfield County Deputies Mohn and Crissman, and J. R. Burdge of J. C. Swartz's undertaking establishment.[17] As to the outcome, the *Daily Avalanche* of July 16 revealed, "While the Avalanche is not authorized to say, it is believed that the examination was unsatisfactory. The dead bandit is yet, in the minds of the wise ones, unidentified."

The *Denver Post*, apparently not concerned about authorization, reported that the body was badly decomposed. A thick black mold covering the body made it very difficult to discern any identifying marks. The only recognizable feature not covered by mold was the large nose.[18] However, a week later there was a report that disagreed with the previous remarks concerning the extent of body decomposition. The *Glenwood Post* of July 23 stated that the body was "somewhat decomposed but not so much so that it would prevent identification had the marks which Logan is said to have had existed."[19]

After taking some measurements of the corpse, Spence expressed the belief that it was the outlaw Kid Curry. Canada and Brunazzi disagreed, citing the lack of scars listed on Pinkerton circulars, such as the gunshot wound near the right wrist. It should be remembered that this scar was originally noted by Spence as being slight. In fact the detective believed any scars on the body could have been made invisible owing to decomposition.[20] Dr. Macalester had earlier listed scars found on the dead bandit that were not known to be present on Curry. Although Pinkerton circulars were not always terribly accurate or comprehensive, the newspapers made much of these discrepancies. What is surprising is that these same newspapers did not consider the one distinct scar that Curry was known to have beyond any doubt, but was not listed on the Pinkerton circular. That was the three-inch cut he had received from a Knoxville police billy club which opened the top of his scalp to the bone. The physical features noted of the dead man before he was buried and later published in the *Denver Post*, matched this with a "Scar back of head running toward neck."[21] Even modern researchers seldom make any mention of this fact.[22]

There was also some circumstantial evidence that, for some reason, was not considered seriously. Curry's well known preference for suits with a Denver trademark was reflected in the label of the dead bandit's clothing.[23] One of the revolvers that had been found on his body was the same one Curry had taken from Charles Judd, a Colt salesman, during the train robbery at Wilcox, Wyoming.[24] This, along with identical physical characteristics, which included a missing lower front tooth, and the telltale billy club scar on top of the head, should be enough to be reasonably certain that "the unknown" was Kid Curry. This conclusion is only strengthened by the fact that the vast majority of Knoxville officials identified the corpse in the photographs as the famous outlaw who had spent a good deal of time in their county jail.

Despite this evidence, Globe Express Company special agent R. Brunazzi believed without a doubt that the dead bandit was Tap Duncan. The D. & R.G. conducted an investigation in Texas concerning the Duncan family, as well as other outlaw families, such as the Kilpatricks, Sheffields, and Ketchums. The Duncans ranched near the latter family in San Saba County. It was learned that Tap Duncan and his brothers Dick and Bige were frequently on the wrong side of the law. Bige was married to a sister of Tom Ketchum, and oldest brother Dick had been hanged in 1892 for murdering a family during a home break-in at Eagle Pass, Texas. A railroad agent showed photos of the dead bandit buried at Glenwood Springs to Duncan's friends and relatives.[25] Although Brunazzi reported that they identified the body as that of Tap Duncan, it is now known the identifications were wrong or possibly intentionally misleading. A recently located death certificate gives proof that he died when hit by a car in Kingman, Arizona, on November 18, 1944.[26]

Duncan married a niece of Tom Ketchum in 1892, and moved to the Three Creek area in Idaho about the middle of the decade. In 1898 he had to leave for Arizona to escape local retribution after killing a man in a barroom brawl.[27] He was ranching with his family in that state when, according to the railroad agent, he was supposedly seen leaving Texas with George Kilpatrick and Dan Sheffield in March 1904. As Dan Buck points out, this would lend credence to Spence's assertion that the Tap Duncan who accompanied Kilpatrick and Sheffield was actually Kid Curry using the name as an alias.[28] A Denver Pinkerton operative report of July 24, 1904, stated that Duncan had fled to Utah to avoid arrest for various charges including cattle rustling. It also named Kilpatrick, Sheffield, and Duncan, or maybe Curry as Duncan, as the three Parachute train robbers.[29] Another Pinkerton letter reveals that an operative discovered Tap Duncan living in Arizona in mid-1905 under his name G. (George) T. (Taplin) Duncan.[30]

A supposed acquaintance of Tap Duncan, named John Ring, surfaced in Glenwood Springs in late August 1904. He told a reporter that a picture of the dead bandit he had seen displayed in the window of a photographic gallery was that of Duncan. He had often seen the man in Des Moines, Iowa, and in Waco, Texas. Ring described Duncan as a disagreeable fellow who had few friends, and was a gambler who followed the county fair circuit. He confided that the nickname "Tap" came from the practice of "tapping the pot" (taking poker winnings) whether or not he had the winning hand.[31] This anecdote actually betrays Ring's real lack of familiarity concerning Duncan, since his nickname almost certainly is derived from his middle name of Taplin.

Why did the real Tap Duncan's friends and relatives, including Ola Kilpatrick, identify him in the photographs? In view of his lawless background in Texas, and his hurried departure from Three Creek, Idaho, for a murder, his supporters may have conspired to throw the law off his trail. However, this wouldn't explain why the sheriff at Brady, Texas, also insisted the man in the photos was Duncan. The autopsy report clearly stated that the dead bandit had a distinctive nose scar and buckshot wounds on his abdomen. The Brady sheriff said the corresponding nose wound on Duncan had been inflicted when he resisted arrest several years earlier. A deputy sheriff named Joe Arkey (most likely referring to San Saba County Sheriff Joe Harkey) had struck him in the face with his gun. In addition, he said the buckshot wounds were caused by the authorities shooting Duncan from his horse while fleeing arrest.[32]

Charlie Siringo received a letter soon after the Parachute robbery that convinced him Kid Curry was not dead. It had been sent by Curry's friend Jim Ferguson, who was living near Palisade, Colorado, not far from the robbery site. The letter was addressed to Harry Blevins, Siringo's outlaw alias, telling him of the controversy in the newspapers concerning the identity of the dead robber. "The man who was killed, stopped with me up to the time the train was held up," stated Ferguson, "and I know he was not 'Kid Curry'." Siringo forwarded the letter to the superintendent of the Burns Detective Agency in Los Angeles, California, as proof that the dead bandit was not Kid Curry. "He [Ferguson] had no reason to write me a falsehood," Siringo later said, "as he supposed I was an outlaw."[33] However, it is entirely possible that Ferguson, and other Wild Bunch associates such as Jack Ryan and Jim Hanson, were aware that Siringo was an undercover Pinkerton detective, and were obliged to feed him false information.

On July 25, 1904, John C. Houk, Curry's defense attorney, sent off a letter to Jim Thornhill in Montana stating his belief that Jim's friend was dead. "Enclosed find picture of the man I believe to be Harvey Logan. What do you say? ... Robber though he was, I learned to like him and I am sorry to believe he is really dead."[34] Thornhill's reply of August 9 said, "I don't think that friend is dead although the picture favors him greatly. [H]e woulden have shot himself as long as there was any body else to shoot and that possie was coming up from the rear and if he was able to shoot him self he could have shot one or more of them and had company over the divide."[35] Houk took exception in his next letter of August 22. "I will state that I think you are mistaken in thinking that Logan still lives. I have no doubt in the world that he is dead ... I shall never believe without positive proof that there was the slightest understanding between Logan and the Jail Officials or any of them. Logan got away himself, remarkable escape though it was … Logan had the nerve while those in charge of him did not have it and he walked out as the result of his cunning and dare devil determination to die or escape. The people here do not want to believe that Logan is dead but I think you will be convinced in the course of time that he did 'pass over the divide'."[36]

Many years later, after Lowell Spence had retired, he revealed in a letter to his former employers that "I've been laughed at a number of times because of this identification, but I know it was Logan's body. Mr. Canada saw Logan but once, then behind the bars in the Knoxville jail. I have seen and talked to Logan a dozen times, have seen him awake and asleep in the jail, on the streets of Knoxville going to and from the courthouse, and sitting in the courtroom hours at a time … I've seen a number of reports that Logan was known to be here, there, and everywhere, including South America, but I know his body was buried in Glenwood Springs, Colorado."[37]

In 1949, Lowell Spence told the story of his investigations concerning the identification of Curry's body to James D. Horan. He concluded: "I had known Kid Curry better, I think, than any other officer in the West. I had hunted him day and night for years, as Assistant Superintendent of the Chicago office of the Agency, I had helped direct others in hunting him.

"In Knoxville I was at his side from the moment he was put into his cell until the day he was found guilty by the jury and then sentenced to prison.

"I knew the man intimately. I knew his face, how he talked, his features—and I am certain now as I was so many years ago, that the dead man buried as Tap Duncan was Harvey Logan.

"I think it is significant that we never heard from Harvey Logan again." (Author's emphasis)[38]

CHAPTER 30

South American "Sightings"

owell Spence's statement is true in that there were never any more official sightings of Kid Curry, at least nothing that could be proven, after the suicide in Colorado. But many people could not accept the fact that the infamous outlaw was gone, and continued to attribute later bank robberies to the Curry gang (despite the fact that Curry's criminal career clearly shows he much preferred robbing trains).

One of these was the attempted robbery by two men of the First National Bank of Cody, Wyoming, on November 1, 1904. The holdup was thwarted when the larger of the two bandits shot down the cashier when he ran out into the street. There was speculation that of the two robbers, the shorter, slender one was Kid Curry. This could not be considered seriously after the November 3 *Cody Enterprise* reported that during the holdup, "the slender one was plainly rattled, throwing his gun around and shooting almost at random." This was not the actions of a veteran outlaw of the Wild Bunch. After trading shots with the citizens of Cody, the robbers raced out of town with a posse following close behind. Although the posse eventually gave up the chase near Thermopolis, law officials continued the hunt for the bandits. During the year following the robbery, a number of suspects were arrested. They were all able to provide an alibi or witnesses at the time of the robbery and were ultimately released.[1]

Most stories of Kid Curry in South America usually place him on the continent some time in 1905. One story, however, has him traveling there not long after his escape from jail in Knoxville in June 1903. The story can be found, with slight variations, in several sources. Its origin was most likely an article by Edgar Young in the June 1927 issue of *Frontier Times* entitled "The End of Harvey Logan." Young was managing a logging camp (a gold mine in a later version) in Brazil, when a sickly tramp came to his camp looking for work. The man had escaped from jail in Buenos Aires, Argentina, traversing the vast pampas and Brazilian jungles to Young's camp. When he was well enough, Young put him to work as an assistant foreman. One day a former employee who had been fired attempted to stab Young in the back. The tramp, who had allegedly told Young he was Harvey Logan, intervened and saved his life. One version said he killed the Brazilian Indian or Hispanic attacker.[2]

Curry told Young of his adventures prior to his arrival at the Brazilian logging camp. After his escape from Knoxville, Curry made his way to Minnesota to visit his sister.[3] He then hopped a westbound Great Northern passenger-freight, stopping for a time in Montana, before continuing on to Seattle. Here he was able to hire onto a sailing ship going to South America. He jumped ship when it docked at Valparaiso, Chile, and was a very busy man for the next several months. He worked for a time in a Chilean copper mine, before crossing the Andes into Argentina where he robbed several railroad stations. To avoid arrest, he returned to Valparaiso and took ship to Punta Arenas in southern Argentina. In nearby Rio Gallegos he staked a claim and panned for gold from the beach sand. He was jailed at Punta Arenas after a drinking spree, but easily escaped his confinement. He then walked north across Patagonia robbing ranches and trading posts. When he eventually reached the transcontinental railroad he robbed several more railroad stations. Making his way to Buenos Aires, he fell in with a gang of international counterfeiters. Thrown in jail after another one of his revels, he again escaped and worked his way to Young's logging camp in Brazil. Curry told Young that in all that time he never met up with either Butch Cassidy or the Sundance Kid.[4]

After working for Young a few months, he returned to Buenos Aires, and in time reached Punta Arenas again. Here he robbed some citizens, and when he was arrested this time, he was identified as Harvey Logan alias Kid Curry. Supposedly, out of fear of the infamous American outlaw, the citizens waited until he was in a drunken sleep, and then tied him onto a horse. He was taken fifty miles north into a wild and desolate region, and left on foot, never to be seen again.[5]

Of course none of the incidents in this narrative can be verified. In addition, this individual did not possess any of Kid Curry's traits or abilities. As Gary Wilson states, Young portrayed him as being "stupid, slow-witted, slow on the draw, and a poor rider—just the opposite of the real Logan."[6] In any case he was back in the U.S. and officially sighted in a Denver hotel in mid-February 1904. It would have been a very short time frame for all of these adventures to take place, not to mention the vast distances traveled on foot.

There are stories that place Curry back in South America in early 1905. Some have credited him with helping Butch and Sundance rob the bank at Rio Gallegos, Santa Cruz Territory, Argentina, on February 14.[7] The Pinkertons disputed his participation, and rightly so, since recent evidence proves that at the time of the robbery, Butch, Sundance, and Ethel were in the vicinity of their ranch in Cholila, Argentina, 750 miles north of Rio Gallegos.[8] However, the Pinkertons were at least indirectly responsible for Butch and Sundance returning to outlawry, and for the reported sightings of Curry in South America.

In March 1903, one of their agents, Frank Dimaio, was in Brazil trailing an international criminal. He was ordered to Buenos Aires to investigate reports of Butch and Sundance ranching somewhere in Argentina. From an informant Dimaio learned Butch, Sundance, and Ethel were ranching at Cholila in the Chubut Territory. Before setting sail to the U.S. in May 1903, he supplied the Argentine police with Spanish versions of the trio's Pinkerton wanted circulars.[9] Although the agency had no evidence of Curry in South America, it has been stated that Dimaio decided to also include his photo and description.[10] The Argentine authorities suspected Butch and Sundance for the robbery at Rio Gallegos, and an order was issued for their arrest. A friend tipped them off before any police action could be taken. In early May 1905, they sold their ranch holdings in Cholila, and traveled with Ethel to Chile.[11]

About the latter part of 1905 or possibly early 1906, Will Coburn, Abe Gill, and other Montana ranchers visited southern Argentina for several months to investigate the prospect of ranching in Patagonia. They heard rumors that Curry, Cassidy, and Sundance were operating a ranch (under assumed names) in that country. Walt Coburn thought that Gill notified authorities in Buenos Aires and the Pinkerton Agency of the outlaws' presence, but his efforts met with little response. Leaving Gill in Buenos Aires, Will Coburn took it upon himself to travel deep into the interior with a pack outfit, to get a closer look at a South American cattle operation.[12] Joseph Kinsey Howard stated in his book *Montana: High, Wide, and Handsome*, that Will Coburn visited Kid Curry in Patagonia.[13] Walt Coburn responded, "I have no way of knowing where Howard got the information that Will Coburn paid a visit to Kid Curry at Patagonia, South America. For all I know, Will might have visited the Kid when he made the pack trip into the vast *Pampa* country. I was a kid at that time and too young to share in any confidential talk among my three half-brothers, who were fifteen to twenty years my seniors, but I do vaguely recall that Will did see Kid Curry on this trip."[14]

Gary Wilson provides a May 1906 date for Will Coburn's return to the United States. He adds that in October 1906, Montana newspapers reported Curry having been seen in South America by a "Montana man" sometime in the previous six months. Although the author does not specify any of these newspapers, he infers that the "Montana man" must have been Will Coburn.[15] In a 1936 *Great Falls Tribune* article, John Ritch stated that the Kid and Butch Cassidy were in the Argentine republic "Some time in 1905," and that "During their stay there some Montana stockmen visited the Argentine and reported to have seen Curry."[16]

Nevertheless, supposing the stories of Curry actually being in the company of his three friends at this time were true, disregarding all the evidence against Curry still being alive, this visit could not have occurred in Patagonia. As already stated, Butch, Sundance, and Ethel had fled their ranch the previous May to escape to Chile. They returned to Argentina briefly to rob the bank in Villa Mercedes, San Luis Province, on December 19, 1905.[17] There were reports that Ethel participated in the heist, along with an unidentified fourth bandit, possibly a Texan named Dey.[18] The December 24, 1905, issues of Buenos Aires newspapers *La Prensa* and *La Nacion* reported that Butch, Sundance, Ethel, and Kid Curry were suspected of the holdup.[19] Pinkerton file photographs of the four were shown to the owner of a bar which the bandits had frequented before the robbery. He readily recognized all of the people in the photos except for Curry.[20]

After 1906 the Pinkertons appeared divided in opinion that Curry was alive and in South America. In a January 15, 1907, memorandum, Robert Pinkerton states, "It is our belief that Logan joined Cassidy and Longabaugh in the Argentine."[21] Later the same year, William Pinkerton, in an address to the annual convention of the International Association of Chiefs of Police in Jamestown, Virginia, said, "'Butch' Cassidy with Harry Longbaugh and Etta Place, a clever horsewoman and rifle shot, fled to Argentine Republic, South America, where they, *it is said*, have been joined by Logan ... During the past two years, they committed several 'hold-up' bank robberies in Argentina in which Etta Place, the alleged wife of Harry Longbaugh, *it is said*, operated with the band in male attire." (Italics added)[22] It is obvious from these statements that William Pinkerton was not entirely sure of the involvement of Kid Curry and Ethel Place in any bank robberies in Argentina. (The Pinkertons referred to Ethel Place as Etta.)

It is generally believed Ethel took ship to San Francisco in early 1906, and remained in the United States. About April of that year, Sundance returned to the Cholila ranch to sell the livestock that had been left in the care of a friend and neighbor named Daniel Gibbon. He then worked his way to the central Bolivian Andes to join Butch, who had found employment at the Concordia Tin Mine.[23] In 1970, Buenos Aires journalist, Justo Piernes, wrote that Curry parted with Butch and Sundance, and joined two other North American outlaws operating in Patagonia named Robert Evans and William Wilson. He accompanied Evans and Wilson in their December 1909 holdup of the Chubut Cooperative store in Arroyo Pescado, in which the company agent was murdered. It was believed Curry had been killed by his companions a few months later near the Gulf of Corcovado on the Chilean coast.[24] Pearl Baker said he was reportedly killed by a wild mule in South America in 1909.[25]

The *Steamboat Pilot* of Steamboat Springs, Colorado, carried an eastern news dispatch in its February 23, 1910, issue that reported on Wild Bunch activities in Argentina: "Three of the most noted train robbers in the history of the West are masters of a great cattle ranch, and at the same time the leaders of a gang of brigands so powerful that the government of the Republic is forced to pay them tribute, according to a dispatch to the State Department in Washington. The bandits are George [Robert] LeRoy Parker, alias Butch Cassidy, Harry Longabaugh, alias The Sundance Kid, and, last but not least, Harvey Logan, who was the leader of the Wild Bunch, a gang which infested the Hole-in-the-Wall country ... The best men of the Pinkerton Detective Service have been detailed to capture the leaders from time to time, but have failed. They have had all three men killed or in prison, according to the reports, several times over, but each day they bobbled up in some other place."[26]

The State Department immediately asked the Pinkertons for a report on the bandits. Kid Curry had been specifically mentioned as operating in Argentina in a report from the Embassy in Buenos Aires.[27] As part of the requested information, the agency's New York office sent a February 1910 letter to William Pinkerton which stated, "We have never been advised that Harvey Logan's photograph has been identified as being in the Argentine Republic."[28]

After the robbery and murder at the store in Arroyo Pescado, and the kidnapping of a prominent Chubut rancher in March 1911, authorities began an inquiry into the activities of Evans, Wilson, and fellow gang members Andrew J. Duffy and Mansel Gibbon (the son of Daniel Gibbon). According to authors Daniel Buck and Anne Meadows, "Several Argentines interviewed during the inquiry believed that Andrew Duffy ... was Harvey Logan, alias Kid Curry. That supposition undoubtedly arose from the circulation in Argentina of Pinkerton wanted flyers that showed photographs of Butch, Sundance, Ethel ... and Harvey Logan ... How the Argentines settled on Duffy as Logan is unclear. According to the Pinkertons, no one in Argentina ever recognized Logan's photograph, and several other disreputables in the Chubut region could have qualified just as easily as Duffy ... In any event, correspondence in the record undermines the theory that Duffy was Logan." The difference in their ages was one discerning factor. Duffy was described as a young man in late 1907, while Curry would have attained forty years by that date.[29]

Furthermore, the circumstances of Duffy's death closely mirror those attributed to Curry at the hands of his companions. Witness testimony

revealed that Robert Evans and Mansel Gibbon had admitted killing
Duffy in August 1910, very close to the time of Curry's purported death.
"We killed him because he was too cruel," Gibbon said. His body was
seen near Rio Pico, south of Cholila, not far from where Curry was said
to have been killed by his companions.[30]

At the Concordia Tin Mine Butch and Sundance became close friends
with manager Percy Seibert. One day Butch began telling Seibert about
his lawless exploits in the United States and South America. He told
Seibert that he had tried to persuade Kid Curry to come with him to
South America, but he had refused. Butch added that he considered
Curry to be the bravest man he had ever known.[31] Butch and Sundance
quit their jobs at the tin mine in 1908, and traveled to southern Bolivia.
On the morning of November 4, 1908, they robbed the Aramayo company mine payroll. They died two days later in a gun battle with soldiers
and police in the small mining town of San Vicente, Bolivia. Witnesses
reported it was evident that Butch had shot a badly wounded Sundance
in the forehead, before shooting himself in the temple. They were buried
in the local cemetery as "unknowns."[32] Interestingly, Robert Evans and
William Wilson also died in a similar shootout near Rio Pico, Chubut,
Argentina, in December 1911.[33]

It is apparent that news of some American outlaws dying violently in
South America reached the United States, although the details were necessarily confused. Montana pioneer Arthur J. Jordan, writing of events
that occurred during the winter of 1906, said: "A few years afterwards,
the news reached Montana—which appears to be authentic—that [Mon-
tana outlaw] George Whitney, 'Kid' Curry, and two other outlaws had
met their death at a cabin in the interior of the Argentine Republic. After a bank holdup they had been hard pressed by Argentine police and
soldiers. After a battle of three days, the soldiers and police rushed the
cabin, discovering the four outlaws lying on the cabin floor; they had
taken their own lives, each having saved his last cartridge for himself."[34]

Inevitably, there were rumors and sightings of Kid Curry back in the
United States. In late August 1906, Abe Gill, having returned to Montana
from South America, was in the process of selling his ranch and cattle

to the Coburns. At the Circle C ranch, a tally was being made of Gill's cattle by livestock and brand inspector George Hall. Walt Coburn was on his school break, and was present during a conversation between Gill and Hall:

"When the stock inspector dropped the name of Kid Curry, I had both ears cocked. It was George Hall's opinion that Kid Curry had left South America, if he had ever gone there, and was back in the Hole-in-the-Wall country and that one of these days he would show up in the Little Rockies at his hideaway or at Jim Thornhill's ranch.

"Abe Gill was dead serious when he admitted that was one reason he was selling his ranch holdings and going back East. He said he knew if he stayed on, it would only be a matter of time until Kid Curry or one of his gang shot him down in the same manner in which Jim Winters had been murdered ...

"Just after Abe Gill sold his ranch [in fall of 1906] to the Coburn Cattle Company, he mysteriously disappeared. He supposedly rode away from his ranch on his favorite horse, White Cloud, and neither he nor his horse were ever seen again."[35]

Gary Wilson suggests the Coburns wanted Gill's land, and Hall was part of a conspiracy to scare Gill into selling his ranch. In addition, the absence of the U.S. Land Commissioner would make it much easier for the Coburns to run off unwelcome homesteaders.[36] As to what happened to Gill, he may have been murdered, or he may have met with an accident while out riding alone; no one knows for sure to this day.

"Curry Gang Again Active in Montana," reported the *Havre Plain Dealer* of October 3, 1908. The Kid Curry gang had stolen some horses and mules from a U.S. Geological survey party at Fort Peck Indian Reservation in eastern Valley County, Montana, to dispose of in Canada.[37] In his writings, John B. Ritch told of Curry visiting a few trusted friends in the Little Rockies area in summer 1910, and of hearing that the Kid had died of pneumonia in a Denver hospital in early winter of the same year.[38]

When the Gila Valley Bank at Morenci, Arizona, was held up by a lone robber on September 6, 1910, the Burns Detective Agency hired retired Pinkerton agent Charles A. Siringo to investigate. The bandit had secured

$3,000 cash, and after a short gun battle in the street with the bank manager and two employees, he raced out of town. He delayed two deputies who had followed, by jumping his horse over a cliff twelve feet high. They couldn't, or wouldn't, make the jump, and had to detour around the cliff. The posse soon lost the robber's trail on the San Francisco River, seven miles south of Morenci. Siringo concluded, after his investigation, that the daring bandit was Kid Curry. "Out in the hills I found some men who had seen him before the robbery," he wrote in *A Lone Star Cowboy*, "and their descriptions tallied with that of 'Kid Curry'." He had swarthy skin, a lean face, and dark hair and beard. His height was about five feet eight inches, and his roughly 150-pound frame was all muscle. Curry was always reported as having dark eyes; however this bandit's eyes were said to be deep-blue or brownish-gray. Siringo also said that Curry's "old pals," Butch Cassidy and Elzy Lay, had been seen together not long before the holdup.[39] This is not very definitive proof, especially since Cassidy had been lying in a grave in Bolivia for almost two years. The Morenci bank robbery was the last holdup attributed to Kid Curry.

Walt Coburn said it was about 1916, Walter Duvall estimated about 1922, when Jim Thornhill moved with his family to Globe, Arizona, and started a small ranch.[40] Here, author/illustrator Ross Santee became a good friend and confidant to Jim. One day they were sitting together on a curb in Globe, and Thornhill began telling Santee of his friend Kid Curry. Finally he chuckled and said, "Kid's still alive, of course; we don't dare write but I've had word of him."[41] Walt Coburn wrote, "In recent years Jim Thornhill told me that Kid Curry, Butch Cassidy, and the Sundance Kid had gone to South America to go into the cattle business."[42]

During the teens, twenties, and thirties, Curry allegedly visited friends all over Montana and northern Wyoming. One of these visits was supposedly witnessed by Mike O'Neil at the Mint Saloon in Great Falls during Prohibition. This was the same Great Northern Railway fireman who had testified against Curry during his Knoxville trial. While playing cards he noticed two men in conversation standing at the bar. After careful scrutiny, he determined one of the men was Kid Curry and the other was one of his old friends. Needless to say, O'Neil quickly exited the saloon without bothering to introduce himself to Curry.[43]

There have been many statements concerning his death, including one from his friend, Augusta Chamberlain, who said Kid Curry had died in an asylum in 1937 (possibly in Washington State).[44] Various stories, including one from the Kolczak family, have Curry dying of natural causes some time in the late 1950s, and buried in a cemetery in Spokane, Washington. Of course the grave cannot be found because he had been buried under an unknown assumed name.[45]

In 1959, former stagecoach driver, Ruel Horner, told the *Great Falls Tribune* that he had met Elfie Curry when she visited the Little Rockies a few years previous. She told him that the Kid had died in a car accident in Washington State "not too many years ago."[46] The *Chinook Opinion* of July 4, 1957, reported on Elfie's visit to Landusky. "The historical little mining town of Landusky vibrated with memories during the past week. A motor car drew up in front of the old Wimberly building (known as the old Wimberly saloon) and a tall stately lady, aged 78 years, and her sister stepped forth, back to their old home in the gay nineties." She introduced herself to Postmaster Ted Duvall as the wife of the late Lonie Logan. Mrs. Duvall served lunch to Elfie and her sister, during which much early local history was discussed. While taking a tour of the town, Elfie remarked on the absence of many of the old buildings, but recognized several including the summer home that had been built by her step-father, Pike Landusky. Outside of town she visited her step-father's grave, as well as those of John Curry and Jim Winters.[47]

There really isn't any verifiable proof concerning the stories of Kid Curry going to South America, or that he was seen in the United States after his reported death by suicide in Colorado in 1904. As the saying goes, "Everyone loves a good mystery," and people do not want to admit the finality that is death for someone whose life has held a great fascination. A popular folk song titled "Harvey Logan" was recorded in 1927, but by no stretch of the imagination can Kid Curry be considered a folk hero like Jesse James, Billy the Kid, and Butch Cassidy.[48] However, like them, his admirers have not allowed him to die when there is overwhelming evidence to the contrary. Hardened career criminals cannot give up their professions easily. The fact that there were no more robberies, especially of trains, which could with any certainty be attributed to Curry, should be additional proof that it was his body buried in the Glenwood Springs, Colorado, cemetery.

This author sent a letter to the editor of *The Journal*, a publication of the Western Outlaw-Lawman History Association, suggesting that Curry's body should be exhumed and its DNA compared to his living relatives. The letter appeared in the Winter 2002 issue, but it generated no response. Recently it has been stated that a Logan descendent was in favor of settling the whole matter by digging up the body of the man known as "J. H. Ross." However, when informed that the grave could not be located owing to lost plot records and past landslides, the idea was given up.[49] If he had been buried in a potter's field section of the cemetery as reported, there most likely wouldn't have been a record of the burial anyway. Still, when this author visited the Glenwood Springs Cemetery on New Year's Day 1999, he found a nondescript grave marked with a small metal tag, not far from Doc Holliday's elaborate headstone, with the name "Harvey Alexander Logan" crudely inscribed.

Author at supposed grave of Harvey Alexander Logan in Glenwood Springs, Colorado, cemetery. New Year's Day, 1999. (Author's Collection)

Endnotes

PREFACE

[1]Richard F. Selcer, *Hell's Half Acre: The Life and Legend of a Red-Light District* (Fort Worth: Texas Christian University Press, 1991), 318, endnote 8.

[2]Charles A. Siringo, *A Cowboy Detective: A True Story of Twenty-two Years with a World-Famous Detective Agency* (1912; repr., Lincoln: University of Nebraska Press, 1988), 351, 355.

[3]Harvey Logan Papers, Small Collection 2063, Montana Historical Society Archives, in John A. Lamb, "Harvey Logan's Lost Journal," *True West*, October 1994, 20.

[4]Facsimile of inquest into the death of James Winters, in Shirley Gillespie, *Goin' to 'Dusky* (Chandler, AZ: Two Dogs Publishing, 2007), 116.

[5]Robert West Howard, ed., The Westerners Chicago Corral, *This is the West* (New York: Rand McNally & Co., 1957), 122.

[6]James D. Horan, *The Great American West* (New York: Crown Publishers, 1978), 237.

[7]*Knoxville Journal and Tribune*, December 17, 1901, in Sylvia Lynch, *Harvey Logan in Knoxville* (College Station, TX: Creative Publishing, 1998), 62.

[8]*Richmond Democrat*, November 20, 1879, in William A. Settle Jr., *Jesse James Was His Name: Or, Fact and Fiction Concerning the Careers of the Notorious James Brothers of Missouri* (Columbia: University of Missouri Press, 1966), 105.

CHAPTER 1

[1]Bruce E. Logan Jr., "Kid Curry, A.K.A. Harvey Logan," website, 1999; Jesse Cole Kenworth, *Storms of Life: In Search of Kid Curry* (Bozeman, MT: Self published, 1990), 12–14, 55.

[2]Ibid., 12–13, 61. Earlier Kid Curry biographers did not find much information on his ancestors. Brown Waller, *Last of the Great Western*

Train Robbers (New York: A. S. Barnes and Co., 1968), 17–18, states that "Records in the state archives at Frankfort [Kentucky] disclose little on the family of Harvey Logan. But the Logans of Kentucky are many. They came from Ireland and settled in Virginia in early Colonial days, and were among the first settlers in the wilderness country of Kentucky, at that time a part of Virginia." He later says, "The Logans of Rowan County were prominent people—lawyers, doctors, business men ..." Horan, *Great American West*, 230, says he received details of Kid Curry's background from a family member who wished to remain anonymous. "Kid Curry came from an established Kentucky family that had links to the Lees of Virginia and produced Richard Merton Johnson, eighth vice-president of the United States. Johnson, a celebrated Kentucky lawyer, had been a congressman and senator for many years and a friend of Andrew Jackson. He served under Van Buren from 1838 to 1841."

[3]Jim Dullenty, "George Currie and the Curry Brothers," NOLA *Quarterly*, October 1979, 4–5. Dullenty traced the Logan children's ancestors through their grandmother to one William Crosthwait, married to an Ann B. After William's death, she married a Joseph Christy. Ann B. Christy died in 1786, leaving a daughter also named Ann B. The latter married Jacob Powers and gave birth to Elizabeth Ray Powers, Harvey's grandmother; Kenworth, *Storms of Life*, 13, 61; Logan, "Kid Curry."

[4]Kenworth, *Storms of Life*, 12–13, 17, 50, 61; Logan, "Kid Curry." Waller, *Last of the Great*, 19, states that the mother's first name was Amanda. The Fleming County, Kentucky, census of 1850 shows an Amanda that appears to be an older sister of the Logan children's mother, Eliza Jane.

[5]Kenworth, *Storms of Life*, 13.

[6]Ibid., 14, 17–18, 55, 61. By interviews and family records, Kenworth established that three girls born between the births of Hank and Harvey, in 1863, 1864, 1865, all died as babies or infants. Also, there were twin girls who, it is believed, died in childbirth in 1869 between the births of John and only surviving sister Arda.

[7]Dullenty, "George Currie," 5. Some writers spell Loranzo's name as Lorenzo; however Kenworth, *Storms of Life*, 18, says baptismal records

show it as Loranzo. Also, that is the way it is spelled on his gravestone in Forest Hill Cemetery in Kansas City, Missouri.

[8]Gary A. Wilson, *Tiger of the Wild Bunch: The Life and Death of Harvey "Kid Curry" Logan* (Helena, MT: TwoDot, 2007), 2–4. The author worked with Sharon Moran, the grandniece of Lonie Logan, to record what little remains of family remembrances.

[9]Kenworth, *Storms of Life*, 17.

[10]Ibid., 13, 61; Logan, "Kid Curry."

[11]Waller, *Last of the Great*, 19.

[12]Wilson, *Tiger*, 2.

[13]Dullenty, "George Currie," 5, 7. Dullenty came up with an exact birth date for Elizabeth from family sources and a death certificate. Federal census records for 1850, 1860, 1870 and 1880, various states and counties, contain errors which could make the birth year in 1827, 1828 or 1829. Also the Oct. 7, 1849, marriage date from the Marriage Records of Fleming County, Ky., 1798–1851, appears to be much more accurate than the Aug. 1, 1832, date given by Kenworth, *Storms of Life*, 13, 61, and Bruce E. Logan Jr., "Kid Curry." That would make Hiram about seven years old and Elizabeth between three and four years old when they were married. Information concerning the Lees' movements was ultimately obtained by Dullenty from a "History of Jackson County, Mo., 1881," 997; Kenworth, *Storms of Life*, 13, 53–54. The 1860 census record for Shawnee Township, Johnson County, Kansas, and the 1870 census for Dodson Post Office, Lee's Summit Township, Jackson County, Missouri, corroborate the destinations and timing of the Lees' moves stated by Dullenty.

[14]Horan, *Great American West,* 231.

[15]Dullenty, "George Currie," 5.

[16]Kenworth, *Storms of Life*, 54; Logan, "Kid Curry."

[17]Horan, *Great American West,* 231. Wilson, *Tiger*, 3, says the Logan family believes that Arda and Lonie remained with the Lees, while Harvey and Johnny were sent to live with other relatives, at least for a time, in Marion County, Kansas, near Peabody.

[18]Howard, *This Is the West*, 117.

[19]Horan, *Great American West,* 231.

[20]*Kansas City Star*, February 28, 1900.

[21]James D. Horan, and Paul Sann, *Pictorial History of the Wild West* (New York: Crown Publishers, 1954), 198.

[22]Stella Frances James, *In the Shadow of Jesse James* (Thousand Oaks, CA: Revolver Press, 1990), 111, 117.

[23]Howard, *This is the West*, 117.

[24]Waller, *Last of the Great*, 19, 22.

[25]Samuel K. Phillips Jr., *Fallen Branches on Montana Soil* (Lewistown, MT: Ballyhoo Printing and Design, 2005), 49, 52.

[26]Wilson, *Tiger*, 3–5.

CHAPTER 2

[1]Waller, *Last of the Great*, 19, 22; Kenworth, *Storms of Life*, 20.

[2]Charles A. Siringo, *A Lone Star Cowboy* (Santa Fe: Siringo, 1919), 234–35.

[3]A. V. Cheney, "Kid Curry and His Brothers," *True West*, April 1962, 69.

[4]John B. Ritch, "Kid Curry, 'Bad Man'," Part 1; *Great Falls Tribune*, June 21, 1936, 14.

[5]Waller, *Last of the Great*, 22; E. C. Abbott, and Helena Huntington Smith, *We Pointed Them North: Recollections of a Cowpuncher* (Norman: University of Oklahoma Press, 1971), vii. Map titled "The Texas Trail": "The route indicated is that of the Western Trail, which succeeded the Chisholm Trail in the late seventies."

[6]Dullenty, "George Currie," 4–5.

[7]Kenworth, *Storms of Life*, 24–25; Phillips, *Fallen Branches*, 49.

[8]Alva Josiah Noyes, *In the Land of Chinook; or, The Story of Blaine County* (Helena, MT: State Pub. Co., 1917), 115.

[9]Michael S. Kennedy, ed., *Cowboys and Cattlemen* (New York: Hastings House, Publishers, 1964), 239.

[10]Ibid., 241.

[11]Phillips, *Fallen Branches*, 49, 53.

[12]Noyes, *Land of Chinook*, 115; Kenworth, *Storms of Life*, 25.

[13]Ibid.

[14]Noyes, *Land of Chinook*, 115. In Dullenty, "George Currie," 6, the author states that Kid Curry worked in the store of Vincent Gies in

Maiden, Montana, just northeast of Lewistown, that winter. (See end-notes 24, 30, 43, on p. 7.)

[15]Walt Coburn, *Pioneer Cattleman in Montana: The Story of the Circle C Ranch* (Norman: University of Oklahoma Press, 1968), 54; Truman McGiffin Cheney, with Roberta Carkeek Cheney, *So Long, Cowboys of the Open Range* (Helena, MT: Falcon Publishing, Inc., 1990), 94–95.

[16]Ritch, "Kid Curry, 'Bad Man'," Part 1, 14.

[17]Kenworth, *Storms of Life*, 25. Paraphrases A. J. Davis' statements made in the 1920s.

[18]Con Price, *Memories of Old Montana* (Hollywood: The Highland Press, 1945), 85–86.

[19]Ritch, "Kid Curry, 'Bad Man'," Part 1, 14.

[20]Coburn, *Pioneer Cattleman*, 54.

[21]Thornhill's 1904 application for marriage to Lucy Tressler shows he was born in Jackson County, Missouri (Kenworth, *Storms of Life*, 118.) It's interesting that writers still assert to this day that Jim Thorn-hill was really Frank "Dad" Jackson of the old Sam Bass outlaw gang of Texas. The source of this misconception was Pinkerton Detective Charlie Siringo who wrote of his belief in at least two of his books. Thornhill himself told Walt Coburn (*Pioneer Cattleman*, 108) that he was too young to be Jackson. This is true because Thornhill's 1904 application for marriage to Lucy Tressler indicates his birth year as 1864 (November). As Jesse Cole Kenworth (*Storms of Life*, 15–16, 118–19) points out, Thornhill would have only been thirteen years old in 1878 when the Sam Bass Gang met its end in Round Rock, Texas.

[22]Granville Stuart, *Forty Years on the Frontier*, vol. 2 (Harrisburg, PA: The National Historical Society, 1994), 230.

[23]Waller, *Last of the Great*, 24; Stuart, *Forty Years*, 213–14, 231–32. In the spring of 1885, the DHS (Davis, Hauser, and Stuart) had a change of ownership. Granville Stuart and Conrad Kohrs became sole owners, and incorporated under the name Pioneer Cattle Company.

[24]Ritch, "Kid Curry, 'Bad Man'," Part 1, 14.

[25]Donna B. Ernst, *Sundance, My Uncle* (College Station, TX: Creative Publishing Co., 1992), 33–35, hereafter cited as *SMU*; Vivian A. Pala-din, ed., *From Buffalo Bones to Sonic Boom* (Glasgow, MT: Glasgow Jubilee Committee, 1962), 5.

[26]*Daily Yellowstone Journal*, June 9, 1887, in Mary Garman, *Harry Longabaugh—The Sundance Kid, The Early Years, 1867–1889* (Pamphlet published by Crook County Museum, 1978), 3–4. From a letter to the newspaper that Harry Longabaugh wrote after his arrest.

[27]*The Sundance Gazette*, March 18, 1887, in Garman, *Harry Longabaugh*, 1.

[28]Garman, *Harry Longabaugh*, 1–5; Ernst, *SMU*, 40–45.

[29]Horan, *Great American West*, 232.

[30]Donna B. Ernst, *Harvey Logan, Wildest of the Wild Bunch* (Kearney, NE: Morris Publishing, 2003), 9.

[31]Ernst, *SMU*, 35; Roberta Carkeek Cheney, *Names on the Face of Montana: The Story of Montana's Place Names* (Missoula, MT: Mountain Press Publishing Co., 1983), 22–23, states that McNamara and Marlow owned a freight depot in Big Sandy.

[32]Coburn, *Pioneer Cattleman*, 15, 18, 54, 69–70.

[33]Ibid., 70.

[34]"Kid Curry," *The Lewistown Democrat*, December 19, 1902, in Phillips, *Fallen Branches*, 51.

[35]Ritch, "Kid Curry, 'Bad Man'," Part 1, 14; Kenworth, *Storms of Life*, 28.

[36]Charles Greenfield, "How the Logan Boys Got That Way," *Golden West*, September 1969, 15–16. Cites an unpublished manuscript in the Montana Historical Library.

[37]Floyd Hardin, *Campfires and Cowchips* (Great Fall, MT: Privately published, 1972), 73–74.

[38]Ritch, "Kid Curry, 'Bad Man'," Part 1, 14.

[39]Waller, *Last of the Great*, 25–26.

[40]Noyes, *Land of Chinook*, 29.

[41]Ritch, "Kid Curry, 'Bad Man'," Part 1, 14.

[42]Eugene Cunningham, *Triggernometry: A Gallery of Gunfighters* (Caldwell, ID: The Caxton Printers, Ltd., 1941), 438–39.

[43]Gillespie, *Goin' to 'Dusky*, 128–29; Phillips County Historical Society, *The Yesteryears* (Havre, MT: Griggs Printing & Publishing, 1978), 85–86, 100–1.

[44][Gladys Costello], *The Golden Era of the Little Rockies: Stories Written by Gladys Costello* (Privately published, n.d.), 24.

[45]Phillips County, *Yesteryears*, 86, 101; Dorothy M. Johnson, "Durable Desperado Kid Curry," *Montana: The Magazine of Western History*, April 1956, 23; John Willard, *Adventure Trails in Montana* (Billings, MT: Privately printed, 1971), 143.

[46]Gillespie, *Goin' to 'Dusky*, 128–29.

[47]Phillips County, *Yesteryears*, 75–77.

[48]Edward M. Kirby, *The Rise and Fall of the Sundance Kid* (Iola, WI: Western Publications, 1983), 37, 39. Donna Ernst believes there isn't any evidence that Sundance worked in Montana at this time, but that he went to Canada almost directly after leaving jail in Sundance, Wyoming, in early February 1889. Author's phone conversation with Donna B. Ernst on January 12, 2012.

[49]BLM homestead records: Fergus County, Township 19N and Range 18E. http://www.glorecords.blm.gov

[50]Noyes, *Land of Chinook*, 116; Horan, *Great American West*, 233.

[51]*Lewistown News Argus*, July 21, 1892, and *The Chinook Opinion*, August 25, 1892, in Phillips, *Fallen Branches*, 52. The author states that the doctors waited a month before finally deciding to amputate John Curry's right arm, with his brother Harvey and James Thornhill giving their consent; Gary A. Wilson, *Outlaw Tales of Montana* (Havre, MT: High-Line Books, 1995), 137–38; Waller, *Last of the Great*, 179–80; Horan, *Great American West,* 233. Horan does not cite a source, but says John Curry's arm was amputated on July 20, 1892. However, in James D. Horan, *The Authentic Wild West: The Gunfighters* (New York: Crown Publishers, Inc., 1976), 298, endnote 10, Horan traces this story to the *Fort Benton River Press*, February 3, 4, 5, 1896, which reported John Curry's death in a gun battle with rancher James Winters on February 1, 1896. This report is over three and one-half years after the supposed altercation with Olson occurred. In fact Horan states, "No other newspaper, particularly those who reported the Winters-Curry shooting, described Curry as having one arm."

[52]Waller, *Last of the Great*, 25; Kenworth, *Storms of Life*, 14.

[53]Kenworth, *Storms of Life*, 14–15; Willard, *Adventure Trails*, 139.

[54]Phillips, *Fallen Branches*, 52–53.

[55]Wilson, *Tiger*, 2, 4, 32; Horan, *Great American West*, 231.

⁵⁶Wilson, *Tiger*, 32; Waller, *Last of the Great*, 25.

⁵⁷Wilson, *Tiger*, 4, 32; Horan, *Great American West*, 230.

CHAPTER 3

¹John B. Ritch, "True Story of Pike Landusky Better than Beadles's Best Thriller," *Great Falls Tribune*, January 20, 1935; ["Teddy Blue" Abbott], "Pike Landusky, Trapper, Woodhawk and Gold Miner," *The Boulder Monitor*, n.d.

²*The River Press* (Fort Benton), January 9, 1895; Gillespie, *Goin' to 'Dusky*, 41, 43. Cites a July 4, 1949, Earl Talbott letter, Small Collection 2079, Montana Historical Society, Helena, Montana.

³Phillips, *Fallen Branches*, 29; Gillespie, *Goin' to 'Dusky*, 41. This date is also inscribed at his gravesite on his old ranch near the town of Landusky.

⁴*The River Press* (Fort Benton), January 9, 1895. Places Landusky's arrival in Fort Benton in July 1868; Gillespie, *Goin' to 'Dusky*, 43. The author says specifically July of 1868, citing a July 4, 1949, Earl Talbott letter, Small Collection 2079, Montana Historical Society, Helena, Montana; Eugene Lee Silliman, ed., *We Seized Our Rifles: Recollections of the Montana Frontier* (Missoula, MT: Mountain Press Publishing Co., 1982), 76. J. H. Boucher, a friend of Landusky's, says Pike came to Last Chance Gulch in 1868.

⁵*The River Press* (Fort Benton), January 9, 1895; Ritch, "True Story."

⁶Silliman, *We Seized*, 76; Muriel Sibell Wolle, *Montana Pay Dirt: A Guide to the Mining Camps of the Treasure State* (Denver: Sage Books, 1963), 75, 82; Waller, *Last of the Great*, 61.

⁷Abbott and Smith, *We Pointed*, 173–74; Ritch, "True Story."

⁸[Abbott], "Pike Landusky"; Phillips, *Fallen Branches*, 31. Cites the June 1880, Montana Territory census, listing Landusky as a thirty-one-year-old, white male, and his occupation as a wood chopper.

⁹Silliman, *We Seized*, 180; Wolle, *Montana*, 372; [Abbott], "Pike Landusky."

¹⁰Ibid.; Silliman, *We Seized*, 76-84; Ritch, "True Story."

¹¹Abbott and Smith, *We Pointed*, 172.

¹²[Abbott], "Pike Landusky"; Gillespie, *Goin' to 'Dusky*, 44.

[13]Abbott and Smith, *We Pointed*, 177; Kenworth, *Storms of Life*, 29, 60. Cites 1900 census for Landusky Township, Chouteau County, Montana; Gillespie, *Goin' to 'Dusky*, 11, 44, 53, 55–57, 64.

[14]Phillips, *Fallen Branches*, 32–33.

[15]Ibid., 35. Cites *The Mineral Argus* (Maiden), July 14 and 17, 1884.

[16]Noyes, *Land of Chinook*, 32–34; Ritch, "True Story"; Wolle, *Montana*, 370, 372–73.

[17]Phillips, *Fallen Branches*, 36–37. Cites *The Mineral Argus* (Maiden), March 12, May 7, and November 19, 1885, *The Helena Independent*, November 5, 1885, and *United States vs. Pike Landusky*, United States Court District of Montana. From the National Archives, Seattle, Washington.

[18]Abbott and Smith, *We Pointed*, 171–72.

[19]Ibid., 176; Waller, *Last of the Great*, 67.

[20]Gillespie, *Goin' to 'Dusky*, 43, 45.

[21]Ibid., 45, 53.

[22]Wolle, *Montana*, 373; Ritch, "True Story"; Waller, *Last of the Great*, 66.

[23]Walter W. Duvall, with Helen Duvall-Arthur, *Memories of a Filly Chaser* (Privately published, 1992), 171. From a March 19, 1958, letter written by Augusta Chamberlain to a friend in Harlem, Montana.

[24]Wolle, *Montana*, 373-74.

[25]Ritch, "True Story"; *The Havre Advertiser*, July 19, 1894, in Phillips, *Fallen Branches*, 23–24, 39, 55.

[26]Gillespie, *Goin' to 'Dusky*, 11; Phillips, *Fallen Branches*, 40.

[27]Ernst, *Harvey Logan*, 12; Wilson, *Outlaw Tales*, 139; Dullenty, "George Currie," 5; Kenworth, *Storms of Life*, 22.

[28]Duvall and Duvall-Arthur, *Memories*, 166, 169, 171–72, 303. From a March 19, 1958, letter written by Augusta Chamberlain to a friend in Harlem, Montana.

[29]*The Chinook Opinion*, October 18 and November 15, 1894, in Phillips, *Fallen Branches*, 40, 55; *The Havre Advertiser*, July 19, 1894, article printed in Wolle, *Montana*, 374. Although some authors claim Lee left Missouri to go to Montana with cousins Hank and Harvey Logan in 1884, or had later accompanied younger cousins John or Lonie in 1888/1889, it is not certain when he came west. His name is conspicuously absent at the time the Currys were cowboys and when they were

building their ranch on Rock Creek. In fact, except for the tidbit of information mentioned in the Havre newspaper, there is a complete lack of historical records and family history that would place Lee in Montana any time before 1899. The first known instance of his presence in the west is about 1896, when he was living in Cripple Creek, Colorado, employed in mining and saloon work.

³⁰Wilson, *Tiger*, 23–24; Phillips, *Fallen Branches*, 57–58. (Remembrances from Landusky's step-daughter Elfie, who wrote her memoirs in an undated manuscript, entitled "Life of Elfie Dessery Logan.")

³¹Noyes, *Land of Chinook*, 116.

³²Ritch, "True Story." "Many new men came to the camp and into the mountains and the cowpunchers whooped it up plenty."

³³"Tells of Curry Gang," *The Lewistown Democrat*, December 5, 1902, in Phillips, *Fallen Branches*, 53, 71; Wilson, *Outlaw Tales*, 135–36.

³⁴C. W. Duvall, "Milk River Bill," *Great Falls Tribune*, November 17, 1935, 10–12.

³⁵Phillips County, *Yesteryears*, 6–7, 84–85.

³⁶Robert W. Lind, *From the Ground Up: The Story of "Brother Van" Orsdel, Pioneer Montana Minister* (Montana: Treasure State Publishing Co., 1961), 153–56.

³⁷Ibid., 156-57.

³⁸Kenworth, *Storms of Life*, 29, 61. Elfie's baptismal name was Cindinilla Athanissa Dessery. She was born on November 18, 1878, in Colorado.

³⁹Coburn, *Pioneer Cattleman*, 57.

⁴⁰Ritch, "True Story."

⁴¹Duvall and Duvall-Arthur, *Memories*, 173. From a March 19, 1958 letter, written by Augusta Chamberlain to a friend in Harlem, Montana.

⁴²Kenworth, *Storms of Life*, 31-32. Sometimes it is stated that the cattle were owned by Jim Winters, a neighbor of the Currys'. In yet other accounts Jim Thornhill is also charged, and Lonie is substituted for John.

⁴³Ibid., 15; Duvall and Duvall-Arthur, *Memories*, 178. Information from an article by Charles W. Duvall, "The Disappearance of Abram Ditmars Gill," circa 1940.

⁴⁴Dullenty, "George Currie," 7; Kenworth, *Storms of Life*, 19. In 1889 the couple and their two children located on some land in Chouteau

County near her brothers. They also had some extra money to invest in the Curry ranch. For some reason the couple began to become estranged, with Lee blaming the brothers' interference in their marriage. (Wilson, *Tiger*, 15, 24.) Also, Allie found that she did not like Montana, and she may have become overwhelmed by the family's feud with Landusky and its tragic results. Whatever the reason, she returned to Missouri in 1895 and divorced Lee. By spring of 1896 Allie had met and married Manuel R. Rodriguez, and they were living in the Kansas City area. (Kenworth, *Storms of Life*, 19.) They later changed their place of residence to Noel, McDonald County, in the very southwest corner of Missouri. (Wilson, *Tiger*, 175; Gillespie, *Goin' to 'Dusky*, 78.) Lee Self died in Malta of a heart attack on June 21, 1913. (Kenworth, *Storms of Life*, 19, 63; Gillespie, *Goin' to 'Dusky*, 78.)

45File case no. 1107, District Court records, Chouteau County, Montana.

46*The Chinook Opinion*, September 27 and October 16, 1894, in Phillips, *Fallen Branches*, 40; Gillespie, *Goin' to 'Dusky*, 45, 103.

47Noyes, *Land of Chinook*, 116-17; Coburn, *Pioneer Cattleman*, 57. Coburn has Lonie Curry as a prisoner instead of his brother John Curry.

48Noyes, *Land of Chinook*, 117; Wilson, *Tiger*, 34.

49Ibid.

50Duvall and Duvall-Arthur, *Memories*, 168; Coburn, *Pioneer Cattleman*, 58, 60.

51Ibid., 60.

52*The River Press* (Fort Benton), December 7, 1894, in Phillips, *Fallen Branches*, 57.

53Kenworth, *Storms of Life*, 32.

54*The River Press* (Fort Benton), November 28, 1894, and *The Chinook Opinion*, December 6, 1894, in Phillips, *Fallen Branches*, 40, 58; File case no. 1111, District Court records, Chouteau County, Montana, cited in Ernst, *Harvey Logan*, 11, 83.

55Ibid.

56Kenworth, *Storms of Life*, 32.

57Ibid., 31.

58Horan, *The Gunfighters*, 192.

59Noyes, *Land of Chinook*, 116–17.

60Duvall and Duvall-Arthur, *Memories*, 102; Ritch, "True Story."

[61]Ibid.

[62]Ibid. (Wilson, *Outlaw Tales*, 136, says Dad Marsh may have financed John Curry's new barn. Marsh sued the Curry brothers for defaulting on a loan of $932.70 in September 1893.)

[63]Wilson, *Tiger*, 35.

[64]Ritch, "True Story."

[65]Ibid. Bill Kellerman described a different scene concerning the Curry boys' behavior during the Christmas season of 1894. Kellerman was a fifteen-year-old orphan when he arrived in the Little Rockies in October 1894. He had come out from Missouri with Pike Landusky when the latter made the trip to bring back a number of his relatives to Montana. Kellerman is quoted in [Costello], *Golden Era*, 24: "A Christmas dance was being held in Landusky. That night the Curry Gang shot up the town, including the dance hall. They shot the piano to splinters, broke guitars over the musicians' heads and generally wrecked the place." This and other sensational stories he recites are to be read with caution. Many of his statements are inaccurate to say the least. For example, he includes the presence of Harry Longabaugh, the Sundance Kid, at Kid Curry's confrontation with Pike Landusky on December 27, 1894. There is no evidence of this in the contemporary sources, which includes court records.

[66]Wilson, *Tiger*, 36.

CHAPTER 4

[1]Phillips, *Fallen Branches*, 18–22. Cites *Great Falls Tribune*, November 17, 1891, and March 5, 8, and 14, 1893, *The River Press* (Fort Benton), November 18, 1891, and December 28, 1891, and *Lewistown News Argus*, March 16, 1893. Harris was charged with assault with intent to commit murder, found guilty, and sentenced to one year at the Montana State Penitentiary at Deer Lodge.

[2]Ritch, "True Story"; Kenworth, *Storms of Life*, 35–36.

[3]The recounting of the fight is taken from sworn witness testimony given at the December 31, 1894, coroner's inquest concerning the death of Powell "Pike" Landusky on December 27, 1894. When quoting, I left the spelling and phrasing in its original form; some punctuation has been added for clarity.

[4]Even though Hogan was a friend of Jacob Harris, he called it as he saw it when giving evidence. He (and other witnesses) did not back testimony from Harris and Landusky's miner friends who had stated that Lonie and Thornhill held guns and threatened to kill anyone who interfered in the fight.

[5]Testimony in the case of *The State of Montana vs. James Thornhill*, File case no. 1188, District Court records, Chouteau County, Montana. The record clearly shows that Charles Annis (Hogan) was willing to swear that "During the progress of the fight, Curry's pistol fell to the floor out of his pocket, and was picked up by the defendant, who held it in his hand, grasping it by the barrel, at the same time calling the attention of the bystanders to the fact, that he was not drawing any pistol, he continued to hold the pistol in his hand, in such manner, that he could not have discharged it."

[6]Most accounts say that Landusky pulled a handkerchief from his pocket to wipe his face. This statement is not part of the coroner's inquest testimony, but is included in File case no. 1188, District Court records, Chouteau County, Montana.

[7]There has been much conjecture concerning the make and type of gun that Landusky drew from his pocket, a possibility being it was a new (1893) semiautomatic Borchardt pistol he wasn't familiar with. (Kenworth, *Storms of Life*, 39.) His step-daughter Elfie stated that Landusky, when returning to Montana with relatives he had brought from Missouri in October 1894, bought a "special gun" in Chinook. (Gillespie, *Goin' to 'Dusky*, 70.) This could be so; however, the testimony just describes the gun as a revolver.

[8]Landusky never got to move in according to local residents. The author verified the home was still standing as of July 1999.

[9]Wilson, *Tiger*, xiv, 36–37.

[10]Waller, *Last of the Great*, 70–71.

[11]Coburn, *Pioneer Cattleman*, 67–68; BLM map #16, Zortman, Montana, N4730-W10800, 1987. (This author visited the site of Kid Curry's Hideaway in July 1999 with local resident, Mr. Winston Mitchell. There is nothing left of the cabin except possibly a few boards on the ground.)

[12]Duvall and Duvall-Arthur, *Memories*, 167.

[13]File case nos. 1155 and 1157, District Court records, Chouteau County, Montana, cited in Ernst, *Harvey Logan*, 83–84, 86. Not long after the

killing of Pike Landusky (at least by mid-March 1895), Lonie Curry's name began to appear on legal documents as "Louis" Curry. Also, as discovered by Jim Dullenty, Lonie signed a Chouteau County election registrar in 1896 as Louis Curry. (See Dullenty, "George Currie," 5.)

[14]Noyes, *Land of Chinook*, 117–18.

[15]Gillespie, *Goin' to 'Dusky*, 79, 151.

[16]Noyes, *Land of Chinook*, 118; Copy of the "Summary of the acquittals of Louis [Lonie] Curry and James Thornhill in the death of Pike Landusky." Chouteau County Records, Fort Benton, Montana, in Phillips, *Fallen Branches*, 60.

CHAPTER 5

[1]Coburn, *Pioneer Cattleman*, 68, 107.

[2]Waller, *Last of the Great*, 26; Alan Lee Brekke, *Kid Curry: Train Robber* (Harlem, MT: Privately published, 1989), 32–33.

[3]Ross Santee, *Lost Pony Tracks* (1953; New York: Bantam Books, 1956), 142.

[4]Copy of the "Summary of the acquittals of Louis [Lonie] Curry and James Thornhill in the death of Pike Landusky." Chouteau County Records, Fort Benton, Montana, in Phillips, *Fallen Branches*, 60; File case no. 1188, District Court records, Chouteau County, Montana.

[5]Chicago *Herald*, April 16, 1892, in Helena Huntington Smith, *The War on Powder River: The History of an Insurrection* (New York: McGraw-Hill Book Company, 1966), xi.

[6]Pearl Baker, *The Wild Bunch at Robbers Roost* (New York: Abelard-Schuman, 1965), 186; Waller, *Last of the Great*, 37.

[7]Ibid.

[8]Joe LeFors, *Wyoming Peace Officer; An Autobiography* (Laramie, WY: Laramie Printers, Inc., 1953), 103–4.

[9]Waller, *Last of the Great*, 37.

[10]Kennedy, *Cowboys and Cattlemen,* 262, note 16.

[11]*Cheyenne Daily Sun*, August 6, 1893, and *The Laramie Boomerang*, December 4, 1896, in Mike Bell, "The Friends and Enemies of the Notorious Nutcher Brothers," WWHA *Journal*, August 2010, 40–41.

[12]Richard Patterson, *Butch Cassidy, a Biography* (Lincoln: University of Nebraska Press, 1998), 50–53, 124.

[13]Baker, *Wild Bunch*, 186.

[14]Buffalo Centennial Committee, *Buffalo's First Century* (Buffalo, WY: Buffalo Bulletin, Inc., 1984), 34–35, 74; Margaret Brock Hanson, ed., *Powder River Country: The Papers of J. Elmer Brock* (Kaycee, WY: Self published, 1981), 277, 383.

[15]Kenworth, *Storms of Life*, 23.

[16]Patterson, *Butch Cassidy*, 46, 53, 60–67, 71, 78.

[17]Matt Warner, *The Last of the Bandit Riders* (New York: Bonanza Books, 1950), 292–93.

[18]Grace McClure, *The Bassett Women* (Athens, OH: Swallow Press/ Ohio University Press, 1985), 57.

[19]Dick DeJournette and Daun DeJournette, *One Hundred Years of Brown's Park and Diamond Mountain*, 2nd ed. (Vernal, UT: DeJournette Enterprises, 1997), 223–24. Daun DeJournette interview with Josie Bassett Morris in the 1950s.

[20]McClure, *Bassett Women*, 58–59. Quotes Ann Bassett letter to Esther Campbell. Ann indicated that the Thanksgiving dinner took place in 1895; however Butch was still in prison in Wyoming at that time.

[21]Charles Kelly, *The Outlaw Trail: A History of Butch Cassidy and His Wild Bunch* (New York: The Devin-Adair Company, 1959), 95–96, 135, 137–40. Contrary to what Kelly stated, Donna Ernst says there is no evidence that the Castle Gate robbers went to Robbers Roost after the holdup. She believes they spent a few months at Powder Springs, Colorado, before celebrating in Baggs, Wyoming, in late July 1897. Author's phone conversation with Donna B. Ernst on January 12, 2012.

[22]Ibid., 141.

[23]Patterson, *Butch Cassidy*, 112; Kirby, *Rise and Fall*, 41; Ernst, *SMU*, 23–25, 53.

[24]Garman, "Harry Longabaugh," 4–5.

[25]Donna B. Ernst, *The Sundance Kid: The Life of Harry Alonzo Long-abaugh* (Norman: University of Oklahoma Press, 2009), 49, 53; Patterson, *Butch Cassidy*, 117–18.

[26]Ibid., 119–22; Kirby, *Rise and Fall*, 46-48; Ernst, *Sundance*, 54–59.

[27]Kirby, *Rise and Fall*, 41, 48.

[28]Ernst, *SMU*, 35; Paladin, *From Buffalo Bones*, 6.

[29]Ernst, *Sundance*, 61–62.

[30]*Craig Courier*, January 9 and 16, 1897, in Ernst, *Sundance*, 64.

[31]John Rolfe Burroughs, *Where the Old West Stayed Young* (New York: Bonanza Books, 1962), 43; Kelly, *Outlaw Trail*, 130; Ernst, *Sundance*, 23; Waller, *Last of the Great*, 89.

[32]Dullenty, "George Currie," 4.

[33]Kelly, *Outlaw Trail*, 113.

CHAPTER 6

[1]Duvall and Duvall-Arthur, *Memories*, 176–77. Quoted from an article by Charles W. Duvall, "The Disappearance of Abram Ditmars Gill," circa 1940. Dan Tressler, a ranching neighbor of the Currys', had taken part in the initial gold rush into the Little Rockies in 1884. After this short-lived boom, with only a small amount of placer gold being found, Tressler eventually quit mining to take up ranching south of the Little Rockies. About 1888 he squatted or homesteaded on what was to become a valuable piece of land, and built a roomy log house on it. (See Marvin M. Morin, "Two Graves in Montana," *True West*, March 1984, 54.)

[2]Morin, "Two Graves," 54.

[3]Noyes, *Land of Chinook*, 116.

[4]Morin, "Two Graves," 54–55; Wilson, *Outlaw Tales*, 143.

[5]Wilson, *Outlaw Tales*, 144, 146–47. Winters came to Montana in 1884 after working the previous seven years for some of the most famous cattle ranches in Texas. (Duvall and Duvall-Arthur, *Memories*, 177–78.) He first worked for cattle outfits along the Yellowstone River, and then went north to work for an outfit in Valley County riding range. He tried his hand at operating a harness shop in Malta for several years, before moving to Landusky and meeting Dan Tressler. (Waller, *Last of the Great*, 178–79.)

[6]Kenworth, *Storms of Life*, 33.

[7]Coburn, *Pioneer Cattleman*, 72; Waller, *Last of the Great*, 179-80.

[8]Wilson, *Tiger*, 43.

[9]Horan, *The Gunfighters*, 194–95.

[10]Coburn, *Pioneer Cattleman*, 72–74.

[11]W. W. Lampkin testimony in facsimile of coroner's inquest into the death of John Curry, February 1, 1896, in Phillips, *Fallen Branches*, 108; Phillips County, *Yesteryears*, 79–80; Coburn, *Pioneer Cattleman*,

73, 76. Credits: *Chinook Opinion*, February 6, 1896; Waller, *Last of the Great*, 180; Horan, *Great American West*, 236–37.

[12]Facsimile of coroner's inquest into the death of John Curry, February 1, 1896, in Gillespie, *Goin' to 'Dusky*, 84; Noyes, *Land of Chinook*, 116. The quote is from Dad Marsh's account of the killing of John Curry. It is possibly an indication that John may not have been one-armed. (See Horan, *The Gunfighters*, 298, endnote 10.) It is definitely not conclusive evidence; however it would seem quite awkward for a man with one arm to ride one horse while leading another, in addition to engaging in a shootout. It is curious that Dad Marsh, a close friend of the Currys', never mentioned John as having only one arm in his reminiscences.

[13]Facsimile of coroner's inquest into the death of John Curry, February 1, 1896, in Gillespie, *Goin' to 'Dusky*, 85–86; *The Chinook Opinion*, February 6, 1896, *The River Press* (Fort Benton), February 12, 1896, *The Fergus County Argus*, February 1896 (No date cited), in Phillips, *Fallen Branches*, 61; Coburn, *Pioneer Cattleman*, 74; Noyes, *Land of Chinook*, 116.

[14]"The Curry Shooting," *The Daily River Press* (Ft. Benton), February 5, 1896; Coburn, *Pioneer Cattleman,* 74–75; Horan, *Great American West*, 236.

[15]Facsimile of coroner's inquest into the death of John Curry, February 1, 1896, in Gillespie, *Goin' to 'Dusky*, 83–86. James D. Horan briefly questioned whether John Curry really had his right arm amputated after his 1892 fight with the sheepherder. It is tantalizing to read through the February 1, 1896, coroner's inquest report into the death of John Curry. Unfortunately, although it states that "The body lay face upward with left arm outstretched," and also relates the positions of his left and right legs to their surroundings, there is no mention of his right arm, missing or otherwise. On the other hand, maybe this actually answers the question; Phillips, *Fallen Branches*, 61; Horan, *Great American West*, 236–37.

[16]Waller, *Last of the Great*, 180–81.

[17]"The Curry Shooting," *The Daily River Press* (Ft. Benton), February 5, 1896.

[18]Waller, *Last of the Great*, 71.

[19]Wilson, *Tiger*, 45.

[20]Coburn, *Pioneer Cattleman*, 76–77.

[21]Waller, *Last of the Great*, 71.

[22]Gillespie, *Goin' to 'Dusky*, 67, 72. Unfortunately the author does not cite her sources for this elopement and marriage. She admits her queries have not located a marriage record.

CHAPTER 7

[1]May Gardner letter to the *Buffalo Voice*, December 15, 1922, in F. Bruce Lamb, *Kid Curry: The Life and Times of Harvey Logan and the Wild Bunch* (Boulder: Johnson Publishing, 1991), 335, chapter 16, endnote 1. Lamb's book was written as fiction based on fact. Nevertheless, it includes endnotes citing primary and secondary sources. His book is cited only a few times in this volume, and these are taken exclusively from historic material in his endnotes. The majority of the citations reflect his use of primary sources, the remainder from secondary sources as indicated.

[2]Hanson, *Powder River*, 209, 435–36.

[3]Thelma Gatchell Condit, "The Hole-in-the-Wall," *Annals of Wyoming*, October 1959, 192–93. (This author visited the site of the Grigg post office in September 2009. All that is left are the cement steps that the present owners of the property use at the back door of their modern log home.)

[4]Waller, *Last of the Great*, 73–74.

[5]Larry Pointer, *In Search of Butch Cassidy* (Norman: University of Oklahoma Press, 1977), 124–25. Cites Millicent James interview with James K. Dullenty at Kaycee, Wyoming, April 1974. Pointer's book is based on a manuscript entitled "The Bandit Invincible, the Story of Butch Cassidy," written by William T. Phillips. Put simply, the manuscript claimed that Cassidy did not die in Bolivia, but escaped and came back to the U.S. to start a new life (as Phillips according to Pointer). Disregarding this false thesis, Pointer otherwise did much valid research concerning events in the real Cassidy's life, and this is reflected in his endnotes. The book is cited infrequently in this volume; the majority of references are based on Pointer's use of primary sources.

[6]Waller, *Last of the Great*, 74. Although Waller made use of many old newspapers in writing his book on Kid Curry, he does not cite his sources for this incident.

[7]*Buffalo Bulletin*, April 22, 1897, in Pointer, *In Search of Cassidy*, 125.

[8]Waller, *Last of the Great*, 74.

[9]Hanson, *Powder River*, 435–36. This and other accounts are at odds with Charles Kelly's assertion that Deane's "killers then roped his body and dragged it through the sagebrush until it was unrecognizable." (Kelly, *Outlaw Trail*, 119.)

[10]Ibid., 436.

[11]Waller, *Last of the Great*, 74–75.

[12]Kelly, *Outlaw Trail*, 119.

[13]*Wyoming Tribune*, February 13, 1942, in Pointer, *In Search of Cassidy*, 125.

[14]Kelly, *Outlaw Trail*, 118, 121.

[15]Hanson, *Powder River*, 438-39.

[16]Ibid., 437.

[17]Phillips, *Fallen Branches*, 63.

[18]Gillespie, *Goin' to 'Dusky*, 68.

[19]*The Lewistown Democrat*, March 11 and 18, 1897, and *Great Falls Tribune*, March 6, 1897, in Phillips, *Fallen Branches*, 25–26, 63–64.

[20]*The Fergus County Argus*, August 4, 1897, and *Lewistown News Argus*, August 26, 1897, in Phillips, *Fallen Branches*, 26, 64.

[21]Alfred James Mokler, *History of Natrona County Wyoming 1888–1922* (Casper, WY: Mountain States Lithographing, Centennial Edition, 1989), 323–24.

CHAPTER 8

[1]Baker, *Wild Bunch*, 97–98.

[2]R. I. Martin, "A Lively Day in Belle Fourche," *True West*, April 1962, 43, 47. Martin was a witness to the robbery.

[3]Tim McCoy, with Ronald McCoy, *Tim McCoy Remembers the West* (Lincoln: University of Nebraska Press, 1988), 69.

[4]Edward J. Farlow, *Wind River Adventures: My Life in Frontier Wyoming* (Glendo, WY: High Plains Press, 1998), 110.

[5]Hanson, *Powder River*, 440.

[6]Kirby, *Rise and Fall*, 55–56.

[7]Dullenty, "George Currie," 6.

[8]Facsimile of a Pinkerton wanted poster, in Ernst, *SMU*, 84.

[9]Baker, *Wild Bunch*, 97.

[10]Horan, *The Gunfighters*, 205.

[11]Local Belle Fourche author Doug Engebretson is one exception. In Doug Engebretson, *Empty Saddles, Forgotten Names: Outlaws of the Black Hills and Wyoming* (Aberdeen, SD: North Plains Press, 1982), 177, he insists that Kid Curry was not one of the Butte County Bank robbers, and doesn't mention Lonie Curry at all.

[12]Pointer, *In Search of Cassidy*, 127, and 266, chapter 12, endnote 10. Cites an 1896 settler census.

[13]Ernst, *SMU*, 85–86; Kirby, *Rise and Fall*, 55.

[14]Donna B. Ernst, "The Sundance Kid: My Uncle. Researching the Memories of Snake River Residents," *Frontier Magazine*, August 1997, 6. Ernst cites an unpublished manuscript in the University of Wyoming archives written by a Little Snake River Valley rancher named John F. Gooldy. He claimed to have been a friend of Sundance, and that he (Sundance) was working for ranching neighbor, A. R. Reader, during the time of the Belle Fourche robbery, as late as August 28, 1897. This would support Sundance's claim (See Kirby, *Rise and Fall*, 61, 63) after he was captured that he was in Carbon County, in southern Wyoming, on the day of the robbery. He listed several friends as witnesses, including Al Reder (Reader) as stated in the manuscript; In Ernst, *Sundance*, 69–70, the author also cites a October 12, 1897, letter from Little Snake River Valley resident David Gillespie to his mother, which says his friend (Sundance) was working at Al Reader's ranch on June 28, the day of the robbery. Gillespie writes of Sundance being wounded in the arm while resisting arrest for the robbery, and having a horse shot from under him. This incident actually happened to Kid Curry when he refused to surrender to the posse.

[15]Kirby, *Rise and Fall*, 57.

[16]Martin, "Lively Day," 47.

[17]Kirby, *Rise and Fall*, 57. Some authors have stated that O'Day was sent to Belle Fourche a few hours or as much as one day ahead of the rest of the gang, in order to case the town. He goes to Sebastion's Saloon, gets thoroughly drunk, and forgets to report back to his chums. Subsequently, the robbery is pulled off without him.

[18]Ibid., 57; Ernst, *SMU*, 87; Kelly, *Outlaw Trail*, 120. Kelly quotes "A dispatch from Deadwood, dated June 28, 1897." The original bank

building is gone, and a modern Wells Fargo Bank was built on the old bank's foundation. A two-story limestone building opposite on Sixth Avenue may be period, and looks much like the original bank building.

[19]Kirby, *Rise and Fall*, 57; Engebretson, *Empty Saddles*, 172; Waller, *Last of the Great*, 76.

[20]Butte County Court Records, and Deadwood *Pioneer-Times*, June 29 and July 29, 1897, in Engebretson, *Empty Saddles*, 172–73.

[21]*Belle Fourche Times*, July 1, 1897, in Engebretson, *Empty Saddles*, 172; Kelly, *Outlaw Trail*, 120. Kelly quotes "A dispatch from Deadwood, dated June 28, 1897."

[22]Martin, "Lively Day," 47.

[23]Ibid., 47; Butte County Court Records, and Deadwood *Pioneer-Times*, June 29, 1897, in Engebretson, *Empty Saddles*, 173; Waller, *Last of the Great*, 76.

[24]*The Billings Gazette*, September 28, 1897, in Ernst, *SMU*, 87.

[25]Kelly, *Outlaw Trail*, 120. Kelly quotes "A dispatch from Deadwood, dated June 28, 1897"; Martin, "Lively Day," 47.

[26]Kirby, *Rise and Fall*, 59; Ernst, *SMU*, 87–88; Butte County Court Records, and Deadwood *Pioneer-Times*, June 29, 1897, in Engebretson, *Empty Saddles*, 173, 175.

[27]Martin, "Lively Day," 47–48.

[28]Butte County Court Records, and Spearfish *Queen City Mail*, June 30, 1897, in Engebretson, *Empty Saddles*, 173, 175; Kirby, *Rise and Fall*, 58–60.

[29]Butte County Court Records, *Belle Fourche Times*, July 1, 1897, and Deadwood *Pioneer-Times*, June 29, 1897, in Engebretson, *Empty Saddles*, 173, 175; Kirby, *Rise and Fall*, 59–60.

[30]*Belle Fourche Times*, July 1, 1897, and Deadwood *Pioneer-Times*, June 29, 1897, in Engebretson, *Empty Saddles*, 176; Waller, *Last of the Great*, 77–78.

[31]Lamb, *Kid Curry*, 337, chapter 17, endnote 3, quotes from: "Hot On Their Trail," *The Daily Pioneer-Times* (Deadwood, S.D.), June 30, 1897; Waller, *Last of the Great*, 77; Kirby, *Rise and Fall*, 60, asserts that George Fuller got close enough to shoot the horse from under the Sundance Kid. Posse member W. R. Glassie took possession of the Kid's saddle. It is unfortunate that the author does not give his source

for this incident, because if it could be substantiated, it would definitely place Sundance at the robbery.

[32]Lamb, *Kid Curry*, 337, chapter 17, endnotes 1 and 3, quotes from: "Hot on Their Trail," *The Daily Pioneer-Times* (Deadwood, S.D.), June 30, 1897.

[33]July 31, 1897, letter from Bob Devine to his boss Ed David, from Tisdale's Ranch, Wyoming, in Hanson, *Powder River*, 447.

[34]Butte County Court Records, and Deadwood *Pioneer-Times*, June 29, 1897, in Engebretson, *Empty Saddles*, 177.

[35]*The Sundance Gazette*, July 2, 1897, in Ernst, *SMU*, 84, 89.

CHAPTER 9

[1]Kennedy, *Cowboys and Cattlemen*, 256.

[2]Waller, *Last of the Great*, 88.

[3]Hanson, *Powder River*, 434. R. M. Divine to E. T. David, January 1, 1897.

[4]Kennedy, *Cowboys and Cattlemen*, 256–58.

[5]Ibid., 258, 260–61.

[6]Donna B. Ernst, "A Deadwood Jail Break," *True West*, January 2000, 13.

[7]Kelly, *Outlaw Trail*, 159–60.

[8]Anne Goddard Charter, *Cowboys Don't Walk: A Tale of Two* (Billings, MT: Western Organization of Resource Councils, 1999), 51.

[9]Ernst, *Sundance*, 71; Stacy W. Osgood, "Butch Cassidy Never Held Up a Train!" *The Westerners Brand Book* 21, no. 4, Chicago Corral of Westerners, June 1964, 26.

[10]Charter, *Cowboys Don't Walk*, 48; Ernst, *Sundance*, 62. Cites the Gooldy memoirs for Sundance's employment at Ora Haley's Two Bar Ranch.

[11]Kelly, *Outlaw Trail*, 160; *Rawlins Republican*, July 30, 1897, in Ernst, *Sundance*, 71.

[12]Siringo, *Cowboy Detective*, 363; Ernst, *Sundance*, 71. Ernst states that Ryan bought the Con Quinlin Saloon on Fifth Street.

[13]Baker, *Wild Bunch*, 188.

[14]Kelly, *Outlaw Trail*, 129–30, 187; Waller, *Last of the Great*, 89; James D. Horan, *Desperate Men*, rev. ed. (New York: Doubleday & Company, Inc., 1962), 216. Jeffrey Burton asserts that Lost Soldier Pass is

a geographic feature that does not exist, and Mae Urbanek's *Wyoming Place Names* does not list it. The latter does list a Lost Soldier Creek in Carbon County, and a Fillmore Station in Albany County. Wyoming pioneer Edward Farlow, in his *Wind River Adventures*, mentions that Lost Soldier Creek was about forty miles north of Rawlins, and a footnote states that a Lost Soldier stage station existed near there at the base of the Green Mountains. See Jeffrey Burton, *The Deadliest Outlaws: The Ketchum Gang and the Wild Bunch* (Denton: University of North Texas Press, 2009), 439, endnote 18; Mae Urbanek, *Wyoming Place Names* (Missoula, MT: Mountain Press Publishing Co., 1988), 66, 126; Farlow, *Wind River*, 55.

[15]Waller, *Last of the Great*, 79–80.

[16]Horan, *Desperate Men*, rev. ed., 218–19. Horan states that the syndicate was recognized by the Pinkertons in an official report, although depending on which of his books is referred to, he isn't sure if Denver superintendent J. P. McPharland (McParland) or William Pinkerton wrote it. (See also Horan and Sann, *Pictorial History*, 199.) The organization was also recognized by the newspapers at some point. For example, in James D. Horan, *The Authentic Wild West: The Outlaws* (New York: Crown Publishers, 1977), 301, endnote 8, the author cites "Breaking Up the Train Robbers Syndicate," *Denver Republican*, September 20, 1903; Kelly, *Outlaw Trail*, 130–31, 187.

[17]Ernst, *Sundance*, 72.

[18]*Billings Times*, September 30, 1897, in Ernst, *SMU*, 89–90; Waller, *Last of the Great*, 80.

[19]Harry J. Owens, "The Thrilling Capture of the Sundance Kid and Kid Curry," NOLA *Quarterly*, Spring 1986, 9.

[20]Ibid.

[21]*Fremont Clipper*, October 1897, in Ernst, *SMU*, 90.

[22]*The Billings Times*, September 30, 1897, and *The Billings Gazette*, September 24, 1897, in Ernst, *SMU*, 90–91.

[23]*The Billings Gazette*, September 24, 1897, in Ernst, *SMU*, 91; Owens, "Thrilling Capture," 9.

[24]Ibid.; *The Billings Times*, September 30, 1897, in Ernst, *SMU*, 92.

[25]Ibid.

[26]*Queen City Mail*, September 29, 1897, and *Sturgis Weekly Record*, October 1, 1897, in Ernst, *SMU*, 92–93; Waller, *Last of the Great*, 81.

CHAPTER 10

[1]Lamb, *Kid Curry*, 338, chapter 17, endnote 8, quotes from: "Robbers Arrive at Deadwood," *The Daily Pioneer–Times* (Deadwood, S.D.), September 30, 1897.

[2]Hanson, *Powder River*, 449. R. M. Divine to E. T. David, November 5, 1897.

[3]Ernst, *SMU*, 92.

[4]Deadwood *Daily Pioneer-Times*, October 2, 1897, in Ernst, "Jail Break," 14.

[5]Kirby, *Rise and Fall*, 61.

[6]Ibid., 61, 63; Ernst, "Jail Break," 14–15.

[7]Lamb, *Kid Curry*, 338, chapter 17, endnote 9. Quotes from John C. Fraser, Pinkerton Report, June 7, 1900, Frank A. Hadsell Papers, Research Collection H70–18, Wyoming State Archives and Historical Department, Cheyenne, Wyoming.

[8]Waller, *Last of the Great*, 140.

[9]Ibid., 81–82; *Sturgis Weekly Record*, November 5, 1897, in Engebretson, *Empty Saddles*, 177; Deadwood *Daily Pioneer–Times*, November 2, 1897.

[10]Ibid.; Waller, *Last of the Great*, 82; Ernst, "Jail Break," 15.

[11]Ibid., 13, 15; Waller, *Last of the Great*, 82–83; Deadwood *Daily Pioneer-Times*, November 2, 1897.

[12]Ibid.

[13]Ibid., November 2 and 3, 1897. (Donna Ernst writes that a deposition contained in Sheriff Hadsell's private papers indicates the horses left in Spearfish Canyon may have been supplied by Lonie Curry. Frank Hadsell Papers, H70–18/107–125, Wyoming State Archives, in Ernst, *SMU*, 94.)

[14]Ibid., November 3, 1897; Spearfish *Queen City Mail*, November 3, 1897, in Engebretson, *Empty Saddles*, 177.

[15]Waller, *Last of the Great*, 84–85.

[16]Billings *Gazette*, April 1, 1898, in Pointer, *In Search of Cassidy*, 132.

[17]Spearfish *Queen City Mail*, March 20, April 14, 1898, and Deadwood *Pioneer–Times*, April 13, 1898, in Engebretson, *Empty Saddles*, 179.

[18]*Belle Fourche Times*, March 31, 1898, Deadwood *Pioneer–Times*, March 24, 1898, and Lawrence County Court Records, in Engebretson, *Empty Saddles*, 179.

CHAPTER 11

[1]*Denver News*, March 6, 1898, in Kelly, *Outlaw Trail*, 208–9.

[2]Kelly, *Outlaw Trail*, 211.

[3]Frank Hadsell files, Wyoming State Archives, Cheyenne, Wyoming, in Ernst, *Sundance*, 77.

[4][Frank Lamb], Alan Swallow, ed., *The Wild Bunch* (Denver: Sage Books, 1966), 67–69. At his 1902 trial in Knoxville, Tennessee, Curry tried to establish an alibi for the July 3, 1901, Great Northern train robbery in Montana by claiming he was in France from June 5 to August. (See Lynch, *Harvey Logan*, 117; also Waller, *Last of the Great*, 220)

[5]*Denver News*, February 27, 1898, in Kelly, *Outlaw Trail*, 188.

[6]Frank Murray to Frank Hadsell, June 7, 1900, Frank Hadsell Papers, in Wayne Kindred, "The Wilcox Robbery: Who Did It?" WOLA *The Journal*, Spring 1999, 11.

[7]*Denver News*, March 6, 1898, in Kelly, *Outlaw Trail*, 209–11.

[8]As part of a posse, Hoy had been shot from ambush by desperado and Utah State Penitentiary escapee Harry Tracy, in company with fellow convict Dave Lant, and cowboy rustler Patrick Johnson. Johnson had shot and killed a sixteen-year-old boy named Willie Strang at Valentine Hoy's Red Creek Ranch, supposedly by accident, on February 17. See Jim Dullenty, *Harry Tracy: The Last Desperado* (Dubuque, IA: Kendall/Hunt Publishing Co., 1996), 29–31; Douglas W. Ellison, *David Lant: The Vanished Outlaw* (Aberdeen, SD: Midstates Printing, Inc., 1988), 68–69, 81–84; Diana Allen Kouris, "The Lynching Calamity in Brown's Park," *True West*, September 1995, 22–24.

[9]*Denver News*, March 11, 1898, reproduced in full in Kelly, *Outlaw Trail*, 201–4; Also reproduced in full in Ellison, *David Lant*, 113–15.

[10]Kelly, *Outlaw Trail*, 211; *Fremont Clipper*, March 25, 1898, in Pointer, *In Search of Cassidy*, 141, 143.

[11]Kelly, *Outlaw Trail*, 212.

[12]*Fremont Clipper*, March 25, 1898, in Pointer, *In Search of Cassidy*, 143–44.

[13]*Wyoming State Tribune*, June 16, 1939, in Pointer, *In Search of Cassidy*, 147.

[14]Ibid., 147–48.

[15]Kelly, *Outlaw Trail*, 212.

[16]Ibid., 174–76; *Eastern Utah Advocate*, May 19, 1898, in Patterson, *Butch Cassidy*, 137–38; Baker, *Wild Bunch*, 76–81. Baker believes Walker's gun was under his pillow, and he was shot in the head before he could reach for it.

[17]Kelly, *Outlaw Trail*, 177–78; *Eastern Utah Advocate*, May 19, 1898 in Patterson, *Butch Cassidy*, 138–39; Baker, *Wild Bunch*, 81–82. Sanford "Sang" Thompson and associates George Currie, Tom O'Day, and Nate Champion, were already located in the Hole-in-the-Wall area when Butch Cassidy took up residence in 1890. Walt Punteney may not have arrived until a few years later. Cassidy settled on a piece of land a few miles northwest of Sang Thompson on Blue Creek. Thompson was a rustler who was notorious enough to have been included on the cattlemen's hit list with Nate Champion during the Johnson County War of 1892. (See Hanson, *Powder River*, 335.)

[18]Waller, *Last of the Great*, 85; Wilson, *Tiger*, 74; Kelly, *Outlaw Trail*, 127–28. Brown Waller indicates only two men were involved, one said to be Kid Curry, although he was still being referred to as a Roberts brother at this time. The second man was most likely the Sundance Kid. Waller doesn't state the timing of this episode, other than spring 1898 at the earliest. Wilson says it occurred in August; however he does not give his source. It is frustrating that his book does not contain endnotes citing sources that would validate his statements.

[19]Waller, *Last of the Great*, 86; Kelly, *Outlaw Trail*, 128. According to Curry's cousin, Bob Lee, after they broke jail in Deadwood "Harvey and Scramble [an alias for Sundance] went to Montana and went then to Lonnie Logan's ranch and got horses from Lonnie." This is indeed possible since the Little Rockies are just east and a little south of the Bear Paw Mountains. See William A. Pinkerton report to John C. Fraser, June 7, 1900, Frank Hadsell Papers, in Kindred, "Wilcox Robbery," 10.

[20]Waller, *Last of the Great*, 86.

[21]Kelly, *Outlaw Trail*, 128. Waller and Kelly also differ in the dates and timing of the post office robberies, the flight east through Gillette, and the gun battle in the Bear Paw Mountains. I have followed Waller's chronology for the most part. Kelly has the battle with the posse in Hole-in-the-Wall occurring on December 15, 1897.

[22]Burton, *Deadliest Outlaws*, 135–37, 142–144, 147. The Galveston, Harrisburg & San Antonio was the Texas division of the Southern Pacific.

[23]Ibid., 145.

[24]Ibid., 91–92. Cites Concho County, Texas, *Herald*, in *San Angelo Standard*, January 16, 1897.

[25]Ibid., 92.

[26]Dick and Vivian Dunham, *Our Strip of Land: A History of Dagget County, Utah* (Manila, UT: Dagget County Lions Club, 1947), 78, 80. The little town of Linwood was located about five miles east of Manila on the Wyoming border, and is now under the waters of the Flaming Gorge Reservoir.

[27]Baker, *Wild Bunch*, 100; Kirby, *Rise and Fall*, 65.

[28]Stanley Wood, *Over the Range to the Golden Gate* (Chicago: R. R. Donnelley & Sons Co, Publishers, 1895), 153.

[29]*The Weekly Independent* (Elko), July 15, July 22, 1898, and *Tuscarora Times*, July 14, 1898, in Donna B. Ernst, "George S. Nixon," WOLA *The Journal*, Summer 2001, 44.

[30]Ibid., 44–45, and 47, endnote 3.

[31]Ibid., 45.

[32]Ernst, "George S. Nixon," 45.

[33]Robert K. DeArment, *George Scarborough: The Life and Death of a Lawman on the Closing Frontier* (Norman: University of Oklahoma Press, 1992), 209.

[34]*The Free Press* (Elko), April 29, 1899, in Ernst, *SMU*, 102–3; Ernst, "George S. Nixon," 45–46. Cites Pinkerton Detective Agency Archives.

[35]*San Angelo Standard*, August 5, 1899, in Burton, *Deadliest Outlaws*, 147.

[36]Donna B. Ernst, "Before the Wild Bunch Struck a Bank in Winnemucca, Nev., They Hit a Store in Three Creek, Idaho," *Wild West*, December 2001, 10.

[37]Burton, *Deadliest Outlaws*, 92–93, 146.

[38]Ibid., 147.

[39]Ibid., 52, 95, 148, 151–52.

[40]Ibid., 152; Joseph "Mack" Axford, *Around Western Campfires* (Tucson: University of Arizona Press, 1969), 41–42.

[41]Burton, *Deadliest Outlaws*, 152–53; William French, *Some Recollections of a Western Ranchman* (1927; repr., Silver City, NM: High–Lonesome Books, 1997), 257.

[42]Axford, *Western Campfires*, 42–43, 47–48.

[43]French, *Recollections*, 271.

[44]Ibid., 258–60

[45]Burton, *Deadliest Outlaws*, 105, 113–14; DeArment, *George Scarborough*, 176–78.

[46]Walter C. Hovey, "Black Jack Ketchum Tried to Give Me a Break," *True West*, March–April 1972, 48.

[47]Burton, *Deadliest Outlaws*, 127–28; DeArment, *George Scarborough*, 184–85.

[48]Jeff Burton, *Dynamite and Six–Shooter* (Santa Fe: Palomino Press, 1970), 180. Actually, even before this there was confusion, as Pinkerton Detective Charlie Siringo wrote in a 1919 autobiography, *A Lone Star Cowboy*, 241: "'Kid Curry' knew every foot of this whole country, as he had been a cowboy along the line of New Mexico and Arizona, under the name of Tom Capehart."

[49]Ernst, "The Sundance Kid," 17.

[50][Lamb], *Wild Bunch*, 67. The author places Cassidy and Lay in New Mexico about a year too early.

[51]Axford, *Western Campfires*, 41–43.

[52]Ibid., 108.

[53]Ibid., 22.

CHAPTER 12

[1]Kirby, *Rise and Fall*, 66.

[2]*The Free Press* (Elko), April 8, 1899, and September 29, 1900, in Ernst, *SMU*, 104.

[3]Kindred, "Wilcox Robbery," 11.

[4]Ernst, *SMU*, 104–5.

[5]*The Elko Free Press*, April 8, 1899, in Ernst, *SMU*, 105; Kirby, *Rise and Fall*, 66; Baker, *Wild Bunch*, 101.

[6]Ernst, *Sundance*, 81–82. The author states her belief that the saloon robbery was not their style and not in character for Sundance, Flatnose,

and Kid Curry. However, it was a relatively short time previous to this that they had been robbing post offices and sheep camps.

[7]Baker, *Wild Bunch*, 101.

[8]*Wyoming Derrick*, June 22, 1899, in Kindred, "Wilcox Robbery," 11.

[9]*Cheyenne Daily Sun–Leader*, June 13 and 17, 1899, in Kindred, "Wilcox Robbery," 11.

[10]French, *Recollections*, 259–65.

[11]Burton, *Deadliest Outlaws*, 154–55.

[12]Kelly, *Outlaw Trail*, 26–27; Ken Jessen, *Colorado Gunsmoke: True Stories of Outlaws and Lawmen on the Colorado Frontier* (Loveland, CO: J. V. Publications, 1986), 163–74. The actual robbers were two brothers named Jack and Bob Smith, and two other men named Bob Boyle (alias Wallace) and Ed Rhodes. Gunnison County Sheriff Cyrus Wells "Doc" Shores and Pinkerton agent Charles A. Siringo were instrumental in their capture. (See Siringo, *Cowboy Detective*, 66–69.)

[13]Burton, *Deadliest Outlaws*, 105–8.

[14]Pinkerton Archives, Ryan file, in Ernst, *Sundance*, 91.

[15]*Rawlins Republican*, June 3 and 8, 1899, in Ernst, *Sundance*, 91.

[16]*The Denver Times*, June 2, 1899; Donna B. Ernst, "The Wilcox Train Robbery," *Wild West*, June 1999, 34.

[17]*Buffalo Bulletin*, June 8, 1899, in Pointer, *In Search of Cassidy*, 149. Quotes mail clerk Robert Lawson's statement to the press.

[18]Ernst, "Wilcox Robbery," 34, 36.

[19]Charlotte Babcock, *Shot Down! Capital Crimes of Casper, Wyoming* (Glendo, WY: High Plains Press, 2000), 71. Depending on the account, at some point the fireman Dietrick attempted to remove the mask of one of the robbers to see his face. The robber threatened to shoot him if he tried it again.

[20]Kirby, *Rise and Fall*, 68.

[21]*Buffalo Bulletin*, June 8, 1899, in Pointer, *In Search of Cassidy*, 149–50.

[22]Ibid., 150.

[23]Waller, *Last of the Great*, 95.

[24]*Wyoming Derrick*, June 8, 1899, in Babcock, *Shot Down*, 73. Quotes mail clerk Robert Lawson's statement to the press; Waller, *Last of the Great*, 97.

[25]*The Denver Times*, June 2, 1899.

[26]Waller, *Last of the Great*, 97; Ernst, "Wilcox Robbery," 36, 38–39; Horan, *The Outlaws*, 251.

[27]Ernst, "Wilcox Robbery," 36.

[28]*Wyoming Derrick*, June 8, 1899, in Babcock, *Shot Down*, 73.

[29]*The Denver Times*, June 2, 1899.

[30]Kelly, *Outlaw Trail*, 235, 241; *Buffalo Bulletin*, June 8, 1899, in Ernst, *SMU*, 112. Some writers believe that there had to be more than three robbers involved in the holdup, since someone would have been needed to hold the horses. This isn't necessarily so, since the horses were left a short distance from the holdup site with sufficient constraints.

[31]*Wyoming Derrick*, June 8, 1899, in Babcock, *Shot Down*, 73.

[32]Ernst, "Wilcox Robbery," 34; Waller, *Last of the Great*, 97–98.

[33]*Carbon County Journal*, June 3, 1899, in Ernst, *SMU*, 112; Waller, *Last of the Great*, 97–98.

[34]Kelly, *Outlaw Trail*, 242.

[35]Witness testimony at Bob Lee's trial in U.S. Court, Cheyenne, Wyoming, for May 24, 1900, in Brekke, *Kid Curry*, 61–63; *Wyoming Derrick*, June 8, 1899, in Kindred, "Wilcox Robbery," 9.

[36]Facsimile of reward poster in Charles "Pat" Hall, *Documents of Wyoming Heritage* (Cheyenne, WY: Wyoming Bicentennial Commission, 1976), 104.

[37]Mokler, *Natrona County*, 318.

[38]Waller, *Last of the Great*, 99–100; *Idaho Daily Statesman*, June 3–12, 1899 in Arthur Soule, *The Tall Texan: The Story of Ben Kilpatrick* (Deer Lodge, MT: TrailDust Publishing, Inc., 1995), 30–31.

[39]Mokler, *Natrona County*, 318–19.

[40]Babcock, *Shot Down*, 77.

[41]Ibid., 77–78; Mokler, *Natrona County*, 319.

[42]Babcock, *Shot Down*, 78; Ernst, *SMU*, 112.

[43]Babcock, *Shot Down*, 78.

[44]Mokler, *Natrona County*, 319; Waller, *Last of the Great*, 101–2.

[45]*Natrona County Tribune*, June 8, 1899, in Pointer, *In Search of Cassidy*, 151–52; Mokler, *Natrona County*, 319; Waller, *Last of the Great*, 102.

[46]*Wyoming Derrick*, June 8, 1899, in Kindred, "Wilcox Robbery," 8; Paul and Donna Ernst, "Wild Bunch Shootout Sites," WOLA *The Journal*, Fall 1999, 50–51; Waller, *Last of the Great*, 102.

[47]Ibid., 103; Hanson, *Powder River*, 453.

[48]Mokler, *Natrona County*, 319–20. Although many writers single out Kid Curry as the killer of Sheriff Josiah Hazen, it would be very difficult to substantiate. The posse was ambushed; the men did not know the outlaws were in the immediate vicinity. Hazen and Dr. Leeper were the targets of a fusillade from the bandits, using smokeless powder cartridges, making it virtually impossible to determine which of the three outlaws mortally wounded the sheriff. Pinkerton wanted posters only stated that the murder was committed by the gang.

It is interesting that a diary entry from Frank A. Hadsell, a U.S. Marshal when he joined the Wheeler posse, states, "(Charles) Woodward [Woodard] says White River Charlie, Jack McKnight, and Hank Boyed alias Longbaugh killed Hazen." (Frank Hadsell Papers, H83–62/28, Wyoming State Archives, in Ernst, *SMU*, 113.)

[49]Waller, *Last of the Great*, 104.

[50]Ibid., 103–4; *Idaho Daily Statesman*, June 3–12, 1899, in Soule, *Tall Texan*, 31.

[51]*Natrona County Tribune*, June 8, 1899, in Pointer, *In Search of Cassidy*, 152.

[52]*Natrona County Tribune*, June 8, 1899, in Babcock, *Shot Down*, 80.

[53]Waller, *Last of the Great*, 104.

[54]*The Denver Republican*, June 8, 1899, in Patterson, *Butch Cassidy*, 301, endnote 22.

[55]Hanson, *Powder River*, 456.

[56]*Cheyenne Daily Sun–Leader*, June 3, 1899, in Kindred, "Wilcox Robbery," 8.

[57]*Wyoming Derrick*, June 8, 1899 in Kindred, "Wilcox Robbery," 8. Mokler, *Natrona County*, 319, 323–24, states: "[I]t was later learned that they [the robbers] were George Currie ..., Harve Logan, and one of the Roberts boys, three of the worst outlaws in the west." It was his belief that the "Roberts Brothers" were "Tom and George Dickson, alias Tom and George 'Jones'." (It should be remembered that Kid Curry and Sundance gave their names as Tom and Frank Jones while in custody for the Belle Fourche robbery.)

[58]William A. Pinkerton report to John C. Fraser, June 7, 1900, Frank Hadsell Papers, in Kindred, "Wilcox Robbery," 11. This report, written a year after the Wilcox robbery, noted that when authorities from

Montana, South Dakota, Wyoming, and Utah, were shown a photograph of Kid Curry, they all identified him as the *shorter* Roberts brother. Since Lonie was shorter than Harvey, this would appear to exclude him as one of the Roberts brothers, and the taller brother would be identifiable as the similarly dark complexioned Harry Longabaugh, the Sundance Kid.

[59]Facsimile of a Union Pacific and Pacific Express reward poster dated Omaha, Nebraska, June 10, 1899, in Horan, *The Outlaws*, 252; Facsimile of a Union Pacific and Pacific Express reward poster dated Omaha, Nebraska, June 10, 1899, in Horan, *The Gunfighters*, 208. This is a similar poster to the one printed in *The Outlaws*, but includes details of the posse's pursuit of the bandits and Sheriff Hazen's death, and descriptions of the three captured horses.

[60]*Cheyenne Daily Sun–Leader*, June 10, 1899, and June 13, 1899, in Kindred, "Wilcox Robbery," 9.

[61]Waller, *Last of the Great*, 105–6. Waller is in error when he states that the man who separated from his two partners was Elzy Lay.

[62]Mokler, *Natrona County*, 320. Charles Kelly and Brown Waller both stated that DeVore recognized them as George Currie and Harvey Logan. Kelly actually included Lonie Logan by specifying the "Logan brothers." Harvey's real identity was not known at this time, and he was always described as one of the "Roberts brothers." (See Kelly, *Outlaw Trail*, 244; and Waller, *Last of the Great*, 105.)

[63]Waller, *Last of the Great*, 105–6; Mokler, *Natrona County*, 245.

[64]*Cheyenne Daily Sun–Leader*, June 12, 1899, in Kindred, "Wilcox Robbery," 8.

[65]Waller, *Last of the Great*, 106.

[66]Ibid.

[67]Frank Murray to Frank A. Hadsell, March 6, 1901, Hadsell Files, in Ernst, *Sundance*, 90–91.

[68]Waller, *Last of the Great*, 107.

[69]LeFors, *Wyoming Peace Officer*, 109–10; Chip Carlson, *Joe LeFors, "I Slickered Tom Horn"* (Cheyenne, WY: Beartooth Corral LLC., 1995), 145, 147. A history of Joe LeFors based on the handwritten manuscript of his autobiography. Included are some comments that were deleted from the published book, such as LeFors' disparagements of other lawmen's abilities to enhance his own. The author

corrected misspellings, and changed LeFors' syntax to "improve readability." Valuable additional material is included, such as letters and newspaper accounts.

[70]Ibid., 147–49; LeFors, *Wyoming Peace Officer*, 110–12.

[71]Hanson, *Powder River*, 453–55.

[72]Ibid., 454, 456.

[73]*Wyoming Derrick*, June 15, 1899, in Kindred, "Wilcox Robbery," 8.

[74]Hadsell file in Carlson, *Joe LeFors*, 157–58.

[75]Ibid.

[76]Ibid., 159.

[77]LeFors, Joe, *Wyoming Peace Officer*, 112–13.

[78]Waller, *Last of the Great*, 108, 110–11.

[79]Ibid., 109–10; *Wyoming Derrick*, June 22, 1899, in Babcock, *Shot Down*, 84.

[80]LeFors, *Wyoming Peace Officer*, 113–14; Carlson, *Joe LeFors*, 151–52. From LeFors' autobiography.

[81]Ibid., 152–53; LeFors, *Wyoming Peace Officer*, 114–15; Babcock, *Shot Down*, 84–85; *Wyoming Derrick*, June 29, 1899, in Kindred, "Wilcox Robbery," 8.

[82]Federal Writers' Project of the WPA, *Wyoming: A Guide to Its History, Highways, and People* (New York: Oxford University Press, 1948), 332.

[83]Larry K. Brown, *The Hog Ranches of Wyoming* (Glendo, WY: High Plains Press, 1995), 41–42.

[84]Will Frackelton and Herman Seely, *Sagebrush Dentist* (Pasadena, CA: Trail's End Publishing Co., Inc., 1947), 78.

[85]Ibid., 76–77.

[86]Ibid., 67–68, 77.

[87]Waller, *Last of the Great*, 116.

[88]DeJournette and DeJournette, *One Hundred Years*, 302–3. Facsimile of letter from probate file of Isam Dart (courtesy Wyoming State Archives.)

[89]Siringo, *Cowboy Detective*, 305–7. In the author's email correspondence with Robert G. McCubbin on January 11, 2012, he suggested that W. O. Sayles was not the detective's real name. McCubbin has an original photograph depicting Siringo and Sayles, with Siringo's notation on the back indicating his fellow Pinkerton detective's name was

W. B. Sayers. Siringo changed the names of many persons in his books
to hide their real identities.

[90]Ibid., 307–10.

[91]Ibid., 310–12.

[92]Ibid., 312. Alvin Darkbird's name is suspiciously quite similar to that
of Arthur Sparhawk mentioned in Joe LeFors' autobiography. Of the
latter LeFors said, "I am sure this Sparhawk belonged to some secret
agency ..." (See Carlson, *Joe LeFors*, 151.) It is difficult to refrain from
speculating on the possibility that they were the same person. Siringo
frequently changed the names of persons in his books to hide their
identities.

[93]Siringo, *Cowboy Detective*, 312; Baker, *Wild Bunch*, 102.

[94]Siringo, *Cowboy Detective*, 342; Kelly, *Outlaw Trail*, 248.

[95]Ernst, *SMU*, 114.

[96]Siringo, *Cowboy Detective*, 312.

[97]Ibid., 312–13. William E. Webb asserts that "Cunny" was the nick-
name of Elton A. Cunningham, a confidant of members of the Wild
Bunch in New Mexico. It is doubtful then, that he would have given
Siringo any useful information pertaining to the outlaws. (William E.
Webb, "Elton A. Cunningham, a Member of the Wild Bunch," *The
Outlaw Trail Journal*, Summer 1994, 18, endnote 12.)

[98]Ibid., 313–14. Canyon City is spelled as Canon City on modern maps,
sometimes with a "~" over the first "n".

[99]Ibid., 314–24.

CHAPTER 13

[1]French, *Recollections*, 260; Burton, *Deadliest Outlaws*, 154.

[2]Ibid.

[3]Hadsell Files, Bob Lee deposition, in Ernst, *Harvey Logan*, 34.

[4]Donna B. Ernst, "The Real Tom Capehart," WOLA *The Journal*,
Summer 2000, 39. From a transcript furnished by Jeff Burton: "*The
Territory of New Mexico versus William H. McGinnis*, Cause No.
2419—Murder." Concerning the shootout in Turkey Creek Canyon,
Ernst states: "[T]he transcript from Lay's trial clearly indicates that
Will Carver—not Logan—was the shooter."

In Kelly, *Outlaw Trail*, 249, the author obviously refused to believe that Butch Cassidy and Elzy Lay were not at the Wilcox robbery. He sidesteps the evidence against it by stating: "They [he includes Kid Curry] arrived in Alma, New Mexico, just over the line from Arizona, in such a short space of time that it seemed impossible they could have been present at the Wilcox robbery. It was one of the longest rides they ever made ... The date of their arrival was almost an alibi."

[5]French, *Recollections*, 260–61.

[6]Burton, *Deadliest Outlaws*, 155.

[7]Ibid., 154–55,162. (In Axford, *Western Campfires*, 62, the author states that all the members of the Ketchum gang carried the powerful .30–.40 box magazine Winchester rifles. It was the first time he had seen guns of this caliber. Actually, the carbine was more widely used by outlaws as a saddle gun.)

[8]Ibid., 162–165; Miguel Antonio Otero, *My Nine Years as Governor of the Territory of New Mexico 1897–1906* (Santa Fe, NM: Sunstone Press, 2007), 114–15.

[9]Burton, *Deadliest Outlaws*, 167, 179, 186, 190, 235.

[10]Otero, *My Nine Years*, 115–16, 129. Otero, who attended Elzy Lay's trial, stated: "From all of the evidence given at the trial, I came to the conclusion that Franks [Carver] killed both Sheriff Farr and H. N. Love, as both McGinnis [Lay] and Ketchum were down and out after the first volley of bullets fired by the posse"; Burton, *Deadliest Outlaws*, 155, 171–76. The author asserts that Elzy Lay, during a brief moment of consciousness, shot Farr. He bases this mainly on evidence gathered on the field of battle by the sheriff's brother, David E. Farr, and on the description of the fight that Joseph "Mack" Axford received later from Will Carver and supposedly Sam Ketchum. Axford and David Farr both concluded that the killer of Ed Farr was the man firing in a position lower down on the hill, presumed to be Lay. (See Burton, *Deadliest Outlaws*, 176, 228, and 413–14, endnote 14; Axford, *Western Campfires*, 256–58); *San Angelo Standard*, July 17, August 5, 1899, in Ed Bartholomew, *Black Jack Ketchum, Last of the Hold-Up Kings* (Houston: The Frontier Press of Texas, 1955), 68–70; Unnamed newspaper accounts (Springer, N.M.), July 18, July 21, 1899, reprinted in B. D. Titsworth, "Hole-in-the-Wall Gang," *Badman*, Fall 1972, 8–9.

[11]*Las Vegas Daily Optic*, July 21, 1899, reprinted in Titsworth, "Hole-in-the-Wall Gang," 9–10.

[12]Unnamed newspaper account (Santa Fe, N.M.), July 25, 1899, reprinted in Titsworth, "Hole-in-the-Wall Gang," 10; Otero, *My Nine Years*, 116.

[13]Titsworth, "Hole-in-the-Wall Gang," 40.

[14]Otero, *My Nine Years*, 117.

[15]French, *Recollections*, 266–67.

[16]Burton, *Deadliest Outlaws*, 200.

[17]Otero, *My Nine Years*, 117–18; Burton, *Deadliest Outlaws*, 199, 201–5; Unnamed newspaper account (Carlsbad, N.M.), August 17, 1899, reprinted in Titsworth, "Hole-in-the-Wall Gang," 39–40.

[18]French, *Recollections*, 266–68.

[19]Otero, *My Nine Years*, 111, adds to the confusion by stating (never mentioning Capehart) that the Ketchum gang included "Will Carver, alias G. W. Franks, whose real name I believed to be Harvey Logan."

[20]*Trinidad Chronicle News*, August 23, 1899, reprinted in Titsworth, "Hole-in-the-Wall Gang," 40; Otero, *My Nine Years*, 118–20.

[21]Ibid., 125, 127, 129–31; Burton, *Deadliest Outlaws*, 233, 238–44, 298–99, 309–11, 324.

[22]Hadsell Files in Ernst, *Sundance*, 93–95.

[23]Hadsell Files in Donna B. Ernst, *Women of the Wild Bunch* (Kearney, NE: Morris Publishing, 2004), 96, endnote 115.

[24]In Ernst, *SMU*, 155, endnote 1, the author states that "[A]ccording to Sheriff Frank Hadsell's private papers ... Sundance was known to visit the Galveston, Texas area on numerous occasions."

[25]Burton, *Deadliest Outlaws*, 249.

[26]French, *Recollections*, 271.

[27]Ernst, *Sundance*, 212, chapter 17, endnote 7.

[28]Lamb, *Kid Curry*, 346, chapter 22, endnote 20, quotes from Fraser Report, June 7, 1900, Frank A. Hadsell Papers, Research Collection H70–18, Wyoming State Archives, Cheyenne, Wyoming.

CHAPTER 14

[1]Facsimile of Union Pacific and Pacific Express reward poster dated Omaha, Nebraska, January 12, 1900, in Horan and Sann, *Pictorial*

History, 213; Facsimile of Pinkerton reward poster dated Denver, Colo., February 23, 1900, in Horan, *The Gunfighters*, 207.

[2]Patterson, *Butch Cassidy*, 147.

[3]Brekke, *Kid Curry*, 37–38.

[4]Gillespie, *Goin' to 'Dusky*, 68.

[5]Facsimile of land transfer, in Kenworth, *Storms of Life*, 98. Lonie had acquired the land through the Desert Land Act under the name Louis A. Curry.

[6]Gillespie, *Goin' to 'Dusky*, 74–75.

[7]Phillips County, *Yesteryears*, 137–38.

[8]*Harlem Enterprise*, June 5, 1900, in Horan, *The Gunfighters*, 196, 202; Brekke, *Kid Curry*, 46; Wilson, *Tiger*, 97–98.

[9]Brekke, *Kid Curry*, 46.

[10]Montana Parade, "Where Was Loney Curry at Train Holdup?" *Great Falls Tribune*, November 17, 1957.

[11]Witness testimony at Bob Lee's trial in U.S. Court, Cheyenne, Wyoming, for May 25, and 26, 1900, in Brekke, *Kid Curry*, 65–69.

[12]*The Enterprise* (Harlem), July 8, 1899, in Phillips, *Fallen Branches*, 64; Montana Parade, "Where Was Loney"; Brekke, *Kid Curry*, 50.

[13]Waller, *Last of the Great*, 134–35; Brekke, *Kid Curry*, 49–51, 69.

[14]William A. Pinkerton report to John C. Fraser, June 7, 1900, Frank Hadsell Papers, in Kindred, "Wilcox Robbery," 10; Hadsell Files, Bob Lee deposition, in Ernst, *Sundance*, 92–93.

[15]Waller, *Last of the Great*, 135; Brekke, *Kid Curry*, 52.

[16]William A. Pinkerton report to John C. Fraser, June 7, 1900, Frank Hadsell Papers, in Kindred, "Wilcox Robbery," 9, 12, endnote 19; Waller, *Last of the Great*, 135–36.

[17]Ibid., 136; *The Enterprise* (Harlem), December 2, 1899, in Phillips, *Fallen Branches*, 64.

[18]Brekke, *Kid Curry*, 53; Gillespie, *Goin' to 'Dusky*, 68.

[19]*Harlem Enterprise*, June 5, 1900, in Horan, *The Gunfighters*, 202; Testimony at Bob Lee's trial in U.S. Court, Cheyenne, Wyoming, for May 25, 1900, in Brekke, *Kid Curry*, 65–66.

[20]Superintendent Sayles' testimony at Bob Lee's trial in U.S. Court, Cheyenne, Wyoming, on May 25, 1900, in Brekke, *Kid Curry*, 64.

[21]Siringo, *Cowboy Detective*, 324.

[22]Facsimile of *Harlem Enterprise* article, n.d., in Horan, *The Outlaws*, 253. Chouteau County District Judge Dudley DuBose said he unwittingly helped Lonie obtain his train fare to a point near the Wilcox robbery, when he helped him cash a fifty-dollar check in Helena. DuBose's statements should be read with caution, since he also claimed that Kid Curry had traveled to Paris, France. (See "Tells of Curry Gang," *The Lewistown Democrat*, December 5, 1902, in Phillips, *Fallen Branches*, 71, and Wilson, *Outlaw Tales*, 143, 149.) There is no evidence to support this claim, and it is highly unlikely that he took such a trip.

[23]Waller, *Last of the Great*, 136–37; Frank K. Baird's testimony at Bob Lee's trial in U.S. Court, Cheyenne, Wyoming, on May 25, 1900, in Brekke, *Kid Curry*, 64. It is uncertain at this point as to the disposition of the old Curry ranch on Rock Creek in the Little Rockies. Frank Baird, part-time bartender for the Curry Brothers Saloon, testified, "Loney had sixty horses on a ranch to the south and a partner there [presumably Thornhill]"; Al Brekke, "Curry Boys Leave Their Mark on Blaine County," *Harlem Enterprise*, n.d.

[24]Ibid.; Montana Parade, "Where Was Loney."

[25]Waller, *Last of the Great*, 136; Horan, *The Gunfighters*, 196.

[26]Waller, *Last of the Great*, 137; *Rocky Mountain News* (Denver), March 1, 1900, in Kindred, "Wilcox Robbery," 9.

[27]Ibid., 9; Waller, *Last of the Great*, 137–38, 140.

[28]Siringo, *Cowboy Detective*, 324–25.

[29]Waller, *Last of the Great*, 138.

[30]*Kansas City Star*, February 28, 1900; *Lexington Times*, n.d., in "Lonnie Logan," "Old West Gravesites," website, 2002.

[31]*Kansas City Star*, February 28, 1900; Horan, *Desperate Men*, rev. ed., 261; Waller, *Last of the Great*, 140. Waller briefly mentions (p. 141) that some later accounts place Kid Curry at his aunt's home at about the time Lonie was gunned down, with one "stating that as he [Kid Curry] shot his way out he was wounded in the arm and shoulder; but the [contemporary] reports on the death of his brother do not mention it." (One of these later reports was in the *Chicago Inter Ocean* of October 6, 1904.)

[32]Montana Parade, "Where Was Loney"; Brekke, *Kid Curry*, 59; Gillespie, *Goin' to 'Dusky*, 81, says it was (Chouteau County) Undersheriff (Charles) Crawford who went to Kansas City to identify Lonie's body.

[33]*Kansas City Star*, March 9, 1900.

[34]Waller, *Last of the Great*, 140; Horan, *The Gunfighters*, 203.

[35]Kenworth, *Storms of Life*, 18, 27, 30; Wilson, *Outlaw Tales*, 151; Gillespie, *Goin' to 'Dusky*, 68, 74.

[36]*Knoxville Journal and Tribune*, November 17, 1902, in Lynch, *Harvey Logan*, 122.

[37]Siringo, *Cowboy Detective*, 325–29.

[38]Ibid., 329–31, 337.

[39]Kenworth, *Storms of Life*, 16, 57, 64–65. Facsimile of the marriage certificate appears on p. 119. Lucy Tressler was listed as a "boarder" in the 1900 federal census for Chouteau County.

[40]Ibid., 57, 64–65. Kenworth says little Harvey's middle initial was "L"; however his obituary and other sources show it as "D."

[41]Siringo, *Cowboy Detective*, 330–31. Records indicate little Harvey was born 13 August; however the exact year of his birth is questionable. His obituary, U.S. Census records, and other records do not agree, and list his birth year variously as 1895, 1896, and 1897. (Gillespie, *Goin' to 'Dusky*, 137, 141; Pinal County, AZ, Archives Obituaries for Harvey Thornhill, from "Harvey Thornhill Dies in Florence," *Eloy Enterprise*, March 9, 1972. File at: http://files.usgwarchives.org/az/pinal/obits/t/thornhil3ob.txt)

A birth date of August 13, 1897, would obviously not be correct, since Sarah was born in November of that year. Siringo says the boy was three years old at the time of his visit with Thornhill in late winter 1900. An August 1896 birthdate would put his age at 3 ½ years old at this time. Kenworth says Lucy and her husband Dan had separated for a period in 1895–1896. Their final divorce decree wasn't until August 1, 1902. It is apparent they were back together sometime in early 1897 to conceive Sarah, before Dan finally deserted his wife. (Kenworth, *Storms of Life*, 33, 65.) Some accounts suggest that little Harvey's father was John Curry and not Dan Tressler. (Gillespie, *Goin' to 'Dusky*, 137.)

[42]Siringo, *Cowboy Detective*, 332–35.

[43]Santee, *Lost Pony Tracks*, 143.

[44]Siringo, *Cowboy Detective*, 335–37, 339.

[45]Ernst, *Harvey Logan*, 35. Upon his release, Lee returned to Kansas City, Missouri, where he reportedly operated a saloon. The 1910 U.S.

Census for Jackson County, Washington Township, revealed him to be forty-two years old, unmarried, with the occupation of pool hall owner. (Wilson, *Tiger*, 103–4.) Some writers have stated that Lee committed suicide in 1911. (Soule, *Tall Texan*, 38. Correspondence with Jesse Cole Kenworth.) However Jim Dullenty acquired a copy of Lee's death certificate, which showed he was a construction superintendent for Jackson County, Missouri, at the time he died on December 17, 1912. He left behind a wife, Minnie M. Lee, whom he had married sometime after returning to Kansas City from prison, and a daughter, Lucy Lee. (Dullenty, "George Currie," 7. Cites Missouri Vital Records Bureau, and Interment record, Forest Hill Cemetery, Kansas City.) Gillespie, *Goin' to 'Dusky*, 87, states that Lee married Minnie Ferguson (apparently years earlier), the union producing two children, one born in 1892, and the other in 1897. She does not cite her source for this.

[46]William A. Pinkerton report to John C. Fraser, June 7, 1900, Frank Hadsell Papers, in Kindred, "Wilcox Robbery," 9–10.

[47]Ibid.

[48]Kindred, "Wilcox Robbery," 11. With Lonie naming his brother as one of the robbers, there would be no reason for him to lie about not knowing George Currie. If this is the case, it would place great doubt on Lonie participating in the 1897 Belle Fourche bank robbery as one of the Roberts brothers, and also the Deane killing in Wyoming, since it is almost certain that Currie was one of the shooters. Could it have been Will Roberts or the Sundance Kid instead?

[49]Harvey Logan Papers, Small Collection 2063, Montana Historical Society Archives, in Lamb, "Logan's Lost Journal," 20, 26. A collection of Curry's writings, referred to as a journal, surfaced in 1994. It contains several undated letters to the editor of a Knoxville, Tennessee, newspaper, written in a bookkeeping ledger sometime after his 1903 escape from the Knox County jail, and were never mailed. The collection also includes several pages of strong criticisms towards, but not limited to, W. A. Pinkerton, Sheriff James W. Fox, Circuit Judge Joseph Sneed, and Curry's attorneys. The journal somehow ended up being given to Curry's old friend, Jim Thornhill. At some point Thornhill loaned it to Bob Coburn, who apparently never returned it. It was eventually passed down to Coburn's nephew, Coburn Maddox, and

recently his daughter, Mary Grandell, donated the journal to the Montana Historical Society.

[50]Ibid., 26.

CHAPTER 15

[1]French, *Recollections*, 270–74; Siringo, *Cowboy Detective*, 354.

[2]French, *Recollections*, 271–72, 274.

[3]Ibid., 274–76; Siringo, *Cowboy Detective*, 354–56; Philip J. Rasch, *Desperadoes of Arizona Territory* (Laramie, WY: NOLA, Inc., 1999), 54.

[4]Ibid., 53–54.

[5]Ibid., 54–55; Donna B. Ernst, "A Deadly Year for St. Johns Lawmen," NOLA *Quarterly*, January–March 2001, 18–19.

[6]Ibid., 19; Rasch, *Desperadoes*, 55–56. There has been some confusion concerning these murders up to the present day. At some point in time the two Mormon men were designated as "the Norman brothers," and their deaths attributed to Kid Curry. Some modern chroniclers of Kid Curry continue to repeat this error.

[7]French, *Recollections*, 276–77; Ernst, "Deadly Year," 19; Rasch, *Desperadoes*, 54.

[8]Holbrook *Argus*, April 14, 1900 in Rasch, *Desperadoes*, 56.

[9]*Arizona Bulletin*, April 13, 1900, in Burton, *Deadliest Outlaws*, 260.

[10]Rasch, *Desperadoes*, 57.

[11]Dudley Cramer, ed., "The Killing of George Scarborough," *The Haley Library Newsletter*, summer 2000, 4. Based on an Interview by J. Evetts Haley with Walter Birchfield, El Paso, Texas, November 2, 1939; Rasch, *Desperadoes*, 57.

[12]Cramer, "Killing of Scarborough," summer 2000, 4–5, and fall 2000, 4.

[13]Ibid., summer 2000, 5.

[14]Ibid.

[15]*St. Johns Herald*, May 26, 1900, in Rasch, *Desperadoes*, 59–60.

[16]DeArment, *George Scarborough*, 241–42.

[17]*St. Johns Herald*, May 26, 1900, in Rasch, *Desperadoes*, 60.

[18]Siringo, *Cowboy Detective*, 355, 369. The DeJournettes mention the presence of a Sessions family on Diamond Mountain in Utah. See DeJournette and DeJournette, *One Hundred Years*, 193.

[19]*St. Johns Herald*, March 31, 1900, in DeArment, *George Scarborough*, 239.

[20]Horan, *The Gunfighters*, 208.

[21]Burton, *Dynamite*, 132–35; Rasch, *Desperadoes*, 58.

[22]Ibid., 65, 70.

[23]Ibid., 60.

[24]*Silver City Independent*, April 17, 1900, in DeArment, *George Scarborough*, 238–39.

[25]Burton, *Deadliest Outlaws*, 268.

[26]Wilson, *Tiger*, 103. Quotes from Fraser Report, June 7, 1900, Frank A. Hadsell Papers.

[27]Rasch, *Desperadoes*, 58–59; DeArment, *George Scarborough*, 232.

[28]Phoenix *Arizona Republic*, May 7, 1900, in Rasch, *Desperadoes*, 66–67.

[29]DeArment, *George Scarborough*, 246.

[30]Socorro *Chieftain*, April 28, May 5, May 12, 1900, in Ernst, "Deadly Year," 19–20.

[31]Burton, *Deadliest Outlaws*, 269.

[32]Socorro *Chieftain*, April 13, 1901, in Ernst, "Deadly Year," 20; Rasch, *Desperadoes*, 67.

[33]French, *Recollections*, 282–83.

[34]Burton, *Deadliest Outlaws*, 269, 325–26; H. A. Hoover, *Tales from the Bloated Goat: Early Days in Mogollon* (1958; repr., San Lorenzo, NM: High-Lonesome Books, n.d.), 52–53.

[35]Baker, *Wild Bunch*, 178–80; Pointer, *In Search of Cassidy*, 253–54; Otero, *My Nine Years*, 131.

CHAPTER 16

[1]Waller, *Last of the Great*, 145; Baker, *Wild Bunch*, 86.

[2]Kelly, *Outlaw Trail*, 261–62; Waller, *Last of the Great*, 145–46.

[3]Ibid., 146–47.

[4]Kirby, *Rise and Fall*, 74.

[5]Kelly, *Outlaw Trail*, 262.

[6]Kirby, *Rise and Fall*, 75.

[7]Ibid.

[8]Dullenty, "George Currie," 6–7.

[9]Waller, *Last of the Great*, 147.

[10]Rasch, *Desperadoes*, 62.

[11]Waller, *Last of the Great*, 147–48; Kelly, *Outlaw Trail*, 263.

[12]Ibid.; Waller, *Last of the Great*, 148; *Grand Valley Times*, June 1, 1900, reprinted in Baker, *Wild Bunch*, 87–88.

[13]Ibid.; Waller, *Last of the Great*, 148–49; Kelly, *Outlaw Trail*, 263–64.

[14]Ibid., 264–65; Waller, *Last of the Great*, 148–52; Rasch, *Desperadoes*, 62.

[15]Waller, *Last of the Great*, 147–49; Rasch, *Desperadoes*, 62.

[16]DeArment, *George Scarborough*, 234–36.

[17]*Arizona Weekly Journal Miner*, June 20, 1900, in DeArment, *George Scarborough*, 236.

[18]Siringo, *Cowboy Detective*, 353.

[19]Kelly, *Outlaw Trail*, 265.

[20]Bartholomew, *Black Jack Ketchum*, 82, 84.

[21]Burton, *Deadliest Outlaws*, 273.

[22]Silver City *Independent*, April 17, 1900 in Rasch, *Desperadoes*, 65.

[23]Siringo, *Cowboy Detective*, 367–68.

[24]Burton, *Deadliest Outlaws*, 272, and 438, endnote 16.

[25]Ibid., 274.

[26]Mike Bell, "Winnemucca Revisited," WOLA *The Journal*, Spring 2000, 6. This article reprints a story in the *Buenos Aires Standard* of April 17, 1912, purported to be the Sundance Kid's account of the Winnemucca bank robbery told to a third party some time prior to his death in Bolivia in 1908. (An earlier printing of this article has been recently located by Mr. Bell as published in the *Anaconda* (Montana) *Standard* of July 10, 1910. He speculates that Sundance's story had been brought to the United States by a friend he met in South America, Frank Aller, who served as American vice–consul in Antofagasta, Chile, from 1903 to 1906. See Bell, "Winnemucca Revisited," WWHA *Journal*, April 2010.)

[27]Ibid., 6, 11.

CHAPTER 17

[1]Frank Hadsell Papers, Wyoming State Archives, in Ernst, "Deadly Year," 20.

[2]Donna B. Ernst, "Secret Link with the Wild Bunch," website, 1999.

[3]Siringo, *Cowboy Detective*, 361–62.

[4]Charter, *Cowboys Don't Walk*, 48, 59.

[5]Pinkerton Detective Agency Archives, Tipton report, in Ernst, *Harvey Logan*, 39, 41. Born in Texas, Cruzan had served three years in the Colorado State Penitentiary, Canon City, for grand larceny, and was discharged on May 12, 1898. Marvin and Macy Cruzan, "The Cruzan Rogues' Gallery," website, 2002; William Cruzan's Pinkerton file, reproduced in Horan and Sann, *Pictorial History*, 192–93.

[6]Horan, *The Outlaws*, 244.

[7]Pinkerton Detective Agency Archives, Tipton report, in Ernst, *SMU*, 126–27.

[8]Siringo, *Cowboy Detective*, 361.

[9]Ernst, *Harvey Logan*, 39, 41.

[10]Siringo, *Cowboy Detective*, 361.

[11]Pinkerton Detective Agency Archives, Tipton report, in Ernst, *SMU*, 126–27.

[12]*Rawlins Republican*, December 12, 1900, in Ernst, *Sundance*, 100.

[13]Siringo, *Cowboy Detective*, 362.

[14]Pinkerton Detective Agency Archives, Tipton report, in Horan, *The Gunfighters*, 212. Facsimile of a list titled "Tipton Witnesses" gathered by Pinkerton agent Lowell Spence, who trailed Kid Curry for years. Four of the words attributed to witness Courtney A. Joyce, "the dark complected man," are underlined.

[15]Rawlins *Republican*, September 1, 1900, in Carlson, *Joe LeFors*, 177–78.

[16]*Rocky Mountain News* (Denver), August 31, 1900, quoted in Pointer, *In Search of Cassidy*, 167–68.

[17]Waller, *Last of the Great*, 153.

[18]*Rocky Mountain News* (Denver), August 31, 1900, in Pointer, *In Search of* Cassidy, 168. Some reports indicated there were two express cars: a Pacific Express car, and an Oregon Short Line Express car, which may have been partitioned for baggage.

[19]Rawlins *Republican*, September 1, 1900, in Carlson, *Joe LeFors*, 179.

[20]Ibid., 178–79.

[21]Kirby, *Rise and Fall*, 79–80; Ernst, *SMU*, 119, 126.

[22]LeFors, *Wyoming Peace Officer*, 123.

[23]*The Denver Republican*, September 2, 1900, in Patterson, *Butch Cassidy*, 163.

[24]Ernst, *SMU*, 126.

[25]*The Denver Republican*, September 2, 1900, in Patterson, *Butch Cassidy*, 163.

[26]Facsimile of reward poster in Hall, *Documents of Wyoming*, 105.

[27]Butch Cassidy's Pinkerton file, reproduced in Horan and Sann, *Pictorial History*, 196.

[28]Ben Kilpatrick's arrest and prison records from Pinkerton file, reproduced in Horan, *The Gunfighters*, 204–5.

[29]Burton, *Dynamite*, 210.

[30]Facsimile of reward poster in Hall, *Documents of Wyoming*, 105.

[31]William Cruzan's Pinkerton file, reproduced in Horan and Sann, *Pictorial History*, 192–93.

[32]*St. Louis Daily Globe-Democrat*, November 6, 1901, in Soule, *Tall Texan*, 60.

[33]Facsimile of reward poster in Hall, *Documents of Wyoming*, 105.

[34]Rawlins *Republican*, September 1, 1900, in Carlson, *Joe LeFors*, 179.

[35]Carlson, *Joe LeFors*, 321, endnote 97. In an attempt to make a tentative link with the McCarty outlaw family, the author states: "The only Perry accounted for in records of the Wild Bunch (to whom the robbery has been attributed) was Anne Perry, who was married to Tom McCarty's brother, Billy."

[36]Frackelton and Seely, *Sagebrush Dentist*, 68, 76–77, 142–44.

[37]Hanson, *Powder River*, 440.

[38]Rawlins *Republican*, September 1, 1900, in Carlson, *Joe LeFors*, 180; Kelly, *Outlaw Trail*, 275.

[39]LeFors, *Wyoming Peace Officer*, 118–19.

[40]Rawlins *Republican*, September 1, 1900, in Carlson, *Joe LeFors*, 180; Kelly, *Outlaw Trail*, 275.

[41]Rawlins *Republican*, September 1, 1900, in Carlson, *Joe LeFors*, 181; LeFors, *Wyoming Peace Officer*, 118.

[42]Ibid., 118–19.

[43]Facsimile of Tipton reward poster, in Ernst, *SMU*, 116.

[44]LeFors, *Wyoming Peace Officer*, 119–21.

[45]Ibid., 121–22.

[46]Ibid., 123.

[47]Ibid., 121, 123–24.

[48]Ibid., 124–25, 128.

[49]Rawlins *Republican*, September 5, 1900, in Carlson, *Joe LeFors*, 181. When working undercover for the Pinkertons in Rawlins, Charles Siringo went on a wild horse hunt with saloon owner and Wild Bunch confidant Jack Ryan. They went "into the Haystack Mountains, where Jack R. [Ryan] kept a hired man and a pile of grub to feed the 'Wild Bunch' when passing through the country." (Siringo, *Cowboy Detective*, 369.)

[50]Pinkerton Detective Agency Archives, in Horan, *The Gunfighters*, 212. Facsimile of "Logan's Log" kept by Pinkerton agent Lowell Spence on the Menger Hotel letterhead, San Antonio, Texas; Siringo, *Cowboy Detective*, 361.

[51]Ibid., 359.

[52]Ibid., 339, 361. It is not known what became of Cruzan. The *Kansas City Times*, July 11, 1904, reported, "[William] Cruzans has been reported dead, but the rumor was never verified."

[53]Ibid., 340–41.

[54]Ibid., 342. There is a persistent legend that the robbers buried at least part of the Tipton loot somewhere around Powder Springs or Brown's Hole. In fact it has been stated that Ben Kilpatrick returned to the Powder Springs area in the winter of 1910–1911, and established a trapper's camp. He spent the next few months digging and trying to locate the buried loot. Old-timers in Baggs supposedly recognized Kilpatrick when he came to town to buy groceries. He left in the spring of 1911 with nothing to show for all of his digging. (Burroughs, *Where West Stayed Young*, 133.) The main problem with this story is that Kilpatrick was still serving a prison sentence during this time.

[55]Siringo, *Cowboy Detective*, 342–43. A Pinkerton file on Frank Elliott (the rancher Siringo visited?), alias Bert Curtis, indicates his arrest for robbery in 1891, and that he was a "pal of Rob't. Eldredge, alias Peg Leg." (Reproduced in Horan and Sann, *Pictorial History*, 196.) They were members of the McCoy gang who robbed the Denver and Rio Grande Train No. 4 between Cotopaxi and Texas Creek, Colorado, on August 31, 1891. See Richard Patterson, *The Train Robbery Era: An Encyclopedic History* (Boulder, CO: Pruett Publishing Co., 1991), 49–50.

[56]Ibid., 345.

[57]Ibid., 346.

[58]Ibid., 347.

[59]Ibid., 347–48, 354. Frank Lamb ([Lamb], *Wild Bunch*, 131) explained why the Wilcox money had been distributed so widely: "[T]he Wilcox robbery was the first robbery after the Spanish American War. During that war, the Wild Bunch had decided to lay low. Consequently, their income had been low and they were in need of money. For this reason, the unsigned currency was distributed among the entire membership of the Wild Bunch."

[60]Ibid., 355–61.

[61]Facsimile of Winnemucca reward poster, in Ernst, *SMU*, 128. The Pinkerton reward poster listed the take as $31,000 in $20 gold coins, $1,200 in $5 and $10 gold coins, and the balance in currency.

[62]*The Silver State*, September 20, 1900, in Ernst, *SMU*, 133, 136–38.

[63]Bell, "Winnemucca Revisited," 9.

[64]Ernst, "Wild Bunch Struck a Bank," 64.

[65]Bell, "Winnemucca Revisited," 10; Donna B. Ernst, and Paul D. Ernst, "The Last Hurrah of the Notorious Wild Bunch," *Wild West*, October 2002, 16.

CHAPTER 18

[1]Carolyn Bullion McBryde, "Love Behind Bars: The Thorny Rose," *True West*, April 1992, 21–23; Donna B. Ernst, "The Wild Bunch in Texas," NOLA *Quarterly*, October–December 1999, 31–32.

[2]Ernst, *Women of Wild Bunch*, 32.

[3]Lillie Davis Statement, Pinkerton Archives, printed in Ernst, *Women of Wild Bunch*, 38.

[4]Ernst, "Wild Bunch in Texas," 34.

[5]*Nashville American*, October 16, 1901, in Wayne Kindred, "The Trials and Travels of Annie Rogers," *Old West*, Winter 1995, 26.

[6]Richard F. Selcer, "The Women Who Loved the Wild Bunch," *Wild West*, December 1994, 54.

[7]Ernst, "Wild Bunch in Texas," 34.

[8]*Nashville American*, October 28, 1901, printed in Lynch, *Harvey Logan*, 34; Kindred, "Trials and Travels," 27. Some earlier writers thought

Maud Walker and Annie Rogers were two different women. It is interesting to note, according to a statement made to the Pinkertons by Lillie Davis, Lewis Walker was a relative of Fannie Porter's, and whose
maiden name was Walker. (See Ernst, *Women of Wild Bunch*, 42.)

[9]Ibid.; Horan and Sann, *Pictorial History,* 220. Curry's (Logan's) father
had a middle name of Neville.

[10]Ibid., 221; Selcer, *Hell's Half Acre*, 250.

[11]Ernst, "Wild Bunch in Texas," 32–33; Ernst and Ernst, "Last Hurrah,"
16.

[12]Barbara Barton, *Den of Outlaws* (San Angelo, TX: Rangel Printing,
2000), 56, 58.

[13]Lillie Davis Statement, Pinkerton Archives, printed in Ernst, *Women
of Wild Bunch*, 39.

[14]Ernst, "Wild Bunch Struck a Bank," 64.

[15]Ernst, *Sundance*, 121–22.

[16]Ernst and Ernst, "Last Hurrah," 16. Cites David Gillespie letters and
John Gooldy memoirs.

[17]Ibid., 16, 18; Selcer, *Hell's Half Acre*, 246–47, 255–56.

[18]Ibid., 255.

[19]Pinkerton files, Logan's Log; Bartholomew, *Black Jack Ketchum*, 85;
Selcer, *Hell's Half Acre*, 258.

[20][Lamb], *Wild Bunch*, 86.

[21]Selcer, *Hell's Half Acre*, 260.

[22]Pinkerton files cited in Ernst, *SMU*, 149. Although Pinkerton archives
support this, why did Dodge not mention this event in his journals and
letters? The reason could be that his published memoirs, *Under Cover
for Wells Fargo: The Unvarnished Recollections of Fred Dodge*, end in
1893, at least seven years before the Fort Worth Five photo was taken;
Kelly, *Outlaw Trail*, 281; Bartholomew, *Black Jack Ketchum*, 85.

[23]Selcer, *Hell's Half Acre*, 262.

[24]Kelly, *Outlaw Trail*, 281; Pinkerton files cited in Ernst, *Harvey Logan*,
44–45. Curry was interviewed in 1903 by the *Knoxville Sentinel* while
incarcerated in the Knox County jail. He told reporter W. P. Chandler that "One day one of us saw a Pinkerton detective on the street
and in thirty minutes the apartment was empty." They were in such a
hurry, the gang left behind a print of the Fort Worth Five picture for the

Pinkertons to find. Richard F. Selcer has some problems with this story as does this author. One of the points he makes is that it is remarkable the Pinkerton agent has never been named in any Wild Bunch literature or the Pinkerton Archives. I believe the gang's subsequent movements do not show any great concern for being apprehended in Fort Worth by the Pinkertons or any law enforcement agencies. (Selcer, *Hell's Half Acre*, 256, 263. Also 321, 323, endnotes 47, 69, 70; Horan, *The Gunfighters*, 299, endnote 29.)

[25]Richard Selcer, and Donna Donnell, "Last Word on the Famous Wild Bunch Photo," *Wild West*, December 2011, 29, 31.

[26]Roy D. Holt, "The End of Will Carver," *True West*, May–June 1970, 91.

[27]Ernst and Ernst, "Last Hurrah," 18.

[28]Register of Marriages, State of Texas, County of Tarrant, page 121, No. 9965 in Soule, *Tall Texan*, 42. A Justice of the Peace was found, license granted, filed, and recorded on the same day; Lillie Davis Statement, Pinkerton Archives, printed in Ernst, *Women of Wild Bunch*, 38–40.

[29]Ibid., 39.

[30]Wayne Kindred, "The Hunt for the Great Northern Train Robbers," website, 2000, 5–6.

[31]Lillie Davis Statement, Pinkerton Archives, printed in Ernst, *Women of Wild Bunch*, 40.

[32]Pinkerton files, Logan's Log; Selcer, *Hell's Half Acre*, 254.

[33]Lillie Davis Statement, Pinkerton Archives, printed in Ernst, *Women of Wild Bunch*, 39–40.

[34]Kindred, "Trials and Travels," 27.

[35]Pinkerton files, Logan's Log.

[36]Holt, "End of Will Carver," 87.

[37]Pinkerton files, Logan's Log.

[38]Holt, "End of Will Carver," 87.

[39]Pinkerton files, Logan's Log.

[40]John A. Loomis, *Texas Ranchman: The Memoirs of John A. Loomis* (Chadron, NE: The Fur Press, 1982), 67.

[41]Burton, *Deadliest Outlaws*, 282; Ernst, *Harvey Logan*, 49–50.

[42]Pinkerton files, Logan's Log.

[43]*San Angelo Standard*, April 6, 1901, quoted in Bartholomew, *Black Jack Ketchum*, 90, and printed in John Eaton, *Will Carver, Outlaw* (San Angelo, TX: Anchor Publishing Co., 1972), 130.

[44]Pinkerton files, Logan's Log.

[45]Edward M. Kirby, *The Saga of Butch Cassidy and the Wild Bunch* (Palmer Lake, CO: The Filter Press, 1977), 48.

[46]Ibid., 55, 64.

[47]Soule, *Tall Texan*, 46.

[48]Pinkerton files, Logan's Log.

[49]*Devil's River News* (Sonora), April 6, 1901, printed in Eaton, *Will Carver*, 12; *San Angelo Standard* and *Devil's River News*, April 6, 1901, in Burton, *Deadliest Outlaws*, 283.

[50]Pinkerton files, Logan's Log.

[51]Loomis, *Texas Ranchman*, 67.

[52]Ernst, *Sundance*, 135.

[53]Anne Meadows, and Dan Buck. "The Last Days of Butch and Sundance," website, 2002, 4, part 1.

[54]Pinkerton files, Logan's Log; *Devil's River News* (from *San Angelo Standard*), April 6, 1901, printed in Eaton, *Will Carver*, 61–62, 66.

[55]Bartholomew, *Black Jack Ketchum*, 86; Eaton, *Will Carver*, 70; Soule, *Tall Texan*, 2–3, 48.

[56]*Devil's River News* (from *San Angelo Standard*), April 6, 1901, printed in Eaton, *Will Carver*, 66–67; Bartholomew, *Black Jack Ketchum*, 86.

[57]Loomis, *Texas Ranchman*, 66.

[58]*Devil's River News* (from *San Angelo Standard*), April 6, 1901, printed in Eaton, *Will Carver*, 66–67; Bartholomew, *Black Jack Ketchum*, 86; Waller, *Last of the Great*, 162. In a 1963 interview, barber John Waide (he was ninety-two years old at the time) said that he helped prepare Thornton's body for burial. He claimed that there was only one wound in the body. This was a well-placed bullet hole that entered the front of the chest. (Eaton, *Will Carver*, 69–70.) A contemporary newspaper account contradicts Waide's details of the shooting. The report stated that Thornton had been shot twice, one bullet entered the forehead and "came out at the back of the head," and the other went "clear through the body going in at one side and out at the other." (*San Angelo Standard*, March 30, 1901, reprinted in *Devil's River News*, April 6, 1901, quoted in Burton, *Deadliest Outlaws*, 286; *Devil's River News* (from

San Angelo Standard), April 6, 1901, printed in Eaton, *Will Carver*, 67.)

[59] *San Angelo Standard*, March 30, 1901, reprinted in *Devil's River News*, April 6, 1901, quoted in Burton, *Deadliest Outlaws*, 286; Waller, *Last of the Great*, 163.

[60] *Devil's River News* (from *San Angelo Standard*), April 6, 1901, printed in Eaton, *Will Carver*, 68.

[61] *Devil's River News* (Sonora), April 6, 1901, printed in Eaton, *Will Carver*, 10; *San Angelo Standard* and *Devil's River News*, April 6, 1901, in Burton, *Deadliest Outlaws*, 286.

[62] Burton, *Deadliest Outlaws*, 286.

[63] *Devil's River News* (from *San Angelo Standard*), April 6, 1901, printed in Eaton, *Will Carver*, 67; Barton, *Den of Outlaws*, 113; Waller, *Last of the Great*, 162–63. Mary's maiden name was Steen, and she was the daughter of an ex-judge of Concho County. See Eaton, *Will Carver*, 69. On page 110 Eaton quotes the *Devil's River News* of April 6, 1901: "L. N. Steen, son of ex-judge of Concho County was in Sonora Wednesday ... Mr. Steen was a brother-in-law of Thornton who was killed at Paint Rock last week." It should be remembered that Ben Kilpatrick used an alias of Mack Steen.

[64] Soule, *Tall Texan*, 46–47.

[65] The Pinkerton ID card for Harvey Logan does show Bob McDonald as an alias at this time, but not Walker. Reproduced in Ernst, *Harvey Logan*, 63.

[66] Waller, *Last of the Great*, 162; Barton, *Den of Outlaws*, 185; *St. Louis Daily Globe-Democrat*, December 12, 1901, reprinted in *San Angelo Standard*, December 21, 1901, in Burton, *Deadliest Outlaws*, 286–87.

[67] Loomis, *Texas Ranchman*, 67.

[68] Bartholomew, *Black Jack Ketchum*, 70–72, 83–84, 87.

[69] Soule, *Tall Texan*, 46.

[70] Eaton, *Will Carver*, 75.

[71] Loomis, *Texas Ranchman*, 66–67.

[72] Soule, *Tall Texan*, 2, 194.

[73] From a March 26, 1905, letter to Ben Kilpatrick from his mother when he was in the federal penitentiary at Atlanta, Georgia, printed in James D. Horan, *The Wild Bunch* (New York: Signet, New American Library, 1958), 183–84.

[74]Holt, "End of Will Carver," 87; *Devil's River News* (from *San Angelo Standard*), April 6, 1901, printed in Eaton, *Will Carver*, 67. Eaton states that the rubber-tired buggy and "fancy Fort Worth toggery" were left behind, and the three men were on horseback leading an extra mount and a pack horse (p. 87).

[75]*San Angelo Standard*, April 6, 1901, reprinted in *Devil's River News*, April 13, 1901, in Burton, *Deadliest Outlaws*, 287. Burton adds that Carver actually left the saddle horses in a pasture near Sherwood, sixty miles west of Eden, in Irion County. They were intended to be used for an escape relay after the gang had robbed the Sonora bank. He says the contemporary reports were wrong in surmising "that the horses had been abandoned on April 4 by the men who had fled from Sonora on the night of the 2nd." (Burton, *Deadliest Outlaws*, 287, and 442, endnote 40. Cites the *San Angelo Standard*, April 13, 1901.)

[76]*San Angelo Standard* and *Devil's River News* (Sonora), April 6, 1901, in Ernst, *Harvey Logan*, 50.

[77]*Devil's River News* (from *San Angelo Standard*), April 6, 1901, printed in Eaton, *Will Carver*, 67.

[78]Ballinger *Banner-Leader*, April 6, 1901, in Ernst, *Harvey Logan*, 50; Eaton, *Will Carver*, 70.

[79]*Devil's River News* (Sonora), April 6, 1901, printed in Eaton, *Will Carver*, 12, 68; *San Angelo Standard* and *Devil's River News*, April 6, 1901, in Burton, *Deadliest Outlaws*, 287.

[80]Burton, *Dynamite*, 141.

[81]Holt, "End of Will Carver," 87; *Devil's River News* (Sonora), April 6, 1901, printed in Eaton, *Will Carver*, 11–12; Burton, *Deadliest Outlaws*, 287–88. This is not to be confused with the Half-Circle Six ("Sixes") ranch on Dove Creek near Knickerbocker, where Carver, Ben Kilpatrick, Sam and Tom Ketchum, and Dave Atkins worked together. (See Burton, *Deadliest Outlaws*, 374, endnote 28; also Holt, "End of Will Carver," 38; and Soule, *Tall Texan*, 14. He mistakenly calls it the T Half Circle Six.)

[82]Holt, "End of Will Carver," 87.

[83]*Devil's River News* (Sonora), April 6, 1901, printed in Eaton, *Will Carver*, 12; Burton, *Deadliest Outlaws*, 288.

[84]*Devil's River News* (Sonora), April 6, 1901, printed in Eaton, *Will Carver*, 7–8, and diagram of Sonora and the probable route of the

outlaws, p. 100; *San Angelo Standard*, April 6, 1901, quoted in Bartholomew, *Black Jack Ketchum*, 90.

[85]Ibid.; *Devil's River News* (Sonora), April 6, 1901, printed in Eaton, *Will Carver*, 8, and copy of Will Carver's death certificate, 141; Holt, "End of Will Carver," 87.

[86]Burton, *Deadliest Outlaws*, 291; Eaton, *Will Carver*, 94.

[87]*San Angelo Standard*, April 6, 1901, quoted in Bartholomew, *Black Jack Ketchum*, 90–92; *Devil's River News* (Sonora), April 6, 1901, printed in Eaton, *Will Carver*, 8, 11–12; Burton, *Deadliest Outlaws*, 291–92; Waller, *Last of the* Great, 164–65.

[88]Holt, "End of Will Carver," 87

[89]*San Angelo Standard*, April 6, 1901, quoted in Bartholomew, *Black Jack Ketchum*, 91–92; *Devil's River News* (Sonora), April 6, 1901, printed in Eaton, *Will Carver*, 8–9; Burton, *Deadliest Outlaws*, 292.

[90]*Devil's River News* (Sonora), April 6, and July 6, 1901, printed in Eaton, *Will Carver*, 11–12, 110–12.

[91]Holt, "End of Will Carver," 91; Eaton, *Will Carver*, 21.

[92]*Devil's River News* (from *San Angelo Standard*), April 13, 1901, printed in Eaton, *Will Carver*, 111; Donna B. Ernst, "Will Carver, alias Will Casey," *Old West*, Fall 1995, 25.

[93]*Devil's River News* (Sonora), April 6, 1901, printed in Eaton, *Will Carver*, 9.

[94]Ibid., 9–10.

[95]*Devil's River News* (Sonora), June 22, 1901, printed in Eaton, *Will Carver*, 111.

[96]Selcer, *Hell's Half Acre*, 253.

[97]*Devil's River News* (from *San Angelo Standard*), April 13, 1901, printed in Eaton, *Will Carver*, 110–11.

[98]*Devil's River News* (Sonora), April 6, 1901, printed in Eaton, *Will Carver*, 10.

[99]Bartholomew, *Black Jack Ketchum*, 86–87, 92; Barton, *Den of Outlaws*, 115, 122.

[100]*San Angelo Standard*, April 6, 1901, quoted in Bartholomew, *Black Jack Ketchum*, 89, and printed in Eaton, *Will Carver*, 129.

[101]Pinkerton files, Logan's Log.

[102]*Devil's River News* (Sonora), April 27, 1901, printed in Eaton, *Will Carver*, 111; *Devil's River News* (Sonora), April 27 and May 4, 1901, in Soule, *Tall Texan*, 50.

[103]Concho County Court Records, *The State of Texas vs. George Kilpatrick*, *The State of Texas vs. Ed Kilpatrick*, File No's 479 and 480 respectively, in Soule, *Tall Texan*, 47.

[104]*Devil's River News* (Sonora), April 6, 1901, printed in Eaton, *Will Carver*, 11.

[105]Ernst, *Harvey Logan*, 51.

[106]Facsimile of *St. Louis Post-Dispatch*, November 7, 1901, in Horan, *The Outlaws*, 260; Ernst, *Women of Wild Bunch*, 22. Cites *St. Louis Post-Dispatch* of November 7, 1901, and Pinkerton Archives; Waller, *Last of the Great*, 188–89; *St. Louis Post-Dispatch*, November 7, 1901, and *St. Louis Republic*, November 8, 1901, in Burton, *Deadliest Outlaws*, 317.

[107]Lillie Davis Statement, Pinkerton Archives, printed in Ernst, *Women of Wild Bunch*, 40.

CHAPTER 19

[1]Facsimile of Pinkerton's Wagner reward poster dated August 5, 1901, in Horan and Sann, *Pictorial History*, 218–19; Richard Murphy, "A Killer with a Hankering for Booze and Brawls, 'Deaf Charley' Hanks Hooked Up with the Wild Bunch," *Wild West*, August 1995, 28, 30.

[2]Pinkerton reward poster, Circular No. 1, dated Denver, Colo., May 15, 1901.

[3]Lillie Davis Statement, Pinkerton Archives, printed in Ernst, *Women of Wild Bunch*, 39–40. Besides identifying her husband Will Carver as Will Casey, and Kid Curry as Bob Nevilles, she knew Ben Kilpatrick as Dan, the Sundance Kid as Harry, and Butch Cassidy as Jim.

[4]Patterson, *Train Robbery Era*, 104–5, 238, 250.

[5]Waller, *Last of the Great*, 176, 178.

[6]Coburn, *Pioneer Cattleman*, 91–92.

[7]Horan, *The Gunfighters*, 299, endnote 29.

[8]Wayne Kindred, "The Ice Wagon Affair," website, 1987, 1.

[9]Facsimile of Pinkerton's Wagner reward poster dated August 5, 1901, in Horan and Sann, *Pictorial History*, 218–19.

[10]*Great Falls Daily Tribune*, July 4, July 9, 1901, in Kindred, "Hunt for Great Northern Robbers," 1–3.

[11]Wayne Kindred, "Who Robbed the Great Northern Express?" *True West*, January 1994, 21; *New York Daily Tribune*, July 5, 1901, in Lynch, *Harvey Logan*, 10. There were out-of-area newspapers that reported a "half-breed," approximating Kid Curry, as the bandit who boarded the train at Malta and held up the engineer and fireman: *Idaho Daily Statesman*, July 5, 1901, in Soule, *Tall Texan*, 55; *Knoxville Journal and Tribune*, July 5, 1901, in Lynch, *Harvey Logan,* 14. Some authors cite Johnson, "Durable Desperado," 28, in which George Campbell of the Circle Diamond outfit claimed he saw Kid Curry in a saloon in Malta, waiting for the arrival of the Great Northern train No. 3.

[12]*New York Daily Tribune*, July 5, 1901, in Lynch, *Harvey Logan*, 10.

[13]Kindred, "Who Robbed Great Northern?" 21. Cites fireman Mike O'Neil's testimony at Harvey Logan's November 1902 trial in Knoxville, Tennessee.

[14]Waller, *Last of the Great*, 170.

[15]Hill County Bicentennial Commission, *Grits, Guts and Gusto: A History of Hill County* (Havre, MT: Bear Paw Printers, 1976), 63. Excerpts from a 1926 interview with Mike O'Neil in the *Havre Daily News*, March 15, 1968.

[16]*The Enterprise* (Malta), July 10, 1901.

[17]Coburn, *Pioneer Cattleman*, 100; Brekke, *Kid Curry*, 79.

[18]Express messenger C. H. Smith's testimony at Harvey Logan's November 1902 trial in Knoxville, Tennessee, printed in Lynch, *Harvey Logan*, 9; C. H. Smith's testimony at Annie Rogers' court appearance for a reduced bond in Nashville, Tennessee, reported by the *Nashville American*, April 22, 1902, printed in Lynch, *Harvey Logan*, 102.

[19]Ibid.

[20]C. H. Smith's testimony at Harvey Logan's November 1902 trial in Knoxville, Tennessee, in Kindred, "Who Robbed Great Northern?" 21; C. H. Smith's testimony at Harvey Logan's November 1902 trial in Knoxville, Tennessee, printed in Lynch, *Harvey Logan*, 9–10.

[21]Ibid., 10.

[22]Mike O'Neil's testimony at Harvey Logan's November 1902 trial in Knoxville, Tennessee, in Kindred, "Who Robbed Great Northern?" 21–22; Hill County, *Grits, Guts and Gusto*, 63.

[23]Phillips County, *Yesteryears*, 47.

[24]Mike O'Neil's testimony at Harvey Logan's November 1902 trial in Knoxville, Tennessee, in Kindred, "Who Robbed Great Northern?" 22.

[25]Kelly, *Outlaw Trail*, 283.

[26]Soule, Arthur, *Tall Texan*, 54. Correspondence with Jesse Cole Kenworth. The fact that there were actually two men named Mike O'Neil, introduces some confusion into these statements. The fireman had a cousin of the same name who had previously worked as a section foreman for the Great Northern, and now owned a ranch on Exeter Creek. Riding to his ranch on the morning of the train robbery, he found the outlaws hiding in his barn. Curry is said to have had a good laugh when the cousin's horse spooked and almost threw him off. O'Neil thought at the time that the man was a hobo, and didn't think anything of the incident. It could be speculated that the gang received information concerning money shipments from one or both of the O'Neils. However, as Gary Wilson points out, neither one was ever implicated as accessories in the robbery. (See Hill County, *Grits, Guts and Gusto*, 64; Wilson, *Tiger*, 134–35.) It is possible that Curry may have enlisted fireman O'Neil's help because he trusted him. When Curry had his attention directed to blowing the safe, it was obvious that he did not trust messenger Smith by the comment he made. He felt more at ease when he switched to O'Neil to hold the dynamite sack. Almost eleven years later, Ben Kilpatrick would be killed when he turned his back on an express messenger.

[27]Waller, *Last of the Great*, 169.

[28]C. H. Smith's testimony at Harvey Logan's November 1902 trial in Knoxville, Tennessee, in Lynch, *Harvey Logan*, 10.

[29]C. H. Smith's testimony at Harvey Logan's November 1902 trial in Knoxville, Tennessee, in Kindred, "Who Robbed Great Northern?" 22–23.

[30]C. H. Smith's testimony at Annie Rogers' court appearance for a reduced bond in Nashville, Tennessee, reported by *Nashville American*, April 22, 1902, printed in Lynch, *Harvey Logan*, 103.

[31]*Knoxville News Sentinel*, July 4, 1901, and *New York Daily Tribune*, July 5, 1901, in Lynch, *Harvey Logan*, 10; Waller, *Last of the Great*, 169–70, 172.

[32]Brekke, *Kid Curry*, 77–78; Patterson, *Butch Cassidy*, 189–90.

[33]C. H. Smith's testimony at Harvey Logan's November 1902 trial in Knoxville, Tennessee, in Lynch, *Harvey Logan*, 10.

34Lynch, *Harvey Logan*, 12. Cites the *Malta Enterprise*, n.d.; Ernst, *Harvey Logan*, 53.

35Patterson, *Butch Cassidy*, 190.

36*New York Daily Tribune*, July 5, 1901, in Lynch, *Harvey Logan*, 12; Waller, *Last of the Great*, 171.

37Facsimile of a Pinkerton's Wagner reward poster, in Lynch, *Harvey Logan*, 23.

38Hill County, *Grits, Guts and Gusto*, 63–64.

39*Knoxville News Sentinel*, July 4, 1901, and *New York Daily Tribune*, July 6, 1901, in Lynch, *Harvey Logan*, 10; Waller, *Last of the Great*, 170, 172–73.

40Facsimile of a Great Northern Express Co. reward poster dated St. Paul, Minn., July 4, 1901, in Horan, *The Outlaws*, 253.

41O. C. Hanks' Pinkerton file, reproduced in Horan and Sann, *Pictorial History*, 193.

42Facsimile of a Great Northern Express Co. reward poster dated St. Paul, Minn., July 4, 1901, in Horan, *The Outlaws*, 253.

43C. H. Smith's testimony at Annie Rogers' court appearance for a reduced bond in Nashville, Tennessee, reported by *Nashville American*, April 22, 1902, printed in Lynch, *Harvey Logan*, 102.

44Kindred, "Hunt for Great Northern Robbers," 2.

45*New York Daily Tribune*, July 6, 1901, in Lynch, *Harvey Logan*, 12.

46Coburn, *Pioneer Cattleman*, 100–1.

47Gillespie, *Goin' to 'Dusky*, 54.

48Coburn, *Pioneer Cattleman*, 101; Kelly, *Outlaw Trail*, 284.

49Kindred, "Hunt for Great Northern Robbers," 2; Waller, *Last of the Great*, 176–77; Brekke, *Kid Curry*, 79, 83. Some accounts state that the Ellis sighting occurred a week later on Wednesday, July 10.

50*Great Falls Daily Tribune*, July 4, 1901, in Kindred, "Hunt for Great Northern Robbers," 2.

51*Great Falls Daily Tribune*, July 4, 1901, in Kindred, "Who Robbed Great Northern?" 22.

52Ibid., July 12, 1901.

53Coburn, *Pioneer Cattleman*, 85, 88–91.

54Ibid., 91–92.

55Ibid., 94–95, 101–2.

[56]The *Anaconda Standard*, July 8, 9, 1901, in Fredie Steve Harris, "Butch Cassidy's Outlaw Horsemen," *Golden West*, May 1969, 62–63.

[57]*Helena Independent*, July 5, 1901, in Kindred, "Hunt for Great Northern Robbers," 3; *Idaho Daily Statesman*, July 5–7, 1901, in Soule, *Tall Texan*, 55; *Knoxville Journal and Tribune*, July 5, 1901, in Lynch, *Harvey Logan*, 14.

[58]Ibid., July 6, 1901.

[59]*Great Falls Daily Tribune*, July 6, 1901, in Kindred, "Hunt for Great Northern Robbers," 3.

[60]Ibid., 5.

[61]Ibid., 3; *Knoxville Journal and Tribune*, July 6, 1901, in Lynch, *Harvey Logan*, 14–15.

[62]*The Enterprise* (Malta), July 10, 1901; *New York Daily Tribune*, July 6, 1901, in Lynch, *Harvey Logan*, 15.

[63]Ibid., 15–16; *The Enterprise* (Malta), July 10, 1901.

[64]Kindred, "Hunt for Great Northern Robbers," 3.

[65]*Helena Independent*, July 9, 1901, in Kindred, "Hunt for Great Northern Robbers," 3.

[66]*Idaho Daily Statesman*, July 8, 1901, in Soule, *Tall Texan*, 55; *Knoxville Journal and Tribune*, July 8, 1901, in Lynch, *Harvey Logan*, 16.

[67]Kindred, "Hunt for Great Northern Robbers," 3–4.

[68]*Knoxville Journal and Tribune*, July 11, July 17, 1901, in Lynch, *Harvey Logan*, 16; Kindred, "Hunt for Great Northern Robbers," 4; Soule, *Tall Texan*, 55–56.

[69]*St. Louis Daily Globe-Democrat*, November 11, 1901, in Soule, *Tall Texan*, 56; Waller, *Last of the Great*, 178.

[70]Facsimile of Pinkerton's Wagner reward poster, in Lynch, *Harvey Logan*, 23; Facsimile of Pinkerton's Wagner reward poster dated August 5, 1901, in Horan and Sann, *Pictorial History*, 218–19.

[71]Lynch, *Harvey Logan*, 16.

CHAPTER 20

[1]Coburn, *Pioneer Cattleman*, 111–12.

[2]Kenworth, *Storms of Life*, 57, 64; Santee, *Lost Pony Tracks*, 136.

[3]Ritch, "Kid Curry, 'Bad Man'," 14, part 2; Joseph K. Howard, *Montana: High, Wide, and Handsome* (New Haven, CT: Yale University Press, 1943), 141; Brekke, *Kid Curry*, 85.

[4]Siringo, *Cowboy Detective*, 336.

[5]"Dastardly Attempt to Murder," *The Daily River Press* (Ft. Benton), July 26, 1901; Horan, *Great American West*, 239; Gillespie, *Goin' to 'Dusky*, 113–14.

[6]Coburn, *Pioneer Cattleman*, 112.

[7]Horan, *Great American West*, 239.

[8]Phillips, *Fallen Branches*, 68–69, and facsimile of inquest into the death of James Winters, 115; Gillespie, *Goin' to 'Dusky*, 113–14; Brekke, *Kid Curry*, 84.

[9]Phillips, *Fallen Branches*, 69–70, and facsimile of inquest into the death of James Winters, 115; Brekke, *Kid Curry*, 84.

[10]"Dastardly Attempt to Murder," *The Daily River Press* (Ft. Benton), July 26, 1901.

[11]Facsimile of inquest into the death of James Winters, in Gillespie, *Goin' to 'Dusky*, 116; Brekke, *Kid Curry*, 84.

[12]"Dastardly Attempt to Murder," *The Daily River Press* (Ft. Benton), July 26, 1901.

[13]Gillespie, *Goin' to 'Dusky*, 114, and facsimile of inquest into the death of James Winters, 116.

[14]Ibid., 114; Coburn, *Pioneer Cattleman*, 114–15.

[15]Gillespie, *Goin' to 'Dusky*, 114; Phillips, *Fallen Branches*, 70.

[16]Facsimile of inquest into the death of James Winters, in Gillespie, *Goin' to 'Dusky*, 116. Several accounts state that Winters was shot with bullets of .30–.30 caliber, however the jury at the inquest found them to be .30–.40.

[17]Gillespie, *Goin' to 'Dusky*, 114; Wilson, *Outlaw Tales*, 156.

[18]"Dastardly Attempt to Murder," *The Daily River Press* (Ft. Benton), July 26, 1901.

[19]Ernst, *Harvey Logan*, 55–56. Cites Montana State Historical Society, file SC 2063.

[20]Duvall and Duvall-Arthur, *Memories*, 179. Quoted from an article by Charles W. Duvall, "The Disappearance of Abram Ditmars Gill," circa 1940.

[21]"Dastardly Attempt to Murder," *The Daily River Press* (Ft. Benton), July 26, 1901.

[22]Gillespie, *Goin' to 'Dusky*, 114; Waller, *Last of the Great*, 182.

[23]Ibid., 181–82; Coburn, *Pioneer Cattleman*, 111; Kindred, "Hunt for Great Northern Robbers," 5.

[24]Greenfield, "How the Logan Boys," 40. The Pike Landusky building that had housed Jake Harris' saloon was damaged by fire in November 1935. It was then completely destroyed by fire in the fall of 1943. (Newspaper clippings in the Phillips County Museum, Malta, Montana, reproduced in Gillespie, *Goin' to 'Dusky*, 15.)

[25]Kindred, "Hunt for Great Northern Robbers," 5; Coburn, *Pioneer Cattleman*, 111; Waller, *Last of the Great*, 182.

[26]Ibid.

[27]Duvall and Duvall-Arthur, *Memories*, 179–80. Quoted from an article by Charles W. Duvall, "The Disappearance of Abram Ditmars Gill," circa 1940.

[28]Wilson, *Tiger*, 141.

[29]Siringo, *Cowboy Detective*, 369–70.

[30]Pinkerton files, Logan's Log, and Tillston Report of December 26, 1901, printed in Ernst, *Harvey Logan*, 47–48. Tillston was a Pinkerton informant. If the chronology is correct, that Curry met Carrie Hunter about seven years previous to the date of the report, it would suggest that he came home for a visit most likely soon after killing Pike Landusky in December 1894, and before he arrived in Hole-in-the-Wall, Wyoming, about mid-1895.

[31]Ibid.

[32]Pinkerton Files, Logan's Log.

[33]Pinkerton files, Criminal History #5067-8, in Ernst, *Women of Wild Bunch*, 22–23.

[34]*San Angelo Standard*, September 14, 21, 28, 1901, in Burton, *Deadliest Outlaws*, 319.

[35]Concho County Court Records, in Ernst, *Harvey Logan*, 59; Soule, *Tall Texan*, 56.

[36]*Nashville American*, October 28, 1901, printed in Lynch, *Harvey Logan*, 34.

[37]Kindred, Wayne. "Trials and Travels," 27; Lynch, *Harvey Logan*, 69.

CHAPTER 21

[1]Horan, *Desperate Men*, rev. ed., 297.

[2]Pinkerton files, Logan's Log.

[3]Horan, *Desperate Men*, rev. ed., 297.

[4]Kindred, "Trials and Travels," 27–28.

[5]Lynch, *Harvey Logan*, 112. Citing witness testimony at Annie Rogers' trial in Nashville, Tennessee, on June 16, 1902.

[6]Ibid., 35.

[7]Ibid., 105. Citing testimony of Annie Rogers at her court appearance for a reduced bond in Nashville, Tennessee, on April 22, 1902.

[8]Ibid., 112. Citing witness testimony at Annie Rogers' trial in Nashville, Tennessee, on June 16, 1902.

[9]Ibid., 20, 35, 105.

[10]Ibid., 105. Citing testimony of Annie Rogers at her court appearance for a reduced bond in Nashville, Tennessee, on April 22, 1902.

[11]Kindred, "Trials and Travels," 28.

[12]Ibid.; Lynch, *Harvey Logan*, 103–4. Citing witness testimony at Annie Rogers' court appearance for a reduced bond in Nashville, Tennessee, on April 22, 1902.

[13]Ibid., 35, 103, 105.

[14]Kindred, "Trials and Travels," 28.

[15]Lillie Davis Statement, Pinkerton Archives, printed in Ernst, *Women of Wild Bunch*, 41.

[16]*Nashville American*, October 16, 1901, printed in Lynch, *Harvey Logan*, 18.

[17]Kindred, "Trials and Travels," 26; Lynch, *Harvey Logan*, 18, 102, 104. Citing witness testimony at Annie Rogers' court appearance for a reduced bond in Nashville, Tennessee, on April 21, 22, 1902.

[18]Ibid., 20. State of Tennessee, Davidson County warrant.

[19]Ibid., 19–20.

[20]Kindred, "Trials and Travels," 26.

[21]Horan, *The Outlaws*, 248.

[22]Kindred, "Trials and Travels," 26–27; *Nashville American*, October 18, 1901, in Lynch, *Harvey Logan*, 20–21.

[23]Ibid.; Kindred, "Trials and Travels," 27.

[24]Kindred, "Trials and Travels," 27–28; Lynch, *Harvey Logan*, 104–5. Citing witness testimony at Annie Rogers' court appearance for a reduced bond in Nashville, Tennessee, on April 22, 1902.

[25]Kindred, "Trials and Travels," 28, 30; Lynch, *Harvey Logan*, 35, 103–4. Citing witness testimony at Annie Rogers' court appearance for a reduced bond in Nashville, Tennessee, on April 22, 1902.

[26]*Nashville American*, October 31, 1901, in Lynch, *Harvey Logan*, 35.

[27]Ibid.

[28]Lynch, *Harvey Logan*, 104. Pinkerton Detective Charlie Siringo wrote that Kid Curry came directly to Rawlins, Wyoming, after Annie Rogers had been arrested, for the purpose of digging up the Great Northern money he had cached on Jim Hanson's Twenty–mile ranch. This information came from saloon owner and Wild Bunch confidant Jack Ryan. Curry supposedly needed the money to hire lawyers for Annie's defense. He would hardly have needed to travel all the way to Wyoming for more of the incomplete (unsigned) banknotes, when he had thousands of dollars of these same notes on his person while traveling through the South. Siringo was also told that Kid Curry had seen him in a Rawlins saloon, and became suspicious of him. Curry supposedly said that Siringo "looked too bright and wide-awake for a common rounder." When Ryan assured Curry that Siringo (going by the name of Harry Blevins) was all right, Curry was supposedly satisfied. Just as Jim Thornhill knew that Siringo was a Pinkerton agent, it is quite possible that Jack Ryan was also aware of this, and enjoyed feeding him false information. (Siringo, *Cowboy Detective*, 370)

[29]Ibid., 22.

[30]Ibid.

[31]*Nashville American*, October 26, 1901, in Lynch, *Harvey Logan*, 24–25.

[32]*Nashville American*, October 28, 1901, printed in Lynch, *Harvey Logan*, 32.

[33]Ibid., 27, 29, 31.

[34]Pinkerton files, Logan's Log.

[35]*Nashville American*, October 28, 1901, printed in Lynch, *Harvey Logan*, 27; Kindred, "Ice Wagon Affair," 2.

[36]*Nashville American*, October 28, and 29, 1901, printed in Lynch, *Harvey Logan*, 27, 36. Statement of Detective Dwyer in issue of 29th.

[37] Ibid., October 28, 1901, 27–28.

[38] Ibid., 28.

[39] Ibid., 28–31; Kindred, "Ice Wagon Affair," 3–4.

[40] *Nashville American*, October 28, 1901, printed in Lynch, *Harvey Logan*, 28–30.

[41] *Nashville American*, October 29, 1901, in Lynch, *Harvey Logan*, 35–36; Waller, *Last of the Great*, 186–87.

[42] *Nashville American*, October 28, 1901, printed in Lynch, *Harvey Logan*, 29.

[43] *Nashville American*, October 30, 1901, in Lynch, *Harvey Logan*, 37–38.

[44] Ibid., November 1, 1901, 39.

[45] Waller, *Last of the Great*, 187.

[46] *Nashville American*, October 29 and 30, 1901, in Lynch, *Harvey Logan*, 34–35.

[47] *St. Louis Daily Globe-Democrat*, November 7, 1901, in Soule, *Tall Texan*, 56.

[48] Barton, *Den of Outlaws*, 175; Ernst, *Women of Wild Bunch*, 24.

[49] *St. Louis Daily Globe-Democrat*, November 7, 1901, in Soule, *Tall Texan*, 59.

[50] *Nashville American*, November 3, 1901, in Lynch, *Harvey Logan*, 50.

[51] Pinkerton files, Logan's Log.

[52] *St. Louis Daily Globe-Democrat*, November 8, 1901, in Soule, *Tall Texan*, 59; Barton, *Den of Outlaws*, 168.

[53] *St. Louis Daily Globe-Democrat*, November 6, 1901, in Soule, *Tall Texan*, 60.

[54] Ibid., November 7, 1901; Barton, *Den of Outlaws*, 170–71.

[55] Ibid., 173, 175, 179–80, 183; *St. Louis Daily Globe-Democrat*, November 7, 8, and 18, 1901, in Soule, *Tall Texan*, 61–62; *San Antonio Express*, November 7, 1901, in Ernst, *Women of Wild Bunch*, 26.

[56] Soule, *Tall Texan*, 65. Cites Case No. 4666 *United States vs John Arnold and Laura Causey*; Pardon Case No. 26–349, B. A. Kilpatrick; Barton, *Den of Outlaws*, 178.

[57] Pinkerton files, Logan's Log.

[58] Lillie Davis Statement, Pinkerton Archives, printed in Ernst, *Women of Wild Bunch*, 40–41.

[59] Ibid., 41–42.

[60]Soule, *Tall Texan*, 66, 68. Cites Case No. 4666 *United States vs John Arnold and Laura Causey*; Barton, *Den of* Outlaws, 178, 183, 186, 192.

CHAPTER 22

[1]Wayne Kindred, "Kid Curry—The Missing Months," WOLA *The Journal*, Fall/Winter 1997, 29.

[2]*Knoxville Sentinel*, December 14, 1901, in Lynch, *Harvey Logan*, 47; Waller, *Last of the Great*, 205; Dick North, "When the Tiger of the Wild Bunch Broke Out of the Knoxville Jail!" *Frontier Times*, September 1975, 17.

[3]Waller, *Last of the Great*, 212; Lynch, *Harvey Logan*, 62.

[4]Ibid., 45–46, 119; Waller, *Last of the Great*, 200, 204–5, 219. The police later searched Curry's room at the Central Hotel, finding the two grips and his clothes, which included some expensive suits, shirts, and underwear. Sylvia Lynch states that these items were taken to police headquarters, but then there was no further mention of them in the newspapers or in court testimony.

[5]North, "When the Tiger Broke Out!" 16–17; *Knoxville Journal and Tribune*, December 15, 1901, in Lynch, *Harvey Logan*, 45–46; Waller, *Last of the Great*, 204–5; Horan, *The Gunfighters*, 205.

[6]Ibid., 205–6.

[7]Lynch, *Harvey Logan*, 43; Waller, *Last of the Great*, 204.

[8]*Knoxville Sentinel*, February 2, 1902, in Lynch, *Harvey Logan*, 90. Interview with William Dinwiddie; Waller, *Last of the Great*, 220. Dinwiddie's testimony at Harvey Logan's November 1902 trial in Knoxville, Tennessee.

[9]*Knoxville Journal and Tribune*, December 15, 1901, in Lynch, *Harvey Logan*, 45–46; Waller, *Last of the Great*, 205.

[10]Lynch, *Harvey Logan*, 62–63; Waller, *Last of the Great*, 212.

[11]Wayne Kindred, "Capturing a Train Robber: Kid Curry's Escapades in Knoxville, Tennessee," website, 1996, 1; Waller, *Last of the Great*, 200–1, 205; Lynch, *Harvey Logan*, 42–43. Uses the *Knoxville Journal and Tribune*, December 14, 1901, for the most part.

[12]Ibid., 43; Kindred, "Capturing a Train Robber," 1–2.

[13]Lynch, *Harvey Logan*, 43. Uses the *Knoxville Journal and Tribune*, December 14, 1901, for the most part.

[14]Kindred, "Capturing a Train Robber," 2; Waller, *Last of the Great*, 201–2; North, "When the Tiger Broke Out!" 17; Lynch, *Harvey Logan*, 43–44. Uses the *Knoxville Journal and Tribune*, December 14, 1901, for the most part.

[15]Ibid., 44, 66; Waller, *Last of the Great*, 202–3; North, "When the Tiger Broke Out!" 17.

[16]Waller, *Last of the Great*, 202–3; North, "When the Tiger Broke Out!" 17–18; Lynch, *Harvey Logan*, 44–45. Uses the *Knoxville Journal and Tribune*, December 14, 1901, for the most part.

[17]Ibid., 45; Waller, *Last of the Great*, 203; Kindred, "Capturing a Train Robber," 2.

[18]*Knoxville Sentinel*, December 14, 1901, and *Knoxville Journal and Tribune*, December 15, 1901, in Lynch, *Harvey Logan*, 46; Waller, *Last of the* Great, 203–4.

[19]Ibid., 204, 208; *Knoxville Journal and Tribune*, December 15, 1901, in Lynch, *Harvey Logan*, 53.

[20]Waller, *Last of the Great*, 204; Kindred, "Capturing a Train Robber," 3.

[21]*Knoxville Sentinel*, December 14, 1901, and *Knoxville Journal and Tribune*, December 15, 1901, in Lynch, *Harvey Logan*, 47, 53; Waller, *Last of the* Great, 204, 206.

[22]*Knoxville Sentinel*, December 14, 1901, and *Knoxville Journal and Tribune*, December 15, 1901, in Lynch, *Harvey Logan*, 47–48; Kindred, "Capturing a Train Robber," 3.

[23]Ibid.; *Knoxville Sentinel*, December 14, 1901, and *Knoxville Journal and Tribune*, December 15, 1901, in Lynch, *Harvey Logan*, 47–48.

[24]Kindred, "Capturing a Train Robber," 3; Lynch, *Harvey Logan*, 48, 50.

[25]Ibid., 48.

[26]Ibid., 50; Kindred, "Capturing a Train Robber," 3.

[27]Lynch, *Harvey Logan*, 53.

[28]Kindred, "Capturing a Train Robber," 4.

[29]Waller, *Last of the Great*, 205–6; Lynch, *Harvey Logan*, 54.

[30]Ibid.; Kindred, "Capturing a Train Robber," 4; Waller, *Last of the Great*, 206.

[31] *Knoxville Journal and Tribune*, December 16, 1901, in Lynch, *Harvey Logan*, 54–55; Kindred, "Capturing a Train Robber," 4; Waller, *Last of the Great*, 206–7; North, "When the Tiger Broke Out!" 18–19.

[32] *Knoxville Sentinel*, December 16, 1901, in Lynch, *Harvey Logan*, 55.

[33] Ibid.; North, "When the Tiger Broke Out!" 18; Kindred, "Capturing a Train Robber," 4.

[34] *Knoxville Sentinel*, December 16, 1901, in Lynch, *Harvey Logan*, 56–57; Waller, *Last of the Great*, 207; Kindred, "Capturing a Train Robber," 4.

[35] North, "When the Tiger Broke Out!" 18; Kindred, "Capturing a Train Robber," 4; Waller, *Last of the Great*, 207; Lynch, *Harvey Logan*, 57.

[36] Ernst, *Harvey Logan*, 62. Pinkerton files.

[37] Lynch, *Harvey Logan*, 57–58; Kindred, "Capturing a Train Robber," 5; Waller, *Last of the Great*, 208.

[38] North, "When the Tiger Broke Out!" 18.

[39] Waller, *Last of the Great*, 208; *Knoxville Journal and Tribune*, December 16, 1901, printed in Lynch, *Harvey Logan*, 55, 58; Kindred, "Capturing a Train Robber," 5.

[40] *Knoxville Journal and Tribune*, December 16, 1901, printed in Lynch, *Harvey Logan*, 58.

[41] Ibid., 59–60, 80; Waller, *Last of the Great*, 208–9.

[42] Ibid., 207–8, 213; Lynch, *Harvey Logan*, 60.

[43] North, "When the Tiger Broke Out!" 19.

[44] Ibid., 18; Waller, *Last of the Great*, 207–8.

[45] Ibid., 208; Kindred, "Capturing a Train Robber," 5; Lynch, *Harvey Logan*, 60.

[46] Ibid., 60–61; Waller, *Last of the Great*, 209.

[47] Ibid., 212–13; Lynch, *Harvey Logan*, 62–64; North, "When the Tiger Broke Out!" 18; Kindred, "Capturing a Train Robber," 5. It would not be unreasonable to assume that Curry wasn't just haphazardly traveling through the southern and eastern parts of the country, hiding from the law. It is entirely possible his purpose in traveling to such cities as Cincinnati, Asheville, Chattanooga, and Knoxville, was to make contact with people who could exchange the stolen money for "good" money.

[48] *Knoxville Journal and Tribune*, December 16, 1901, in Lynch, *Harvey Logan*, 62; Waller, *Last of the Great*, 210.

[49]North, "When the Tiger Broke Out!" 18; *Knoxville Journal and Tribune*, December 17, 1901, in Lynch, *Harvey Logan*, 62.

CHAPTER 23

[1]*Knoxville Journal and Tribune*, December 16, 1901, and *Knoxville Sentinel*, December 16, 1901, in Lynch, *Harvey Logan*, 70–71; North, "When the Tiger Broke Out!" 18–19.

[2]Ibid., 19; *Knoxville Journal and Tribune*, December 29, 1901, in Lynch, *Harvey Logan*, 71.

[3]Lynch, *Harvey Logan*, 71–72.

[4]Ibid., 64; Waller, *Last of the Great*, 213.

[5]Ibid., 213–14; Lynch, *Harvey Logan*, 64–65.

[6]Ibid., 64–65; Waller, *Last of the Great*, 214; North, "When the Tiger Broke Out!" 19.

[7]Ibid.; Lynch, *Harvey Logan*, 66; Waller, *Last of the Great*, 208; Kindred, "Capturing a Train Robber," 5.

[8]North, "When the Tiger Broke Out!" 19; Lynch, *Harvey Logan*, 66–67; Waller, *Last of the Great*, 213.

[9]Ibid., 210; Kindred, "Capturing a Train Robber," 5; Lynch, *Harvey Logan*, 65–66.

[10]Ibid., 66; North, "When the Tiger Broke Out!" 18–19; Kindred, "Capturing a Train Robber," 5. James Horan tells of a woman of "a good family" named Catherine Cross, who became infatuated with Curry. She visited him in jail as often as she could, "showing him much attention." Horan writes: "Catherine Cross is a mystery figure in the story of Logan's period in Knoxville. She appears to have been a daily visitor to the jail—along with other women—but there are no newspaper photographs or physical description of her ... She was later murdered by an infuriated drunk or madman because she insisted on singing a ballad about the Kid and his exploits." (Horan, *The Gunfighters*, 188, 218, and 298, endnote 24.)

[11]Ibid., 5–6; Waller, *Last of the Great*, 210–11; Lynch, *Harvey Logan*, 67–68. Uses the *Knoxville Sentinel*, December 17, 1901, for the most part.

[12]Ibid., 68; Waller, *Last of the Great*, 211; Kindred, "Capturing a Train Robber," 6.

[13]Lynch, *Harvey Logan*, 68.

[14]Ibid., 68–69; Kindred, "Capturing a Train Robber," 6.

[15]Waller, *Last of the Great*, 206; Lynch, *Harvey Logan*, 97.

[16]Ibid., 70.

[17]Ibid., 69; Waller, *Last of the Great*, 212–13.

[18]Ibid.; Lynch, *Harvey Logan*, 70; Kindred, "Capturing a Train Robber," 5.

[19]Ibid.

[20]Waller, *Last of the Great*, 213; Lynch, *Harvey Logan*, 70.

[21]Ibid.; Kindred, "Capturing a Train Robber," 4.

[22]Waller, *Last of the Great*, 213; Lynch, *Harvey Logan*, 70.

[23]*Knoxville Sentinel*, December 18, 1901, in Lynch, *Harvey Logan*, 75–76.

[24]Lynch, *Harvey Logan*, 78; Waller, *Last of the Great*, 214, 216.

[25]Lynch, *Harvey Logan*, 80–81.

[26]*Knoxville Journal and Tribune*, December 18, and December 23, 1901, in Lynch, *Harvey Logan*, 70, 76; North, "When the Tiger Broke Out!" 19.

[27]*Knoxville Journal and Tribune*, December 20, 1901, in Lynch, *Harvey Logan*, 76–77; Waller, *Last of the Great*, 214.

[28]*Knoxville Journal and Tribune*, December 20, 1901, in North, "When the Tiger Broke Out!" 46.

[29]Lynch, *Harvey Logan*, 79; Waller, *Last of the Great*, 211–12, 214; Kindred, "Capturing a Train Robber," 6.

[30]*Knoxville Sentinel*, December 23, 1901, in Horan, *The Gunfighters*, 211–12.

[31]*Knoxville Journal and Tribune*, December 23, 1901, in Lynch, *Harvey Logan*, 76; Waller, *Last of the Great*, 215–216.

[32]Ibid., 216.

[33]Ibid., 215; Lynch, *Harvey Logan*, 83.

[34]Ibid.; Kindred, "Capturing a Train Robber," 6.

[35]Waller, *Last of the Great*, 215.

[36]Lynch, *Harvey Logan*, 113. Morgan Roop's testimony at Annie Rogers' trial in Nashville, Tennessee, on June 17, 1902; Ernst, *Women of Wild Bunch*, 54. James Horan states that he has copies of Annie's love letters to the Kid that had been smuggled into the jail. (Horan, *The Outlaws*, 249.)

[37]Lynch, *Harvey Logan*, 80.

[38]Wayne Kindred, "The Logan, Houk, Thornhill Letters," WOLA *The Journal*, Fall 2002, 34; Waller, *Last of the Great*, 216.

[39]*Knoxville Sentinel*, December 30, 1901, in Lynch, *Harvey Logan*, 82–83.

[40]Waller, *Last of the Great*, 216–17; Lynch, *Harvey Logan*, 81.

[41]Ibid., 81, 83.

[42]*Knoxville Sentinel*, February 11, 1902, in Kindred, "Logan, Houk, Thornhill," 34.

[43]*Knoxville Journal and Tribune*, January 6, 1902, in Lynch, *Harvey Logan*, 84–85; Waller, *Last of the Great*, 214–15.

[44]Ibid., 214; *Knoxville Sentinel*, January 16, 1902, in Lynch, *Harvey Logan*, 87–88.

[45]Ibid., January 20, 1902, 89.

[46]Lynch, *Harvey Logan*, 89.

[47]*Knoxville Sentinel*, January 30, and February 2, 1902, in Lynch, *Harvey Logan*, 90.

[48]Ibid., February 11, 1902, 93–94; *Knoxville Sentinel*, February 11, 1902, in Kindred, "Logan, Houk, Thornhill," 34–35.

[49]*Knoxville Journal and Tribune*, February 10, 1902, and *Knoxville Sentinel*, February 5, 1902, in Lynch, *Harvey Logan*, 92–93.

[50]*Knoxville Journal and Tribune*, February 14, 1902, in Lynch, *Harvey Logan*, 94; Waller, *Last of the Great*, 217.

[51]*Knoxville Sentinel*, March 8, 1902, in Lynch, *Harvey Logan*, 97.

[52]*Knoxville Journal and Tribune*, March 13, 1902, in Lynch, *Harvey Logan*, 98.

[53]Ibid., March 24, 1902, 99.

[54]Lynch, *Harvey Logan*, 99.

CHAPTER 24

[1]Waller, *Last of the Great*, 198.

[2]*The San Antonio Express*, April 20, 1902, in Chuck Parsons, "O. C. Hanks and the Texas Connection," *The Outlaw Trail Journal*, Summer 1994, 26.

[3]Ibid., 27.

[4]Murphy, "Killer with a Hankering," 24.

[5]Ibid., 34; *San Francisco Chronicle*, April 20, 1902, in Burton, *Deadliest Outlaws*, 321.

[6]Bartholomew, *Black Jack Ketchum*, 100; Waller, *Last of the Great*, 198.

[7]*The San Antonio Express*, April 20, 1902, in Soule, *Tall Texan*, 72; Bartholomew, *Black Jack Ketchum*, 100.

[8]Parsons, "O. C. Hanks," 24, 26.

[9]Ibid., 25–26; *The San Antonio Express*, April 17, 1902, in Soule, *Tall Texan*, 72–73; Murphy, "Killer with a Hankering," 24; Bartholomew, *Black Jack Ketchum*, 99–100.

[10]Ibid., 100; *The San Antonio Express*, April 17–18, 1902, in Soule, *Tall Texan*, 72–73; Murphy, "Killer with a Hankering," 24; Parsons, "O.C. Hanks," 25–26.

[11]Ibid.; *The San Antonio Express*, April 17–18, 1902, in Soule, *Tall Texan*, 73; Murphy, "Killer with a Hankering," 24; Bartholomew, *Black Jack Ketchum*, 100.

[12]Waller, *Last of the Great*, 198; Lynch, *Harvey Logan*, 100.

[13]Parsons, "O. C. Hanks," 26–27; Murphy, "Killer with a Hankering," 24.

[14]Parsons, "O. C. Hanks," 26–27. Cites *The San Antonio Express*, April 18–25, 1902; Kindred, "Hunt for Great Northern Robbers," 8.

[15]Ibid.; Parsons, "O. C. Hanks," 26–27.

[16]*Nashville American*, April 21, 1902, in Lynch, *Harvey Logan*, 100.

[17]Kindred, "Hunt for Great Northern Robbers," 8; Parsons, "O. C. Hanks," 27.

[18]*The San Antonio Express*, April 24, 1902, in Soule, *Tall Texan*, 73; *The San Antonio Express*, April 25, 1902, in Parsons, "O. C. Hanks," 27.

[19]*Knoxville Sentinel*, April 18, 1902, in Lynch, *Harvey Logan*, 100.

[20]*Nashville American*, April 20 and 22, 1902, in Lynch, *Harvey Logan*, 101–2; Ernst, *Women of Wild Bunch*, 54; Kindred, "Trials and Travels," 28.

[21]*Nashville American*, April 22, 1902, in Lynch, *Harvey Logan*, 102–3. C.H. Smith's testimony as reported in the newspaper; Ernst, *Women of Wild Bunch*, 54–55; Kindred, "Trials and Travels," 29.

[22]Ibid.; Lynch, *Harvey Logan*, 103–4; Ernst, *Women of Wild Bunch*, 55.

[23]Ibid.; Lynch, *Harvey Logan*, 104.

[24]Ibid., 104–105; Kindred, "Trials and Travels," 29; Ernst, *Women of Wild Bunch*, 55.

[25]Ibid.; Lynch, *Harvey Logan*, 105, 107; Kindred, "Trials and Travels," 29.

[26]*Knoxville Journal and Tribune*, April 24, 1902, in Lynch, *Harvey Logan*, 105–6; Waller, *Last of the Great*, 218.

[27]Michael Rutter, *Wild Bunch Women* (Helena, MT: TwoDot, 2003), 7, 11.

[28]*Knoxville Journal and Tribune*, April 27, 1902, printed in Lynch, *Harvey Logan*, 106.

[29]*Knoxville Sentinel*, April 26, 1902, printed in Lynch, *Harvey Logan*, 106.

[30]Lynch, *Harvey Logan*, 107.

[31]*Knoxville Sentinel*, May 1, 1902, in Lynch, *Harvey Logan*, 108.

[32]Wayne Kindred, "Harvey Logan's Escape," *True West*, May 1986, 25.

[33]Kindred, "Logan, Houk, Thornhill," 35. Cites Jim Thornhill to Reuben L. Cates, April 22, 1902, and Harvey Logan to Jim Thornhill, May 11, 1902, McClung Historical Collection.

[34]*Knoxville Sentinel*, May 13 and 14, 1902, in Lynch, *Harvey Logan*, 108–9.

[35]Lynch, *Harvey Logan*, 109.

[36]*Knoxville Journal and Tribune*, May 18, 1902, in Lynch, *Harvey Logan*, 108.

[37]*Knoxville Sentinel*, June 4, 1902, in Lynch, *Harvey Logan*, 109–10.

[38]Ibid., June 3, 1902, 110; Waller, *Last of the Great*, 217; *Knoxville Sentinel*, June 3, 1902, in Kindred, "Logan, Houk, Thornhill," 35.

[39]Ibid.; Lynch, *Harvey Logan*, 110.

[40]*Knoxville Sentinel*, June 11, 1902, in Lynch, *Harvey Logan*, 110–11.

[41]Ernst, *Women of Wild Bunch*, 56; Kindred, "Trials and Travels," 29; Lynch, *Harvey Logan*, 111–12.

[42]Ibid., 112.

[43]Ibid.; Kindred, "Trials and Travels," 29–30.

[44]Lynch, *Harvey Logan*, 112–13; Ernst, *Women of Wild Bunch*, 56; Kindred, "Trials and Travels," 30.

[45]Ernst, *Women of Wild Bunch*, 56; Lynch, *Harvey Logan*, 113.

[46]Ibid.; Ernst, *Women of Wild Bunch*, 56; Kindred, "Trials and Travels," 30.

[47]Ibid.

[48]Ibid.; *Nashville American*, June 19, 1902, in Lynch, *Harvey Logan*, 113; Ernst, *Women of Wild Bunch*, 56–57.

[49]Ibid., 57; Kindred, "Trials and Travels," 30; Lynch, *Harvey Logan*, 130.

[50]Ernst, *Women of Wild Bunch*, 57. Gary Wilson believes the mysterious woman was Curry's devoted admirer Catherine Cross. (Wilson, *Tiger*, 166.) However, Alan Lee Brekke fixes the date of her murder on February 6, 1902, making it impossible for her to have put in an appearance at Curry's September 1902 hearings. (Brekke, *Kid Curry*, 87.)

[51]Horan, *The Outlaws*, 248–49.

CHAPTER 25

[1]Kindred, "Logan, Houk, Thornhill," 35–36. Cites Jim Thornhill to Charles Johnson, August 15, 1902, McClung Historical Collection. In Noyes, *Land of Chinook*, 119, Dad Marsh states that Jim Thornhill sold a band of horses he owned to raise money for Curry.

[2]Kindred, "Logan, Houk, Thornhill," 36.

[3]*Knoxville Journal and Tribune*, August 18, 1902, in Lynch, *Harvey Logan*, 114.

[4]*Knoxville Journal and Tribune*, September 6, 1902, in Kindred, "Logan, Houk, Thornhill," 36; Lynch, *Harvey Logan*, 115–16.

[5]Kindred, "Logan, Houk, Thornhill," 36. Cites Harvey Logan Papers, Small Collection #2063, Montana Historical Society Archives, Helena, Montana.

[6]*Knoxville Journal and Tribune*, September 14, 1902, printed in Lynch, *Harvey Logan*, 116.

[7]Lynch, *Harvey Logan*, 117.

[8]Ibid.; Waller, *Last of the Great*, 220.

[9]Lynch, *Harvey Logan*, 117–18.

[10]Ibid., 118.

[11]Ernst, *Harvey Logan*, 64; *Knoxville Sentinel*, September 17, 1902, in Lynch, *Harvey Logan*, 118–19.

[12]North, "When the Tiger Broke Out!" 47; Kindred, "Logan, Houk, Thornhill," 36–37.

[13]Ibid., 37. Cites Harvey Logan Papers, Small Collection #2063, Montana Historical Society Archives.

[14]Lynch, *Harvey Logan*, 119–21. Note printed in full from the *Knoxville Sentinel*, September 20, 1902; Waller, *Last of the Great*, 219; Facsimile

of a September 20, 1902, news story titled "Sheriff Makes Timely Discovery," in Horan, *The Gunfighters*, 214.

[15]Kindred, "Capturing a Train Robber," 6; Lynch, *Harvey Logan*, 121.

[16]Ibid., 122–23.

[17]Ibid., 116, 130–31; Waller, *Last of the Great*, 221.

[18]Lynch, *Harvey Logan*, 123.

[19]Ibid., 123–24.

[20]Ibid., 124; Horan, *The Gunfighters*, 213.

[21]Lynch, *Harvey Logan*, 124.

[22]Ibid., 124–25; Horan, *The Gunfighters*, 213–14; Waller, *Last of the Great*, 220.

[23]Ibid.; Lynch, *Harvey Logan*, 125–27.

[24]Ibid., 118, 128.

[25]Ibid., 127–28.

[26]*Knoxville Journal and Tribune*, November 21, 1902, in Lynch, *Harvey Logan*, 128; Waller, *Last of the Great*, 220.

[27]Lynch, *Harvey Logan*, 128.

[28]Ibid., 128–29, 131; Kindred, "Logan, Houk, Thornhill," 37. Cites case no. 1187, *United States vs. Harvey Logan,* Federal Records Center, East Point, GA; Ernst, *Harvey Logan*, 65–66.

[29]Kindred, "Missing Months," 24–25. Cites William Wright to Department of Justice, September 11 and 19, 1902, and November 24, 1902, Record Group 060, National Archives, College Park, MD.

[30]*Lewistown Democrat News*, December 5, 1902, in Horan, *The Gunfighters*, 214–15.

[31]Ernst, *Harvey Logan*, 66; Lynch, *Harvey Logan*, 131.

[32]*Knoxville Sentinel*, December 4, 1902, in Lynch, *Harvey Logan*, 131–32; Waller, *Last of the Great*, 221; Ernst, *Harvey Logan*, 66–67. Cites Pinkerton Archives, Criminal History Record.

[33]*Knoxville Journal and Tribune*, November 22, 1902, in Lynch, *Harvey Logan*, 130.

[34]Lillie Davis Statement, Pinkerton Archives, printed in Ernst, *Women of Wild Bunch*, 41–42; Horan, *The Outlaws*, 248. Annie Rogers' mother may have moved from Texas to St. Louis, Missouri, sometime after her daughter's arrest in Nashville.

[35]Ernst, *Women of Wild Bunch*, 57. Cites Pinkerton Archives, Criminal Histories #5063 and #5064.

[36]Kindred, "Missing Months," 25–26. Cites William Wright to Department of Justice, December 4, 1902, Record Group 060, National Archives.

[37]Lynch, *Harvey Logan*, 132–33.

[38]Ibid.; Waller, *Last of the Great*, 221–22.

[39]*Knoxville Journal and Tribune*, January 8, 1903, in Lynch, *Harvey Logan*, 133, and in Ernst, *Harvey Logan*, 66.

[40]Waller, *Last of the Great*, 221; Lynch, *Harvey Logan*, 133.

[41]Ibid., 133–34.

[42]Kindred, "Logan, Houk, Thornhill," 37. Cites Charles Johnson to John C. Houk, January 30, 1903, McClung Historical Collection.

[43]Kindred, "Logan, Houk, Thornhill," 38.

[44]*Knoxville Sentinel*, March 10, 1903, in Lynch, *Harvey Logan*, 134.

[45]Ibid., April 6, and May 6, 1903.

[46]Kindred, "Logan, Houk, Thornhill," 38. Cites case no. 1187, *United States vs. Harvey Logan*, Federal Records Center; Horan, *The Gunfighters*, 215, and 299, endnote 28. Cites copy of Logan's appeal in the U.S. Circuit Court of Appeals, *Harvey Logan alias Harvey Curry, Kid Curry, etc. vs. the United States*. Docket no. 1187. The James D. Horan Civil War and Western Americana Collection; Lynch, *Harvey Logan*, 135.

CHAPTER 26

[1]This account of Curry's escape is taken from the *Knoxville Sentinel* of June 29, 1903, unless otherwise noted.

[2]James D. Horan, *Desperate Men* (1949; repr. New York: Bonanza Books), 270.

[3]*Knoxville Journal and Tribune*, June 28, 1903, in Lynch, *Harvey Logan*, 138; Horan, *Desperate Men,* Rev. ed., 305.

[4]Waller, *Last of the Great*, 234; Lynch, *Harvey Logan*, 140–41.

[5]Waller, *Last of the Great*, 233; Kindred, "Missing Months," 28–29. The endnotes in Kindred's article are not numbered in the text owing to a printing error. However it can be determined that he used the following newspapers as sources for Curry's escape: *Knoxville Sentinel*, June

30, and July 1, 1903. *Knoxville Journal & Tribune*, June 28, and June 29, 1903.

[6]Ibid., 28; Waller, *Last of the Great*, 234.

[7]Ibid.; Horan, *Desperate Men,* rev. ed., 307; Kindred, "Logan's Escape," 23–24.

[8]Waller, *Last of the Great*, 234–35; Kindred, "Missing Months," 28.

[9]Ibid., 28–29.

[10]Horan, *Desperate Men,* rev. ed., 307.

[11]Waller, *Last of the Great*, 235.

[12]Facsimile of Pinkerton reward poster, in Ernst, *Harvey Logan*, 69.

[13]Waller, *Last of the Great*, 233, 242; Kindred, "Missing Months," 29.

[14]Ibid.; Waller, *Last of the Great*, 236–37.

[15]Ibid., 236.

[16]Ibid., 235–36.

[17]*Knoxville Sentinel*, July 4, 1903, in Lynch, *Harvey Logan*, 147; Waller, *Last of the Great*, 236.

[18]Horan, *Desperate Men,* rev. ed., 307.

[19]*Knoxville Sentinel*, July 4, 1903, in Lynch, *Harvey Logan*, 147; Kindred, "Missing Months," 29.

[20]Waller, *Last of the Great*, 238.

[21]Ibid., 236; Kindred, "Missing Months," 29.

[22]North, "When the Tiger Broke Out!" 47; Lynch, *Harvey Logan*, 142.

[23]Kindred, "Missing Months," 26, 29. Cites sworn statement of R. W. Austin, January 1, 1903, RG 060, National Archives; North, "When the Tiger Broke Out!" 47.

[24]Horan, *Desperate Men*, 274; Waller, *Last of the Great*, 237.

[25]Ibid., 239; Horan, *Desperate Men*, 274–75.

[26]Lynch, *Harvey Logan*, 144; Waller, *Last of the Great*, 237–38.

[27]Ibid., 238.

[28]Lynch, *Harvey Logan*, 141–42.

[29]Waller, *Last of the Great*, 238.

[30]Horan, *Desperate Men,* Rev. ed., 309.

[31]Kindred, "Missing Months," 44. Cites case no. 1339, *United States vs. J. W. Fox*, Federal Records Center, East Point, GA; Lynch, *Harvey Logan*, 152.

[32]Ibid.

[33]Ernst, *Harvey Logan*, 70. Cites Pinkerton Archives.

³⁴Kindred, "Logan's Escape," 25; Waller, *Last of the Great*, 226.

³⁵John C. Houk to James Thornhill, August 22, 1904, Harvey Logan Papers, Small Collection 2063, Montana Historical Society Archives, in Lamb, "Logan's Lost Journal," 27.

³⁶Ernst, *Harvey Logan*, 68, 70. Cites Pinkerton Archives.

³⁷Harvey Logan Papers, Small Collection 2063, Montana Historical Society Archives, in Lamb, "Logan's Lost Journal," 20.

³⁸Harvey Logan Papers, Small Collection 2063, Montana Historical Society Archives, in Wayne Kindred, "Harvey Logan's Secret Letters," *True West*, October 1994, 37.

³⁹Lynch, *Harvey Logan*, 144–45; Waller, *Last of the Great*, 239.
    The following account of the Pinkertons' pursuit of Curry is taken from Lynch, *Harvey Logan*, 148–50, and Kindred, "Missing Months," 29, 43–44, unless otherwise noted. The endnotes in Kindred's article are not numbered in the text owing to a printing error. However it can be determined that he used the following newspapers as sources: *Knoxville Sentinel*, July 21, and July 23, 1903. *Knoxville Journal & Tribune*, July 23, 1903. Lynch used the *Knoxville Sentinel*, July 21, 1903, and the *Knoxville Journal & Tribune*, July 21, 22, and 23, 1903.

⁴⁰Waller, *Last of the Great*, 239.

⁴¹Kindred, "Logan, Houk, Thornhill," 40. Cites Jim Thornhill to John C. Houk, August 20, 1905, McClung Historical Collection.

⁴²*Knoxville Sentinel*, August 30, 1904, in Lynch, *Harvey Logan*, 151–52.

CHAPTER 27

¹Kindred, "Missing Months," 44; Waller, *Last of the Great*, 244.

²Ibid.

³Mokler, *Natrona County*, 322.

⁴Lamb, *Kid Curry*, 356, chapter 31, endnote 1, and 357, endnote 7. For Stevens the author cites an anonymous, unpublished manuscript furnished by Wanda Ramage, "The Outlaws," Lysite, Wyoming, 1971. For W. H. Howland he cites Baker, *Wild Bunch*, 186.

⁵Buffalo Centennial, *Buffalo's First Century*, 35. As to the existence of a Charles Stevens, there are a few brief references in the sources. One is in a letter dated August 12, 1899, from the Sweetwater County prosecuting attorney to U.S. Marshal Frank Hadsell, concerning the sighting

of Wilcox robber George Currie near Powder Springs. The attorney closed his letter by informing the marshal that Tom O'Day and Charles Stevens, alias White River Charley, were seen in the area. A diary entry from Hadsell's private papers named White River Charley as one of Sheriff Josiah Hazen's killers. (DeJournette and DeJournette, *One Hundred Years*, 303. Facsimile of letter from probate file of Isam Dart. Courtesy Wyoming State Archives.) Charles Kelly also makes a brief mention of Charles Stevens, alias Waterhole Charley, in connection with the robbery of Charley Guild's post office-store-saloon on June 15, 1897, in Fort Bridger, Wyoming. (Kelly, *Outlaw Trail*, 162–63.) Joe LeFors referred to one Charlie *Stephens*, who the Hole-in-the-Wall boys knew as Old Charlie. (LeFors, *Wyoming Peace Officer*, 100.)

[6]Mokler, *Natrona County*, 322. In a conversation with the present owners of the Kenneth McDonald ranch (now called the Willow Creek Ranch) in September 2009, the author was told that the cowboys were eating in the cookhouse when the horses were stolen. The owners have painstakingly restored the 1890s log cookhouse, converting it to a bunkhouse for guests.

[7]Ibid. Although Punteney was not averse to helping his outlaw friends when they were in a bind, he did not go back to the outlaw life. He was married in January 1907 and continued to ranch on Bridger Creek in the Lost Cabin country until 1912. He moved with his wife and daughter to Pinedale, Wyoming, where he died on April 19, 1950. (See Donna B. Ernst, "Walt Punteney and Tom O'Day, Two Early Wild Bunch Members, Lived Long But Out of the Spotlight," *Wild West*, April 2004, 72.)

[8]Lamb, *Kid Curry*, 357, chapter 31, endnote 7. Quotes from an anonymous, unpublished manuscript furnished by Wanda Ramage, "The Outlaws," Lysite, Wyoming, 1971; Gillespie, *Goin' to 'Dusky*, 96. Quotes from Larry Pointer's typed interview with Ray Picard. Neither citation can be verified by any other reliable sources; therefore this material may not be factual.

[9]Mokler, *Natrona County*, 322–23.

[10]Ibid., 323. According to Mokler, Dr. Julius A. Schuelke of Thermopolis was the source of this story. It had to have taken place before August 7, 1903, because that is the day in which the doctor reportedly died of an overdose of morphine. One story suggests his death may have been

caused by poison administered by his mistress. (See Jean A. Mathisen, "A Handsome Man," *True West*, October 1994, 62.)

[11]Lamb, *Kid Curry*, 357, chapter 31, endnote 7. Quotes from an anonymous, unpublished manuscript furnished by Wanda Ramage, "The Outlaws," Lysite, Wyoming, 1971; Tacetta B. Walker, *Stories of Early Days in Wyoming: Big Horn Basin* (Casper, WY: Prairie Publishing Co., 1936), 155–56; Gillespie, *Goin' to 'Dusky*, 96. Quotes from Larry Pointer's typed interview with Ray Picard.

[12]Walker, *Early Days in Wyoming*, 155-56.

[13]Gillespie, *Goin' to 'Dusky*, 96. Quotes from Larry Pointer's typed interview with Ray Picard.

[14]Wilson, *Tiger*, 182; Gillespie, *Goin' to 'Dusky*, 96.

[15]Waller, *Last of the Great*, 244–46; Brekke, *Kid Curry*, 91.

[16]Ibid., 91; Waller, *Last of the Great*, 245.

[17]Hill County, *Grits, Guts and Gusto*, 480–481.

[18]Gladys Costello, "Former Stagecoach Driver Recalls Little Rockies Boom," *Great Falls Tribune*, Montana Parade Supplement, November 22, 1959.

[19][Costello], *Golden Era*, 28–29; Gillespie, *Goin' to 'Dusky*, 95. From an oral interview on file at the Montana Historical Society in Helena.

[20]Mokler, *Natrona County*, 327–28; Jean A. Mathisen, "The Montgomery Ward Badman," WOLA *The Journal*, Spring 2001, 26–28. O'Day was released in June 1908, after serving less than four and a half years. He lived in a dugout near Lost Cabin for a few years before moving to South Dakota. He married an Indian woman there, and was killed at Fort Pierre in 1930 when his wagon was overturned by a runaway team. (Mathisen, "Montgomery Ward," 28.)

[21]"'Kid' Curry in City of Denver," *Great Falls Daily Tribune*, February 16, 1904.

[22]Daniel Buck, "New Revelations About Harvey Logan Following the Parachute Train Robbery," WOLA *The Journal*, Spring 1997, 11; Soule, *Tall Texan*, 48. Cites Concho County Court Records; *The Denver Post*, July 11, 1904: "For more than six months the Pinkertons have been watching a suspicious 'bunch' of men rendezvousing at Ozona, Sheffield and other towns in southern Texas ... The movements of three of them have been traced carefully and it was this trio that robbed the

Rio Grande train. Logan and George Kilpatrick were two of the men. The identity of the third is not revealed."

[23]Burton, *Deadliest Outlaws*, 328; Ernst, *Harvey Logan*, 72. Ernst interviewed two Sheffield descendants, Sam Herrell and Ed Chastain, in December 1994. It was their belief, from family stories, that Dan Sheffield was involved in the Parachute train robbery, as well as George Kilpatrick. See Ernst, *Harvey Logan*, 94, endnote 105. (See also Soule, *Tall Texan*, 74. He adds that Edward Chastain was the son of Willora Justain (Sheffield) Chastain, a sister of Dan Sheffield.)

To family history can be added investigations that were conducted by the Pinkertons and Globe Express Company special agent R. Brunazzi. They were positive that the two accomplices in the train holdup were George Kilpatrick and Dan Sheffield. Ernst agrees, citing Pinkerton Archives. (See also Buck, "New Revelations about Logan," 11–12, and 39, endnote 39, cites undated Pinkerton memorandum; Wilson, *Outlaw Tales*, 165–66.)

[24]*Knoxville Journal and Tribune*, July 9, 1904, in Buck, "New Revelations about Logan," 7.

[25]*The Denver Republican*, August 20, 1904, in Soule, *Tall Texan*, 73, and in Buck, "New Revelations about Logan," 11–12; Horan, *The Gunfighters*, 299, endnote 30.

CHAPTER 28

[1]This account of the Denver & Rio Grande train robbery near Parachute is taken from the following newspapers unless otherwise noted: The Glenwood Springs, Colo., *Daily Avalanche*, June 8, 9, 10, 11, and July 16, 1904; Glenwood Springs *Avalanche Echo*, June 10, 1904; *The Denver Republican*, June 9 and 10, 1904; *Glenwood Post*, June 11, 1904; *Salida Mail*, June 10, 1904.

[2][Lamb], *Wild Bunch*, 115.

[3]Ibid., 123.

[4]*The Glenwood Post*, June 11, 1904.

[5]Dave Fishell, "They Robbed the Wrong Train," Grand Junction, Colorado, Westworld, December 10, 1978, 8.

[6]Ibid.; Erlene Durrant Murray, *Lest We Forget: A Short History of Early Grand Valley, Colorado, Originally called Parachute, Colorado* (Grand Junction, CO: Quahada, Inc., 1974), 131.

[7]Ibid.; Donna B. Ernst, "The Parachute Train Robbery," *Old West*, Winter 1996, 13.

[8]*The Denver Republican*, June 9, 1904.

[9]Ibid., June 10, 1904.

[10]*The Daily Avalanche*, June 10, 1904.

[11]*The Glenwood Post*, June 11, 1904. At least one newspaper reported the name as "Tom."

[12]*The Daily Avalanche*, June 10, 1904.

[13]Ibid., June 11, 1904.

[14]Nellie Duffy, "The Ballad of Tap Duncan: The County's Historic Train Heist," *The Glenwood Post*, March 7, 1973.

[15]Waller, *Last of the Great*, 254.

[16]J. C. Swartz is sometimes spelled as Schwarz. The former spelling is the same as John Swartz, the photographer in Fort Worth, Texas, where the Wild Bunch had their picture taken in November 1900. The Swartz View Company was indirectly responsible for Kid Curry's identification at that time, and the Swartz Mortuary was the scene of the later debate over the identification of his corpse.

[17]Waller, *Last of the Great*, 254.

[18]Murray, *Lest We Forget*, 130; Wilson, *Tiger*, 189–90.

[19]Soule, *Tall Texan*, 77. Cites the Glenwood Springs, Co., *Avalanche Echo*, June 23, 1904; Waller, *Last of the Great*, 250. Waller makes a vague reference to a posse confrontation on upper Divide Creek at the Schweitzer ranch.

[20]Soule, *Tall Texan*, 88–89. Cites Ben Kilpatrick's Atlanta, Georgia, Federal Penitentiary prison file.

[21]Ibid., 101; Dale T. Schoenberger, "Love Behind Bars: The Tall Texan," *True West*, April 1992, 28.

[22]Soule, *Tall Texan*, 102. Cites Ben Kilpatrick's Atlanta, Georgia, Federal Penitentiary prison file.

[23]Ibid., 87; Horan, *Wild Bunch*, 183–84; Horan, *Desperate Men,* rev. ed., 360–62.

[24]Burton, *Deadliest Outlaws*, 328, and 377, endnote 71, and 455, endnote 59.

²⁵Soule, *Tall Texan*, 87.

²⁶Horan, *Wild Bunch*, 183; Horan, *Desperate Men,* Rev. ed., 360; Soule, *Tall Texan*, 87; McBryde, "Love Behind Bars," 24.

²⁷Ernst, *Harvey Logan*, 95, endnote 110. Sheffield was convicted of horse theft in March of 1905, sentenced to serve two years in the Texas state prison at Huntsville, and released on April 25, 1907. (Soule, *Tall Texan*, 87. Cites records of Crockett County Court House, Ozona, Texas, and Texas Department of Criminal Justice, Huntsville, Texas.) He murdered Felix Kilpatrick in New Mexico on June 30, 1913, but his trial on April 1, 1914, ended in acquittal. (Soule, *Tall Texan*, 193–95. Cites the *Carrizozo News*, July 4, 1913, and Lincoln County District Court records.) He is reported to have died in Van Horn, Texas, in about 1938. (Soule, *Tall Texan*, 198. Cites correspondence with Boone Kilpatrick's son, Bill.)

²⁸Donna B. Ernst, "Death along Baxter's Curve," *True West*, June 2000, 28; Soule, *Tall Texan*, 164.

²⁹Concho County Court Records, *The State of Texas vs. Ben Kilpatrick*, Case No. 414½, in Soule, *Tall Texan*, 141, 143, 147, 149.

³⁰McBryde, "Love Behind Bars," 25–26.

³¹Soule, *Tall Texan*, 163–64, 174; Ernst, "Baxter's Curve," 28, 30.

³²Soule, *Tall Texan*, 164, 166-67, 170-74; Ernst, "Baxter's Curve," 30–31.

³³Ibid., 31; Soule, *Tall Texan*, 175.

³⁴McBryde, "Love Behind Bars," 27.

CHAPTER 29

¹*The Glenwood Post*, June 11, 1904, and *The Daily Avalanche*, June 10, 1904.

²*The Daily Avalanche*, June 10, 1904.

³Ibid., June 13, 1904.

⁴*The Denver Post*, July 11, 1904.

⁵Ibid.

⁶Duffy, "Ballad of Tap Duncan."

⁷Horan, *Desperate Men*, 277.

⁸*The Denver Post*, July 12, 1904, in Buck, "New Revelations about Logan," 9–10. This would argue against Jesse Cole Kenworth's statements

that railroad officials, who claimed the body was not Curry's, did so because they did not want to pay out the large rewards. (See Kenworth, *Storms of Life*, 43, 45.)

[9]*Knoxville Journal and Tribune*, July 9, 1904, in Buck, "New Revelations about Logan," 7.

[10]Pointer, *In Search of Cassidy*, 271, endnote 21. William Pinkerton to Robert Pinkerton, July 9, 1904, Pinkerton Archives.

[11]*The Denver Post*, July 11, 1904.

[12]*Knoxville Journal and Tribune*, December 18, 1901, in Buck, "New Revelations about Logan," 9.

[13]Ibid., June 29, 1903.

[14]*Knoxville Journal and Tribune*, December 18, 1901, and June 28, 1903, in Buck, "New Revelations about Logan," 9.

[15]Buck, "New Revelations about Logan," 10.

[16]*Rifle Telegram*, July 15, 1904, in Buck, "New Revelations about Logan," 10; Ernst, *Harvey Logan*, 77.

[17]*The Daily Avalanche*, July 16, 1904; Horan, *The Gunfighters*, 219. From Horan's interview with Lowell Spence in 1949.

[18]*The Denver Post*, July 16, 1904, in Buck, "New Revelations about Logan," 10.

[19]*The Glenwood Post*, July 23, 1904, in Buck, "New Revelations about Logan," 10.

[20]Horan, *The Gunfighters*, 219-20. From Horan's interview with Lowell Spence in 1949.

[21]*The Denver Post*, July 11, 1904.

[22]In Kenworth, *Storms of Life*, 43–44, Kid Curry researcher Jesse Cole Kenworth is one of the few writers to note the significance of the scar in identifying the body as Curry's.

[23]*Knoxville Journal and Tribune*, August 28, 1904, in Buck, "New Revelations about Logan," 12.

[24]Horan, *The Outlaws*, 258.

[25]*The Denver Republican*, August 20, 1904, in Buck, "New Revelations about Logan," 11–12; Horan, *The Gunfighters*, 299, endnote 30.

[26]Buck, "New Revelations about Logan," 12. Cites the Arizona Office of Vital Records, Phoenix, Arizona.

[27]Ernst, "Wild Bunch Struck a Bank," 10; Buck, Daniel, "New Revelations about Logan," 11–12.

[28]Ibid., 12.

[29]Wilson, *Tiger*, 194.

[30]Ernst, *Harvey Logan*, 77. Cites a June 10, 1905, Pinkerton letter from J. Fraser to J. McParland.

[31]*The Glenwood Post*, August 27, 1904, in Buck, "New Revelations about Logan," 11.

[32]*The Denver Republican*, August 20, 1904, in Buck, "New Revelations about Logan," 12; Horan, *The Gunfighters*, 299, endnote 30.

[33]Siringo, *Lone Star Cowboy*, 235–36.

[34]John C. Houk to James Thornhill, July 25, 1904, Harvey Logan Papers, Small Collection 2063, Montana Historical Society Archives, in Lamb, "Logan's Lost Journal," 27, and Kindred, "Logan, Houk, Thornhill," 39.

[35]Jim Thornhill to John C. Houk, August 9, 1904, McClung Historical Collection, in Kindred, "Logan, Houk, Thornhill," 39.

[36]John C. Houk to James Thornhill, August 22, 1904, Harvey Logan Papers, Small Collection 2063, Montana Historical Society Archives, in Lamb, "Logan's Lost Journal," 27; Ernst, *Harvey Logan*, 79-80. Cites Small Collection 2063, Montana Historical Society Archives.

[37]Buck, "New Revelations about Logan," 12. Cites an undated (c. 1940) Lowell Spence memorandum in the Pinkerton Archives; Horan, *Desperate Men*, 276–77.

[38]Horan, *The Gunfighters*, 220. From Horan's interview with Lowell Spence in 1949.

CHAPTER 30

[1]Jeremy Johnston, "We Want Them Dead Rather Than Alive: Buffalo Bill the Lawman," WWHA *Journal*, December 2011, 4–5, 13–14.

[2]Wilson, *Tiger,* 177. Cites Edgar Young. "The End of Harvey Logan." *Frontier Times*, June 1927; Gillespie, *Goin' to 'Dusky*, 99-100. Cites a letter postmarked January 26, 1942, from Charles T. Kemper to E. P. Lamborn. Kemper tells Lamborn of a letter he received "a number of years past" from Edgar Young. Young's letter recounted his meeting with Harvey Logan in Brazil. (E. P. Lamborn Papers, 1913–1970, Kansas State Historical Society, Manuscript Collection No. 156, Topeka, Kansas.)

[3]Actually, his only sister, Arda "Allie" was living in Missouri with husband Manuel Rodriguez. She later moved to Houston, Texas, where she died in 1955 at about eighty-seven years of age. See *Kansas City Times*, February 2, 1955, in Gillespie, *Goin' to 'Dusky*, 79.

[4]Wilson, *Tiger*, 177-178. Cites Edgar Young. "The End of Harvey Logan." *Frontier Times*, June 1927; Gillespie, *Goin' to 'Dusky*, 98. Gillespie found this portion of the story in an unidentified, undated newspaper article, entitled "The End of Kid Curry," in the University of Wyoming archives in Laramie. It is known that John B. Ritch wrote an article reciting this story; Waller, *Last of the Great*, 259–60.

[5]Ibid., 260. Waller makes the statement that several people in Montana claimed to have received cards from Kid Curry during his sojourn in South America. (In Johnson, *Durable Desperado*, 30, the author said she heard that several men in the north central part of Montana claimed to have received post cards from the Kid, as well as the "good widow Coalchak" in Landusky.) Gillespie, *Goin' to 'Dusky*, 98. Cites unidentified, undated newspaper article, entitled "The End of Kid Curry," in the University of Wyoming archives in Laramie.

[6]Wilson, *Tiger*, 178. Cites Edgar Young, "The End of Harvey Logan." *Frontier Times*, June 1927.

[7]Anne Meadows, *Digging Up Butch and Sundance* (New York: St. Martin's Press, 1994), 67. Cites a 1970 three-part series of articles titled "Butch Cassidy in Patagonia" in the Buenos Aires daily *Clarin*, by Justo Piernes.

[8]Daniel Buck and Anne Meadows, "New Wild Bunch Documents Surface," *True West*, August 1997, 7–9.

[9]Horan, *The Outlaws*, 263–65, 268–70. Author's interview with retired Pinkerton operative Frank Dimaio in the late 1940s. In this interview Dimaio said he showed photographs of the Sundance Kid, Cassidy, and Etta (Ethel), to Dr. Robert Newberry (actually Dr. George Newbery), a Buenos Aires dentist who owned a ranch next to the trio's, and to the president of the London River Platte Bank where the bandits had an account. They readily identified them by their aliases, Mr. and Mrs. Harry Place, and James Ryan. There was no mention of Harvey Logan or any of his known aliases by Dimaio in this interview. However, in Horan, *The Gunfighters*, 299, endnote 31, published a year before

The Outlaws, the author states that Dimaio also included Curry's photograph. Neither informant was able to identify this fourth American bandit.

[10]Meadows, *Digging up Butch*, 42–43. This is curious since Curry was still in the Knox County jail at this time. He did not escape until the day of June 27, 1903. It is difficult to believe that Dimaio would have been so ill informed. Curry may not have been included in the circulars until a later version was printed, possibly not until circular no. 4 that was issued on January 15, 1907. The latter is reproduced in Horan, *The Outlaws*, 266–67. See also pp. 273, and 302, endnote 27. (Recently, a three-page circular issued in January 1906 by the Buenos Aires police, showing Butch, Sundance, Ethel, and Kid Curry, was reproduced in Daniel Buck, "Gone But Not Forgotten: Butch and Sundance Wanted Poster in Patagonia," WWHA *Journal*, June 2008, 44–47.)

[11]Meadows and Buck, "Last Days of Butch," 4–5, part 1; Daniel Buck and Anne Meadows, "Leaving Cholila: Butch and Sundance Documents Surface in Argentina," *True West*, January 1996, 24–25, 27.

[12]Coburn, *Pioneer Cattleman*, 119, 223.

[13]Howard, *Montana*, 141.

[14]Coburn, *Pioneer Cattleman*, 224–25.

[15]Wilson, *Tiger*, 197.

[16]Ritch, "Kid Curry, 'Bad Man'," 15, part 2.

[17]Meadows and Buck, "Last Days of Butch," 5, part 1.

[18]Kelly, *Outlaw Trail*, 289; Horan, *Desperate Men,* rev. ed., 335–36.

[19]Ernst, *SMU*, 180.

[20]Meadows, *Digging up Butch*, 80, 83.

[21]Pinkerton files, Robert Pinkerton, memorandum, New York, January 15, 1907, cited in Pointer, *In Search of Cassidy*, 271, endnote 22.

[22]William A. Pinkerton, *Train Robberies, Train Robbers, and the "Holdup" Men* (New York: Arno Press, 1974), 79.

[23]Meadows and Buck, "Last Days of Butch," 5, part 1; Patterson, *Butch Cassidy*, 209–10. Recently, Donna B. Ernst has discovered the name of a Mrs. E. Place on a passenger manifest for the S.S. *Seguranca*, which arrived in New York City on July 29, 1905. (Donna B. Ernst, "Ethel Place—A Look at the Possibility She Came Home Alone," WOLA *The Journal*, Spring 2007, 30.)

[24]Pointer, *In Search of Cassidy*, 202. Cites a three-part series of articles by Justo Piernes in 1970, titled "Butch Cassidy in Patagonia," in the Buenos Aires daily *Clarin*. Piernes made use of Chubut Province police reports for his articles; Buck and Meadows, "Leaving Cholila," 24. Judicial records confirm the robbery of the store in Arroyo Pescado, but Curry is not mentioned.

[25]Baker, *Wild Bunch*, 108.

[26]*The Steamboat Pilot*, February 23, 1910, reprinted in Burroughs, *Where West Stayed Young*, 133; Meadows, *Digging up Butch*, 110.

[27]Horan, *Desperate Men,* rev. ed., 346. Not surprisingly, fifteen years after writing this, Horan contradicts himself in *The Outlaws*, 303, endnote 30, by stating, "There is no evidence in the State Department Archives to show that it requested the aid of the Pinkertons to hunt down Cassidy, the Sundance Kid, and Etta Place, nor is there any evidence that any South American country complained to the State Department about their robberies."

[28]Meadows, *Digging up Butch*, 43.

[29]Buck and Meadows, "Leaving Cholila," 24–26.

[30]Ibid., 26.

[31]Kelly, *Outlaw Trail*, 292.

[32]Meadows and Buck, "Last Days of Butch," 6–7, part 1; 1–6, part 2; 1–5, part 3.

[33]Buck and Meadows, "Leaving Cholila," 25.

[34]Arthur J. Jordan, *Jordan* (Missoula, MT: Mountain Press Publishing Co., 1984), 178.

[35]Coburn, *Pioneer Cattleman*, 121–23.

[36]Wilson, *Outlaw Tales*, 172-74.

[37]Gillespie, *Goin' to 'Dusky*, 97.

[38]Ritch, "Kid Curry, 'Bad Man'," 15, part 2.

[39]Siringo, *Lone Star Cowboy*, 234, 236–41; Waller, *Last of the Great*, 261–63.

[40]Coburn, *Pioneer Cattleman*, 58, 280; Duvall and Duvall-Arthur, *Memories*, 51.

[41]Santee, *Lost Pony Tracks*, 142.

[42]Coburn, *Pioneer Cattleman*, 226. Thornhill died on July 6, 1936, followed less than a year later by his wife Lucy on May 20, 1937. They

are buried in a plot in the old section of the Globe Cemetery. (Gillespie, *Goin' to 'Dusky*, 139, 142.) Their son Harvey D. "Man" Thornhill died on March 6, 1972, in Florence, Arizona, and was buried in Eloy. He was a World War I veteran, had done ranch work in Arizona for forty years, and had owned a small cattle spread near Florence. (Pinal County, AZ, Archives Obituaries for Harvey Thornhill, from "Harvey Thornhill Dies in Florence," *Eloy Enterprise*, March 9, 1972. File at: http://files.usgwarchives.org/az/pinal/obits/t/thornhil3ob.txt)

[43]Wilson, *Tiger*, 200-1.

[44]Duvall and Duvall-Arthur, *Memories*, 166.

[45]Gillespie, *Goin' to 'Dusky*, 93–94.

[46]Costello, "Stagecoach Driver."

[47]"California Matron Visits Her Early Day Home in Landusky," *The Chinook Opinion*, July 4, 1957, reprinted in Gillespie, *Goin' to 'Dusky*, 71. Elfie died on October 12, 1965, in Oroville, California, at the age of 86, and was buried in Paradise, California. She was preceded in death by her children, Mrs. Maime C. Moran, on February 14, 1962, in Great Falls, Montana, and Lonie L. Logan on August 16, 1965, in Paradise. According to his obituary, Lonie served in the Navy for a few months near the end of World War I. (Gillespie, *Goin' to 'Dusky*, 70, 73–74. Quotes from *The Chinook Opinion*, February 15, 1962, for Maime Moran's obituary.)

[48]Lynch, *Harvey Logan*, 152. The song told of Harvey Logan's famous escape from the Knox County jail.

[49]Wilson, *Tiger*, 204.

Bibliography

BOOKS AND ARTICLES

Abbott, E. C., and Helena Huntington Smith. *We Pointed Them North: Recollections of a Cowpuncher.* 1939. Repr., Norman: University of Oklahoma Press, 1971.

[Abbott, "Teddy Blue," from facts furnished by.] "Pike Landusky, Trapper, Woodhawk and Gold Miner." *The Boulder Monitor,* n.d. Vertical file, Montana Historical Society, Helena.

Axford, Joseph "Mack." *Around Western Campfires.* 1964. Repr., Tucson: University of Arizona Press, 1969.

Babcock, Charlotte. *Shot Down! Capital Crimes of Casper, Wyoming.* Glendo, WY: High Plains Press, 2000.

Baker, Pearl. *The Wild Bunch at Robbers Roost.* New York: Abelard-Schuman, 1965.

Bartholomew, Ed. *Black Jack Ketchum, Last of the Hold-Up Kings.* Houston: The Frontier Press of Texas, 1955.

Barton, Barbara. *Den of Outlaws.* San Angelo, TX: Rangel Printing, 2000.

Bell, Mike. "The Friends and Enemies of the Notorious Nutcher Brothers." Wild West History Association (WWHA) *Journal,* August 2010.

———. "Winnemucca Revisited." WOLA *The Journal,* Spring 2000.

Betenson, Lula Parker, as told to Dora Flack. *Butch Cassidy, My Brother.* Provo, UT: Brigham Young University Press, 1975.

Brekke, Al. "Curry Boys Leave Their Mark on Blaine County." *Harlem Enterprise,* n.d.

Brekke. Alan Lee. *Kid Curry: Train Robber.* Harlem, MT: Privately published, 1989.

Brown, Larry K. *The Hog Ranches of Wyoming.* Glendo, WY: High Plains Press, 1995.

Bryan, Howard. *Robbers, Rogues and Ruffians: True Tales of the Wild West in New Mexico.* Santa Fe: Clear Light Publishers, 1991.

Buck, Daniel. "Gone But Not Forgotten: Butch and Sundance Wanted Poster in Patagonia." *Wild West History Association (WWHA) Journal*, June 2008.

———. "New Revelations About Harvey Logan Following the Parachute Train Robbery." WOLA *The Journal*, Spring 1997.

———, and Anne Meadows. "Leaving Cholila: Butch and Sundance Documents Surface in Argentina." *True West*, January 1996.

———, and Anne Meadows. "New Wild Bunch Documents Surface." *True West*, August 1997.

Buffalo Centennial Committee, comp. *Buffalo's First Century*. Buffalo, WY: Buffalo Bulletin, Inc., 1984.

Burroughs, John Rolfe. *Where the Old West Stayed Young*. New York: Bonanza Books, 1962.

Burton, Jeff. *Dynamite and Six-Shooter*. Santa Fe: Palomino Press, 1970.

Burton, Jeffrey. *The Deadliest Outlaws: The Ketchum Gang and the Wild Bunch*. 2nd ed. Denton: University of North Texas Press, 2009.

Carlson, Chip. *Joe LeFors, "I Slickered Tom Horn."* Cheyenne, WY: Beartooth Corral LLC., 1995.

Charter, Anne Goddard. *Cowboys Don't Walk: A Tale of Two*. Billings, MT: Western Organization of Resource Councils, 1999.

Cheney, A. V., as told to Mrs. A. V. Cheney. "Kid Curry and His Brothers." *True West*, April 1962.

Cheney, Roberta Carkeek. *Names on the Face of Montana: The Story of Montana's Place Names*. Missoula, MT: Mountain Press Publishing Company, 1983.

Cheney, Truman McGiffin, with Roberta Carkeek Cheney. *So Long, Cowboys of the Open Range*. Helena, MT: Falcon Publishing, Inc., 1990.

Coburn, Walt. *Pioneer Cattleman in Montana: The Story of the Circle C Ranch*. Norman: University of Oklahoma Press, 1968.

Condit, Thelma Gatchell. "The Hole-in-the-Wall." *Annals of Wyoming*, October 1959.

Costello, Gladys. "Former Stagecoach Driver Recalls Little Rockies Boom." *Great Falls Tribune*, Montana Parade Supplement, November 22, 1959.

[Costello, Gladys.] *The Golden Era of the Little Rockies: Stories Written by Gladys Costello.* Privately published, n.d.

Cramer, Dudley, ed. "The Killing of George Scarborough." *The Haley Library Newsletter*, Summer and Fall 2000.

Cruzan, Marvin, and Macy Cruzan. "The Cruzan Rogues' Gallery." 2002. Website: http://users.mo-net.com/mcruzan/Wild_Bill.htm

Cunningham, Eugene. *Triggernometry: A Gallery of Gunfighters.* Caldwell, ID: The Caxton Printers, Ltd., 1941.

DeArment, Robert K. *George Scarborough: The Life and Death of a Lawman on the Closing Frontier.* Norman: University of Oklahoma Press, 1992.

———. "Bad Month for Badmen." *True West,* August 1990.

DeJournette, Dick, and Daun DeJournette. *One Hundred Years of Brown's Park and Diamond Mountain.* 2nd ed. Vernal, UT: DeJournette Enterprises, 1997.

Devine [*sic*, Divine], Bob. Edited by John Boessenecker. "We Raided Hole-In-The-Wall." *Real West*, January 1980.

Drago, Harry Sinclair. *The Great Range Wars: Violence on the Grasslands.* 1970. Repr. Lincoln: University of Nebraska Press, 1985.

Duffy, Nellie. "The Ballad of Tap Duncan: The County's Historic Train Heist." *The Glenwood Post*, March 7, 1973.

Dullenty, Jim. "George Currie and the Curry Brothers." NOLA *Quarterly*, October 1979.

———. *Harry Tracy: The Last Desperado.* Dubuque, IA: Kendall/Hunt Publishing Company, 1996.

———, and Ben Garthofner. "New Gold Rush in the Little Rockies." *True West*, March 1984.

Dunham, Dick, and Vivian Dunham. *Our Strip of Land: A History of Dagget County, Utah.* Manila, UT: Dagget County Lions Club, 1947.

Duvall, C. W. "Milk River Bill." *Great Falls Tribune*, November 17, 1935.

Duvall, Walter W., with Helen Duvall-Arthur. *Memories of a Filly Chaser.* Privately published, 1992.

Eaton, John. *Will Carver, Outlaw.* San Angelo, TX: Anchor Publishing Co., 1972.

Ellison, Douglas W. *David Lant: The Vanished Outlaw*. Aberdeen, SD: Midstates Printing, 1988.

Engebretson, Doug. *Empty Saddles, Forgotten Names: Outlaws of the Black Hills and Wyoming*. Aberdeen, SD: North Plains Press, 1982.

Ernst, Donna B. "Before the Wild Bunch Struck a Bank in Winnemucca, Nev., They Hit a Store in Three Creek, Idaho." *Wild West*, December 2001.

———. "A Deadly Year for St. Johns Lawmen." NOLA *Quarterly*, January–March 2001.

———. "A Deadwood Jail Break." *True West*, January 2000.

———. "Death along Baxter's Curve." *True West*, June 2000.

———. "Ethel Place—A Look at the Possibility She Came Home Alone." WOLA *The Journal*, Spring 2007.

———. "George S. Nixon." WOLA *The Journal*, Summer 2001.

———. *Harvey Logan, Wildest of the Wild Bunch*. Kearney, NE: Morris Publishing, 2003.

———. "John Dunn." WOLA *The Journal*, Winter 2002.

———. "The Parachute Train Robbery." *Old West*, Winter 1996.

———. "The Real Tom Capehart." WOLA *The Journal*, Summer 2000.

———. "Secret Link with the Wild Bunch." 1999. Website: www.flash .net/~pggreen/WOLA/wildbnch.htm

———. *The Sundance Kid: The Life of Harry Alonzo Longabaugh*. Norman: University of Oklahoma Press, 2009.

———. "The Sundance Kid: My Uncle. Researching the Memories of Snake River Residents." *Frontier Magazine*, August 1997.

———. *Sundance, My Uncle*. College Station, TX: Creative Publishing Company, 1992.

———. "Walt Punteney and Tom O'Day, Two Early Wild Bunch Members, Lived Long But Out of the Spotlight." *Wild West*, April 2004.

———. "The Wilcox Train Robbery." *Wild West*, June 1999.

———. "The Wild Bunch in Texas." NOLA *Quarterly*, October–December 1999.

———. "Will Carver, alias Will Casey." *Old West*, Fall 1995.

———. *Women of the Wild Bunch*. Kearney, NE: Morris Publishing, 2004.

———, and Paul D. Ernst. "The Last Hurrah of the Notorious Wild Bunch." *Wild West*, October 2002.

Ernst, Paul, and Donna Ernst. "Wild Bunch Shootout Sites." WOLA *The Journal*, Fall 1999.

Ernst, Paul D. "The Winnemucca Bank Holdup." *Wild West*, June 1998.

Farlow, Edward J. *Wind River Adventures: My Life in Frontier Wyoming.* Glendo, WY: High Plains Press, 1998.

Federal Writers' Project of the Works Progress Administration, American Guide Series. *Wyoming: A Guide to Its History, Highways, and People.* New York: Oxford University Press, 1941.

Fishell, Dave. "They Robbed the Wrong Train." Copy of article in the Glenwood Springs Historial Society headed: Grand Junction, Colorado, Westworld, Sunday, December 10, 1978.

Frackelton, Will, and Herman Seely. *Sagebrush Dentist.* 1941. Revised, Pasadena, CA: Trail's End Publishing Co., 1947.

Frandsen, Joel. "The Burial of Joe Walker and Butch Cassidy." WOLA *The Journal,* Fall 2001.

French, William. *Some Recollections of a Western Ranchman.* 1927. Repr., Silver City, NM: High-Lonesome Books, 1997.

Garman, Mary. *Harry Longabaugh—The Sundance Kid, The Early Years, 1867–1889.* Pamphlet published by Crook County Museum, 1978.

Gillespie, Shirley. *Goin' to 'Dusky.* Chandler, AZ: Two Dogs Publishing, 2007.

Greenfield, Charles. "How The Logan Boys Got That Way." *Golden West*, September 1969.

Hall, Charles "Pat." *Documents of Wyoming Heritage.* Cheyenne, WY: Wyoming Bicentennial Commission, 1976.

Hanson, Margaret Brock, ed. *Powder River Country: The Papers of J. Elmer Brock.* Kaycee, WY: Margaret Brock Hanson, 1981.

Hardin, Floyd. *Campfires and Cowchips.* Great Falls, MT: Privately published, 1972.

Harris, Fredie Steve. "Butch Cassidy's Outlaw Horsemen." *Golden West*, May 1969.

Hill County Bicentennial Commission, comp. *Grits, Guts and Gusto: A History of Hill County.* Havre, MT: Bear Paw Printers, 1976.

Holt, Roy D. "The End of Will Carver." *True West*, May–June 1970.

Hoover, H. A. *Tales from the Bloated Goat: Early Days in Mogollon.* 1958. Repr., San Lorenzo, NM: High-Lonesome Books, n.d.

Horan, James D. *The Authentic Wild West: The Gunfighters.* New York: Crown Publishers, 1976.

———. *The Authentic Wild West: The Outlaws.* New York: Crown Publishers, 1977.

———. *Desperate Men.* New York: G. P. Putnam's Sons, 1949. Repr., New York: Bonanza Books. Rev. ed., New York: Doubleday & Company, Inc., 1962.

———. *The Great American West.* Rev. ed. New York: Crown Publishers, 1978.

———. *The Wild Bunch.* New York: Signet, New American Library, 1958.

———, and Paul Sann. *Pictorial History of the Wild West.* New York: Crown Publishers, 1954.

Hovey, Walter C., edited by Doris Sturges. "Black Jack Ketchum Tried to Give Me a Break." *True West*, March–April 1972.

Howard, Joseph K. *Montana: High, Wide, and Handsome.* New Haven, CT: Yale University Press, 1943.

Howard, Robert West, ed. *This is the West.* The Westerners, Chicago Corral. New York: Rand McNally & Co., 1957.

James, Stella Frances. *In the Shadow of Jesse James.* Edited by Milton F. Perry. Thousand Oaks, CA: Revolver Press, 1990.

Jessen, Ken. *Colorado Gunsmoke: True Stories of Outlaws and Lawmen on the Colorado Frontier.* Loveland, CO: J. V. Publications, 1986.

Johnson, Dorothy M. "Durable Desperado Kid Curry." *Montana: The Magazine of Western History*, April 1956.

Johnston, Jeremy. "We Want Them Dead Rather Than Alive: Buffalo Bill the Lawman." Wild West History Association (WWHA) *Journal*, December 2011.

Jordan, Arthur J. *Jordan.* Missoula, MT: Mountain Press Publishing Company, 1984.

Kelly, Charles. *The Outlaw Trail: A History of Butch Cassidy and His Wild Bunch.* New York: The Devin-Adair Company, 1959.

Kennedy, Michael S., ed. *Cowboys and Cattlemen.* New York: Hastings House, Publishers, 1964.

Kenworth, Jesse Cole. *Storms of Life: In Search of Kid Curry.* Bozeman, MT: Self published promotional copy number 5. 1990.

"Kid Curry file." Glenwood Springs (Colorado) Historical Society.

Kindred, Wayne. "Capturing a Train Robber: Kid Curry's Escapades in Knoxville, Tennessee." 1996. Website: http://home.att.net/~wk354/capture.html. Originally published in the WOLA *Journal*, Fall–Winter 1996.

————. "Harvey Logan's Escape." *True West*, May 1986.

————. "Harvey Logan's Secret Letters." *True West*, October 1994.

————. "The Hunt for the Great Northern Train Robbers." 2000. Website: http://home.att.net/~wk354/Great.html. Originally published in the NOLA *Quarterly*, January–March 2000.

————. "The Ice Wagon Affair." 1987. Website: http://home.att.net/~wk354/IceWagon.html. Originally published in *True West*, February 1987.

————. "Kid Curry—The Missing Months." WOLA *The Journal*, Fall/Winter 1997.

————. "The Killing of Pike Landusky." 1999. Website: http://members.aol.com/_ht_a/Waynek423/Pike.html

————. "The Logan, Houk, Thornhill Letters." WOLA *The Journal*, Fall 2002.

————. "The Trials and Travels of Annie Rogers." *Old West*, Winter 1995.

————. "Who Robbed the Great Northern Express?" *True West*, January 1994.

————. "The Wilcox Robbery: Who Did It?" WOLA *The Journal*, Spring 1999.

Kirby, Edward M. *The Rise and Fall of the Sundance Kid.* Iola, WI: Western Publications, 1983.

————. *The Saga of Butch Cassidy and the Wild Bunch.* Palmer Lake, CO: The Filter Press, 1977.

Kouris, Diana Allen. "The Lynching Calamity in Brown's Park." *True West*, September 1995.

————. *The Romantic and Notorious History of Brown's Park.* 3rd ed. Greybull, WY: Wolverine Gallery, 1988.

Lamb, F. Bruce. *Kid Curry: The Life and Times of Harvey Logan and the Wild Bunch.* Boulder: Johnson Publishing, 1991.

[Lamb, Frank.], Swallow, Alan, ed. *The Wild Bunch.* Denver: Sage Books, 1966.

Lamb, John A. "Harvey Logan's Lost Journal." *True West*, October 1994.

LeFors, Joe. *Wyoming Peace Officer; An Autobiography.* Laramie, WY: Laramie Printers, Inc., 1953.

Lind, Robert W. *From the Ground Up: The Story of "Brother Van" Orsdel, Pioneer Montana Minister.* Montana: Treasure State Publishing Co., 1961.

Logan, Bruce E., Jr. "Kid Curry, A.K.A. Harvey Logan." 1999. Website: freepages.genealogy.rootsweb.com/~blogan/logan3.html

"Lonnie Logan," "Old West Gravesites." 2002. Website: www.dimensional.com/~sgrimm/lonnie_logan.htm

Loomis, John A. *Texas Ranchman: The Memoirs of John A. Loomis.* Chadron, NE: The Fur Press, 1982.

Lynch, Sylvia. *Harvey Logan in Knoxville.* College Station, TX: Creative Publishing, 1998.

McBryde, Carolyn Bullion. "Love Behind Bars: The Thorny Rose." *True West*, April 1992.

McClure, Grace. *The Bassett Women.* Athens, OH: Swallow Press/Ohio University Press, 1985.

McCoy, Tim, with Ronald McCoy. *Tim McCoy Remembers the West.* 1977. Repr., Lincoln: University of Nebraska Press, 1988.

Mac, 'Tana. "The Long Long Trail." *Frontier Times,* Spring 1961.

Martin, R. I. "A Lively Day in Belle Fourche." *True West*, April 1962.

Mathisen, Jean A. "A Handsome Man." *True West*, October 1994.

———. "The Montgomery Ward Badman." WOLA *The Journal*, Spring 2001.

Meadows, Anne. *Digging Up Butch and Sundance.* New York: St. Martin's Press, 1994.

———, and Dan Buck. "The Last Days of Butch and Sundance." 2002. Website: wysiwyg://112/http://americanhistory.about.com/library/prm/bllastdays1.htm Originally published in *Wild West Magazine*, February 1997.

Miller, James O. "Did Butch Cassidy Plan the Wilcox Train Robbery?" WOLA *TheJournal,* Spring 1999.

Mokler, Alfred James. *History of Natrona County Wyoming 1888–1922*. 1923. Repr., Casper, WY: Mountain States Lithographing, Centennial Edition, 1989.

Montana Parade. "Where Was Loney Curry at Train Holdup?" *Great Falls Tribune*, November 17, 1957.

Morin, Marvin M. "Two Graves in Montana." *True West*, March 1984.

Murphy, Richard. "A Killer with a Hankering for Booze and Brawls, 'Deaf Charley' Hanks Hooked Up with the Wild Bunch." *Wild West*, August 1995.

Murray, Erlene Durrant. *Lest We Forget: A Short History of Early Grand Valley, Colorado, Originally Called Parachute, Colorado*. Grand Junction, CO: Quahada, Inc., 1973.

North, Dick. "When the Tiger of the Wild Bunch Broke Out of the Knoxville Jail!" *Frontier Times*, September 1975.

Noyes, Alva Josiah. *In the Land of Chinook; or, The Story of Blaine County*. Helena, MT: State Pub. Co., 1917.

Osgood, Stacy W. "Butch Cassidy Never Held Up A Train!" *The Westerners Brand Book* 21, no. 4, Chicago Corral of Westerners, June 1964.

Otero, Miguel Antonio. *My Nine Years as Governor of the Territory of New Mexico 1897–1906*. 1940. Repr., Sánta Fe, NM: Sunstone Press, 2007.

Owens, Harry J. "The Thrilling Capture of the Sundance Kid and Kid Curry." NOLA *Quarterly*, Spring 1986.

Paladin, Vivian A., ed. *From Buffalo Bones to Sonic Boom*. Glasgow, MT: Glasgow Jubilee Committee, 1962.

Parsons, Chuck. "O. C. Hanks and the Texas Connection." *The Outlaw Trail Journal*, Summer 1994.

Patterson, Richard. *Butch Cassidy, a Biography*. Lincoln: University of Nebraska Press, 1998.

———. *The Train Robbery Era: An Encyclopedic History*. Boulder, CO: Pruett Publishing Company, 1991.

Phillips County Historical Society, comp. *The Yesteryears*. Havre, MT: Griggs Printing & Publishing, 1978.

Phillips, Samuel K., Jr. *Fallen Branches on Montana Soil*. Lewistown, MT: Ballyhoo Printing and Design, 2005.

Pinkerton, William A. *Train Robberies, Train Robbers, and the "Holdup" Men*. 1907. Repr., New York: Arno Press, 1974.

Pointer, Larry. *In Search of Butch Cassidy*. Norman: University of Oklahoma Press, 1977.

Price, Con. *Memories of Old Montana*. Hollywood: The Highland Press, 1945.

Rasch, Philip J. *Desperadoes of Arizona Territory*. Laramie, WY: National Association for Outlaw and Lawman History, Inc., 1999.

Ritch, John B. "Kid Curry, 'Bad Man'." *Great Falls Tribune*, June 21 (part 1), and June 28 (part 2), 1936.

———. "True Story of Pike Landusky Better than Beadle's Best Thriller." *Great Falls Tribune*, January 20, 1935.

Rutter, Michael. *Wild Bunch Women*. Helena, MT: TwoDot, 2003.

Santee, Ross. *Lost Pony Tracks*. New York: Charles Scribner's Sons, 1953. Repr., New York: Bantam Books, 1956.

Schoenberger, Dale T. "Love Behind Bars: The Tall Texan." *True West*, April 1992.

Selcer, Richard F. *Hell's Half Acre: The Life and Legend of a Red-Light District*. Fort Worth: Texas Christian University Press, 1991.

———. "The Women Who Loved the Wild Bunch." *Wild West*, December 1994.

———, and Donna Donnell, "Last Word on the Famous Wild Bunch Photo," *Wild West*, December 2011.

Settle, William A., Jr. *Jesse James Was His Name: Or, Fact and Fiction Concerning the Careers of the Notorious James Brothers of Missouri*. Columbia: University of Missouri Press, 1966.

Silliman, Eugene Lee, ed.. *We Seized Our Rifles: Recollections of the Montana Frontier*. Missoula, MT: Mountain Press Publishing Company, 1982.

Siringo, Charles A. *A Cowboy Detective: A True Story of Twenty-two Years with a World-Famous Detective Agency*. 1912. Repr: Lincoln: University of Nebraska Press, 1988.

———. *A Lone Star Cowboy*. Santa Fe: Siringo, 1919.

———. *Riata and Spurs: The Story of a Lifetime Spent in the Saddle as Cowboy and Detective*. Boston: Houghton Mifflin Company, 1927.

Skovlin, Jon M., and Donna McDaniel Skovlin. *In Pursuit of the Mc-Cartys*. Cove, OR: Reflections Publishing Co., 2001.

Smith, Helena Huntington. *The War on Powder River: The History of an Insurrection*. New York: McGraw-Hill Book Company, 1966.

Soule, Arthur. *The Tall Texan: The Story of Ben Kilpatrick*. Deer Lodge, MT: TrailDust Publishing, 1995.

Stuart, Granville. *Forty Years on the Frontier*. 1925. Repr., Harrisburg, PA: The National Historical Society, 1994.

Titsworth, B. D. "Hole-in-the-Wall Gang." *Badman*, Fall 1972.

Urbanek, Mae. *Wyoming Place Names*. Missoula, MT: Mountain Press Publishing Company, 1988.

Walker, Tacetta B. *Stories of Early Days in Wyoming: Big Horn Basin*. Casper, WY: Prairie Publishing Company, 1936.

Waller, Brown. *Last of the Great Western Train Robbers*. New York: A. S. Barnes and Company, 1968.

Warner, Matt, as told to Murray E. King. *The Last of the Bandit Riders*. 1940. Repr., New York: Bonanza Books, 1950.

Webb, William E. "Elton A. Cunningham, a Member of the Wild Bunch." *The Outlaw Trail Journal*, Summer 1994.

Willard, John. *Adventure Trails in Montana*, Billings, MT: Privately printed, 1964.

Wilson, Gary A. *Outlaw Tales of Montana*. Havre, MT: High-Line Books, 1995.

———. *Tiger of the Wild Bunch: The Life and Death of Harvey "Kid Curry" Logan*. Helena, MT: TwoDot, 2007.

Wolle, Muriel Sibell. *Montana Pay Dirt: A Guide to the Mining Camps of the Treasure State*. Denver: Sage Books, 1963.

Wood, Stanley. *Over the Range to the Golden Gate*. Chicago: R. R. Donnelley & Sons Co., Publishers, 1895.

NEWSPAPERS

Daily Avalanche (Avalanche Echo) (Glenwood Springs, Colorado)
Daily Pioneer-Times (Deadwood, South Dakota)
Daily River Press (Ft. Benton, Montana)
Denver Post

Denver Republican
Denver Times
Glenwood Post (Glenwood Springs, Colorado)
Great Falls (Montana) *Tribune*
Kansas City Star
Knoxville Sentinel
Salida (Colorado) *Mail*
The Enterprise (Malta, Montana)

COURT RECORDS AND MISCELLANEOUS

BLM homestead records: Fergus County, Township 19N and Range 18E. http://www.glorecords.blm.gov

File case no.' s 1107, 1111, 1155, 1157, 1188, District Court records, Chouteau County, Montana.

Pinal County, AZ, Archives Obituaries for Harvey Thornhill. http://files.usgwarchives.org/az/pinal/obits/t/thornhil3ob.txt

State of Montana, County of Chouteau: Sworn witness testimony given before the December 31, 1894, coroner's inquest concerning the death of Powell Landusky.

Index